COVENANTAL RIGHTS

NEW FORUM BOOKS

Robert P. George, Series Editor

A list of titles

in the series appears

at the back of

the book

COVENANTAL RIGHTS

A STUDY IN JEWISH POLITICAL THEORY

David Novak

NEW
FORUM

PRINCETON UNIVERSITY PRESS   PRINCETON, NEW JERSEY

Copyright © 2000 by Princeton University Press
Published by Princeton University Press, 41 William Street,
Princeton, New Jersey 08540
In the United Kingdom: Princeton University Press, Chichester, West Sussex
All Rights Reserved

Library of Congress Cataloging-in-Publication Data
Novak, David, 1941–
Covenantal Rights : a study in Jewish political theory. David Novak
p. cm. — (New Forum Books)
Includes bibliographical references and index.
ISBN: 0-691-02680-7 (cl.: alk. paper)
1. Civil rights (Jewish law) 2. Jews—Politics and government—Philosophy.
3. Human rights—Religious aspects—Judaism—History of doctrines. I. Title. II. Series.
LAW   296.3'82—dc21   99-032287

This book has been composed in Times Roman

The paper used in this publication meets the minimum requirements
of ANSI/NISO Z39.48-1992 (R1997) (*Permanence of Paper*)

http://pup.princeton.edu

Printed in the United States of America

1 3 5 7 9 10 8 6 4 2

To Noam Yigal Stadlan, M.D.

HE SHALL SURELY HEAL.

(Exodus 21:19)

Contents

THIS BOOK is a study in Jewish political theory. Jewish political theory can mean one of two things: either it conceives how a Jewish polity is to be constituted or it conceives how the Jewish political tradition can contribute to a multicultural polity. In some ways this book is both of these kinds of studies, and in other ways it is neither of them.

Covenantal Rights is a study of Judaism itself as a full system of rights and correlative duties. In principle, that full system is the everlasting covenant (*berit*) between God and Israel. That alone is the true polity of the Jews, the polity in which God is the only sovereign (Exodus 15:18; Judges 8:23). In fact, though, that full system could only be the messianic kingdom, since as Maimonides rightly emphasized, only then and there could the full law of the covenant (*torah*) that regulates these rights and correlative duties possibly be operative (*Mishneh Torah*: Melakhim, 11.1). Such a full Jewish polity is something to which Jews are to always aspire. For many Jews, a minimal condition of such a full Jewish polity in the modern world is a Jewish nation-state, something with which the Jewish people today are now blessed in the State of Israel. Some have even seen this blessing literally as the first step in full messianic redemption (*r'eheet tsemihat ge'ulatenu*), although others are not willing to make such an immediate connection between the present state, however important, and the optimal Jewish polity. Nevertheless, authentic Jewish polity does not require this kind of formal political independence as any kind of sine qua non. Formal political independence is preferable, but surely not necessary. Wherever Jews live together in a community that is self-consciously Jewish, there is a Jewish polity having to struggle with how it draws upon the Jewish tradition for its internal governance. As long as there are Jews who look to the Jewish tradition for authority, the covenant between God and Israel is still operative, however partially.

In the diaspora, that polity is partial because Jews are participants in a larger non-Jewish polity, one that usually has the autonomy of national sovereignty; it is partial because we have no real consensus as to what the authority of the Jewish tradition is to be here. And, in the State of Israel, despite the fact that the majority there is Jewish, even there one sees no real consensus as to what the authority of the Jewish tradition is to be. So any Jewish political position, whether in the diaspora or in Israel, has to be partisan—at least at present. The Jewish political situation in both locations is, therefore, unsettled. For this reason, Israeli Jews have something significant in common with the political situation of diaspora Jews, and vice versa. And that is why Israeli Jews have a right to participate in diaspora discussions of what Jewish community is to

be, and that is why a diaspora Jew like myself has a right to participate in
similar discussions about the State of Israel—even without a vote.

Full Jewish polity means much more than a particular group of Jews forcing
their interpretation of the covenant on everyone else by some sort of coup
d'état. Full Jewish polity is possible only when the covenant between God and
Israel has been reaffirmed by the whole Jewish people. Such a reaffirmation
could only be messianic, and many believe it will also include all the other
peoples on earth affirming the Lord God of Israel as their king (Zephaniah
3:9). That is why Jews can live under our law here and now without any
constitution in the modern sense of that institution.

In contemporary Jewish discourse, rights talk is either used in non-Jewish
ways or it is eschewed because it is taken to be essentially non-Jewish. In this
book, I hope to show that rights talk is appropriate for inter-Jewish political
discourse, both for the diaspora and for the State of Israel, but that it must be
seen within the full context of the Jewish tradition. As such, it is broader than
many liberals want to see and deeper than many conservatives want to see.

Covenantal Rights is also an attempt to enter some insights from the Jewish
political tradition into current political discourse in general, a discourse that
heretofore has been primarily concerned with rights and that shows no signs
of losing such concern. Here too, many liberals have insisted that rights are
the achievement of secularity, and, therefore, there can be no religious contribution to rights talk since that achievement is in spite of religious traditions
not because of them in any way. Accepting this very same conclusion, many
conservatives have attempted to belittle rights talk or even remove it from
political discourse, whereby they think we can return to what is taken to be
the premodern concern with duty and virtue. Not only is it very doubtful
whether rights talk can be eliminated from political rhetoric in our own time;
there is also a false assumption that rights have no place in premodern religious
traditions, traditions that despite all the secularist claims from the Enlightenment on are alive and well in modernity and beyond. This book is my attempt
to show that Judaism provides a broader meaning of rights than the one provided by liberalism and a deeper meaning of rights than the one denied by
conservatism. Indeed, I even attempt the more ambitious task of showing Judaism itself to be constituted by rights at all levels from top to bottom.

One need not be a Jew to appropriate the insights of the Jewish tradition
about rights. Since this book brings in as many biblical texts as possible, it
should be most readily appropriable by Christians, whose view of polity must
come from this primary source of their faith in order to be authentic. And,
indeed, it has been in the area of ethics and politics (which cannot be separated
one from the other) where Judaism and Christianity have the most in common.
In fact, one could say that Christianity consciously appropriated Jewish ethical
and political teaching without qualification. Most Jewish teachers who have
been aware of this appropriation and its extent have heartily approved of it,

even though it has always been a partial appropriation of Judaism in all its fullness, and with all the dangers inherent in any such selection. Moreover, even those who are not Jews or Christians can recognize that political theory in any society must be conducted with a sense of historical continuity, and that attempts to create polity, indeed humanity, de novo have wreaked political and human havoc, especially in this century cursed with too many totalitarian regimes. Surely, Judaism is an indispensable component of the political history of the West, one that should be studied by all who are concerned with the survival of our civilization and its societies. And that civilization not only has some reliance on Judaism, it is also where the overwhelmingly number of Jews, both in Israel and the diaspora, live and want to continue to live—even after the Holocaust.

Nevertheless, *Covenantal Rights* is not an attempt to provide any immediate solutions to the very real political dilemmas of either the Jews or the larger world in which Jews live today. It is a work of theory, not of public policy, much less of legal injunction. This is in keeping with the Jewish legal tradition (Halakhah), where practical rulings are not immediately derived from theories about the law (which are always theories about polity: the culture in which law operates) but, rather, from much more concrete legal experience. At best, legal/political theory informs these rulings by providing some overall guidance as to how the law might be read in situ. That is why it would be inappropriate of me here to draw any specific practical conclusions for questions that either Jews among ourselves, Jews in the larger world in which we live, or non-Jews in general raise. However, if anyone finds a bit of guidance for any practical political/legal decision, I will have been glad to have been of some help to them. Being no stranger to political discussions and disputes myself, I certainly have been helped by the theories of other thinkers, both Jews and non-Jews, in my own practical/political decisions. Hence my fond hope here is that I can do for others what others have done for me. But whether or not that actually happens is for others, not for me, to judge.

Even at the level of theory, though, I have been fortunate to have had others call upon me to develop my own theories. In fact, that fits in nicely with the main point of this book, namely, our acts are to be in response to what others claim from us. In the case of *Covenantal Rights*, that call originated in the invitation of my friend Professor John Witte of Emory University Law School to deliver a paper at a conference, "Religious Human Rights," that he was hosting in Atlanta in October 1994. My paper, "Religious Human Rights in Judaic Texts," was delivered at that memorable conference, and the final version of it benefited from the critical discussion that followed it. The paper was subsequently published in the volume *Religious Human Rights in Global Perspective: Religious Perspectives*, ed. John Witte, Jr., and Johan D. van der Vyver (The Hague, 1996). It also appeared in Italian translation as "I diritti religiosi dell'uomo nella tradizione ebraica," in *Conscienza e Libertà*, no. 27

(1996); and in German translation as "Religiöse Menschenrechte in der jüdischen Tradition," in *Gewissen und Freiheit*, nos. 46–47 (1996). Also, parts of two other published papers of mine were reworked and rewritten for this book: "Is There a Concept of Individual Rights in Jewish Law?" in *Jewish Law Association Studies*, vol. 7, ed. S. M. Passamaneck and M. Finley (Atlanta, 1994); and "Religious Communities, Secular Society, and Sexuality: One Jewish Opinion," in *Sexual Orientation and Human Rights in American Religious Discourse*, ed. Martha C. Nussbaum and Saul M. Olyan. (Copyright © 1998 by Oxford University Press. Used by Permission of Oxford University Press.)

In preparing my original paper on rights for publication, I became aware that it had raised issues which surely required a full length monograph. Around this time, another friend, Professor Robert George of Princeton University, asked me if I would be interested in writing something for the series in political theory he was editing for Princeton University Press. This inquiry was fortuitous for me because it indicated that there would be an audience of readers for my thoughts on rights and the Jewish tradition. The inquiry became an invitation, and this book is my concrete response to it. Professor George, like Professor Witte earlier, has my gratitude for enabling me to direct my thoughts on this important topic. I am also grateful to Ann Wald, the editor in chief at Princeton University Press, and her colleagues for publishing *Covenantal Rights* with the distinguished imprimatur of the Press. My thanks are due to such friends and colleagues as Avi Bernstein-Nahar, Eugene Borowitz, Kenneth Green Robert Gibbs, Mary Ann Glendon, Martin Golding, Lenn Goodman, Kenneth Green, Russell Hittinger, Alan Mittleman, Richard John Neuhaus, Peter Ochs, Kenneth Seeskin, Robert Tuttle, Robert Wilken—and others, for discussions too numerous to be mentioned in any detail, but that have very much contributed to my thinking on this question.

Finally, the dedication. Dr. Noam Yigal Stadlan is my son-in-law, the beloved husband of my daughter Marianne Novak. If rights are all personal claims, as this book asserts, then Noam excels in answering the claims of others, whether it be to God who calls upon him to live the life of a complete Jew, or to his family who come to him for love and guidance, or to his friends who come to him for help and encouragement, or to his patients who come to him for care and cure. We are privileged that he has come to our family as well, that we may call upon him too.

Toronto, Ontario
November 1998

Abbreviations Used in Text

B.   Babylonian Talmud (Bavli)
M.   Mishnah
R.   Rabbi
S.   Tosefta
Tos. Tosafot
Y.   Palestinian Talmud (Yerushalmi)

COVENANTAL RIGHTS

Introduction

INDIVIDUALS AND SOCIETIES: RIGHTS AND DUTIES

In modern discussions of political theory, the favored terms seem to be "individual *and* society" or "society *and* individual." Indeed, the very ordering of these terms by any modern political theorist quickly shows on which side of the great debate over the priority of one entity to the other he or she stands. The debate is usually framed in terms of this essential question: Are the demands of *a* society to be justified by criteria coming from *the* individual, or are the demands of individual*s* to be justified by criteria coming from *the* society?

At present, those who favor the first version of the question are usually called "liberals"; those who favor the second version are usually called "communitarians." Each side initially addresses two real political fears, both of which are very much part of contemporary experience, even though by no means unique to it. Liberals address the fear of tyranny; communitarians address the fear of anarchy. Liberals fear that communitarian theory has no way of preventing all rights from being ultimately vested in society and its rulers. The threat of a Hitler or a Stalin seems not to have been sufficiently considered.[1] Communitarians fear that liberal theory has no way of recognizing any real community at all.[2] Liberals seem to regard the right to privacy as supreme, which is "the right to be let alone," in the famous words of Louis D. Brandeis.[3] Thus each side accuses the other of either ignoring or underestimating the primary fear it addresses. Yet could it be that both liberals and communitarians are seeing only parts of a bigger picture? Perhaps we need to search for that bigger picture in order to address their legitimate concerns, while we simultaneously transcend their respective myopia.

Could we start from *the* individual? But where could we possibly find any individual who is actually separate from a society? If that individual speaks, as most do, then that itself, as philosophers from Aristotle to Habermas have

---

[1] See Lloyd L. Weinreb, *Natural Law and Justice* (Cambridge: Harvard University Press, 1987), 253f., especially his charge that the influential communitarianism of Alasdair MacIntyre cannot explicitly argue against Hitler except by internal German criteria, which most people would regard as morally insufficient. Along somewhat similar lines, contra relativism, see Leo Strauss, *Natural Right and History* (Chicago: University of Chicago Press, 1953), 4, 42f. Cf. Luc Ferry, *Political Philosophy*, vol. 1, trans. F. Philip (Chicago: University of Chicago Press, 1990), 21.

[2] See David Selbourne, *The Principle of Duty* (London: Sinclair-Stevenson, 1994), 5; also, John Finnis, *Natural Law and Natural Rights* (Oxford: Clarendon Press, 1980), 210.

[3] Samuel D. Warren and Louis D. Brandeis, "The Right to Privacy," *Harvard Law Review* 4 (1890): 193. This reflects the influence of John Stuart Mill's *On Liberty*, in *Utilitarianism, Liberty, and Representative Government* (London: Everyman Library, 1993), 196. Cf. Mary Ann Glendon, *Rights Talk* (New York: Free Press, 1991), 47ff.

continually pointed out, is the most immediate evidence that humans are inevitably social beings.[4] Thus as one of the early Rabbis despaired when he found himself in a community where he could no longer engage in discourse because his own voice was no longer recognized there: "either fellowship (*haveruta*) or death."[5] And even those individuals who do not or cannot speak could not survive, however minimally, if they are not or have not been included in some way or other in a society of speakers.

Could we start from *society*? But where could we possibly find any society that is actually distinct from the individuals who comprise it? As history in its record of the rise and fall of various human cultures shows, when the formal institutions of society become too separate from the lives of the individual participants in the culture that sustains them, they crumble. Unlike physical power, where an active subject stands over a passive object, political power is not just transitive; it is also a *transaction*, where some active subjects empower other equally active subjects. Thus they make themselves into objects for the other, as philosophers from Plato to Hobbes have pointed out.[6] As such, political power is something between subjects and not something external to them and over and above them in principle, however much social institutions might come to look like impersonal external forces. As philosophers from Maimonides to Hegel have pointed out, one's claims to the exercise of political power (as distinct from the exercise of physical power, however much it might accompany it) are intelligible only when the objects of that power are free persons, that is, those whom one can verbally command.[7]

Of course, it is necessary for discursive purposes to continue to use polar terms like individual and society. They are just too much a part of our ordinary political vocabulary to be dropped altogether. Yet it is not at all helpful, I think, to reduce all political discourse to the relation between these two abstract poles. There is just too much that lies in between that needs less-abstract terms. If so, then what terms are more appropriate for our theoretical purposes here and now?

I submit that we would be better served by locating the political situation of humankind in the relation of the terms "person" and "community."[8] Is not

----

[4] See Aristotle, *Politics*, trans. H. Rackham (Cambridge: Harvard University Press, 1932), 1253a10; Jürgen Habermas, *Moral Consciousness and Communicative Action*, trans. C. Lenhardt and S. W. Nicholsen (Cambridge: MIT Press, 1990), 23ff.

[5] B. Taannit 23a. See Zevahim 117a re Lev. 13:46.

[6] See Plato, *Republic*, trans. P. Shorey, 2 vols. (Cambridge: Harvard University Press, 1930), 338E; D. Novak, *Jewish Social Ethics* (New York: Oxford University Press, 1992), 38f. n. 1; Hobbes, *The Elements of Law*, vol. 1, chap. 15.

[7] See Maimonides, *Mishneh Torah*: Teshuvah, chaps. 5–6; G. W. F. Hegel, *Phenomenology of Spirit*, trans. A. V. Miller (Oxford: Oxford University Press, 1977), sec. 182, p. 112; and Alexandre Kojève, *Introduction to the Reading of Hegel*, trans. J. H. Nichols, Jr. (Ithaca: Cornell University Press, 1969), 5ff.

[8] See Nikolai Berdyaev, *Slavery and Freedom*, trans. R. M. French (New York: Scribner's, 1944), 20ff.; Alfred Schutz, *The Phenomenology of the Social World*, trans. G. Walsh and F. Lehnert (Evanston, Ill.: Northwestern University Press, 1967), 163ff.

the character of a community actually determined by the majority of the persons who comprise it, whether or not they exercise that consent more or less directly? And is not human existence characterized by a person's participation in a series of communities, each related to the other?[9] Thus a person, even when acting singly, is always acting as a member of a community beginning with his or her own family. That is the case whether one is acting inside his or her own immediate community, or outside it by representing it in another community. Thus one is always a son, a daughter, a husband, a wife, a Jew, a Christian, and so forth, whether infracommunally or transcommunally.[10] Furthermore, a person is never only part of one community of which he or she can simply be regarded as a subset. Instead, a person participates in a plurality of communities, the relation of which should be pictured as a series of partially overlapping circles, not as a series of wholly concentric circles.[11] For this reason, a person is not locked into any one community, and can even effect social change in one community based on the standards of another.[12]

A society as distinct from a community might very well be seen as a community that is too large for everyone to personally know every other person in it.[13] Thus societies are abstract constructions stemming from communities. For the sake of more complex order, they require distinctly impersonal institutions to supplement the simpler order of interpersonal contact within smaller, more intimate communities.[14] But when institutionalized societies lose their link with true communities of persons, they crumble. That is why community is a more primal political term than society. Persons in community always need to remain closer to those who know them than to those who do not.

An individual as distinct from a person might very well be seen as a juridical construction. This construction stems from the need for adjudication between litigants, which is a matter requiring equality.[15] Hence we need to abstract from

---

[9] For the dialectical relationship of person and community, see Peter L. Berger, *The Sacred Canopy* (Garden City, N.Y.: Doubleday, 1969), 187, n. 2.

[10] See Michael J. Sandel, "Justice and the Good," in *Liberalism and Its Critics*, ed. M. J. Sandel (Oxford: Blackwell, 1984), 172.

[11] See Michael Walzer, *Spheres of Justice* (Oxford: Blackwell, 1983), 316ff.

[12] See Isaiah Berlin, "Two Concepts of Liberty," in *Four Essays on Liberty* (Oxford: Oxford University Press, 1969), 161, n. 1; also, Luc Ferry and Alain Renaut, *Political Philosophy*, trans. F. Philip (Chicago: University of Chicago Press, 1992), 3:128.

[13] See Aristotle, *Politics*, 1326b15, where the best polity is one in which everyone is personally known to everyone else and decisions can be made based on this personal knowledge. However, Aristotle was also well aware of the fact that political independence (*autarkeia*) requires economic independence (1326b30), and that such independence is impossible when a polity is too small. Optimally, political independence and personal community (*koinōnia*) should go together. But Aristotle is surely suggesting that a less than optimal polity might very well have to sacrifice full communal intimacy for the sake of political survival. In other words, society might have to be constructed by primal communities—for a price, of course.

[14] See Novak, *Jewish Social Ethics*, 212ff.

[15] See B. Shevuot 30a re Lev. 19:15. Regarding courts to handle litigation as being the first political institution, see B. Sanhedrin 56b re Gen. 2:16.

the specific communal identities of different persons inasmuch as equality itself is an abstraction.[16] But when juridical persons lose their link to their own personal identities, becoming components of society in essence, they are unable to be functioning members of the very communities of which societies are abstractions.[17] That is why person is a more fundamental political term than individual. Communities take care of more basic personal needs than societies do.

The relation of the political terms "individual" and "society" is most often seen in the relation of the legal terms "rights" and "duties." The relation of the political terms "person" and "community" is most often seen in the relation of the moral terms "claims" and "responses." This latter set of terms is more primary existentially, and it is closer to the primary normative vocabulary of the Jewish tradition. Nevertheless, the former terms—individual, society, rights, and duties—are by now too prevalent in our ordinary political vocabulary ever to be avoided without paying the price of obscurantism. So, my task in this book is to lead these former terms back to fuller historical origins in the latter terms: person, community, claims, and responses. By doing this, I hope to show that there are richer contexts for rights talk than is provided by current secularist liberalism and denied by many communitarians.

Usually, those who emphasize the priority of rights over duties are also those who emphasize the priority of the individual over society. Rights, for them, are those primal claims the individual person brings with him or her upon entering society. Duties are how society is supposed to subsequently respond to these claims by enforcing them.[18] The price for this correlation of individual rights with social duties is that the individuals who themselves have rights also agree to accept these social duties when the rights of other individuals are at stake. This correlation is made by standards upon which all have agreed or could have agreed upon in advance.[19]

The problem, of course, is that agreements are ultimately promises that require mutual trust.[20] But why should persons whose sole motivation is their

[16] See B. Baba Kama 83b–84a re Lev. 24:22; also, Aristotle, *Nicomachean Ethics*, trans. H. Rackham (Cambridge: Harvard University Press, 1926), 1132a20ff., 1133a30. Hence the roots of society as an impersonal abstraction from community are already found in the communal need for what Aristotle calls "rectifying justice" (*to diorthotikon*).

[17] See Novak, *Jewish Social Ethics*, 225f.

[18] Hence in this view, society has duties to individuals but no rights. See Jack Donnelly, *The Concept of Human Rights* (New York: St. Martin's Press, 1985), 62.

[19] See John Locke, *Second Treatise of Government*, ed. G. Macpherson (Indianapolis, Ind.: Hackett, 1980), chap. 8; also, Alan Gewirth, *The Community of Rights* (Chicago: University of Chicago Press, 1996), 6.

[20] In *Contract as Promise* (Cambridge: Harvard University Press, 1981), Charles Fried writes: "So remarkable a tool is trust that in the end we pursue it for its own sake; we prefer doing things cooperatively when we might have relied on fear or interest or worked alone. —The device that

own individual power trust each other enough to limit their own power for the sake of some greater promised social end? That would even be true in a case where the "social contract" was an actual political event in history—for is not real individual desire a stronger pull on a person than a socially constructed standard, one accepted only under fear of the individual impotence resulting from the isolation that could come from public hostility toward antisocial individuals? Is not the lure of privacy so valued in modernity because it gives us greater opportunity to minimally avoid and maximally cheat on the necessary evil the social contract seems to entail?[21] As Stanley Hauerwas has put it in his critique of liberal rights notions, "Rights are necessary when it is assumed that citizens fundamentally relate to one another as strangers, if not downright enemies."[22] And, surely, the weakness of the social contract is even more evident when it is seen to be only a theoretical construct of some individual philosopher or other, without the support of any communal tradition.

It would seem that the social contract itself is insufficient to protect us from the anarchy most of us correctly fear. The durability of civil society, which is presented as the result of the social contract, would seem to require one of two things. Either antecedent to it there must already be in place communal traditions that themselves are not the results of individual contractural agreement, and that are accepted as communal claims and not merely as necessary instruments for the fulfillment of individual desires;[23] or subsequent to it, institutions must be constructed whose operators are so empowered to have more and more independent authority over the individuals under it, employing fear rather than trust.[24] In either case, though, the whole argument for the social contract, made by lone individuals, being the sufficient foundation to explain and justify civil society, collapses. And if it is not foundational, what heuristic, let alone constructive, value could it pos-

---

gives trust its sharpest, most palpable form is promise" (8). However, if trust is essentially a communal phenomenon, it cannot be rooted in a contract between individuals seeking their own private ends. Trust itself must precede any such contract; it is not a result of it. In the Jewish tradition, contracts between individuals are thus subordinate to the law that governs the covenant, the covenant being rooted in trust: first, between God and Israel; second, between the human members of the covenant (*bnei berit*) themselves. See B. Shevuot 39a re Deut. 29:9–14; M. Baba Metsia 7.11.

[21] See Plato, *Republic*, trans. P. Shorey, 2 vols. (Cambridge: Harvard University Press, 1930), 359Aff.; also, Ferry and Renaut, *Political Philosophy* 3:2.

[22] *Suffering Presence* (Notre Dame, Ind.: University of Notre Dame Press, 1986), 128. See also Martin P. Golding, "The Significance of Rights Language," *Philosophical Topics* 18 (1990): 63f.

[23] See Alasdair MacIntyre, *After Virtue* (Notre Dame, Ind.: University of Notre Dame Press, 1981), 65; Jeffrey Stout, *Morality after Authority* (Notre Dame, Ind.: University of Notre Dame Press, 1981), 234ff.; Vincent Descombes, "The Socialization of Human Action," in *The Public Realm*, ed. R. Schürmann (Albany: State University of New York Press, 1989), 247f.

[24] See Max Weber, "Bureaucracy and Political Leadership," in *Economy and Society* (New York: Bedminster Press, 1968), 3:1401ff.

sibly have? In truth, the social contract presupposes a measure of individual autonomy that communal traditions never recognized or that bureaucratic structures soon suppress. Thus social contract theory and its attendant notion of natural rights simultaneously involves an underestimation and an overestimation of the human condition. It underestimates the natural necessity and priority of discursive community, and it overestimates the importance of individual authority in the natural social order, let alone the covenantal order.

Conversely, those who usually emphasize the priority of duties over rights are also those who emphasize the priority of society over individuals. Duties, for them, are the primal claims society makes on those it enables to be born and nurtured in its midst.[25] Rights are those entitlements society grants to various constituencies within it to justify its benevolent role for their particular interests. The smallest such constituency is the individual person. In this view, however, the highest claim is that of society itself for itself, which is primarily achieved by the exercise of the duty conceived by and for the majority. Only subsequent to this basic duty is the exercise of rights granted by the majority to various minorities within its domain as their entitlements.

The problem, of course, is that the human dignity, which seems to be guaranteed by the concept of rights, also seems to be quite precarious in a system where rights are mere entitlements granted by the society as a matter of largesse instead of something taken as prior to the raw political power of any majority.[26] The experience of recent tyranny alone has taught us to be quite wary of guarantees of respect for the dignity of individual human persons from political power that seems to be more and more self-justifying. What the majority can grant with nothing but self-justification can just as easily be withdrawn by these very same arbitrary criteria. Moreover, with the vast increase in political power brought about by the collective development of technology, it would seem that the benevolent concern of the majority for various minorities, like the family or the individual person, which can be located in older communal traditions, is insufficient in an age when the balance of power between them has been so strongly tipped in favor of larger and larger collectives. One could very well argue that the reason the older benevolence operated at all was simply because those who exercised it lacked the political power that newer social authorities by now have. Hence it would seem that newer protections of minority rights are now called for. So, there would seem to be a new requirement for majority society to see itself as duty bound to enforce even the rights of individual minorities *against* it, and not just the rights of one constituency against another within it as has always been the case. Indeed,

---

[25] See Plato, *Crito*, trans. H. N. Fowler (Cambridge: Harvard University Press, 1914), 50Aff.

[26] See Ronald Dworkin, *Taking Rights Seriously* (Cambridge: Harvard University Press, 1978), 172; Donnelly, *The Concept of Human Rights*, 19.

many have seen this new notion of rights and its correlative notion of duty as a hallmark of modernity as distinct from antiquity.[27]

What we can now begin to see is that just as the phenomena usually designated by the terms "individual" and "society" are better designated by the terms "person" and "community," so the phenomena designated by the terms "rights" and "duties" are better designated by the terms "claims" and "responses." Thus, rights are justified claims; duties are mandated responses to these claims.[28]

When we see the primacy of personal claims, we have better reason to understand the oft-stated point that rights and duties are correlative. That is, without a minimal duty of compliance, the notion of a right makes no sense.[29] Rights are socially sanctioned claims.[30] Minimally, they are claims of noninterference; maximally, they are claims for assistance.[31] All such claims presuppose social reciprocity.[32] For example, in cases where we are obligated to help the poor, the correlation of rights and duties is very much in operation. I am duty bound (obligated) to help the poor because they have a right to my help. Without that justified claim, what they ask of me is nothing but begging. And without that duty, my response to their cry for help is nothing but my subjective largesse. The difference between begging and a right to help, and subjective largesse and a duty to help, is that rights and duties are to be enforced, when necessary, by a third party in the person of society and its authorized agents, whereas begging and subjective largesse cannot invoke such external enforcement. Rights and duties always involve more than simply one-to-one personal relationships. Accordingly, a right without a correlative duty has no socially sanctioned person as the object of the exercise of its claim, and a duty without a correlative right has no socially sanctioned person as the object of its obligation. Law is the formal expression of these relationships.[33]

---

[27] See Emil Brunner, *Justice and the Social Order*, trans. M. Hottinger (New York: Harper and Row, 1945), 54; Nathan Rotenstreich, *Order and Might* (Albany: State University of New York Press, 1988), 219.

[28] See Wesley N. Hohfeld, *Fundamental Legal Conceptions*, ed. W. W. Cook (Westport, Conn.: Greenwood Press, 1964), 38, 60, 71; also, Joel Feinberg, *Rights, Justice, and the Boundaries of Liberty* (Princeton: Princeton University Press, 1980), 140.

[29] Note Samuel Stoljar, *An Analysis of Rights* (London: Macmillan, 1984): "*Ubi jus ibi remedium* is then another . . . way of saying that normative rights and duties are necessarily correlative" (38). See also Bernard Mayo, "What Are Human Rights?" in *Political Theory and the Rights of Man*, ed. D. D. Raphael (London: Macmillan, 1967), 75f.

[30] See Michael Freeden, *Rights* (Buckingham, UK: Open University Press, 1991), 7.

[31] The widely adopted designation of minimal claims as "option-rights" and maximal claims as "welfare-rights" has been made by Martin P. Golding in "The Concept of Rights," in *Bioethics and Human Rights*, ed. E. L. Bundman and B. Bundman (Boston: Little, Brown, 1978), 44f.

[32] See Maimonides, *Commentary on the Mishnah*: Peah, 1.1.

[33] For the primacy of commanded duty over voluntary duty, see B. Kiddushin 31a and Tos., s.v. "gadol."

Thus Joseph Raz aptly notes that "legal personality is the capacity to have rights and duties."[34]

Many have argued that even though a right without a correlative duty is meaningless, there can be duties without rights, nevertheless.[35] But, as I shall illustrate from the Jewish tradition in subsequent chapters, every duty has a correlative right, just as every right has a correlative duty. A duty is something I basically owe someone else. Hence that person has a right to expect the performance of my duty, even if there are times when that duty is not or cannot be legally sanctioned by any human society,[36] for what cannot always be sanctioned by a human society can always be sanctioned by God. The universe itself is the greatest social context for the operation of rights, and duties and the universe is ruled by God, however opaque that rule might be to us oftimes.

Rights are not only correlative with duties, they actually generate them. This can be seen in two ways. One, at the level of creation, God has rights that generate the duties of his creatures. God clearly does not have a duty to create duties. To assume anything like that would lead to the absurd conclusion (at least in Judaism) that God is primarily subordinate to something greater than himself. Two, at the legal level, there are rights for which there are not yet any duties legislated, but which call for such duties to be legislated in the future.[37] Thus, to return to our example of the poor mentioned above, the poor are in need before we have a duty to help them. Hence our duty is for their sake, not for the sake of our own virtue. Whatever virtue we might have is subsequent to the fulfillment of our duty in response to their original right.

This bipolar relation of rights and duties can be seen as the cornerstone of the ethical philosophy of the recently deceased French Jewish philosopher Emmanuel Levinas. He showed quite powerfully that the very presence of other persons (*l'autre*) is itself a claim upon me, minimally obliging me to respect their right to live by not murdering them.[38] We might say that rights are held by the originator of a personal transaction and duties are held by its

---

[34] *The Morality of Freedom* (Oxford: Oxford University Press, 1986), 44.

[35] "There is no *ius* to which is not given, either by nature or by law, some obligation as a companion and guide; so that if need be it can protect itself through a judgment in an action in front of judges (*ministerio iudiciorum*) . . . soliciting the aid of judges (*quae iudicum fidem imploret*). . . . For a *ius* consists of a person, a possession, or the facts from which an obligation springs (*a quo obligatio oritur*)." François Connan, *Commentarium Iuris Civilis Librix* (Paris, 1588), 71r, in Richard Tuck, *Natural Rights Theories* (Cambridge: Cambridge University Press, 1979), 40.

[36] See B. Baba Kama 93a re Gen. 16:5 and Tos., s.v. "d'eeka," where it is emphasized that divine justice for a violation of one's rights may be sought in the absence of a human means to rectify the wrong. For the notion that divine justice comes quicker for those who do not hesitate to protest to God the violation of their rights, see ibid., Tos., s.v. "ehad" re Exod. 22:22–23.

[37] See Raz, *The Morality of Freedom*, 171ff., 249; Gewirth, *The Community of Rights*, 9.

[38] See *Totality and Infinity*, trans. A. Lingis (Pittsburgh: Duquesne University Press, 1969), esp. 187ff.

recipient. Initially, the claim must be made before there can be a subsequent response to it. Thus the primary right/claim creates the duty; in effect, it commands a response by obliging its addressee. But I differ from Levinas by insisting with the Jewish tradition that God, not humans, is the One who makes the primary claim on our response in the world.[39]

Many do not see the full extent of the correlation of rights and duties because they confuse the duty to respond to a claim with the actual capacity of a human society to legally sanction such a claim. However, the true correlation of rights and duties and duties and rights always transcends the limited human capacity to enforce either part of the correlation with legal sanctions.[40] That is why moral claims include more than legally sanctioned rights, moral responses more than legally sanctioned duties.[41] Just as my right is a claim on the duty of someone else, so is my duty a response to the claim of someone else. But God alone is capable of fully enforcing rights or duties or both. That power is concurrent with the truth that all rights are ultimately his and thus all duties are what are owed to him.[42] The human attempt to enforce either too much or too little inevitably leads to a social context in which rights and duties become distorted. When human enforcement is too much, there is too little personal interaction, since impersonal institutions too frequently displace it. At the most extreme level, these institutions and those who control them attempt to replace the ultimate authority of God. And when human enforcement is too little, too much personal interaction loses the protection of social institutions. At the most extreme level, these individual persons attempt to replace the ultimate authority of God. So, as will be argued later, only when God's authority is presented in the covenant do the lesser authority of society and the lesser authority of the individual person find their rightful places respectively and their rightful correlation one with the other.

The ubiquity of the term "rights" in modern political discourse makes any elimination of the term risk elimination from the discourse altogether.[43] Rights by now have become a matter of elementary political vocabulary. But surely this discourse requires rights conceptualization from those who wish not only to participate in it but to contribute to it as well. And I think not only do

[39] See D. Novak, *Law and Theology in Judaism* (New York: KTAV, 1976), 2:15ff.

[40] See, e.g., B. Sanhedrin 37b; Y. Sanhedrin 4.9/22b.

[41] See Martin P. Golding, "The Primacy of Welfare Rights," in *Human Rights*, ed. E. F. Paul, J. Paul, and F. D. Miller, Jr. (Oxford: Blackwell, 1984), 125.

[42] Secularist theories, however, inevitably assume that socially unenforceable duties have no corresponding rights. See, e.g., J. Narveson, "Human Rights: Which If Any Are There?" *Human Rights: Nomos* 23 (1981): 176.

[43] For the notion of convention determining the vocabulary of interhuman discourse, see B. Nedarim 49a; Y. Nedarim 6.1/39c. However, the conceptuality that uses such common vocabulary is determined by the reason exercised by the person who critically employs it for the sake of rational persuasion. See B. Baba Metsia 104a and Tos., s.v. "hayah"; also, Nahmanides, *Hiddushei ha-Ramban* thereon re M. Ketubot 4.6; Y. Ketubot 4.8/28d–29a.

classical Jewish sources lend themselves to rights talk, but they can contribute to it significantly. Indeed, rights conceptualization is a new key for unlocking more of the intelligibility of these sources and drawing new rational suggestions from them. As such, rights talk should not be eschewed by traditionalists, as some communitarians have suggested.[44] It should not only be used by Jewish traditionalists, it should be embraced by us—critically, to be sure—because to discuss rights in a Jewish context is to restore them to their true origin. But that means the exercise of rights talk by Jews must not be confined to the rights of individual persons, who are only one component of the covenant. Rather, rights must now be seen as being exercised by both God and the community as well as by individual persons. As we shall see in the course of this book, constituting all three of these claimants enables us to constitute a truly coherent way to order their conflicting claims. That is the task of this book. Hence this Jewish use of rights talk is not only a rhetorical necessity; it is even more a philosophical desideratum. It is a way of actively entering ideas from the Jewish tradition into contemporary political discourse, a conversation that is happily becoming more pluralistic.

AUTONOMY AND PERSONAL CLAIMS

Although nobody could cogently assert that there are rights without at least the implication of correlative duties, a number of great thinkers have asserted that there are duties without correlative rights. Their arguments are impressive and have been influential, even among Jewish thinkers. These arguments must be critically examined in order to better present, by contrast, the theory of ubiquitous rights advocated here.

As we shall see, all these assertions assume duties are required by autonomous states as distinct from the claims of other persons. That is the only way one can speak of duties without corresponding rights. There seem to be three theoretical forms of such autonomy that have been advocated. Let us briefly look at them in order to discern their ultimately impersonal character, which is so problematic for a biblically based political theory.

First, there is the assertion of autonomy generating these duties as found in those "goods" which are states of active being. This has been posited in one way or another by current natural law theorists who attempt to build on the ethical-legal theory of Thomas Aquinas.[45] Here one can speak of the duties

---

[44] Rights talk is most notably eschewed by Alasdair MacIntyre, who writes, "The truth is plain: there are no such rights, and belief in them is one with belief in witches and unicorns" (*After Virtue*, 67).

[45] Most prominently, see Germain Grisez, *The Way of the Lord Jesus* (Chicago: Franciscan Press, 1983), 1:115ff.; also, Finnis, *Natural Law and Natural Rights*, 59ff.

that follow from one's aspiration to some good, but one cannot speak of that good actually making a claim on one inasmuch as an impersonal claim is at best a metaphor.[46] Only when there is a strong sense of a lawgiver behind natural law can the exercise of a right be seen as normatively foundational, and that requires a more theological basis for natural law theory than even many contemporary natural law theorists, even those who are themselves religious, have been willing to constitute.[47] Moreover, the problem is basically ontological before it is political or ethical, and it goes back to Aquinas himself, indeed back to Hellenistic Judaism. The problem stems from the basically futile attempt to wed the Platonic idea of the Good with the biblical creator God, that is, to equate God with Being.[48] The biblical God is certainly a person; Platonic Being/the Good is certainly not.[49]

Second, there also seems to be a notion of duties without rights in the strongest idea of autonomy constituted by any philosopher, namely, that of Kant. This usually sober philosopher actually becomes rhapsodic when he speaks of duty (*Pflicht*).[50] That is because truly moral persons are authentically autonomous selves, who will an ideal realm of nature for themselves and all other similarly rational selves. That is their duty.[51] Could one not say that this autonomous (or noumenal) self makes a claim on the physically embodied (or phenomenal) self, and that this claim is its right? However, it is difficult to see how an imagined self can actually exercise a claim on a real, embodied one—for *who* is making the claim?[52] In the end, is it not the real,

---

[46] For the priority of good over right (*ius*) in Aquinas, see *Summa Theologiae* 2/2, q. 57, a. 1 and a.2. See also Strauss, *Natural Right and History*, 183f., 297f. for the notion that the primacy of good entails the priority of duty over rights. For an attempt to see the "claims" of goods as more than metaphorical, however, see Hans Jonas, "Ontological Grounding of a Political Ethics: On the Metaphysics of Commitment to the Future of Man," in Schürmann, *The Public Realm*, 158.

[47] For a natural law theorist aware of this problem, see Russell Hittinger, *A Critique of the New Natural Law Theory* (Notre Dame, Ind.: University of Notre Dame Press, 1987), 168ff.

[48] See LXX on Exod. 3:14; also, Aquinas, *Summa Theologiae* 1, q. 2, a. 1. For a discussion of the ontological implications of this equation: God = Being = the Good, see D. Novak, "Buber and Tillich," *Journal of Ecumenical Studies* 29 (1992): 159ff.

[49] See E. LaB. Cherbonnier, "The Logic of Biblical Anthropomorphism," *Harvard Theological Review* 54 (1962): 187.

[50] See *Critique of Practical Reason*, 1.1.2, trans. L. W. Beck (Indianapolis: Bobbs-Merrill, 1956), 1.1.2, p. 89.

[51] See *Groundwork of the Metaphysic of Morals*, trans. H. J. Paton (New York: Harper and Row, 1964), 105ff.

[52] Because of the necessary correlation of rights and duties, which presupposes an *inter*personal relationship, H. L. A. Hart correctly notes: "The expression 'having a duty to Y' . . . indicates the person to whom the person morally bound is bound. This is an intelligible development of the figure of a bond (*vinculum juris: obligare*). . . . So it appears absurd to speak of having duties or owing obligations to ourselves" ("Are There Natural Rights?" *Philosophical Review* 64 [1955]: 181). See also Aristotle, *Nicomachean Ethics*, 1128a5ff.

embodied self who is projecting its own idealized self? The real, embodied self is not only creating an ideal realm of nature for an autonomous self, but is actually making the very autonomous subject of that realm itself its first basic ideal.[53] My idealized future self is more "other" than the real *other person* before me here and now.[54] But how can the product make a claim on its maker? That is why, despite his constant use of the term *Autonomie*, Kant did not mean by it what we mean by "autonomy" today. Instead, he seems to mean what we might call "moral creativity," that is, the human aspiration to create a perfect world for everyone.[55] Here we see a true idealism (in both the ordinary and philosophical senses of the term) that is lacking in more contemporary notions of autonomy, which seem to be concerned with rights only as necessary preconditions for the advancement of individual projects (*bonum sibi*). In his notion of morality ultimately intending what he calls a "kingdom of ends" (*Reich der Zwecke*), Kant clearly meant to constitute a notion of common good (*bonum commune*) that is consistent with the most immediate good, namely, the good of the purely moral will as an end in itself.[56] Isaiah Berlin has astutely designated this whole project as "a form of secularized Protestant individualism, in which the place of God is taken by the conception of rational life."[57]

Third, it is only in some recent liberal theories more closely dependent on social contract theory that a claim *for* autonomy is made to others and can, therefore, be seen as a right. In this sense of autonomy, it is an individual personal claim rather than a desire to be a morally creative god. It does intend a real, other person, somebody already there in the guise of the majority to whom it appeals for maximum noninterference in its own projects or for help

---

[53] Note: "*Freedom* would then be the property . . . of being able to work independently of *determination* by alien causes. . . . The above definition is *negative* and consequently unfruitful as a way of grasping its essence; but there springs from it a *positive* concept. . . . What else can freedom of the will be but autonomy—that is, the property which will has of being a law [to] itself (*sich selbst ein Gesetz zu sein*)?" (Kant, *Groundwork of the Metaphysic of Morals*, 114; the original quote in German is in *Grundlegung zur Metaphysik der Moral*, in *Kants Werke*, Prussian Academy ed., [Berlin: Walter de Gruyter, 1968], 4:446f.) In other words, after external interference has been cleared away by assuming freedom, autonomy as true human/rational substance "flows out."

[54] See D. Novak, *Jewish-Christian Dialogue* (New York: Oxford University Press, 1989), 148ff.

[55] Kant actually suggests that in morality any human being can, as it were, "make himself a God" (*sich einen Gott mache*), indeed, "must make himself one" (*sich einen solchen selbst machen musse*) by comparing this "imaginative representation (*Vorstellung*) . . . with his ideal" (*Religion innerhalb der Grenzen der blossen Vernunft* in *Kants Werke*, Prussian Academy ed. [Berlin: Walter de Gruyter, 1968], 6:168f. n. [my trans.]). For the problem involved in seeing the will as constituting its own object, see Raz, *The Morality of Freedom*, 84; G. Dworkin, *The Theory and Practice of Autonomy* (Cambridge: Cambridge University Press, 1988), 36ff.

[56] See *Groundwork of the Metaphysic of Morals*, 61, 100ff.

[57] "Two Concepts of Liberty," 138.

in achieving them. It is more closely tied to a Lockean type of social contract theory than it is to a strictly Kantian notion of autonomy.[58] However, the expression of such a theory often becomes muddled because most of the liberal theorists advocating this type of right have a tendency to confuse the freedom the exercise of the right presupposes with the autonomy to which it aspires.[59] Here freedom is the right, autonomy the duty. And that duty becomes the highest good itself.[60]

These three types of ethics—that is, social contract, Kantian, and Thomistic—all could be generally termed ethics of aspiration. One can dutifully aspire to attain the highest degree of personal autonomy, or dutifully aspire to participate in a certain state of autonomous good, or dutifully aspire to moral creativity without being claimed by another person. But one cannot be the subject or the object of a right/claim without the presence of another person before him or her. Rights in the modern sense, unlike *right* in the classical sense, seem to be inextricable from the personal subject and the personal object of a claim.[61] That inextricable personal locus of rights makes the concept attractive to a biblically based theology, precisely because persons are irreducible entities in biblical (and rabbinic) teaching.[62] In that sense, such a theology is closer to that of the moderns than it is to that of the ancients whose inspiration ultimately comes from Plato. Therefore, it enables one to formulate a biblically based natural law theory, one that does not fall into the Platonism that makes some natural law theories, whether in more Aristotelian or more Stoic form, so problematic theologically.[63] But it also does that without falling into the trap of subjective autonomy, which either makes

---

[58] Note Kant's critique of a society based on individual rights as distinct from the "ethical commonwealth," where "we have a duty that is *sui generis*, not of men towards men, but of the human race towards itself" (*Religion within the Limits of Reason Alone*, trans. T. M. Greene and H. H. Hudson [New York: Harper and Row, 1960], 89; see note thereon).

[59] See Raz, *The Morality of Freedom*, 369ff., 415, who uses "autonomy" both as the ideal and the condition of the moral life, liberally conceived. Cf. Tara Smith, *Moral Rights and Political Freedom* (Lanham, Md.: Rowman and Littlefield, 1995), 180. Isaiah Berlin's concept of "positive liberty" seems to be identical with autonomy as an ideal (see "Two Concepts of Liberty," 131f.).

[60] Note: "It is, in short, not necessary for autonomy to be the only good thing; it suffices for it to be the best thing that there is" (Bruce Ackerman, *Social Justice in the Liberal State* [New Haven: Yale University Press, 1980], 368f.) See Jürgen Habermas, *Theory and Practice*, trans. J. Viertel (Boston: Beacon, 1974), 84.

[61] See Karl-Otto Apel, "Normative Ethics and Strategical Rationality: The Philosophical Problem of a Political Ethics," in Schürmann, *The Public Realm*, 124.

[62] Thus there is no essence/quiddity of God (see Exod. 3:14) since any such structure would limit the absolute freedom of God. There is no essence/quiddity of human being as the image of God (see Ps. 8:5). In the case of humans, having as they do limited freedom, we assume the conditions making their presence possible, but these conditions do not determine existence. In God's case we assume no such conditions at all (see Ps. 90:1–6). Also, see D. Novak, *The Election of Israel* (Cambridge: Cambridge University Press, 1995), xvii, n. 2.

[63] See Novak, *Natural Law in Judaism*, 154ff.

the self its ultimate object, as in social contract theory, or the self its transcendent creator, as in Kantian ethics. And it also does not fall into the trap of regarding the law of the covenant as a series of merely random commands rather than a system having rational coherence and appeal, which inevitably occurs when duties are emphasized without specific correlation to the rights behind them.

One could argue against all three types of moral aspiration on the same general philosophical grounds, for all three involve the hypostatization of abstract states of being: self-fulfillment, or moral creativity, or transcendent goods. From these hypostatizations norms are then deduced. But it would seem more philosophically cogent to see the source of norms in the transactional claims of real persons to one another in the world.

Of the three concepts, the concept of the good is clearly closest to the observation that morality must be dependent on something external to the self and its projects in order for it to be able to both restrain them and direct them. Furthermore, *good* seems to many to be a more basic moral term than *right*, either in the classical sense ("it *is right* to do that") or in the modern sense ("he or she *has a right* to do that").[64] Nevertheless, it is still insufficient to structure morality in general, and certainly the morality of the Jewish covenantal tradition, for goods are neither states of being *from* which persons derive norms, much less states of being generated *by* the human will. Instead, they are the measure of how adequate to the nature of both the claimant and the respondent, *between* whom the claim operates, that claim really is. Hence these claims/rights are the true criteria of justice. Justice as the order of rights is the more basic ethical-political term than good or *the* Good.[65] Justice is not a whole greater than the sum of its parts in which they participate, but rather justice as the Right is the sum of all the rights—all the justified claims—of the various persons who interact with each other in the world. Justice is in essence immanent. It is what connects all of these rights/claims.[66] Indeed, without an overall theory of justice, we would have no way of distinguishing true from fraudulent rights/claims.[67]

---

[64] For the distinction between these two notions of "right," see Hart, "Are There Natural Rights?" 182; Donnelly, *The Concept of Human Rights*, 3ff.

[65] Since in Judaism all moral terms are ultimately theological (see B. Shabbat 133b re Exod. 15:2; Maimonides, *Mishneh Torah*: Deot, 1.6), this argument can be made theologically: Whereas God's justice (*mishpat*) is always assumed (see Deut. 32:4), God's "goodness" is not always assumed (see Isa. 45:7), for we experience the results of God's acts as both good and bad (see Lam. 2:5). Hence when we experience God's acts as bad (*ra*, but never as "evil"—*resha*—which is only predicated of unjust human beings—see Gen. 18:25; Exod. 9:27; Job 34:1–10), we are still required to praise God's justice (see M. Berakhot 9.5; B. Berakhot 59b; Maimonides, *Mishneh Torah*: Berakhot, 10.4).

[66] For an analysis of *mishpat*, the key biblical term for justice, see Novak, *The Election of Israel*, 124ff.

[67] There is a great debate among political theorists whether the modern notion of natural rights is a development of the ancient notion of natural law or a break with it. For the former view, see

But justice is not transcendent like God.[68] Hence, this view of justice (*mishpat*) combines the strengths of the ancient notion of "Right" (*dikē*) and the modern notion of "rights" (*droits*). Like the ancient notion, its range is cosmic; like the modern notion, its locus is personal.

The proper fulfillment of a right is what is *good*—that is, the duty elicited by the right has been *done well*. It benefits the rights holder or claimant *for* whom it is to be done. Something good has been done on his or her behalf. Only consequently does it benefit the person who has answered someone else's claim. It contributes to the personal virtue of such a commandment keeper by helping designate him or her as a "righteous person" (*tsaddiq*), even though that consequent benefit is not to be one's primary intention in doing his or her duty.[69] One primarily obtains good, what one truly needs, from others, who act *well* for him or her. The good to be done for someone is for the sake of the one who holds the right, who makes the claim.[70] The justice of the claim is what makes the content of the claim good. Hence right precedes good in the sense that persons are prior to their acts and to the things their acts involve.

Berlin, "Two Concepts of Liberty," 129, n. 2; J. R. Pennock, "Rights, Natural Rights, and Human Rights—A General View," *Human Rights: Nomos* 23 (1981): 2; Golding, "The Primacy of Welfare Rights," 126f.; and now, most learnedly, Brian Tierney, *The Idea of Natural Rights* (Atlanta, Ga.: Scholars Press, 1997), 33ff., 214f. For the latter view, see Strauss, *Natural Right and History*, 175ff.; MacIntyre, *After Virtue*, 68. Nevertheless, a biblically based view of natural law can essentially avoid this quarrel by showing that the very idea of "natural law," which the Greeks would have regarded as an oxymoron because it combines the opposites of *physis* and *nomos* (see Plato, *Gorgias*, 482E; also, Leo Strauss, "Natural Law," in *International Encyclopedia of the Social Sciences*, 11:80b), was originally formulated by those who already believed in the biblical idea of God as creator/lawgiver (see Helmut Koester, "NOMOS PHUSEOS: The Concept of Natural Law in Greek Thought," in *Religions in Antiquity: Essays in Memory of Erwin Ramsdell Goodenough*, ed. J. Neusner [Leiden: E. J. Brill, 1968], 521ff.). As such, a retrieval of this biblically based doctrine of natural law supplies the cosmic-theological dimension of natural rights that modern views have eliminated and have thereby made incomplete. It also avoids adopting a Platonic-Aristotelian ontology that is ultimately antithetical to biblical doctrines, however helpful the political insights of Plato and Aristotle often are for us.

[68] Part of the problem with Emmanuel Levinas's attempt to substitute the transcendence/autonomy of ethics for that of God (see Novak, *Natural Law in Judaism*, 86ff.) is his acceptance of Plato's supreme form, the Good in itself (see *Republic*, 517B–C; Levinas, *Totality and Infinity*, 102f.). This is part of Plato's equation of the Good and Being itself (see *Republic*, 509B), which is the attempt to ground ethics in impersonal ontology, the very project Levinas himself so strenuously opposes (see *Totality and Infinity*, 42ff.). For Plato, justice is transcendent, including within itself all that is both divine and human (see *Gorgias*, 508A; *Timaeus*, 29A–C; also, Cicero, *De Legibus*, 1.7.27ff.).

[69] See M. Avot 1.3. Regarding what is good for God, i.e., fulfilling God's covenantal purposes optimally, see, e.g., Deut. 6:18 and commentaries of Rashi and Nahmanides thereon. Regarding what is good for the human other, see, e.g., Deut. 23:17 and *Sifre: Devarim*, no. 259. Regarding what is good for oneself, see, e.g., Hullin 142a re Deut. 22:7 and 5:16 (cf. B. Kiddushin 39b and Tos., s.v. "matnitin"); B. Pesahim 8a-b and Rashi, s.v. "harei zeh tsaddiq gamur" and Tos., s.v. "she-yizkeh."

[70] See Novak, *Natural Law in Judaism*, 164ff.

That is why the modern term "values" well describes the content of rights/claims. Values are what persons designate—evaluate—to be good for them. Values are what rights holders claim from those who are to respond to them. The personal relationship, the transaction itself, is what is evaluative. The closer these values are to the basic rights/claims of persons, the more permanent they are; the farther from them, the more arbitrary they are.[71] But to designate basic moral principles as "values" or "goods" seems to be incorrect because they are derivative. Rights, and justice as the system of all rights, are always what are morally fundamental.

This might well explain why guilt is such a constant feature of human existence and cannot be reduced to something else and, therefore, explained away. It is the subjective result of one's not having responded to a just claim. It explains *why* our moral life is forever bound to just *whom* we are to respond, then *how* we are to respond to that person or community, and, finally, *what* we are to respond with.[72] Guilt is justified when one has not responded at all to a just claim, that is, a claim proper to the nature of the person making it, the nature of the person to whom it is made, and the nature of the community in which it is made. And there is also secondary guilt when one has not responded well to a just claim. Conversely, guilt that psychologists would now call "pathological" is based on an unjustified claim, either unjustified altogether or in terms of improper content.[73] Thus just claims are *true*; unjust claims are *fraudulent*. As we can see, the terms *true* and *just* are more primary than the terms *good* or *valuable*.[74] All these terms are indispensable, but their proper order must be maintained.

In this way of looking at the normative world, *good* functions primarily as an adverb modifying verbs that describe transactions. It is a qualification, not a ground. Thus when a right has been properly made or responded to, one can say "you have have done *right*," where *right* is a synonym for *good* or *well*, which modifies action.[75] Secondarily, *good* functions as an adjective modifying

---

[71] See Walzer, *Spheres of Justice*, 7f. This might be the distinction between what jurists call *ius in rem* and *ius in personam*, viz., the former involve rights that are held by everyone in general and hence are inalienable; the latter involve rights created by individual agreement and hence are alienable. For this analysis of this distinction, see Hohfeld, *Fundamental Legal Conceptions*, 72ff.; Feinberg, *Rights, Justice, and the Bounds of Liberty*, 130ff.; Stoljar, *An Analysis of Rights*, 45ff., 72.

[72] See A. R. White, *Rights* (Oxford: Clarendon Press, 1984), 27f.; also, Feinberg, *Rights, Justice, and the Bounds of Liberty*, 155.

[73] See Martin Buber, "Guilt and Guilt Feelings," trans. M. Friedman, in *The Knowledge of Man*, ed. M. Friedman (New York: Harper and Row, 1965), 121ff.

[74] See Novak, *Jewish Social Ethics*, 14ff. For the primarily aesthetic and only secondarily moral meaning of the terms "good" (*tov*) and "bad" (*ra*), see Maimonides, *Guide of the Perplexed*, 1.2; also, R. Joseph Bekhor Shor, *Commentary on the Torah*: Gen. 1:4, 7, who defines the first use of *tov* in Scripture on aesthetic grounds, viz., what gives pleasure because of its own complete order.

[75] See, e.g., I Kings 8:18.

various things or institutions that function within these transactions for these institutions' sake.[76] For example, one can say about a social institution like marriage, "it is a *good* thing." That is, it functions well by facilitating the natural claims of persons for family life and the community for its own continuity. Thirdly, one can use the abstract noun *a good* to refer to such well-functioning things or institutions themselves. In the aggregate such institutions can be called "goods."[77]

But a biblically based theology should never stretch the use of the term "good" to function as a proper name, that is, "the Good." Moreover, almost everything asserted here about goods can also be asserted about virtues, which have been so emphasized by Alasdair MacIntyre and those whom he has influenced in his critique of the type of political and ethical theory where rights are the central concern.[78] "Virtues" like "goods" usually designate some state of active being.[79] Even more obviously, they are not proper names.[80] They seem, especially, to be more concerned with the character of the dutiful person than with the needs of the rights-bearing person who elicits that duty in the first place.[81] That is why virtues are secondary to rights.

Even when God is taken to be final end of all our desire, his very attractiveness is not because of his autonomous self-sufficiency.[82] Instead, it is because God has already exercised his active claim upon us in both creation and revelation.[83] As such, our desire for God is responsive, not heuristic. In creation, God's claim is experienced negatively, namely, we desire what all of creation lacks. "How indeed could God dwell on earth, for even the highest heavens do not contain you?" (I Kings 8:27). "Who is there for me in heaven? And along with you (*imekha*) I desire (*hafatsti*) no one on earth" (Psalms 73:25). In revelation that claim is experienced positively: "O' Lord, to you (*negdekha*) is my whole desire (*kol ta'avati*)" (Psalms 38:10).[84] "I desire your salvation and your Torah is my delight (*sh'ashu'ai*)" (Psalms 119:174). Accordingly, it is not that God *is good* or *the Good*,[85] but rather that "it is *good to give thanks* to the Lord" (Psalms 92:2). Here "good" (*tov*) describes how

---

[76] See, e.g., Deut. 1:14.

[77] See, e.g., II Kings 25:28.

[78] See *After Virtue*, esp., 137ff.

[79] See Aristotle, *Nicomachean Ethics*, 1103a10.

[80] See ibid., 1096a10ff. where Aristotle differs with Plato over whether there is one overall form, the Good. But, nevertheless, he does see "good" (*t'agathon*) as naming entities (*to onti*) like God (*ho theos*) and intelligence (*ho nous*) as well as functioning as a qualifier (1096a25).

[81] See ibid., 1098b30ff.

[82] Cf. Aristotle, *Metaphysics*, 1072b30–35.

[83] See Novak, *The Election of Israel*, 119f.

[84] See Ps. 73:25ff., 119:35, 40; also, *Selected Religious Poems of Jehudah Halevi*, ed. H. Brody (Philadelphia: Jewish Publication Society of America, 1924), 87.

[85] See B. Megillah 25a and Tos., s.v. "yevarkhukha" (second opinion).

we experience our response to God.[86] What God does for humans is also described as being experienced by us as "good," as for example, "the nearness of God is good for me (*tov li*)" (Psalms 73:28).[87] But God's right always precedes the good he might do for us. As Maimonides most astutely pointed out, valuable qualities predicated of God all describe the effects of God's action, what God has already done *to* the world.[88] But he could not very well say that about God's immediate demands upon his human creatures, his right to oblige us, because that involves God's direct action *for* us and *with* us as our creator.[89] Hence neither in the case of human response nor of divine claim is "the Good" the ultimate *telos* of the transaction. All designations of "good" are *valuable*, that is, they are penultimate and instrumental.[90] Good describes the quality of the personal act, but neither its subject nor its object.

At this point, I agree with John Rawls that rights are prior to goods in a theory of justice[91]—that is the case when a right is exclusively understood as a claim that can be made only by a person to another person. However, as will become apparent in the subsequent chapters, my understanding of persons as rights bearers is much wider than that of Rawls and, consequently, so is my understanding of their interrelationships. In that sense, I disagree with just about everything else he has said about the bases of justice. And, in fact, right is only prior to good, for Rawls, in the political order, where one cannot assume that all the citizens share the same notion of what is good for themselves. That is why society settles for the minimal conditions that enable everyone to pursue his or her own good individually as much as is just for everyone collectively.[92] Like all liberals, he has to see individual autonomy as the primary good, the *telos* of all striving, for which justice is its necessary political precondition. Indeed, it is difficult to see how for any liberal, rights as the *conditio sine qua non* cannot become anything but the *conditio per quam*, that is, the means

---

[86] See Ps. 54:8–9.

[87] See Jer. 33:11; Ps. 119:72.

[88] See *Guide of the Perplexed*, 1.53 re Exod. 33:19 and Gen. 1:31; also ibid. 3.54 re Jer. 9:23.

[89] Note ibid., 3.24, trans. S. Pines (Chicago: University of Chicago Press, 1963), p. 501: "For *Abraham our Father* did not hasten to slaughter *Isaac* because he was afraid that God would kill him or make him poor, but solely because of what is incumbent upon Adamites—namely to love Him and fear Him" (see B. Sanhedrin 56b re Gen. 2:16). In other words, God as he speaks himself to us, not the effects of God's acts, is to be the direct object of human love and fear (See Novak, *Natural Law in Judaism*, 130ff.). When we experience God's justice (either what we are to do or what we are to suffer) as *good for us*, we declare it to be good (e.g., Ps. 119:39; B. Berakhot 5a re Ps. 94:12). But God's judgments (*mishpatim*) are valid even when this is not our experience (see Job 42:1–5; Lam. 3:38).

[90] For the distinction between teleology and instrumentality, see Aristotle, *Nicomachean Ethics*, 1094a1ff.

[91] *A Theory of Justice* (Cambridge: Harvard University Press, 1971), 31.

[92] Ibid., 396; cf. ibid., 560.

inevitably becomes its own end.[93] Thus in the existential order, for Rawls too, the good is prior to rights.[94]

In my view, however, rights are also prior existentially because they are that to which/to whom I am to respond. They are made with a partial response when claimed by a fellow creature; they are made with a total response when claimed by God.[95] *Good* is only the adverb that modifies the way I have so responded, or the adjective that modifies the things I have included in that response. But, clearly, that priority of rights can be constituted only when the first right is God's claim on his human creatures, for whom, in the words of the Protestant theologian Paul Tillich (d. 1965), that claim is to be their "ultimate concern."[96] As Peter Jones states about rights in general, "To possess moral rights is to be not merely an *object* of moral concern, it is to be a *source* of moral concern."[97]

The priority of rights to goods also offers a more convincing solution to the "is/ought problem" that has so bedeviled modern ethical theory. The problem, which was originally formulated by Hume, is that no descriptive proposition ("is") entails any prescription ("ought").[98] What this assumes, however, is that we primarily live in a world of things, *about which* we are basically uninterested. Somehow we must then constitute a world of persons, in whom we are interested and *with whom* we must act in specific ways. But this world is considered epiphenomenal.

The usual philosophical solutions to this problem are: (1) The notion that "goods," which are not themselves things but higher states of being, are built into nature. By their inherent attractiveness, these states of being entail duties ("oughts") for rational subjects.[99] However, this view depends on the ontological assumption of universal teleology, and that is quite impossible to rationally ascertain without reverting to a by now irretrievable scientific cosmology.[100]

---

[93] Along these lines, see A. Ingram, *A Political Theory of Rights* (Oxford: Clarendon Press, 1994), 150, 197, 207.

[94] However, that good ultimately becomes the capacity to have rights. See *A Theory of Justice*, 560.

[95] See B. Berakhot 61b re Deut. 6:5; cf. B. Baba Metsia 62a re Lev. 25:36. This priority of rights over goods, first regarding divine claims on humans and then human claims on one another, was also emphasized by the Protestant reformers in their attempt to return from Aristotelian/ scholastic to more biblical views of polity. See R. V. Andelson, *Imputed Rights* (Athens: University of Georgia Press, 1971), 14.

[96] See his *Systematic Theology*, vol. 1 (Chicago: University of Chicago Press, 1951), 11ff.

[97] *Rights* (New York: Macmillan, 1994), 69.

[98] See *A Treatise of Human Nature*, ed. L. A. Selby-Bigge (Oxford: Clarendon Press, 1888), 3.1.1; cf. G. E. M. Anscombe, "Modern Moral Philosophy," in *The Is-Ought Question*, ed. W. D. Hudson (London: Macmillan, 1969), 175ff.; Novak, *Jewish Social Ethics*, 49ff.

[99] See Thomas Aquinas, *Summa Theologiae*, 2/1, q. 91, a. 3; q. 94, a. 2.

[100] See Strauss, *Natural Right and History*, 8; Jürgen Habermas, *Communication and the Evolution of Society*, trans. T. McCarthy (Boston: Beacon, 1979), 201; MacIntyre, *After Virtue*, 152.

Without rationally determining the existence of a superhuman, self-sufficient being who is the end of all ends, the apex of the whole cosmos, it is quite difficult to argue against Kant's insistence that humans themselves are the only examples of rational teleology in the world, and as such the only ends-in-themselves, for-themselves.[101] (2) The notion that there is a realm of "values" (axiology) that is neither natural nor the product of human projection, which then entails duties for rational subjects.[102] However, this view's very lack of ontological causality (whether adequate or even inadequate as in the solution just mentioned above) makes it ultimately indistinguishable from humanly invented goods.[103] (3) The notion that rational subjects are able to construct an ideal world for themselves. However, this view requires the invention of a god, who is neither discovered in nature nor revealed in history, to ultimately

---

Whereas Habermas rejects the notion of transcendent ends and MacIntyre seems to bracket it, Strauss returns to it. In *What Is Political Philosophy?* (Glencoe, Ill.: Free Press, 1959) he tentatively proposes that human teleology *and* classical (viz., Aristotelian) cosmology are *both* a "quest" for knowledge of the whole rather than a demonstrated cosmology that is "the solution to the cosmological [i.e., teleological] problem" (39). But since, for Strauss, "knowledge of the whole . . . is not at our disposal" (39), yet human teleology is at our disposal ("we know parts . . . knowledge of the ends of human life" [39], would he not have been better advised, based on his own criteria, to more cogently follow Kant's constitution of the autonomous human subject's projective (i.e., immanent) teleology, including its cosmological project of knowledge of the whole (see n. 103 below)? Because of this impasse, the quest for transcendent ends now requires a very different teleology from that of the whole Platonic tradition. Somehow or other, in order for ends to be transcendent, they must *show* themselves. But without a teleological natural science, there is no basis for assuming that the human ends proposed by Plato and Aristotle are not in truth human projects—transcendental in the Kantian sense, but not transcendent, i.e., shown by the human mind but not showing themselves to it (see *Critique of Pure Reason*, A12).

[101] See *Critique of Judgment*, sec. 84; D. Novak, *Suicide and Morality* (New York: Scholars Studies Press, 1975), 90ff. Cf. Novak, *Jewish Social Ethics*, 141f.

[102] See Nicolai Hartmann, *Ethics*, vol. trans. S. Coit (London: G. Allen and Unwin, 1932), 263ff.; Max Scheler, *Formalism in Ethics and Non-Formal Ethics of Value*, trans. M. S. Frings and R. L. Funk (Evanston, Ill.: Northwestern University Press, 1973), 12ff.

[103] In arguing against Leo Strauss's earlier assertion in *Natural Right and History* that a teleological ethics is connected with a teleological natural science (see n. 100 above), John Finnis writes (*Natural Law and Natural Rights*, 52): "There is much to be said for the view that the order of dependence was precisely the opposite—that the teleological conception of nature was made plausible, indeed conceivable, by analogy with the *intro*spectively luminous, self-evident structure of human well-being, practical reasoning, and human purposive action." But if natural teleology is only an analogical human projection, then is it not more reasonable to assume that human morality is such a projection too? Humanly sought goods, for Aristotelian Thomists, are only more than human projects if they are all ordered to a God whose existence is demonstrated by natural teleology (see Thomas Aquinas, *Summa Theologiae*, 1, q. 2., a. 3: 4th way; *Summa Contra Gentiles*, 1.41 and 3.17). As such, Thomistic ethics surely presupposes a teleological natural science and metaphysics, a point that Finnis explictly denies (see *Natural Law and Natural Rights*, 48f.). But is not the attempt to constitute a teleological ethics without a teleologically demonstrated God more convincingly done by Kant's projective teleology than by the various nonmetaphysical moral axiologies that have been proposed, be they either neo-Kantian or neo-Aristotelian or neo-Thomist?

accomplish what is clearly beyond the capacity of finite, mortal humans.[104] It would seem that if one has to employ theology to save ethics, one would be more successful by employing a God discovered by pure reason or a god presented in revelation, neither of whom is invented. Is there not something quite absurd about the maker worshiping what he or she has made for him- or herself?[105]

In each of these solutions to the is/ought problem, the ought follows from a higher state of being, which, unlike the world of things, seems to make claims on persons. But the inadequacy of all of them is that only persons themselves can really make claims on other persons in a truly nonmetaphorical way. Therefore, what a theory of primary rights accomplishes is to make personal claims truly original and not to derive them from an abstract state of being, which, being ideal, is neither person nor thing.

Indeed, the world of things that Hume and so many others have constituted as primary, be these things natural entities or human-made artifacts, is always within the context of interpersonal transactions. As such, we can never stop evaluating things in one way or another. It is not that "is" functions independently of "ought," or that "ought" is constituted after "is," so that it must be derived from a higher state of being that functions as a transcendental base for the deduction of duties. Instead, every "is" functions within a prior world of "oughts," which are personal claims. Things *are found*; persons *claim*. Things themselves are constituted within what Husserl called the "lived world" (*Lebenswelt*). This world can best be seen as the domain of interpersonal transactions.[106] Things that are human artifacts or potential human artifacts ("raw materials") are included in this realm by technology. They are useful; hence, they are to be taken up into our place. Things that are natural entities, which are seen as limits on human praxis to be placed beyond human use, are included in this interpersonal realm by pure science (*theōria*). They are beautiful, hence to be left to exist in their own place.[107] Science itself begins as an aesthetic quest.[108] And works of fine art (*poiēsis*) are also inviolable because they are

---

[104] See Kant, *Critique of Practical Reason*, 1.2.2.5.

[105] See Isa. 44:9ff.

[106] See *The Crisis of European Sciences and Transcendental Phenomenology*, trans. D. Carr (Evanston, Ill.: Northwestern University Press, 1970), 103ff. Husserl does not constitute, however, the realm of the interpersonal until after he has constituted the nonpersonal realm. See *Cartesian Meditations*, trans. D. Cairns (The Hague: M. Nijhoff, 1960), 89ff. Cf. Levinas, *Totality and Infinity*, 67.

[107] This closely follows Heidegger's distinction between "things-at-hand" (*Zuhanden*) and "things-before-hand" (*Vorhanden*). See *Sein und Zeit*, 15th ed. (Tübingen: Max Niemeyer Verlag, 1979), sec. 16. Along these general lines, see Jürgen Habermas, *Knowledge and Human Interests*, trans. J. J. Shapiro (Boston: Beacon, 1971), 113ff.

[108] Note Aristotle, *Metaphysics*, 980a22: "All humans naturally desire to know, which is indicated by our love of our senses. For they are loved for themselves apart from any use . . . even when no action (*prattein*) is intended" (my translation).

imitations of this natural beauty. But the realm of interpersonal transactions is more than technology or pure science or fine art, or even than any combination of all three. It always surrounds them all inclusively. No things are ever beyond the human capacity for categorical description, beyond the capacity for giving common names. Humans themselves, however, receive their proper names as a call from other persons. Only God names himself.[109]

This emphasis of the primacy of personal claims in the moral life also supplies an answer to the frequently invoked question about the idea of natural law: If law qua law requires promulgation, who promulgates natural law?[110] In the case of human-made law, the voice of the human lawgiver is clearly heard and duly recorded, simultaneously noting when and where the law was so promulgated. But if one says that natural law is promulgated by God, who creates and governs the universe, how is that voice heard?[111] Revelation cannot be the answer because even if one holds that natural law is divine law, it is also universal. Conversely, revelation is always to a singular community at a definite point in history.[112] In that general sense, revealed law like human made law is positive law, the specific differences being *who* promulgated it to *whom*, *when* and *where*, not so much *how* it was promulgated. In both these cases, the lawgiver speaks directly to the governed. However, in the case of natural law, the voice of the lawgiver to the governed is mediated. In determining the basic rights of *any* human person and *any* human community, we justify listening to their voices responsively, if these voices make valid universal claims on all of us. So far, we are at the level of universal morality. Moving deeper down to the ontological level, we attribute the justice of these claims to the universal nature God creates by his command. "He spoke and it came to be; he commanded and it endured (*va-ya'amod*)" (Psalms 33:9). Thus human dignity, both personal and communal, reflects the voice of God through the real voices of the humans who make their natural claims upon us here and now. But in the truly original sense, only God can call for our full obedience. Nature itself in general and human nature specifically are the obedient results of God's command. All law must be originally justified by divine law: what is to be obeyed in and of itself.[113] Just humans claims are truly in the image of God,

---

[109] Regarding human descriptive naming of the world, see Gen. 2:19–20. Regarding humans being personally named by others, see Gen. 2:23; also, Novak, *Jewish-Christian Dialogue*, 145ff. Regarding God's self-naming, see Exod. 3:13–15, 6:2–3, 33:17–23.

[110] This was the argument of Hans Kelsen against natural law, viz., "nature has no will" (*The Pure Theory of Law*, trans. M. Knight [Berkeley: University of California Press, 1967], 221). Cf. Novak, *Natural Law in Judaism*, 124, n. 3.

[111] For the view that natural law is divine law, promulgated by God, but through human nature not by historical revelation, see B. Sanhedrin 56b re Gen. 2:16; also, Thomas Aquinas, *Summa Theologiae*, 2/1, q. 90, a. 4.

[112] See Novak, *Jewish-Christian Dialogue*, 129ff.

[113] See Maimonides, *Mishneh Torah*: Melakhim, 8.11; also, Thomas Aquinas, *Summa Theologiae*, 2/1, q. 94, a. 4 ad 1.

which express God's entitlements to his unique human creatures, but which require constant reference to their source: "All is given from the one shepherd" (Ecclesiastes 12:11).[114]

How fundamentally different all this is from seeing natural law as some sort of translation of a higher nature down to the actual affairs of human beings. In that view, there is no primary voice, but only a vision of a polity that might conform to a higher paradigm in the heavens. It is duty without an originating right/claim,[115] for such a right/claim cannot be imagined, but only heard.

The Jewish covenantal tradition, with its attendant legal system of Halakhah, is the best example of a historical community where the correlation of rights and duties and duties and rights seems to be without exception. As we shall see in greater detail, rights generate duties inasmuch as claims generate responses in a way that duties do not generate rights. For *responses* cannot generate the claims made prior to them for them. However, we must see in far greater detail that the notion of rights defended in this book is beholden neither to notions of social contract nor to notions of moral creativity nor to notions of personal autonomy. Furthermore, if one sees all three of these modern views as deconstructions of the biblical covenant, then one can very well retain the term and concept of rights by returning it to its original source and then develop the concept *from* that source and not *against* it.[116] The legacy of Athens is not the only alternative to the individualistic or collectivist excesses of modernity. The voice from Jerusalem makes its own alternative claims, claims that I am convinced are in truth superior.[117]

THE POLITICAL DILEMMA OF MODERN JEWS

Jews can well be seen as one of the chief beneficiaries of modern notions of rights. Rights-based political theories and the polities that they inspired justified the entry of Jews into the uniquely modern nation-states, which began to be constituted in the wake of the French Revolution. Prior to this time, Jews faced the problem of being an alien minority community that was, at best, tolerated by an unsympathetic majority and the culture and societies it controlled; at worst, persecuted by a hostile majority and the cultures and societies

---

[114] See B. Hagigah 3b.

[115] See Plato, *Republic*, 369Cff.; also, Plato, *Timeaus*, 30A–D.

[116] One can see social contract as a reduction of the covenant to a humanly initiated agreement (see Hobbes, *The Elements of Law*, 1.15.9). One can see moral creativity as a substitution of man for God. And one can see personal autonomy as an overelaboration of human free choice, which is integral to the covenant (see Novak, *The Election of Israel*, 163ff.). For the project of retrieving originally biblical doctrines from their modern deconstructions, see 5ff.

[117] Along these lines, see Susan Orr, *Jerusalem and Athens* (Lanham, Md.: Rowman and Littlefield, 1995), 147ff.

it controlled. But with rights-based political theories, there was only the recognition of lone, ahistorical individuals and the particular societies they had constructed for the protection and enhancement of their rights. In theory, anyway, one's religious and cultural distinctions were no longer to be matters of any normative concern. Jews were to be treated like any other individuals.[118] Following this logic in its historical trajectory, its adherents have seen the continued discrimination against Jews in any particular society as attributable to the fact that egalitarian liberty, which is the very project of modern European and North American polities, has not yet been completed. Practice always lags behind theory. Progress is always incremental. As such, this sort of discrimination against the Jews, let alone persecution and genocide, is seen as being due to periodic lapses into older forms of inequality and tyranny. The hope is that these lapses will become fewer and fewer due to higher cultural development and political enlightenment, eventually resulting in a zero sum.

The problem this has raised for Jews, however, is that there seems to be little connection of such a political program to the Jewish tradition, which like any tradition is inherently political, even without having national independence for most of its history.[119] Even though having one's own state is a desideratum of a political tradition, it is not a sine qua non. The community is the smallest self-contained political entity, and Jews have always had some sort of community, even if membership in it has been sustained without the availability of state-enforced sanctions. Indeed, virtually the entire rabbinic tradition developed under circumstances of less than actual national independence. Thus it is to that tradition we must look in constituting what could be termed a Jewish political theory. Maximally, the traditional sources should provide specific source material ready for theoretical development; minimally, that theoretical development should not contradict the specific teachings of these sources.[120] That is, maximally, one's theory should be directly derived from these sources in such a way that its validity is verified by them; minimally, one's theory

[118] For the background of this, see Jacob Katz, *Out of the Ghetto* (Cambridge: Harvard University Press, 1978), 191ff.

[119] See Eugene B. Borowitz, *Renewing the Covenant* (Philadelphia: Jewish Publication Society, 1991), 17f.

[120] See, e.g., Maimonides' *Maamar Tehiyyat ha-Metim*, which is his attempt to show that his theological constitution of the doctrine of "the world-to-come" (*olam ha-ba*) does not contradict the rabbinic designation of the doctrine of the resurrection of the dead as a Jewish dogma (see M. Sanhedrin 10.1). In other words, maximally a theologian's theory should be verified by extensive reference to the scriptural and rabbinic sources; minimally it should not be falsified by these same sources. A Jewish theory of rights in the modern sense would seem to fall in the latter category of validation, as did Maimonides' medieval theory of the world-to-come. That is, at best it can develop only what is implicit within the tradition. It cannot literally derive it from specific sources, however. For the recognition that the answer to every new question cannot be simply deduced from traditional sources, see Nahmanides, *Commentary on the Torah*: Deut. 6:18; R. Vidal of Tolosa, *Magid Mishneh* on Maimonides, *Mishneh Torah*: Shekhenim, 14.5.

should avoid refutation from these sources in such a way that its validity is not falsified by them. In cases of much new theory, the criterion of falsifiability *from* the sources pertains far more often than the stricter correspondence that verifiability *by* the sources entails.[121]

It would seem that the Jewish political tradition has no place for the modern notion of rights. When the question has been raised, some Jewish scholars have pointed out that rights are a foreign import into Jewish legal and political discourse. One of the chief arguments made along these lines is that in Judaism there are duties and anything that could be termed rights is strictly derivative from these duties except, of course, God's primal right to demand all our duties as what is owed to himself.[122] Proof of this is that there are a number of ready-made terms for "duty," most obviously, *hovah* (literally, a "debt"), but there is no real term for a "right."[123] The closest term that comes to mind for the concept of right (and the one used in discussions of rights in modern Hebrew) is *zekh-ut*.[124] But in its original rabbinic setting, a *zekhut* is a privilege, that is, an entitlement. It is not what a person "holds" as much as it is what a person has been granted—and by implication, what can be revoked.[125] The same is true of the term *reshut* (literally, "permission"), which could be defined as that which has not yet been legislated.[126] Thus, whereas duty finds a number of ready-made elementary terms in the traditional system of commandments (*mitsvot*) known by the generic name Halakhah, rights seems to have to borrow one term or other and thus stretch its original meanings considerably, perhaps to the breaking point.[127] Nevertheless, as we shall see, the term that does corre-

---

[121] This closely follows Karl Popper's distinction between verifiability, falsifiability, and conventionalism. Popper correctly shows how the criterion of verifiability alone relies too much on strict correspondence of theory *to* data (what in regard to religious traditons one could call "fundamentalism"), whereas the criterion of conventionalism (which he attributes to Kantianism) makes the data essentially arbitrary (which is much harder to do when the data are from a verbalized tradition, i.e., words, not mute things). The criterion of falsifiability, conversely, makes the data limits on a theory, which it can neither ignore nor simply refer to. That, it seems, is how a religious tradition like Judaism develops with continuity. See "Falsification versus Conventionalism," in *Popper Selections*, ed. D. Miller (Princeton: Princeton University Press, 1985), 143ff.

[122] See Robert M. Cover, "Obligation: A Jewish Jurisprudence of the Social Order," *Journal of Law and Religion* 5 (1987): 66.

[123] Generally, "commandments" (*mitsvot*) are conditional norms; "duties" (*hovot*) are unconditional norms (see Maimonides, *Mishneh Torah*: Berakhot, 11.2). Hence one has an option/right to avoid the conditions that would obligate one to perform a *mitsvah*. Nevertheless, it was often suggested that one should exercise such an option/right since it is more of a privilege (*zekhut*) to be able to observe a *mitsvah* than to avoid one (see, e.g., B. Kiddushin 31a).

[124] Hence "human rights" in modern Hebrew are called *zekhuyot enoshiyot*.

[125] See, e.g., M. Eruvin 7.11; M. Makkot 3.16 re Isa. 42:21; B. Pesahim 19a–b and Rashi, s.v. "zakhinu." For the revocation of such an option/right, see, e.g., B. Kiddushin 12b. Cf. Z. W. Falk, *Law and Religion* (Jerusalem: Meisharim, 1981), 80.

[126] See, e.g., B. Betsah 36b.

[127] See Cover, "Obligation," 65.

spond to rights is a "cry" (*tsa'aqah*) in the language of Scripture, or a "claim" (*ta'anah*) in the language of the Rabbis.[128]

This has led to two divergent Jewish solutions to this theological-political dilemma. On the one hand, that majority of modernity-affirming Jews who did not go over to Marxism (with its denial of the concept of rights) accepted rights as primary, even if that meant a tenuous connection to the Jewish tradition or no connection to it at all.[129] The needs of Jews as individual citizens were seen as taking complete precedence over the needs of the older Jewish communal tradition. But, of course, it is that tradition that makes Jews Jewish. Anything less than it seems to be a ticket to either instant or gradual assimilation, whether individual or collective.

So, on the other hand, there has been a persistent minority of Jews who have basically been adverse to the whole liberal rights culture, attempting to distance themselves from it as much as is politically possible for Jews who, after all, still do not want to live in any of the illiberal polities available in the world today. And when such Jews have gained a measure of political power in the Jewish State of Israel, a state that is still without a written constitution and bill of rights, some of them have been openly contemptuous of the concept of rights—that is, human rights—altogether.[130] In addition, they have often pointed out how indifferent the Western liberal democracies were to the plight of the Jews during the Holocaust, despite the fact that most Jews were enamored of their promise of political equality and opportunity.[131]

Yet at this juncture of our vulnerable history, Jews should realize that only in democracies have we been able to survive, let alone flourish, politically, economically—and even religiously. This certainly explains why the vast majority of Jews, both in Israel and in the diaspora, would not choose to live under any regime but a democratic one. In fact, as is so well known, it is under the other two forms of government available in the modern world—fascism and communism—that Jews have often been the greatest victims of persecution and destruction. Therefore, I think Jews could well conclude from their experience of modernity that what we abhor externally we ought to abhor even on our own communal turf.[132] There is much support for that moral consistency and integrity within the tradition itself. As such, any system of Judaism that cannot factor into its operations at least some of the major democratic principles, most especially the principle of human rights, is attractive only to those who think that Jews can withdraw from the world into the hermetically sealed

---

[128] See, e.g., Job 19:7; M. Ketubot 13.4.

[129] For Marx's rejection of the concept of individual human rights, see "On the Jewish Question," in *The Marx-Engels Reader*, 2nd ed., ed. R. Tucker (New York: W. W. Norton, 1978), 40ff.

[130] See Meir Kahane, *Uncomfortable Questions for Comfortable Jews* (Secaucus, N.J.: L. Stuart, 1987), 45ff., 155ff.

[131] See Meir Kahane, *Never Again* (Los Angeles: Nash, 1971), 5ff.

[132] See B. Sanhedrin 59a and parallels.

safety of a world totally under their own control. Such blindness to contemporary experience is, of course, not unique to Jews. We see examples of it today among Muslims, Christians, Hindus, and Buddhists. The suffering brought by such fanatics on others, even others in their own communities, is obvious to anyone who follows current events.

This theological-political dilemma lies at the heart of the persistent Kulturkampf afflicting the Jewish people throughout the world, most acutely in the Jewish State of Israel but certainly not limited to it. The question is whether it is possible to bridge a commitment to the Jewish tradition and a concern for human rights. It would seem that the only way to do so with integrity would be to locate the concept of human rights *within* the Jewish tradition itself and then develop it from there. The only alternatives to this are either to concede that on *the* major political issue of the modern age Judaism has nothing to say and is thus irrelevant or to simply avoid the issue altogether by reducing it to some sort of pseudo-problem. The first alternative, however, leads to intellectual if not cultural assimilation, for a political vacuum is inevitably filled by something else. The second alternative leads to intellectual and cultural obscurantism. And that obscurantism is anything but benign in the world today. Even the suggestion of a Jewish regime in which the need for rights is denied will inevitably be compared to antiliberal polities already functioning that employ racial or religious coercion. Like it or not, these regimes will be taken as the practical models at hand here and now. But, most importantly, the passion for social justice so obvious in biblical and rabbinic teaching seems to have enough in common with the modern concern for human rights to strongly suggest that looking at the tradition for insight into this whole issue of political theory will by no means be futile.

The philosophical question before us is whether there is some way to avoid—or, better, overcome—the standoff we seem to have between the theocratic principles of the Jewish tradition and the democratic principles of the societies in the world where Jews have survived and flourished.[133] That overcoming cannot be one of a superficial "synthesis," where one simply settles for some questionable similarities between the two political systems. When this happens, what we really have, in effect, is one tradition supplying the principles and the other accommodating itself to it by supplying examples for it—and only convenient examples at that. It is easy to see how Judaism can be used by democratic theorists in this accommodating way.[134] The task for Jewish thinkers, conversely, is to formulate a political theory out of the Jewish tradition that recognizes the institution of rights, but that also does not base

---

[133] Cf. Yeshayahu Leibowitz, *Yahadut Am Yehudi u-Medinat Yisrael* (Jerusalem: Schocken, 1976), 181ff.

[134] This is the problem with most of the essays in the volume *Judaism and Human Rights*, ed. M. Konvitz (New York: W. W. Norton, 1972).

them on principles that are either un-Jewish or anti-Jewish. In order to do that, we must return to the *theocratic* principles of the Jewish covenantal system. And by "theocracy," I do not mean its usual connotation today as basically the dictatorship of clerics, but, rather, its original denotation as "the rule of God."[135] As we shall see, this will also require a critique of the political philosophy of some of those Jewish clerics who speak for the Jewish tradition, even with learning and communal authority behind them. Their philosophy (more often, their ideology) seems to reach the conclusion that the Jewish idea of polity is a dictatorship of rabbis.[136]

The Jewish people has always considered herself to be under the ultimate rule of God who has made a unique and everlasting covenant with her, but the forms of polity she has been able to appropriate have often been borrowed from her historical surroundings. Thus, for example, when the Israelite nation became a monarchy, the motivation behind the choice of this form of government was the people's desire for "a king to judge us like all the nations . . . to go out before us and fight our wars" (I Samuel 8:6, 20). During much of the history of the monarchy in Israel, the task for Jewish thought was to determine the place of this institution, not at all uniquely Jewish, in the uniquely Jewish idea of covenantal theocracy.[137] This led to both an appropriation of a new form of polity and a critical reworking of it.

In the ancient world, the Israelite nation had the choice of being either a monarchy or a tribal confederation. In the modern world, the Jewish people has a choice, collectively as in Israel or individually as in the diaspora, of affirming either a democracy or some type of tyranny, secular or religious. Just as the ancient world offered several basic political options, so does the modern world. And just as the ancient Jewish nation clearly opted for monarchy (with conditional divine approval), so has the modern Jewish people clearly opted for democracy, everywhere (hopefully, with the same conditional divine approval). The real challenge for contemporary Jewish thought is to ground those aspects of democracy it can accept in good faith in the uniquely Jewish covenantal theocracy, and with as much good faith reject those aspects of it that it cannot accept.[138]

Democracy is not just the rule of the majority as opposed to that of an oligarchy. If that were all democracy is, then Nazi Germany or the Soviet

---

[135] The term seems to have been coined by Josephus. See *Contra Apionem*, 2.164ff.

[136] See Isaac Halevy Herzog, *Tehuqah le-Yisrael al-pi Ha-Torah* (Jerusalem: Mosad ha-Rav Kook, 1989), 7ff.

[137] See Yehezkel Kaufmann, *The Religion of Israel*, trans. M. Greenberg (Chicago: University of Chicago, 1960), 266; D. J. Elazar, *Covenant and Polity in Biblical Israel* (New Brunswick, N.J.: Transaction Books, 1995), 295ff.

[138] See S. Federbush, *Mishpat ha-Melukhah be-Yisrael*, 2nd ed., rev. (Jerusalem: Mosad ha-Rav Kook, 1973), 26ff.; Z. W. Falk, *Erkhei Mishpat ve-Yahadut* (Jerusalem: Meisharim, 1980), 40f.

Union would have been a democracy. In both societies, the governing powers surely had the support of the vast majority of the citizens. Instead, democracy combines majority rule with the protection of minority rights, especially the rights of the smallest minority possible, the individual human person, even when these rights are in conflict with the interests of the majority society as a whole. That is the case as long as they do not pose a clear and immediate danger to the survival or liberty of the society itself. Ronald Dworkin has put it quite well: individual rights are what prevent a society and its legal system from becoming "ordered brutality."[139] For today's Jews, this insight is anything but arcane. The question is how to find the justification for these rights in the Jewish tradition.[140] (What they specifically are is itself, of course, a matter of dispute even when the concept of them is accepted in principle.) Those who desire a closer connection between the cultural heritage of the Jewish people and their current political interests ought to be especially motivated to find the concept of rights and elaborate on its philosophical implications. The task, to be sure, is not easy.

The blind spot of many in the Jewish tradition concerning at least the potential for developing a theory of rights out of the tradition might be explained in this way. Most of these opponents of this rights theory uncritically accept the modern assumption that rights pertain exclusively to individual persons. Because an individual person is clearly the smallest component in the covenantal system, it follows that he or she has many more duties than rights, since God and the community have more claims on the individual person than he or she has on them. Hence, this fact has caused many to conclude that there are no rights at all in the covenantal system governed by Halakhah. However, once it is shown that all duties presuppose correlative rights, including duties owed to God or the community, and that individual rights as claims are as valid as those of God or the community, this erroneous dismissal of a Jewish rights theory can be refuted, for it is based on the mistake of assuming that Judaism is nothing but a system of heteronomous duties for their own sake. A theory of rights supplies adequate reasons for these more ostensive duties, and it can be coordinated into a rationally compelling system. In this way, Jewish law, especially as it pertains to interhuman relations, can be seen as based on a theonomous wisdom that avoids the idealism that comes with autonomy and the unintelligibility that comes with heteronomy.[141] Indeed, the insistence that all Jewish duties are correlated with prior rights follows from the assumption that, at least as regards all the commandments pertaining to interhuman rela-

---

For the variety of political systems under which the covenant can function, see D. J. Elazar, ed., *Kingship and Consent* (Washington, D.C.: University Press of America, 1983).

[139] *Taking Rights Seriously*, 205.

[140] Cf. Herzog, *Tehuqah le-Yisra'el al-pi Ha-Torah*, 12, 23, n. 2.

[141] See Novak, *Jewish Social Ethics*, 45ff.

tionships, all these duties have specific reasons (*ta'amei ha-mitsvot*) in addition to being like all the commandments: God's inviolable will.[142] Thus there is a strong link between the discussion of natural law in classical Jewish sources and the modern Jewish concern for human rights. It is, furthermore, no accident that many students of Jewish law who are most suspicious of Jewish rights talk are also advocates of highly hierarchal, authoritarian interpretations and applications of that law, for authoritarianism is equally contemptuous of both reasons and persons. Authority becomes more and more its own justification, requiring no persuasive reasons. It merely asserts that the duties of persons under it are to obey those other persons who possess it. The needs of those persons living under such authority become less and less significant.

HAIM COHN AND THE SECULARIZATION OF JEWISH LAW

The Jewish legal tradition has long been the area where one could engage in the most systematic discourse. Thus it is here that some of the most astute Jewish thinkers have turned to develop a Jewish political theory. This has been the case, most especially, with discussions of rights, since *rights* has such an immediately legal meaning.

To date, the most coherent and learned attempt to incorporate the concern of rights talk into the study of Jewish law has been that of the now retired Israel Supreme Court justice, Haim Cohn. Cohn's project has been basically to argue as follows. In the area of interhuman relationships (*bein adam le-havero*), even though the traditional language of Jewish law is that of obligation—duty (*hovah*) or commandment (*mitsvah*)—these duties do not create subsequent rights but, rather, they recognize rights that are prior to the enactment of the duties that are to be the proper responses to them.[143] One of his prime examples is the obligation to give charity (*tsedaqah*) to the poor. It is not a duty that then creates the right of the poor person to receive it. Instead, it is the recognition of the poor person's right to be helped that leads to the enactment of the proper response to his or her need as a duty on others. This example is one that I too used earlier to demonstrate how a duty presupposes a correlative right. The question regarding Cohn's theory, however, is whether his range of rights and duties extends wide enough.

Using his great erudition in the biblical and rabbinic literary sources, Cohn has made an impressive argument for a new way of looking at Jewish civil and criminal law. However, since the obligations of Jewish law are seen as commandments (*mitsvot*), that is, expressions of God's will, there is a fundamental theological problem with Cohn's theory of human rights in Jewish law.

---

[142] See Novak, *Natural Law in Judaism*, 64ff.

[143] *Human Rights in Jewish Law* (New York: KTAV, 1984), 17f.

It is uncertain, from what he writes, anyway, whether Cohn actually believes in God, and even if he does as a personal matter, whether he sees such belief as legally foundational. Indeed, Cohn seems to explain the religious form of even Jewish civil and criminal law as being the recognition of an essentially human reality, which is then projected onto the level of the divine (*bein adam le-maqom*).[144] This has the effect of giving the laws that protect and enhance human rights a greater sanction, a cosmic status, as it were. Yet it seems that for Haim Cohn, the notion of a divine lawgiver, from whom all rights are gifts and to whom all duties are obligations, functions very much like what Plato called "necessary lies," namely, falsehoods needed to motivate the gullible masses to do what is inherently right.[145] However, what happens when the lie is exposed for what it is: deceit, however well intentioned? At that point, the lie becomes a *myth*, which at best can be remembered nostalgically for what it *once* effected. But how can it ever be retrieved again after the quintessential modern critique of religion expressed by Feuerbach (and after him, mutatis mutandis, by Nietzsche, Marx, and Freud), namely, that religion itself is a projection of human ideals onto a superhuman reality.[146] What is to be retrieved is not that fictitious reality, but the human ideals that lie buried in it. But would not this retrieval lead to a form of polity so antithetical to the whole Jewish tradition as to be forever broken off from it?

Cohn has definitely asked the right questions. Nevertheless, his theory becomes inadequate to the task of constituting a Jewish theory of rights because it cannot locate its foundation in the Jewish tradition itself. If the tradition's constitution of rights has been presented upon a foundation now seen to be fictitious, then it would seem that once that fiction has been uncovered, Jews concerned with rights would have to go elsewhere to find principles that adequately justify rights. As such, the overcoming of the Jewish tradition itself, however fondly it might be remembered, becomes a necessity for anyone concerned with truthfulness as a moral imperative: "Move far away from deceit (*dvar sheqer*)" (Exodus 23:7). Can one consciously lie to himself or herself, however much he or she might lie to others, and still engage in any coherent pursuit?[147]

---

[144] Thus he tellingly writes: "Most talmudical human-rights pronouncements . . . while clothed with divine (or quasi-divine) authority . . . are but normative expressions of their authors' humanitarian creeds . . . the 'divinity' is inherent, so to speak . . . determining the nature of the law as if by legal fiction" (ibid., 5).

[145] See *Republic*, 389B and 414C. Cf. Karl Popper, *The Open Society and Its Enemies*, vol. 1, 5th ed. (Princeton: Princeton Univesrity Press, 1966), 138f. Such a fiction is more than the occasional *fictio juris* present in any legal system. Rather, it can only be seen as the source of a *corpus juris fictionis*. Cf. Novak, *Natural Law in Judaism*, 22f.

[146] See Ludwig Feuerbach, *The Essence of Christianity*, trans. George Eliot (New York: Harper and Row, 1957), 197ff.

[147] See Plato, *Republic*, 351C–D.

Haim Cohn's attempt to secularize Jewish law, especially on the whole question of human rights, is a radical project because it moves away from the root (*radix*) of its tradition. However, it might very well be even more radical to constitute a theory of rights that reaffirms the root of the tradition in such a way as to discover new implications of it for the political needs of our time. In my view, this requires a more explicitly theological way of looking at the law and its sources than is usually the case in the scholarly treatment of Jewish law, either by traditionalists or modernists.[148] That way also has to be more philosophical since its insights are being inserted into general discussions of political *theory*, which itself seems to require the rational rigor of philosophy. Along these lines, I shall attempt to argue that not only is the divine-human relationship the basis of all rights in the Jewish tradition, both those of persons and those of communities, but that it is also the missing link in the current impasse in political theory.

A generation ago, in his introduction to a volume of essays on Judaism and human rights, the Jewish political theorist Milton R. Konvitz correctly noted, "There is no word or phrase for 'human rights' in the Hebrew Scriptures or in any other ancient Jewish text. . . . Yet . . . the absence of these and related words and phrases does not mean the nonexistence of the ideals and values for which they stand or to which they point."[149] Konvitz was right, of course, by arguing against the kind of historicist reduction that would dismiss the question of rights by severing any connection between the issues of the present and the teachings of the past. Nevertheless, the other extreme to be avoided is simply to assume that ancient religious texts can function as precedents for moral and political principles that are already formulated in and for the present. When this is done, the continuing moral necessity of rereading these ancient texts becomes lost because the modern principles of which these texts are precedents are assumed to be true in and of themselves here and now. They are taken to be self-sufficient even if not always self-evident. And, indeed, anything but tangential concern with these ancient precedents might actually be counterproductive by diverting attention from the real and pressing concerns to which moral and political principles are always to be addressed.

A good example of this fallacy, what might be called the "fallacy of immediate relevance," is the simple location in the Jewish tradition of precedents for the modern democratic interest in human rights. Without a critical role for Judaism in its relation to this modern democratic interest, which is a role where it attempts to rethink democracy as to what it is-to-be and not just to confirm it as-it-is—without that critical role I do not see how Judaism would not quickly be turned into a matter of ultimately antiquarian interest. Such a matter is irrelevant when moral and political principles are practically *directed toward*

---

[148] See D. Novak, *Halakhah in a Theological Dimension* (Chico, Calif.: Scholars Press, 1985).
[149] *Judaism and Human Rights*, 13.

the future and not just *traced from* the past parenthetically. In other words, in order for a Jewish thinker to get involved in the conversation about human rights altogether, he or she must insist on being more than a provider of background music, as it were. As the greatest German Jewish philosopher, Hermann Cohen stressed, there is an essential difference between a historical origin of facts (*Anfang*) and a philosophical source (*Ursprung*) of concepts.[150] The task, then, is to look for a definition of rights that can make a bridge between the full vision of rights in the Jewish tradition and the partial vision of rights and duties by both liberals and communitarians today. When this is done, we might be in a better position to see the Jewish tradition in a critical relation to the reality of modern democracy and its concern with human rights. That is, we must see how the Jewish tradition can provide an intelligent viewpoint from which not just to follow contemporary interest in rights, and at best to be patronized by most of its proponents, but to judge it and redirect it. By so doing, we might actually find in and for contemporary democracy those practices that are indispensable for the conduct of a society truly worthy of the moral allegiance of rational human persons, and concurrently reject those practices in it and for it that make a society unworthy of such moral allegiance.

Seeing Judaism as a system of rights, the ensuing chapters will deal with the specific types of rights and correlative duties embedded in seven primary interpersonal relationships. In these relationships, the first term designates the rights bearer, the second the duty bearer. They are: (1) God and human persons; (2) human persons and God; (3) God and covenanted community; (4) covenanted community and God; (5) between human persons; (6) covenanted community and human persons; and (7) human persons and covenanted community.

---

[150] *Religion of Reason Out of the Sources of Judaism*, trans. S. Kaplan (New York: Frederick Ungar, 1972), 10, 63f.

CHAPTER I

God and Human Persons

GOD'S ABSOLUTE POWER

Looking into Scripture, from which all authentic Jewish thought must begin, one sees that at the most primary level, the unlimited power of God is repeatedly asserted. "See now that I, I am He and there is no power (*elohim*) along with me. I kill and I give life; there is no one who can escape my hand" (Deuteronomy 32:39). "I am the first and I am the last, besides me there is no god (*ein elohim*)" (Isaiah 44:6). God has already made everything in the world. That is why no one can stand up against God successfully. "I am the Lord, and there is no other god besides me . . . there is nothing (*efes*) other than me; I am the Lord and no one else" (Isaiah 45:5–6). This difference is brought out by the awareness that everything in creation is mortal and that God transcends creation's essential mortality by his own unique immortality. Scripture emphasizes this as the difference of all differences. Indeed, that seems to be why God has made everything to be mortal. Mortality is inherent within the very nature of every existent created by God. It is the ultimate limit.[1] Being inherent within each existent and not being an eternal entity into which mortal beings are simply dispensable parts, nature is the specific limit of every creature. Mortality is the finality of all finalities. No natural being can escape it. Indeed, the same natural structure that sustains creatures from their beginnings also kills them in the end.[2] Furthermore, not only can no creature claim endless time for

---

[1] For the opinion that mortality is built into the structure of all created being, note: "R. Simon son of R. Lazar sat and interpreted in the name of R. Meir: 'And behold it is very good (*tov m'od*)' (Gen. 1:31)—behold death (*mavet*) is good. . . . R. Hama son of R. Hanina said that it was fitting for the first human not to taste death. So, why was he condemned (*niqnesah*) to death? It was because God foresaw that Nebudchanezzar and Hiram would make themselves into gods in the future, therefore he was condemned to death" (*Beresheet Rabbah* 9.5, ed. Theodor-Albeck, 70). Here the emphasis is on death being decreed so that human immortality not give humans an arrogant reason for sin (see B. Berakhot 5a re Ps. 4:5). For the opinion that death is the result of sin, and can thus be avoided by at least some of the righteous, cf. B. Shabbat 55a–b and Tos., s.v. "arba'ah" and "shema mina"; also, B. Sanhedrin 10a and Rashi, s.v. "malqot."

[2] Hence when humans are told by God that "on the day you eat of the tree of the knowledge of good and evil you shall surely die" (Gen. 2:17), the obvious problem is: They did not die then! However, if one sees this eating as being the entry of humans into the realm of adult, worldly experience, then the warning means that the irrevocable acceptance of this experiential realm is

itself, it cannot claim endless space for itself either.[3] "Heaven and earth and all their formations (*tseva'am*) were enclosed (*va-yekhulu*)" (Genesis 2:1) by God's power. God could have always created more. "Indeed Lord God, surely you have made heaven and earth by your great power and outstretched arm, nothing is too difficult (*lo yipalē*) for you" (Jeremiah 32:17). Accordingly, nothing created is unlimited.[4]

All creation is within time: it has a beginning and an end. "There is a time (*zeman*) and a season (*et*) for every purpose under heaven: a time to be born and a time to die" (Ecclesiastes 3:1–2).[5] Only God is coeval with time, transcending all beginnings and transcending all ends. Everything else occurs within God's lifetime, which limits all creation on both sides: at birth and at death.[6] "Dust (*afar*) you are and to dust you will return" (Genesis 3:19). And this applies not only to animate life on earth, whose deaths we directly experience, but it also applies to inanimate life, both on earth and beyond, whose deaths we do not directly experience. "Before the mountains were born and land and world formed, throughout all time (*me'olam v'ad olam*) you are God" (Psalms 90:2). "All the heavenly company will rot (*ve-namaqqu*) and be rolled up like a scroll, the heavens and all their company will wither away like a leaf from a vine or a fig from a fig tree" (Isaiah 34:4).[7] Creation is thus de novo; it

---

simultaneous with their becoming aware of their own irrevocable mortality. See Nahmanides, *Commentary on the Torah*, thereon.

[3] See B. Rosh Hashanah 11a re Gen. 2:1 and Tos., s.v. "le-qomatan"; *Beresheet Rabbah* 10.1 re Ps. 119:96. For the notion of how the assumption of infinite space entails infinite time, see Alexandre Koyré, *From the Closed World to the Infinite Universe* (Baltimore: Johns Hopkins University Press, 1957), 273ff. But if one assumes that there is not an infinite number of objects in the universe (however astronomical that number might be), then one need not assume an infinite extension of space, for as Kant well argued, the concept of space is meaningless if seen as encompassing more than actual physical objects (see *Critique of Pure Reason*, B195). Nevertheless, since any limiting number of objects in the universe seems to be unknowable, for scientific purposes one can proceed *as if* the universe were infinite and that there is infinite variety therein (see B542–43). In other words, it can be used hypothetically, but not asserted categorically. Theologically, though, it is otherwise, I think. This is not contradictory inasmuch as both the finitude and the infinity of the universe are only plausible assumptions. Neither assumption has been demonstrated to the exclusion of the other. For the difference between scientific and theological cosmology and the need for them not to be mutually exclusive, see Maimonides, *Guide of the Perplexed*, 2.15ff.

[4] See *Beresheet Rabbah* 68.9 re Gen. 28:11.

[5] Note on this verse: "There was a time for the first human to enter the Garden of Eden . . . and a time for him to depart from it" (*Qohelet Rabbati* 3.1). See E. E. Urbach, *Hazal* (Jerusalem: Magnes Press, 1971), 378f.

[6] See D. Novak, *The Election of Israel* (Cambridge: Cambridge University Press, 1995), 200ff., esp., 202, n. 6, contra Maimonides, *Guide of the Perplexed*, 2.13.

[7] See, e.g., B. Berakhot 32a re Exod. 32:13; B. Berakhot 10a and B. Megillah 14a re I Sam. 2:2. But for the opinion that the natural world has perpetuity, see *Sifre: Devarim*, no. 306 re Deut. 32:1, ed. Finkelstein, 335 (cf. ibid., p. 329 re Isa. 65:17 for an opinion of the nonperpetuity of the universe). The most prominent proponent of the perpetuity of the universe was Maimonides,

is an event within the lifetime of God. And because God's lifetime transcends it, creation is to be conceived as having both a beginning and an end.

Because of the constant scriptural emphasis of the transcendence of God, Judaism, quite early in its history (and then Christianity and Islam), interpreted the scriptural accounts of creation as *creatio ex nihilo*.[8] To be sure, it has been a major debate among biblical exegetes, certainly since the Middle Ages, whether the doctrine of "creation out of nothing" (*yesh m'ayin*) is explicitly taught in the text of Scripture, especially in the creation account at the very beginning of Genesis. "In the beginning God created the heavens and the earth. And the earth was an abyss (*tohu ve-vohu*) . . . and God said, 'let there be light' and there was light." (Genesis 1:1–3). It could well be inferred from this text that the "abyss" is some sort of primordial matter out of which God *then* created a world; or to use Platonic language, God engendered cosmos out of chaos.[9] However, this implies that God's power had to share the act of creation with something else primordially.[10] God's power would have to be limited by what is not God. By contrast, *creatio ex nihilo* is a corollary to the monotheism that Judaism from its very origins presented as the alternative to polytheism, where each god's power is limited by the power of some other god with whom he or she has to coexist. In the primordial sense, the logic of strict monotheism requires that God be apprehended as the One who is uniquely "without limit": *Ein Sof* in the language of the Kabbalah.[11]

Were even humans, whom Scripture teaches are the highest of all creatures, to believe themselves to be immortal, that would blur the difference between God and creation.[12] Humans would be the exception to creation instead of

---

Guide of the Perplexed, 2.27. See H. A. Wolfson, *Crescas' Critique of Aristotle* (Cambridge: Harvard University Press, 1929), 424. However, this seems to follow from his view that time is created rather than creation being within time. As such, temporality is a feature of creatures known a posteriori rather than being their a priori condition, as it is in my view.

[8] For perhaps the earliest assertion of *creatio ex nihilo*, which is clearly meant to be in contrast to Hellenic views of the eternity of the universe, see II Maccabees 7:23. For the assumption that this has always been authentic Jewish doctrine, see Maimonides, *Guide of the Perplexed*, 2.13ff.

[9] See Gersonides, *Milhamot ha-Shem*, 4.2.1; also, Jon D. Levenson, *Creation and the Persistance of Evil* (San Francisco: Harper and Row, 1988), 3ff. For Plato's view, see *Timeaus*, 29Eff.

[10] See Langdon Gilkey, *Maker of Heaven and Earth* (Garden City, N.Y.: Doubleday, 1959), 49f.

[11] See Gershom Scholem, *On the Kabbalah and Its Symbolism*, trans. R. Manheim (New York: Schocken, 1969), 35.

[12] This does not, however, deny rabbinic eschatology, because this eschatology is based on faith in God's creative power, which can overcome human mortality and imperfection rather than being based on immortality as an inherent human property. That is how Maimonides argued for the doctrine of the resurrection of the dead (see *Maamar Tehiyyat ha-Metim* in *Igrot ha-Rambam* ed. I. Shailat [Jerusalem: Ma'aliyot, 1987], 1:366f.). Unlike Maimonides, however, who confines this type of reasoning to the doctrine of resurrection (cf. *Mishneh Torah*: Yesodei ha-Torah, 4.8–9; Melakhim, 11.1ff.), I extend it to all of Jewish eschatology (see Novak, *The Election of Israel*, 262f.).

being the pinnacle within creation's limits.[13] Did not the serpent tempt the first human couple with divine power? "And you shall become like God: knowing good and bad" (Genesis 3:5). And did not God assert human mortality as his final response to that tempting lie by expelling the first human couple from the security of the Garden of Eden, with its ignorance of danger? Were the man with the woman to "extend his hand and take from the tree of life and eat and live forever (*l'olam*)" (Genesis 3:22), would they not have proven the serpent to be telling the truth after all? Were humans immortal, being born without having to die, could they not even assume that they have succeeded God in the order of things?[14]

The primary response of humans to the power of God is terror (*pahad*). The way to the tree of life, which humans cannot possess, is guarded by a "fiery sword" (Genesis 3:24). "Will his majesty affright you and his terror (*u-fahdo*) fall upon you?" (Job 13:11). "Therefore I am dismayed by his presence and I am terrified of him" (Job 23:15). Even when Abraham is arguing with God about the question of whether or not God seems to be proposing a just treatment of the people of Sodom and Gomorrah (by the way, a debate made possible by God's invitation to Abraham to be his consultant, not by any impertinence on Abraham's part), Abraham is forced to reiterate: "Here I presume (*ho'alti*) to speak to my Lord, even though I am but dust and ashes" (Genesis 18:27).[15] And after God finally appears to Job after all his complaints and all the conversations with his friends, Job is reduced to utter impotence by God's challenging question: "Where were you when I established the earth?" (Job 38:4). Here the very ground under him, which could alone be the basis of any claim upon God, is bluntly reclaimed by the God who created the earth and Job in it, Job his creature who is now attempting to stand up against God on it. At this point, Job is forced to conclude: "Therefore I abase myself (*em'as*) and withdraw my claim (*ve-nihamti*) [inasmuch as I am standing], on dust and ashes" (Job 42:5). When faced by God directly, Job has no ontological foundation upon which any basic moral claim must ultimately rest.

At this most primary level, however, which must be reiterated whenever humans act as if they were equal, let alone superior, to God, God is not yet exercising his right. A right is not only a power; it is a politically structured claim that calls for duty on the part of someone else. It is a power that cannot be directed to a totally inert object. In order for there to be a right, there must

---

[13] For the notion that awareness of mortality is the distinguishing characteristic of human nature, and for that reason is the Torah revealed to humans, see *Shir ha-Shirim Rabbah* 8.13 and *Tanhuma*: Va-yeshev, no. 4 re Num. 19:14.

[14] Note *Beresheet Rabbah* 19.4, where R. Joshua of Sikhnin puts the following words in the mouth of the serpent speaking to Eve: "He [God] ate of this tree and [then] created the world, so he said to you 'do not eat of it' (Gen. 2:17) in order that you not create other worlds."

[15] Thus at times of public mourning and fasting, the leaders of the community place dust or ashes or both on their heads as a sign of their nothingness before God. See B. Taanit 15b–16a.

be the possibility of an act of duty in free response. A right can be exercised only in the context of a legal system (*Rechtsordnung*), where both the rights holder and the duty holder are active members, however much the rights holder is superior to the duty holder.[16] The legal order structures both the right and the correlative duty proportionally. But at the primary level we have just examined above, humans are as yet in no position to respond to God in any active way. They are too terrified, not yet having any ground under them upon which to stand up before God. At this level, they have not yet been given any ground from God. Here we are painfully aware of the edges of our mortality, where we have no power at all. As one of the most important ancient Rabbis pointed out: "you are necessarily (*b'al korheha*) born . . . and necessarily you die."[17] We are not yet at the level within life itself where God does give us some power as persons. We humans do not have any duties yet, much less any rights.

POWER AS A RIGHT

In order for God's power to be understood as a right, it must be seen as a claim on somebody else, who himself or herself is able to freely respond to that claim. In order for this response to be possible, God must relinquish some of his own space, as it were, to allow his human creatures a place on which to stand before him—but never successfully against him.[18] "There is no wisdom, there is no understanding, there is no counsel to [endure] against (*le-neged*) the Lord" (Proverbs 21:30). Thus Scripture teaches that humans, the only beings whom we know to be addressed by God, are granted a special status at the time of their creation. "And God created humans (*adam*) in his image, in the image of God (*be-tselem elohim*) He made him: male and female He created them" (Genesis 1:27). And when humans leave the otherworldly haven of the Garden of Eden to take their place in this world, God says: "Now humans (*ha'adam*) are one like Us, knowing good and bad" (Genesis 3:22).[19]

There are various opinions about what is meant by the "image of God." Many have seen it as some inherent characteristic of human nature, like reason

---

[16] See H. L. A. Hart, *The Concept of Law* (Oxford: Clarendon Press, 1961), 91ff.

[17] M. Avot 4.22.

[18] Along these lines, we can locate the perennial theological question of the conflict between divine omniscience and human freedom of choice. See Maimonides, *Mishneh Torah*: Teshuvah, 5.4–5. But for a better ontological solution to the problem, see R. Hayyim ibn Attar, *Or ha-Hayyim*: Gen. 6:5; also, B. Megillah 25a and Rashi, s.v. "huts."

[19] Note Rashi, *Commentary on the Torah* thereon: "Indeed, he [humans] is unique (*yahid*) among the lower beings as I am unique among the upper beings—unlike animals and beasts." Also see *Targum Onqelos* thereon and E. E. Urbach, *Hazal* (Jerusalem: Magnes Press, 1971), 283f.; R. Obadiah Sforno, *Commentary on the Torah*, ed. Z. Gottlieb (Jerusalem: Mosad ha-Rav Kook, 1984), thereon; B. Berakhot 10a; Maimonides, *Mishneh Torah*: Teshuvah, 5.1.

or will. In this view, the image of God is a transfer of some divine power, be it reason or will, to a special creature, one who is unlike any other creature in kind. But the problem with seeing the image of God in substantial terms, as some inherent property of human nature, is that such a characteristic can be constituted phenomenologically without reference to God. If God is only the external cause of these characteristics, insight into their phenomenality does not require a causal explanation at all to explain how they essentially appear. What does saying "humans *receive* their reason or their will from God" add to the meaning of the proposition "humans are rational or willful"?[20] In other words, these interpretations lose the intimacy of a relationship *between* God and humans that is suggested by the opening words of God's creation of the human being: "Let us make (*na'aseh*) humans in our image" (Genesis 1:26). The only way one can constitute the intimacy of the relationship *with* God, which Scripture suggests is a possibility *for* humans from the very beginning and continually thereafter, is to see the "image of God" as that which God *and* humans share in what they do *together*.[21]

The Hebrew verb *asoh* as in *na'aseh* (let us make) means both making things and doing acts as, for example, "to do (*la'asot*) the Ten Commandments (*aseret ha-devarim*)" (Deuteronomy 4:13). Similarly, the Hebrew noun *davar* means both a thing and a word as, for example, "the word of our God (*dvar eloheinu*) remains forever" (Isaiah 40:8). Indeed, it has been suggested that this is the source of the correspondence theory of truth (*veritas est adaequatio intellectus ad rem*), for how can a word of ours "correspond" to a wordless thing? Such correspondence requires a mediating factor (*tertium quid*). That factor is the creative word of God: the word that led to a thing (*ens creatum*). Hence our word is adequate to describe a thing after the thing has been made (post factum) because it corresponds to the word of God regarding that thing before it was made (ab initio).[22] In relation to things, humans retrace the words of God by their accurate descriptions. In relation to God and other humans, we respond to God by making a life together when our words correspond to God's word and lead to the constitution of our covenantal world together.[23] The image of God is the active mutuality possible only between God and humans. In the true order of the created world, human action *for* ("ought") precedes human description *of* ("is"). The world we make by our action together is for the sake of each other. God is for us through his commandments; we are for God

---

[20] See D. Novak, *Halakhah in a Theological Dimension* (Chico, Calif.: Scholars Press, 1985), 99.

[21] See Franz Rosenzweig, *The Star of Redemption*, trans. W. W. Hallo (New York: Holt, Rinehart and Winston, 1970), 154f.

[22] See Martin Heidegger, "On the Essence of Truth," trans. J. Sallis, in *Martin Heidegger: Basic Writings*, ed. D. F. Krell (New York: Harper and Row, 1977), 120f.

[23] See M. Avot 2.4.

through our obedience. That is the very heart of God's initial right and our
initial duty demonstrated in the commandments.

Essential human action, which is the practice of the commandments of God,
is unlike all other things that are made *by* the creator. Instead, it is done *along
with* the creator. In rabbinic teaching, even God himself is imagined to observe
the positive commandments of the Torah in order to share with his people the
basic reality of *their* active life together.[24] Even God's autonomy, the only
foundational autonomy Judaism can possibly recognize, is ordered for the sake
of what God has made to be shared in common with us.

The content of the image of God is the normative relationship when humans
recognize that the moral law, which is consistent with their nature, is rooted in
the commandment of God. Authentic duty, which is much more than ordinary
prudence even when leading to the same external acts prudence might dictate,
is the response to God's justified rights upon us.[25] We humans not only owe
God everything for having made us, but more directly and positively we owe
God everything for enabling us to know how to live according to our own
nature and in consistency with the nature of the rest of creation.[26]

Being commanded, however we hear that commandment, is something that
enables us to do well in the world. Without that sense of being commanded,
when our own practical power becomes the measure of all things, we destroy
ourselves and our world. For when this happens, our reason forgets that it is
but a reflection of the wisdom of God who structures the natural world, and
our will forgets that it is but the reflection of God's will who brought the world
into existence. Being commanded is itself what lies at the very core of human
existence and thought, even before we understand what some of its results are
or will be.[27] "And the Lord has commanded us to practice all of these statutes
. . . for our own good (*le-tov lanu*). . . . [I]t is beneficial (*u-tsedaqah*) for us
that we prepare ourselves to practice all this that has been commanded before
the Lord our God as he has commanded us" (Deuteronomy 6:24–25).

At the most fundamental level, the mutual relationship between God and
the human person is normative. It is founded in the expression of God's rights.
Any inkling of the presence of God, however mediated by nature or tradition,
always calls forth a dutiful response or a rebellious refusal on the part of any
human. This can be seen in the first explicit address of God to the first humans
after their creation. "And the Lord God commanded (*va-yitsav*) the human

[24] See Y. Rosh Hashanah 1.3/57b; *Vayiqra Rabbah* 35.5 re Lev. 19:32; also, Novak, *Halakhah
in a Theological Dimension*, 122ff.

[25] See B. Gittin 88b re Exod. 21:1.

[26] Thus our gratitude is not in payment for services already rendered but, rather, proper recognition of the ongoing present-into-the-future life of the covenant. See Novak, *The Election of Israel*,
149ff.

[27] See my late revered teacher, Abraham Joshua Heschel, *Who Is Man?* (Stanford, Calif.: Stanford University Press, 1965), 97ff.

being saying: 'from all the trees of the garden you may surely eat. But from the tree of the knowledge of good and bad you may not eat, for on the day you eat from it you shall surely die' " (Genesis 2:16–17). In the view of the third-century Sage, Rabbi Yohanan bar Nappaha, the human being is both spoken *to* and spoken *about* in this statement, for the Hebrew reads *al ha'adam*, which means both "*to* the human being" and "*about* the human being." From this phraseology, Rabbi Yohanan sees an allusion to the prohibition of murder.[28] This location of the prohibition of murder needs to appear in the scriptural narrative before Cain's murder of his brother Abel. Without such a prohibition—albeit one that is inferred *about* the dignity of human life rather than an explicit proscription—how could Cain be held responsible for Abel's murder? Can one be held responsible for something whose prohibition he or she was unaware of (*nulla poena sine lege*)?[29]

Human dignity is affirmed by the teaching that all human beings are either the subjects or the objects of God's commandments. One's desire, of course, is to be more the subject than the object of these commandments; that is, we want to be more active than passive.[30] Nevertheless, the difference between active subjects and passive objects of these commandments is one of degree rather than one of kind. Even the most active persons need to be passively dependent at times and thus to be the objects of the concern others are commanded (*mitsvah*) to show them in imitation of God.[31] Even the most passive, dependent persons are often able to show some response to the concern of others for them, some form of thankful (even nonverbal) recognition like the way they are to thank God for any benefit.[32]

Accordingly, the ultimate indignity of death is that the dead person is now "free from the commandments," that is, he or she is now totally inert, the total object of the acts of others: to be finally buried and mourned.[33] The dead body is, then, only a remembrance of a life that once was capable of or had the potential for doing something commanded by God: "the shadow of our days on earth" (I Chronicles 29:15). That is why it is the ultimate impurity (*tum'ah*), the final alienation.[34] In death, we are turned into something else; we are made "to return to the dust" (Genesis 3:19). God can exercise his rights only on the

---

[28] B. Sanhedrin 56b.

[29] See D. Novak, *Natural Law in Judaism* (Cambridge: Cambridge University Press, 1998), 31ff.

[30] See, e.g., B. Makkot 10a re Deut. 4:41; B. Shabbat 118a (the statement of R. Akibah) and parallels.

[31] See B. Ketubot 111a re Gen. 50:25.

[32] See *Beresheet Rabbah* 96.5; and Rashi, *Commentary on the Torah*: Gen. 47:29.

[33] Niddah 61b re Ps. 88:6.

[34] A dead body is called "the grandfather of impurity" (*avi avot ha-tum'ah*), viz., the serious cause of impurity either by physical contact or even enclosure therewith. See B. Baba Kama 2b and Rashi, s.v. "ve-tame met" re Num. 19:16; also, *Encyclopedia Talmudit*, 1:23ff., s.v. "avi avot ha-tum'ah."

living. Humans are regarded as sojourners in the world, who can find our true dwelling there only when we realize that our task here is not derived from the world or from ourselves. That identity comes from being related to the One who transcends the world and governs it, the One to whom the world is always immanent. "I am a sojourner (*ger*) on earth; do not hide your commandments from me" (Psalms 119:19).[35] We experience that relationship in our dutiful response to God's rights upon us.

NEGATIVE COMMANDMENTS

In the rabbinic tradition, there are various ways to categorize the commandments of the Torah, even though all of them are considered to be from God in one way or another.[36] At the level of authority, the commandments are divided into two categories: those seen to be derived *from* scriptural revelation itself (*d'oraita*), and those legislated by the Rabbis as the duly recognized communal authorities. The Rabbis are assumed to be authorized *by* Scripture to make rulings *for the sake of* scriptural teaching (*torah*): either for the sake of enhancing specific scriptural laws (*gezerot*) or for the sake of enhancing the overall purposes of life learned from Scripture (*taqqanot*).[37] (I shall employ this categorization more fully in chapter 6, when we explore the rights of the community upon the individual person.) At the level of the direct objects of human action, the commandments are divided into two categories: those whose direct object is God (*bein adam le-maqom*), and those whose direct objects are other humans (*bein adam le-havero*).[38] (I shall employ this categorization more fully in chapter 5, when we explore the rights of persons upon each other.) In the Jewish tradition, the divine-human relationship has a priority over the interhuman relationship, for the ultimate validity of the interhuman relationship depends upon the divine-human relationship, but not vice versa.[39] That is the significance of asserting that humans (and their morality) are created in the image of God rather than asserting (or implying) that God is constructed in the image of human morality.[40] That is why this discussion of rights must begin with God's supreme right to command duties to us and how we experience being so commanded.

At the level of the character of experience of doing the commandments, they are divided into two categories: positive (*mitsvot aseh*), and negative (*mitsvot lo ta'aseh*). This distinction is experienced by the commandment

[35] See Novak, *The Election of Israel*, 128ff., 262f.

[36] See B. Hagigah 3b re Eccl. 12:11.

[37] See B. Shabbat 23a re Deut. 17:11.

[38] See M. Yoma 8.9.

[39] See B. Yoma 87a re I Sam. 2:25.

[40] See Novak, *Natural Law in Judaism*, 82ff. Cf. Kant, *Critique of Pure Reason*, 829B.

keeper even before the specific authorization of any commandment or its external object is determined. Accordingly, it might well be the point at which to begin a phenomenology of the commandments, that is, what it *means* to be commanded as a person. And at this primary level of experience, feelings are most evidently intense. To be commanded is to experience the primary right of God in the world: to feel it, to intelligently accept it, and finally to actively respond to it.

As we shall see in the next section, at the ontological level positive commandments have precedence over negative commandments. However, at the level of experience, we first learn what it means to be commanded when we are told what not to do. Our first experience of being commanded is when we first learn we have to act within limits, limits that are themselves negative demarcations. This point is well brought out by the fact that the most basic word for law in Hebrew, *hoq*, comes from a verb meaning to "carve out" (*haqaq*), and the most basic word for law in Greek, *nomos*, comes from a verb meaning to "apportion" (*nemein*).[41] Also, some have seen the Latin *lex* as coming from *ligare*, meaning "to bind."[42] That is why basic opposition to law itself—antinomianism—takes the form of resentment at being limited by anyone else.[43] Philosophically, this resentment takes the form of the will resenting the necessity of its being limited by reason, that is, its having to justify itself rationally by continual reference to enclosing nature.[44]

The basic human feeling that accompanies this experience of being commanded negatively is fear (*yir'ah*). The negative commandment is itself a warning (*azharah*) that dangerous disorder lies on the other side of the commandment, that is, when one attempts to overcome it (*averah*) rather than living within its limits.[45] However, this fear is not the same as the terror (*pahad*) one experiences when confronted with the raw power of God, for terror paralyzes one, preventing a person from acting at all. By commanding us, conversely, God limits the full range of his power in order to enable us to actively respond to his commandments. Along these lines, the great German scholar of religion Rudolf Otto (d. 1937) made an insightful distinction between the sense of "creaturehood" (*Geschöplichkeit*), which Abraham expresses in his total

---

[41] Re *haqaq*, see Isa. 5:14; Prov. 8:29; Job 26:10. Re *nemein*, see Homer, *Odyssey*, 8.470, where it pertains to finite food rations (cf. Betsah 16a re Gen. 47:22, Prov. 30:8).

[42] See Thomas Aquinas, *Summa Theologiae*, 2/1, q. 90, a. 1.

[43] The classic Jewish characterization of such antinomianism is the phrase put in the mouth of the antinomians: "There is no law (*din*) and there is no judge (*dayyan*)" (*Targum Jonathan ben Uzziel*: Gen. 4:8; see *Vayiqra Rabbah* 28.1 re Eccl. 11:9; also, Ps. 53:2–3).

[44] See Friedrich Nietzsche, *The Will to Power*, trans. W. Kaufmann and R. J. Hollingdale (New York: Vintage Books, 1968), no. 471, p. 262.

[45] That is why negative commandments must be stated ab initio, directly (*azharah*), and not just be inferred from the stipulation of punishment (*onesh*) for their transgression post factum. See, e.g., B. Sanhedrin 54b.

resignation in the presence of God, and the sense of "createdness" (*Geschaffenheit*), which is one's dependence upon the order God has infused in the world as a sign of his wisdom.[46] When the fear of God is understood as our reverential dependence upon the divine order infused in the world, it becomes a concession to us by God. As it is put in the Talmud: "Everything is in the hands of God except the fear of God (*yir'at shamayim*)."[47] That is, our terror of God's power is mostly sublimated into our reverence for God's wisdom. It should reappear only when we are tempted to stand up against God in contempt rather than standing before him in awe.

The fear of God (*yir'at elohim*) in this latter sense is more than a feeling. It leads into cautious action toward God, which is the practical recognition of divine order within the world. By contrast, terror at God's power is pure feeling, which leads to no action at all.[48] Fear of God is respect for the awesome limits God has set down within which humans are to freely choose to live. Furthermore, unlike ordinary fear, where one wants to avoid the object of his or her fear, in the case of fear of God, one is attracted to the object. The restraint of the negative commandments expresses one's fear of being careless at the boundaries any relationship with God must always keep in mind. Scripture speaks of "your servants who desire (*hafetsim*) to fear your name" (Nehemiah 1:11).

Unlike the manifestations of God's power, where all transitive action is on God's part, even the fear accompanying a negative commandment does not prevent a human from engaging in his or her own transitive action. In keeping a negative commandment fearfully, one is required to actively separate himself or herself from that in which one has been forbidden by God's law to partake.[49] This response presupposes that we have enough freedom—enough space of our own, as it were—to either accept or reject the restrictions of the law. That freedom is an entitlement from God (*zekhut*), without which our being commanded by God would make no sense at all.[50] And it seems to be an entitlement that could not be revoked without destroying human nature simultaneously. As such, the giving of the commandment and the acceptance or rejection of the commandment is a permanent transaction between God and humans. Whereas the terror we experience in the face of the power of God takes away the ground from under us and thus leaves us no space around us to act, the fear we experience in the observance of the negative commandment of God demarcates the ground under us and a space around us in which to act. It gives

---

[46] *The Idea of the Holy*, trans. J. W. Harvey (New York: Oxford University Press, 1958), 20f.

[47] B. Berakhot 33b re Deut. 10:12.

[48] See Exod. 20:16; Judg. 13:22; I Sam. 28:20; Ezek. 1:28 (cf. 2:1); Job 13:28–14:2; Dan. 10:15–17.

[49] See *Vayiqra Rabbah* 25.6 re Lev. 19:2.

[50] See Maimonides, *Mishneh Torah*: Teshuvah, 5.1ff.

us a sphere for our own concrete action. That is why the negative commandments cannot be ontologically separated from the positive commandments.
Without the possibility of the positive commandments, the fear accompanying
the negative commandments would revert to the prenomian terror we experience when confronted by God's raw power.[51]

The term "fear of God" (*yir'at elohim*) has a largely moral meaning in Scripture.[52] Thus when Sarah is taken into the harem of the chieftan Abimelech and
Abraham lies about her being his sister rather than his wife, he justifies this
evasion of the truth by telling Abimelech "surely there is no fear of God in
this place" (Genesis 20:11). In other words, the sanctity of marital unions does
not seem to be respected here. It seems that those in power simple take any
woman they fancy, and if she has a husband, they kill him. That is certainly a
violation of the order of the family in the world. It is the overstepping of a
natural boundary that should be recognized everywhere. However, within that
boundary there is a designated space for men and women to marry and bring
children into the world to be reared. Only the boundary is to be feared. But
were this fear the terror we saw above, then it would be impossible for men
and women to do anything concrete together at all. The terror of God is thus
pre-moral, whereas the fear of God is what makes morality possible in a world
ruled by God.

Many Jewish theologians have been concerned that the fear of God be primarily seen as the fear of God's punishment (*onesh*) for our sins. That would
seem to regard the fear of God in exclusively moral terms and in a subordinate
role at that because it relates to God as the enforcer of morality rather than to
God as its true source. Although that punitive fear is certainly mentioned in
the sources from time to time, it does not have God as its direct object. Instead,
it seems to be motivated by the desire to avoid a bad reaction to one's own
actions, actions that have been done for one's own self-interest. Service of God
becomes a means to that selfish end.[53] Perhaps what could be termed the
"higher" fear of God is distinct from the "lower" fear of God in that the higher
fear is the fear of the mighty limits within the world, which is the source of
our reverential restraint in the face of the power of God. That is quite different
from a concern for how the consequences of such restraint might benefit me.
Thus this higher fear could be termed "scientific" inasmuch as it is primarily
concerned with an order whose integrity is to be respected. By contrast, the

---

[51] For this reason too, it seems, human authorities are not to terrorize those for whose practice
they are responsible. They must give them enough leeway to be able to act rationally, with proper
deliberation. See, e.g., B. Gittin 6b–7a; B. Kiddushin 32a re Lev. 19:14.

[52] See Novak, *Natural Law in Judaism*, 47ff.

[53] See B. Avodah Zarah 19a re Ps. 112:1 (the statement of R. Eleazar); Maimonides, *Mishneh
Torah*: Teshuvah, 10.1; also, B. Megillah 25b and Rashi, s.v. "me'ahavah" and "me-yir'ah."

lower fear of God could be termed "technological" inasmuch as it is primarily concerned with how an object can be used.[54]

The true fear of God is awe at the creative and structuring action of God more than fear of ourselves in our capacity to harm ourselves.[55] It is fear of God's action more than fear of God's reaction to our action. It is fear of what is and what will surely be if God's order is violated. In the case of fear of punishment, cognition is for the sake of effect; that is, we learn what to avoid so as not to suffer. In the case of fear of God himself, however, cognition is for the sake of action; that is, our feeling of fearful restraint is to make us of cognizant of God's wisdom and to act accordingly. The recognition of active wisdom calls for an active response proportionally. For this reason, observance of negative commandments motivated by true fear of God intends God directly, whereas observance of negative commandments motivated by the fear of God's punishment intends an external result. In the words of the ancient Sage, Antigonos of Socho, there is a fundamental difference between "serving the master for the sake of payment (*pras*)" and "serving the master not for the sake of payment."[56] As later Rabbis pointed out, this statement should not be interpreted to mean that Antigonos did not believe in divine retribution but, rather, that he made retribution a matter of secondary importance when it came to proper motivation or intent in the observance of the commandments.[57]

Because the positive commandments presuppose the negative commandments, these negative commandments have a wider range in our experience. This point can be best seen in the relation of generally applicable law to specifically applicable law in the Jewish tradition; another division in Jewish law is the difference between Noahide and Mosaic law. Noahide law (*mitsvot benei Noah*) comprises those general norms the Rabbis asserted are required by God of all humankind: the descendants of Noah, those humans who survived the Flood by obeying God.[58] That obedience seems to have first consisted of restraint in the face of those actions considered by Scripture to be perversions of the divinely instituted natural order: "all flesh has destroyed (*hish'heet*) its way on earth" (Genesis 6:12). Secondly, that obedience consisted of their

[54] See R. Isaac Abrabanel, *Commentary on the Torah*: Deut. 10:12, who sees this fear of God as being "rational" (*teva ha-sekhel*).

[55] See *Zohar*: intro., 1:11b–12a; Hayyei Sarah, 1:132b; Aharei-Mot, 3:56a; Behar, 3:112b. The kabbalistic theologian R. Isaiah ha-Levi Horowitz (d. 1630) distinguishes, along these lines, between "inner" fear and "outer" fear. Outer fear is fear of oneself, viz., fear of the retributive consequences of one's acts. Inner fear directly intends God. See *Shnei Luhot ha-Berit*, bk. 1: *Ten Statements*, ed. Amsterdam, 34a. This distinction is also made by a number of Hasidic theologians. See S. Werfel, *Sefer ha-Hasidut* (Tel Aviv: Z. Leinman, 1947), 4b, 9b.

[56] M. Avot 1.3.

[57] See *Avot de-Rabbi Nathan* A, chap. 5, ed. Schechter, 13b.

[58] See D. Novak, *The Image of the Non-Jew in Judaism* (New York: Edwin Mellen Press, 1983), passim.

following God's orders to save themselves from the destructive consequences of that perversion. "And the Lord said to Noah: 'you and your household come to the ark, for I have recognized (*ra'iti*) you as innocent (*tsaddiq*) before me in this generation,' " (Genesis 7:1). However, it is clear from the scriptural narrative that Noah's respect for the divinely instituted natural order long preceded God's reward to him by saving him and his family from the destruction of the Flood.[59]

The seven norms (*sheva mitsvot*), or categories of norms, that the Rabbis discerned from Scripture as binding on all humankind are negative commandments, such as the prohibitions of idolatry, murder, robbery, and adultery.[60] The only positive commandment is the requirement for every human society to have a system of adjudication of disputes (*dinim*).[61] Nevertheless, if one looks upon this commandment as being a second-level procedural rule, designed for the enforcement of the other six primary rules, then its function is derived from the primary rules.[62] It is to prevent or respond to injustices, which are violations of the basic negative norms. The system of adjudication makes some negative commandments, which are to be observed by individual persons, move from the level of moral law to be also included at the level of politically enforceable law. Nevertheless, its own justification is ultimately negative, being for the sake of what are essentially restrictions, rather than being for its own positive sake. (In chapter 6, we shall examine both the negative role of the covenantal polity as society and its positive role as community.) The negative Noahide laws constitute, then, the most generally applicable area of Jewish law inasmuch as their equivalents also apply to Jews as well.[63]

Even those negative commandments that apply only to Jews have a wider range than the positive ones. Most of the positive commandments are limited to specific times (*zeman gerama*), whereas most of the negative commandments apply to all times. The range of positive commandments that apply to men is greater than the range of those that apply to women because women are exempt from most positive commandments.[64] (The question of whether they can observe them anyway, in spite of their initial exemption from them, will be discussed in chapter 7.) But, except for a few negative commandments that seem to be essentially male, women are obligated for all the rest of the negative commandments.[65] Indeed, it seems no accident that of the 613 com-

---

[59] See *Midrash ha-Gadol*: Beresheet re Gen. 6:9, ed. Margulies, 152.

[60] See B. Sanhedrin 58b–59a.

[61] See B. Sanhedrin 56b re Gen. 18:19; Novak, *The Image of the Non-Jew in Judaism*, 53ff.

[62] For the distinction between primary and secondary rules, see Hart, *The Concept of Law*, 113f.

[63] See B. Sanhedrin 59a and Tos., s.v. "leeka."

[64] M. Kiddushin 1.7. For a suggestion of why this is the general principle, see D. Novak, *Law and Theology in Judaism* (New York: KTAV, 1976), 2:137.

[65] M. Kiddushin 1.7.

mandments later rabbinic opinion discerned to be operative in the Mosaic Torah, the majority of them, 365, are taken to be negative.[66] Wider range would seem to imply greater number as well. Negative commandments express the widest range of God's rights.

POSITIVE COMMANDMENTS

The wider range of the negative commandments is because, in effect, they demarcate the area within which valid human relationships may take place. However, no one could possibly live at this level alone. Without positive content within these limits, they would ultimately negate any human capacity for concrete action. They would block human existence at every turn. It could even lead one to hate God. In fact, unless this positive content is taken to have some priority over the negative limits around it, the necessity of the negative would eventually overcome positive content, for without the clear priority of positive content, concrete action can be regarded only as basically optional. It is like saying: what the law does not prohibit, it permits. However, as the history of Jewish law certainly shows, there is nothing to prevent such leeway from being removed by some new negative ruling.[67] That is why the positive commandments have to be more than optional acts in order to endure, let alone triumph. As it is stated several times in the Talmud: "Greater is one who acts because of being commanded (*metsuveh v'oseh*) than one who acts without being commanded."[68] The wider range of negative commandments is counterbalanced by the greater depth of the positive ones. They are essentially far more than what was simply overlooked by the negative commandments.

The inherent connection between the negative commandments and the positive ones can be seen in the unusual connection of fear and love it involves. Usually, we hate those whom we fear, and those whom we love we do not fear. Or, we desire to run away from those we fear, and we desire to draw near to those we love. But as an ancient midrash puts it: "There is no love where there is fear, and no fear where there is love, except in relation to God alone (*be-middat maqom bilvad*)."[69] That is because here fear is for the sake of love, the negative is for the sake of the positive. The positive commandments are to be motivated by love. And they have a priority. This is brought out by the thirteenth-century theologian Nahmanides, commenting on the difference between the positive commandment "remember (*zakhor*) the Sabbath day to hallow it"

---

[66] B. Makkot 23b.

[67] See, e.g., B. Berakhot 26a and Tos., s.v. "ta'ah"; B. Shabbat 9b and Tos., s.v. "le-m'an d'amar"; B. Pesahim 54b and Tos., s.v. "ve-ha'amar"; Hullin 54b and Tos, s.v. "ein" re Arakhin 28b; Y. Pesahim 3.7/30b.

[68] B. Kiddushin 31a and parallels.

[69] *Sifre*: Devarim, no. 32, ed. Finkelstein, 54.

(Exodus 20:8) in the first version of the Decalogue and the negative commandment "guard (*shamor*) the Sabbath day" (Deuteronomy 5:12) in the second
version:

> The truth is that the quality of "remember" is hinted at in the positive command-
> ment (*be-mitsvat aseh*), which comes from the attribute of love and is for the sake
> of the attribute of mercy (*le-middat ha-rahamim*). For one who does what his
> master commands does so because he loves him and his master is merciful to him.
> But the quality of "guard" applies to the negative (*lo ta'aseh*) commandments. It
> is for the sake of the attribute of justice (*din*) and comes from the attribute of
> fear (*yir'ah*). . . . Therefore, a positive commandment is greater than a negative
> commandment inasmuch as love is greater than fear. For one who affirms (*he-
> maqayyem*) and practices what his master wills, both with his body and his prop-
> erty, is greater than one who simply guards himself (*me-ha-nishmar*) from doing
> evil in his [master's] eyes. Accordingly, the Rabbis said that a positive command-
> ment can displace (*ve-dahi*) a negative one.[70]

The principle of a positive commandment displacing a negative one is very
much circumscribed in its actual application by the Talmud.[71] In fact, in rabbinic legislation there are times when consideration of a negative commandment led to the omission of a positive one. Thus, for example, out of concern
for violation of the negative commandment not to carry things on the Sabbath
in public places outdoors (*reshut ha-rabbim*), the Rabbis ruled that the positive
commandment of carrying the four plant species on the festival of Sukkot not
be practiced (*shev v'al ta'aseh*) when the first day of Sukkot falls on the Sabbath.[72] Nevertheless, the theological import of the principle that Nahmanides
is emphasizing above is that God's claim on our love is far more intense and
intimate than his claim on our fear. This is further shown by the fact that in
virtually all the classical discussions of the proper intent (*kavvanah*) for the
performance of a commandment, the intent is connected to the positive commandments. This is what is called "the service of the heart" (*avodat ha-lev*),

[70] *Commentary on the Torah*: Exod. 20:8, ed. Chavel, 399. See the *Commentary on Canticles*
attributed to Nahmanides: Cant. 4:11, *Kitvei Ramban*, ed. C. B. Chavel (Jerusalem: Mosad ha-
Rav Kook, 1963), 2:496f.

[71] See B. Shabbat 132b; B. Yevamot 3b–4a; Y. Betsah 1.3/60b; Y. Nedarim 3.9/38b. In general,
the principle applies when a specific negative commandment somehow or other (and that is debated) is connected to a specific positive commandment; hence the negativity of the former is
overcome by the positivity of the latter. See, e.g., B. Pesahim 41b (re Exod. 12:8) and parallels;
B. Yoma 85b; M. Hullin 12.4; Hullin 141a–b.

[72] B. Sukkah 42b–43a and parallels; also ibid. 41b–42a. Also note how concern for violations
of festival proscriptions led to the postponement of the positive commandment to bury the dead
as soon as possible (B. Sanhedrin 46b and Y. Nazir 7.1/55c re Deut. 21:23; Maimonides, *Mishneh
Torah*: Evel, 12.1 and Radbaz thereon). See B. Betsah 6a and Rashi, s.v. "d'eeka habarei" and
Tos., s.v. "ve-ha'idna."

and that service is derived from the verse "to love the Lord your God and to serve him with all your heart" (Deuteronomy 11:13).[73]

The positive commandments express our love for God, which is in response to God's love for us. That love is only known when it is revealed by God.[74] That is why many of the positive commandments are celebrations of the revealed acts of God, celebrations that occur at regular times.[75] Being the temporally limited creatures we are, God's love for us and our love for God in return are conditioned by history. Everything we do is *sub specie durationis*.[76]

The priority assigned to the positive commandments over the negative commandments is more theological than legal. It is because the priority of love over fear in the covenantal relationship with God is stressed.[77] But the two emotions are still required and the question is how they are related, especially since virtually all the theologians recognize the priority of love.

Some have seen the relation between the two emotions to be hierarchal. That is, fear is taken to be the more primitive emotion, the one that is required to motivate us to obey God at the earlier state of our spiritual development. Love is taken to be the more cultivated emotion, taking more time because of the greater knowledge and commitment it involves. Thus Maimonides, whose approach is highly teleological, writes:

> One who serves [God] out of love engages in the study of the Torah and the performance of the commandments and walks in the paths of wisdom not because of fear of what is bad and not for the sake of some [external] benefit. . . . One who engages in the study of the Torah . . . so that punishment not reach him is not someone who is doing so for its own sake (*she-lo li-shmah*). . . . Therefore, when one teaches children and women and in general the ignorant, they should not be taught to serve God except out of fear (*me-yir'ah*) and to receive a reward . . . until they are able to apprehend him and know him and serve him out of love (*me'ahavah*).[78]

Thus, for Maimonides, we move from the level of observing all the commandments out of fear up to the level of observing all the commandments out of love. Accordingly, the specific connection of fear to the negative commandments and love to the positive commandments is not made in this discussion.

---

[73] *Sifre*: Devarim, no. 41, ed. Finkelstein, 87f.; B. Taanit 2a.

[74] Thus it is God himself who teaches us how to pray, viz., what we can say about him directly to him. See B. Rosh Hashanah 17b re Exod. 34:6; *Sifre*: Devarim, no. 49; B. Berakhot 7a re Isa. 56:7.

[75] See Novak, *The Election of Israel*, 148ff.

[76] See T. Berakhot 1.10; Y. Berakhot 1.9/4a; B. Berakhot 12b re Jer. 23:7–8.

[77] See B. Sotah 31a; B. Yevamot 48b and Rashi, s.v. "me-yir'ah." Also, see J. Faur, "Reflections on Job and Situation Morality," *Judaism* 19 (1970): 221f.

[78] *Mishneh Torah*: Teshuvah, 10.2, 5. See *Guide of the Perplexed*, 3.28. For the notion of doing a commandment for its own sake (*li-shmah*), see B. Pesahim 50b.

However, the notion that the love of God eventually displaces the fear of God when one moves from a lower spiritual level to a higher one seems to be influenced by Maimonides' Platonic emphasis of the love of God being primarily our love of God as the most perfect Being, with whom all intelligent beings strive to be united as much as they can.[79] That perfection entails the notion of divine immutability.[80] Thus all movement, all change, is ours in relation to God, not God's in relation to us, let alone God's in relationship with us. There is little emphasis in Maimonides' theology of God's love for Israel, and that God's love for Israel is what makes Israel's responsive love for God possible. In other words, the transitive activity of God, let alone God's interaction or transactions with Israel, is not constituted theologically by Maimonides. It cannot be theologically constituted in the light of the ontology Maimonides has made the foundation of his theology. In fact, there is little doubt that Maimonides sees the love of God as our desire for a functional, if not substantial, union with God (*unio mystica*).[81] And this comes out in his constant emphasis of the priority of the theoretical or contemplative life over the practical or active life.[82] As such, the love of God, as the affective aspect of the contemplation of God, takes precedence over the actual practice of even the positive commandments, and certainly of the negative commandments.[83]

In this type of theology, the prevalence of the correlation of rights and duties we have been pursuing here is not fundamental. We can see how all duties are directed to God, but we cannot see how God actively exercises his rights when God is taken much more as ultimate object than as prime subject. By contrast, in the theology being developed here, where the rights of God are the foundation of all other rights and duties, contemplation—even the contemplation of God—is for the sake of the practice of the commandments. Even the contemplation of God is thinking about the acts of God as revealed in Scripture, and how the highest practical task is the imitation of those acts God has revealed as normative for us (*mitsvot ma'asiyot*).[84] Outside of the acts of God revealed

---

[79] See *Mishneh Torah*: Yesodei ha-Torah, 2.1ff., Teshuvah, 8.7, 10.6. And, see Plato, *Symposium*, 210B–C.

[80] See Novak, *The Election of Israel*, 237ff.

[81] All of this seems to be love of God as the object *toward* whom we are attracted. It is not love for God as the subject *from* whose acts (the most immediate being God's commanding us) we are able to respond *back* (see *Guide of the Perplexed*, 3.28). As such, our love is to entail the secluded quietude of the *vita contemplativa* (see ibid., 3.51). See Aristotle, *Nicomachean Ethics*, 1177a20ff.

[82] For Maimonides' highly original way of finally constituting the relation between *vita contemplativa* and *vita activa*, see Novak, *Natural Law in Judaism*, 113ff., regarding *Guide of the Perplexed*, 3.54.

[83] See Maimonides, *Mishneh Torah*: Teshuvah, 10.3; *Guide of the Perplexed*, 3.52.

[84] Thus even when learning the Torah (*talmud*) is given a priority over practice of the commandments (*ma'aseh*), its ultimate outcome is to be better intentioned practice. See *Sifre*: Devarim, no. 106 re Deut. 14:23; B. Kiddushin 40b and Tos., s.v. "talmud"; M. Avot 1.17, 2.5; B. Berakhot 17a re Ps. 111:10; R. Joseph Albo, *Iqqarim*, 3.28. Moreover, even the study of the Torah at the ontolog-

to the prophets as directly divine, we know nothing about him. And what is most important for our inquiry here is that only one who is active and involved with other persons, however asymmetrical that relationship might be, has rights.

In the case of fellow humans, conversely, we can sometimes surmise the thoughts behind their acts by analogy to our own thoughts, and because of this we can sometimes predict what they are likely to do.[85] But in the case of God, we have no analogy to our own thoughts. "For my thoughts are not your thoughts, and your ways are not my ways, says the Lord. For as the heavens are higher (*gavhu*) than the earth, so do my ways transcend (*gavhu*) your ways, and my thoughts your thoughts" (Isaiah 55:8–9). Even when God is the object of our acts, it is because he has approached us first as acting subject. We know only what we are told about God; in this case we are told that God's actions for us stem from thoughts infinitely more insightful than our own. "For humans see what appears (*l'einayyim*), but the Lord sees the heart" (I Samuel 16:7). "The heart is most devious and it is wounded; who can know it? I am the Lord who fathoms the heart." (Jeremiah 17:9–10). And God's knowledge, of which we are told of only in its relation to us, seems to be practical, not theoretical, for it intends wonderful acts for our good rather than being contemplation about itself.[86] Therefore, our knowledge of its effectiveness must be essentially practical as well by imitation.[87]

For this reason, it is better to look at the relation between love and fear of God in the same way as the relation between the positive and negative commandments. That relation can be seen as dialectical; that is, each type of commandment offsets what the other lacks.[88] As such, the total relationship with God in the commandments of the Torah involves these two types of commandments and the two types of emotions they involve working in tandem at all levels of conscious action. This comes out in the following rabbinic

---

ical level cannot be Platonic-Aristotelian-Neoplatonic *theōria* inasmuch as it is the remembrance of the acts of God, which are transitive in nature and transactional in the covenant, not the contemplation of God as a self-enclosed object. It is very much, then, *sub specie durationis* rather than *sub specie aeternitatis*. See *Sifre*: Devarim, no. 49 re haggadah as theology.

[85] See B. Betsah 19a; B. Kiddushin 49b and Tos., s.v. "devarim"; M. Baba Kama 10.2; B. Baba Kama 114a; B. Baba Metsia 22b re Deut. 22:3; and Maimonides, *Mishneh Torah*: Gezelah v'Avedah, 11.10.

[86] Cf. Maimonides, *Mishneh Torah*: Yesodei ha-Torah, 2.10; *Guide of the Perplexed*, 1.68; also, Aristotle, *Metaphysics*, 1072b20ff.; and *De Anima*, 430a15–20.

[87] In Isa. 58:8–9, God's thought is called *mahshavah*, which is thought-leading-to-action (*ma'aseh*), i.e., practical reason. See Exod. 31:3–4; Ps. 92:5–6; also, M. Toharot 1.1; M. Makhshirin 6.1; B. Hagigah 10a–b and Rashi, s.v. "mel'ekhet mahshevet" (for the equation of *mahshavah* with *kavvanah*, viz., practical intention); B. Kiddushin 40a re Mal. 3:16. In fact, *mahshavah* could consistently be translated as "plans."

[88] To see how this type of dialectic works in talmudic reasoning, see, e.g., B. Baba Kama 5a–b and Tos., s.v. "le-hilkhoteihem"; Niddah 51b re Lev. 11:9.

observation: "One should act both from love and from fear. Act from love, so if you are coming to hate [God], then know that you love [him] and one who loves does not hate. Act from fear, so that if you come to rebel (*li-v'ot*), then know that you fear and one who fears does not rebel."[89] The sixteenth-century Italian exegete Rabbi Obadiah Bertinoro connects this earlier statement with the distinction between positive and negative commandments. The positive commandments save the fear of God from turning into hatred of the repressive God of the negative commandments, and the negative commandments save the love of God from being our own motivation to approach a passive God whichever way we like.[90] This dialectic holds in balance the desire to approach God with the necessity of being separate from God. Only when this relation is in place can we experience the full range of the rights of God expressed in his demands upon us. That is why viewing the relation between the two types of commandments as dialectical rather than successive seems to be closer to the normative experience of the Jewish people.

In the next chapter, we shall explore whether the claims of God on humans lead to any human claims on God in return.

---

[89] Y. Berakhot 9.5/14b. See Horowitz, *Shnei Luhot ha-Berit*, bk. 3: Ve'ethanan, 81b–82a.
[90] *Commentary on the Mishnah*: Avot 1.3. See also R. Judah Halevi, *Kuzari*, 1.1.

CHAPTER II

Human Persons and God

DEPENDENCE AS THE PRIMARY HUMAN CLAIM ON GOD

At first glance, it surely seems impertinent to assume that humans may make any claims on God. After all, are not humans the creatures and God the creator? How can a creature make a claim on his or her creator? By the time of completed creation, is God not already through with us? On what ground could we possibly stand up to make any such claim? "Ever since the day was, I am He; none can deliver from my hand. When I act, who can turn it back (*yeshiven-nah*)?" (Isaiah 43:13). To make such a claim is to exercise a right, and that assumes God is obliged to respond. And does response not entail at least the possibility that God might change what he had previously decreed for the human being who now calls upon God to act differently for him or her? Does that not mean humans do indeed have an effect on God? But if God is purely active as creator, how can there be any passivity in him so that he be affected by anyone else?[1] "God is not man who lies, nor a human who changes his mind" (Numbers 23:19).[2]

From this point alone, it would seem that the only proper speech to be addressed to God is to praise God for his greatness, but with no hope of any response to us from him whatsoever within time. And since God is beyond any description in words, it would seem that true humility before him should

---

[1] See Maimonides, *Guide of the Perplexed*, 1.55 and 2: intro., no. 18; Abraham Ibn Ezra, *Commentary on the Torah*: Exod. 32:14; R. Isaac Abrabanel, *Commentary on the Former Prophets*: I Sam. 15:29.

[2] In fact, Scripture records God changing his plans much more than God not changing his plans (see, e.g., Gen. 6:6–7; Exod. 32:14; I Sam. 15:11, 35; Jer. 18:10, 42:10; Jon. 3:10; Ps. 106:45). Indeed, to deny God's right to change his plans is to seriously curtail God's transcendent freedom. And, as we shall see later in this chapter, the efficacy of repentance (*teshuvah*) presupposes the mutability of God. But it could also be argued that God's covenantal promises are unchangeable, not because God *could not* change them, but because God *would not* change them (see Exod. 32:12–14; B. Berakhot 32a; Ps. 110:4; B. Yevamot 105a re Dan 10:2; I Sam. 15:29 and R. David Kimhi [Radaq], *Commentary on the Former Prophets* thereon). Hence any proposal to change what *should not* be changed, itself *should* be changed—viz., a double negation reverting to the original immutable promise (see Y. Taaniyot 2.1/65b re Isa. 26:21; Y. Sanhedrin 11.5/30b re Jer. 27:32; *Tanhuma*: Va-yerah, no. 13, Masa'ei, no. 7; Maimonides, *Commentary on the Mishnah*: intro., ed. Kafih, 6; *Mishneh Torah*: Yesodei ha-Torah, 10.4). As for the verse, "I the Lord do not change (*lo shaniti*)" (Mal. 3:6), that means God *does not change into something else*, unlike humans who do change into something else when they die (see Gen. 3:19; Ps. 49:10ff.; Eccl. 12:7; also D. Novak, *The Election of Israel* [Cambridge: Cambridge University Press, 1995], 262f.).

be contemplative silence.³ Nothing should be claimed from him. To be sure, there is a compelling logic to all of this. Unfortunately, though, there are just too many counterexamples. Contemplative silence simply goes against too much of the considerable verbosity of Jewish prayer in Scripture and the rabbinic writings, the elementary sources of all Jewish God talk, especially talk addressed to God.⁴ And most of this verbose prayer is petitionary, not pure adoration. Indeed, all we know about God is what has been revealed to us, not of his actions in general, but only of his actions for us.⁵ The God of Scripture and the Rabbis engages in transitive action, but our concern is always centered on his transactions *with* us. Indeed, if that were not a possibility for human persons, the covenant between God and the people of Israel would have been impossible in the world.

Of course, the possibility of petitionary prayer (*baqashah*) does not mean that God is obliged in any way to grant humans what they request of him. That would suggest that God owes us something as individual persons.⁶ That would suggest that as persons we have some kind of hold on God, some ground from which to claim God's dutiful reply on our specific terms. But as Elihu told Job: "Look to the heavens and see; look to the sky that is higher than you. . . . [I]f you are righteous, what have you given him? What does He take from your hand?" (Job 35:5, 7). And as David said to God: "Who am I and who are my people to have the strength to freely offer like this? For from you comes everything, and from your own hand we are only giving back to you. For we are sojourners (*gerim*) before you, tenants (*toshavim*) like all our ancestors; our days are like a shadow on earth, and there is no gathering place (*ein miqveh*)" (I Chronicles 29:14–16).⁷

³ See Maimonides, *Mishneh Torah*: Yesodei ha-Torah, 7.4; *Guide of the Perplexed*, 3.51, 621. For an excellent study that shows how Maimonides integrated his contemplative emphasis with the petitionary content of much of traditional Jewish prayer, see E. Benor, *Worship of the Heart* (Albany: State University of New York Press. 1995), 63ff. Moreover, contemplation at the highest level is not so much the distinctly human voice addressing God as it is a silent human imitation of the way God "speaks" to himself. It is a participation in divine self-knowledge. Along these lines, see *Zohar*: Va-yigash, 1:209b–210a re B. Berakhot 24b and Rashi, s.v. "hare zeh" re I Kings 18:28; also, Rashi, *Commentary on the Torah*: Num. 7:89.

⁴ For the important difference between language addressed to God (*ansprechen*) and language about God (*aussprechen*), see Martin Buber, *I and Thou*, trans. W. Kaufmann (New York: Scribner's, 1970), 123ff.

⁵ See B. Rosh Hashanah 17a re Exod. 34:5. One could well say that even when God's general creative action in the cosmos is spoken of (e.g. Ps. 19:2–7), it is *via negationis*, viz., God is not exclusively concerned with us. But what God's concrete relationship with the rest of creation outside of our relationship with him is, that is beyond our ken because it is beyond our experience (see Job 38:17–26).

⁶ See B. Berakhot 32b and Tos., s.v. "kol"; B. Shabbat 118b and Tos., s.v. "iyyun"; B. Baba Batra 164b and Rashi, s.v. "iyyun tefillah." For cautious rabbinic speculation that God might even be obligated to grant the petitions of the righteous, see M. Taanit 3.8; Y. Taaniyot 3.10/67a re Job 22:28, etc.; B. Moed Qatan 16b re II Sam. 23:3.

⁷ See Lev. 25:23.

What we do seem to learn from Scripture and the Rabbis is how humans have the right to cry to God, thus believing *that* God will listen to our cry, even though we do not have the right to determine *what* God will actually do to us or for us in response. That is why we are required to acknowledge God's justice for the bad things that happen to us just as we are required to acknowledge God's mercy for the good things that happen to us.[8] For a beneficial response to our prayers, then, we can only hope. In fact, we are required to hope. Thus, immediately after reminding Job how he has no specific claim on God to do for him what Job would do for himself, Elihu then proceeds to castigate those who therefore do not call upon God. "Surely it is false that God does not listen, that the Almighty does not notice. . . . [T]he case (*din*) is before him, so wait for him" (Job 35:13–14).[9] By contrast, passive resignation in the face of what is taken to be the decree of God regarding what we are to experience is the approach of Eli the High Priest, who has lost all hope and who is not worthy to pass the priestly line on to his descendants. Instead of calling upon God to have mercy on him and change the bad decree, Eli abjectly accepts his fate by saying: "Let the Lord do what is good in his eyes" (I Samuel 3:18).[10] That attitude should be sharply distinguished from that of the Psalmist who actively asserts: "O' were it that I be sure to see the goodness of the Lord in the land of the living. Hope towards the Lord; make your heart strong and courageous. Hope towards the Lord" (Psalms 27:13–14).[11] It would seem to be a lack of faith to simply assume that God will not respond because he cannot change his plans. Responding to legitimate human claims presupposes this capacity for change on God's part.

Prayer is the most personal approach to God possible from the human side. It is the overcoming of our lack of certitude about anything God will do to us by our hope that he will act for us in a way we can understand and appreciate. Any certitude that this will actually happen according to our own plans is magic, however.[12] Yet, the opposite extreme is fatalism, which denies we can

---

[8] See M. Berakhot 5.3 and 9.5 re Deut. 6:5; B. Berakhot 33b; M. Megillah 4.9; Y. Megillah 4.10/75c. Indeed, acknowledging only a "good god" might well imply there is a "bad god," viz., gnostic dualism. Cf. B. Taanit 3a and Tos., s.v. "v'ilu."

[9] For the notion that the true theology of the book of Job comes from Elihu rather than Job, see Maimonides, *Guide of the Perplexed*, 3.22–23; Nahmanides, *Commentary on Job*: Job 32:2.

[10] For the attempt of those who considered themselves to be Eli's descendants to overcome his fatalism, see Y. Rosh Hashanah 2.5/58b re I Sam. 3:14. The phrase "let the Lord do what is good in his eyes" also appears in II Sam. 10:12/I Chron. 19:13, but there it is a hope that the *action* of the people in fighting the Ammonites will correspond with God's own plans. In Jer. 38:3, the phrase means *doing* what God has commanded.

[11] See B. Berakhot 4a.

[12] See Martin Buber, *Kingship of God*, trans. R. Scheimann (New York: Harper and Row, 1967), 105f.

hope for anything from God that has not already been eternally decreed. As such, to deny God's responsiveness to the human cri de coeur in the name of God's perfection is to severely limit God's freedom. And freedom is much more closely connected to transcendence than is perfection. One can imagine oneself in union with God's perfection (*unio mystica*) in a way one could never imagine oneself identical with God's freedom.[13] As we saw in the previous chapter, even contemplation is contemplation of God's action, not God's being, God's subjectivity rather than his objectivity.

To pray fundamentally means to beseech God. It presupposes that our primary relationship with God is such that God acts on our behalf and that we act on his behalf responsively. The relationship is one of free persons on both sides. Conversely, both magic and fatalism assume God's necessity. In magic, God is necessarily under our control; in fatalism God is under the control of his own eternity. In magic, God is seen as being manipulated by human freedom so that God is seen within a temporal process of which he is not the first member. In fatalism, God is seen as being without the power to control time by being unable to make changes within time *whenever* he chooses. Thus magic assumes a claim on God we do not in truth have; fatalism denies a claim on God we in truth do have.

This is the so-called God of the philosophers, who (better "which") inevitably turns out to be the God of Aristotle in one way or another: thought thinking itself and nothing else beneath itself. It seems to be its own prisoner. Its self-satisfied perfection breaches no real alterity.[14] As such, this God seems to be limited by a type of fatalism too. In the face of this other God, humans have no rights at all, but only what seem to be duties. Moreover, this other God seems to be too uninterested in us to truly exercise what we would call rights inasmuch as they are personal claims exercised on other persons in specific, temporal situations. Yet duties without rights, as we saw in the introduction, are not really duties at all but, rather, human aspirations to a higher state of being. They are only "duties" metaphorically inasmuch as a duty is real only when it is totally correlated with a prior right. And a right can be exercised only by a person in a transaction with another person to whom he or she is related. A right cannot be exercised by an ultimate object of all contemplative longing. States of being have neither rights nor duties, and we can have no real rights or duties in relation to them. But the covenant, by contrast, is a realm where the correlation of rights and duties is ubiquitous. Hence prayer is part of that correlative scheme of rights and duties. Indeed, it is where the phenomenology of our rights in relation to God should start.

---

[13] For the pretentiousness of human will identifying itself with God's will, confusing the finite with the infinite, see Descartes, *Meditations*, in *The Philosophical Works of Descartes*, trans. E. S. Haldane and G. R. T. Ross (Cambridge: Cambridge University Press, 1967), no. 4, 1:174ff.

[14] See Aristotle, *Metaphysics*, 1072b4, 1074b15–35; Spinoza, *Ethics*, pt. 5, props. 17, 19.

PRAYER: COGNITIVE OR EMOTIVE?

If prayer is the exercise of our claim on God, then we now need to ask whether prayer is essentially cognitive or emotive. That is, do we have to know something about God before we are able to express our feelings of dependence toward him, or do we express these feelings even before we know anything at all about God? An answer to this question might very well get us closer to understanding just how humans really do have a prayerful claim on God, that is, how we are to see our dependence on God. Perhaps we should begin this inquiry by looking at the following rabbinic debate:

> Rabbi Eliezer said that a person should [first] ask for his needs [to be fulfilled] and thereafter pray as Scripture states, "A prayer of the poor one who has despaired, and who pours out his speech (*seeho*) before the Lord" (Psalms 102:1). "Speech" (*seehah*) means prayer (*tefillah*). . . . Rabbi Joshua said that a person should [first] pray and thereafter ask for his needs [to be fulfilled] as Scripture states, "I shall pour out before Him my speeech (*seehi*); my sorrow I shall tell before Him" (Psalms 142:3).[15]

It would seem that for Rabbi Eliezer, the emotive aspect of prayer has priority over the cognitive aspect: we cry before we know. First we need only be aware of our own needs, of our own dependence for their fulfillment. But, for Rabbi Joshua, the cognitive aspect is prior: we must know something beforehand about the One to whom we are crying.[16]

In the ensuing discussion, it is then suggested that Rabbi Joshua derives his approach from the example of Moses, who first praised God for his "greatness" (Deuteronomy 3:24) and then personally beseeched him. But Rabbi Eliezer could easily retort that Moses was vastly different in his personal relationship with God, possessing far greater knowledge of God than do ordinary human beings.[17] Indeed, as Rashi astutely notes in his Talmud commentary thereon, an ordinary human being approaching God with the cognitive certainty of Moses would appear "presumptuous" (*yehora*).[18] After all, only Moses was spoken to by God "face to face as a man speaks to his neighbor" (Exodus 33:11).[19]

[15] B. Avodah Zarah 7b–8a.

[16] This would seem to be the basis of the liturgical order, where God's past redemption of Israel (*ge'ulah*) is to be invoked before our petition for the fulfillment of our present needs in the future (*tefillah*). See B. Berakhot 4b and Rashi, s.v. "zeh ha-someh" re Y. Berakhot 1.1/2d, and Tos., s.v. "d'amar Rabbi Yohanan." See also M. Taanit 1.1; B. Taanit 4b and Tos., s.v. "ve-ha."

[17] B. Avodah Zarah 7b–8a.

[18] B. Avodah Zarah 8a, s.v. "de-rav guvreih."

[19] Yet Moses cannot ever see God directly, but can only communicate with him directly through hearing and speech. See D. Novak, *Jewish-Christian Dialogue* (New York: Oxford University Press, 1989), 145ff.

As for the actual construction of the liturgical order, we follow the view of the Sages, which is presented as the middle view between that of Rabbi Eliezer and that of Rabbi Joshua. They are seen as advocating what is in effect an interchangeable mixture of cognitive praise and emotive petition in the liturgy.[20] Nevertheless, at the theological level, it seems one has to side with either the view of Rabbi Eliezer *or* the view of Rabbi Joshua in their respective phenomenologies of prayer as the human approach to God. And I side here with the view of Rabbi Eliezer, especially because it better illustrates how a human exercises his or her right to call upon God initially in feeling.[21] Thus when the Israelites "groaned from their labor and their cry ascended to God" (Exodus 2:23), it seems that their cry was without any certainty that anyone was actually listening.[22] In fact, Moses had to subsequently reintroduce them to their God. "And He said to say to the children of Israel: 'I who will be there with you (*ehyeh*) has sent me to you' " (Exodus 3:14).[23]

A further indication of the theological profundity of Rabbi Eliezer's view of the priority of affective need over cognitive apprehension of its object is how we primarily constitute our temporality. Usually, we assume that we look at time as a continuum moving from the past through the present into the future. That is what Rabbi Joshua seems to be teaching: namely, consider what God has already done for you in the past, then make your request to God to continue to do so now in the present and on to the future. As the Mishnah puts it: "One is to give thanks by acknowledging (*noten hoda'ah*) [what has been done in] the past (*al she'avar*), and one is to cry (*tso'eq*) for [what is to be

---

[20] B. Avodah Zarah 8a and Tos., s.v. "im" re B. Berakhot 34a; R. Joseph Karo, *Shulhan Arukh*: Orah Hayyim, 112.1.

[21] This suggests an affinity to the famous thesis of the early-nineteenth-century Protestant theologian Friedrich Schleiermacher, viz., that piety is grounded in what he calls "the consciousness of being absolutely dependent" or "the feeling of dependence" (*The Christian Faith*, trans. H. R. Mackintosh and J. S. Stewart [Edinburgh: T. and T. Clark, 1960], no. 4, pp. 12f.), which he states is prior to "some previous knowledge of God" (17). As far as a phenomenology of religious consciousness—i.e., a psychology of religion—goes, this is an important insight. However, ontologically, the Torah is not grounded in human feeling for God but in God's word to us. Hence on the ontological level, cognition of God's word is prior to our feelings of dependence on God's action. That is why the full covenantal relationship with God is prior to any relationship with God centered on human feeling. This is a far cry from Schleiermacher's assertion that "religion's essence is neither thinking nor acting, but intuition and feeling. It wishes to intuit the universe . . . in childlike passivity" (*On Religion*, trans. R. Crouter [Cambridge: Cambridge University Press, 1988], 102). Phenomenology without ontology, especially as regards religious phenomena, inevitably becomes an objectless psychology. See Buber, *I and Thou*, 94f., 129ff.

[22] It is important to note that this verse does not say that the people themselves directed their cry to God. It seems to be saying that the cry itself reached God. Along these lines, see S. R. Hirsch, *The Pentateuch: Translated and Explained*, 2nd ed., vol. 2, translated by I. Levy (New York: Judaica Press, 1971), Exod. 2:23, p. 23; Novak, *Natural Law in Judaism*, 173.

[23] See B. Berakhot 9b; *Shemot Rabbah* 3.7; Nahmanides, *Commentary on the Torah* thereon; also, D. Novak, *Law and Theology in Judaism* (New York: KTAV, 1974), 1:147ff.

done in] the future (*al ha'atid*)."[24] But if the expression of need is our first expression beginning in earliest childhood, then that is not the way we primarily constitute our temporality at all. A child has no past to know before feeling his or her need and expressing his or her desire. A child feels the need in the present and impatiently wants it fulfilled in the immediate future.[25] It is only during the process of maturity that the child begins to have any experience upon which to cognitively draw, and begins to have the capacity to learn about his or her collective past in the history of the community within which he or she makes any claim, especially a claim made directly to God.[26] And even as adults, we think in the present as extending into the future and only then draw upon the past to contribute to our drive. Our experience of the past is always in one way or another a retrojection from our present projection into the future.[27] This being the case, Rabbi Eliezer's teaching about the order of prayer implies the priority of petition (*baqashah*) over even thankful acknowledgment (*hoda'ah*).[28] As such, his phenomenology of our prayer life indicates that we are to exercise our right to call upon God to act before we have to exercise our duty to praise him for what he has already done.

At the most elementary human level, we are needy creatures.[29] Indeed, we come into the world crying. And this is precisely the genesis of rights: a need expressed in desire calling for a recognizable response in a community within which both the rights holder and the intended respondent are members—in one way or another. The experience of need and the desire for its expression and fulfillment from another person are so elementary in humans that they precede the experience of any gender distinctions. In fact, the presexual experience of need might well have some important things to contribute to the discussion of gender distinctions, which is one of the most intense areas of rights talk today, especially in religious communities. It might, furthermore, have something important to contribute to the even more theologically complicated issue of gender language in prayer as regards God, as we shall soon see.

Prayer can be best understood as both a duty and a right. It is a duty in the sense that God wants to hear from us. "He turns to the prayer of the destitute

[24] M. Berakhot 9.4. See B. Berakhot 31a re I Kings 8:25.

[25] Hence even a Torah scholar (*talmid hakham*) is to end the day by beseeching God as a child would for the future. See B. Berakhot 5a re Ps. 31:6.

[26] In the version of the questions of the four sons of the Passover Seder in the Palestinian Talmud, only the wise son is capable of being introduced to the collective past (Y. Pesahim 9.4/ 37d re Exod. 13:14). The other three sons are not mature enough; hence, they are answered at the level of present experience alone.

[27] See Martin Heidegger, *Being and Time*, trans. J. Stambaugh (Albany: State University of New York Press, 1996), sec. 74, pp. 352f.

[28] If one can see the essence of prayer in the shortest prayer in Scripture, that of Moses on behalf of his sister Miriam in her illness (Num. 12:13), that prayer is pure petition (see B. Berakhot 34a).

[29] See B. Berakhot 44b re Deut. 7:14. Cf. Tos., s.v. "she-lo" thereon re Job 26:7, and Hullin 89a for a more cognitive emphasis.

and does not despise their prayer" (Psalms 102:18). "The Lord is near to all who call upon him, to all who truly (*b'emet*) call upon him" (Psalms 145:18). "And it shall be that even before (*terem*) they call I shall answer, while they are still (*od*) speaking I shall hear" (Isaiah 65:24).[30] But even before we know that duty, in prayer we exercise our right to call upon God to listen to us and care for us. At the most elementary level, prayer is spontaneous, indeed, as spontaneous as the experience of the needs that are expressed in our desire for God's aid.[31] It is our feeling that the One who has made us has responsibility for our needs as well. That is the price God has to pay, so to speak, for creating this loquacious human creature.

Prayer assumes that God is still concerned with the world he has created, especially with the only creature who seems to be concerned with him and for his personal care. In that sense, God and humans occupy a common world, albeit a world that humans occupy in a restricted way and God occupies in a most unrestricted way. The right to pray, then, might very well be seen as God's first entitlement to his human creatures, which is our claim on God that he consider cosmic changes on our behalf. It is the claim on God to dwell with us in the world. Thus when King Solomon dedicated the First Temple in Jerusalem, he states, "How could God possibly (*ha'umnam*) dwell on earth, even the heavens, the very highest heavens cannot contain you (*yekhalkelu-kha*)?" but then immediately asks God to "listen to the praise (*ha-rinah*) and the prayer (*ha-tefillah*) which your servant is praying before you today" (I Kings 8:27–28). How could God listen and respond to this prayer without interposing himself in the world with his creatures?[32]

The duty to pray, though, is more accurately the duty to engage in prescribed worship (*avodah*), with its own public liturgical order (*matbea shel tefillah*).[33] And at this level, Jewish tradition teaches a profound difference between men and women, one so profound that the very sense of public liturgical time is seen to be different for women than for men. Thus women are considered to be exempt from most positive commandments that are to be performed at a specific time (*she-ha-zeman grama*).[34] Because of this great difference, the Talmud supposes how one could well think that women need not pray, prayer being a male need and obligation. But the Mishnah specifically states that women are obligated to pray—even though subsequent halakhic development indicates that their prayer can be much more informal than the regular prayer prescribed for men as worship. The reason given for this in the same talmudic discussion is that women, like men, "are seekers of mercy" (*de-rahamei*

---

[30] See *Shemot Rabbah* 15.29.

[31] See Y. Berakhot 4.3/8a (the statement of R. Aha in the name of R. Yose).

[32] See *Shemot Rabbah* 34.1 re Exod. 25:8; *Pesiqta Rabbati*, chap. 16 re Exod. 25:22, ed. Fried-mann, 84b; *Pesiqta de-Rav Kahana*, sec. 23 re Ps. 89:16, ed. Mandelbaum, 2:337.

[33] See Y. Berakhot 6.2/10b.

[34] M. Kiddushin 1.7.

neenhu).[35] In another talmudic discussion, it is also assumed that both women and men are "seekers of life" (*ba'ei hayyei*).[36] And the need for life and for love long precede the need to be ordered by public events. In fact, it is sort of ironic that in rabbinic tradition, the etiquette of formal prayer is learned from the spontaneous prayer of Hannah, a woman whose prayer for a child was so fervent that Eli the High Priest of Israel thought it to be the irreverent ravings of a drunkard.[37]

Now the terms used in both these talmudic discussions are significant. The term for "mercy" (*rahamim*) comes from the word for "womb" (*rehem*). And the most intimate connection to life for both females and males is to their mother. Our first—and often last—cry for loving mercy is made to our mother. Indeed, the first woman, Eve (*Hava*), is given that name by her husband because he sees her as "mother of all life" (*em kol hei*—Genesis 3:20), even of his own life, he who was literally brought forth from the earth motherless.[38] The most basic dependence of all humans is on our mother. Indeed, the awareness of her gender precedes the awareness of our own: we know her breast long before we know our own genitals.

In the Talmud, there are various criteria for distinguishing an adult, who is subject to formal responsibility, from a child, who is exempt from it. These criteria vary from context to context, since adulthood cannot be univocally constituted.[39] Nevertheless, the earliest religious responsibility placed on any Jewish child is to dwell in the *sukkah*, the special hut open to the sky set up for the week of the festival of Sukkot. In fact, Shammai the Elder even required infants to dwell in the *sukkah*.[40] However, the other Sages see this as the obligation of a child who is already beyond infancy, one who no longer "needs his mother" (*sh'eino tsarikh l'immo*). According to the Talmud, such a child must be mature enough to be able to wake up at night and not have to cry, "Mama, Mama!" Nevertheless, it is recognized that this is a difference of degree rather than one of kind, for even adults can be seen as calling to their mother when frightened by the night.[41] Thus the Psalmist says: "On You have I depended since the womb, from my mother's innards You are my strength; for You my praise is continual" (Psalms 71:6). It is not that one literally praises God in utero, but from one's very beginnings at conception he or she is dependent on God. One's connection to mother is the most primary locus of that need.[42]

[35] B. Berakhot 20b re M. Berakhot 3.3.

[36] B. Kiddushin 34a re Deut. 11:21.

[37] B. Berakhot 31a–b.

[38] See *Midrash ha-Gadol*: Beresheet re Gen. 24:67, ed. Margulies, 411f.

[39] See, e.g., M. Hagigah 1.1; B. Hagigah 6a; B. Gittin 65a; B. Baba Metsia 12b; M. Avot 5.21.

[40] M. Sukkah 2.8.

[41] B. Sukkah 28b. See Eruvin 82a. Cf. Y. Sukkah 2.8/53b.

[42] See Niddah 31a and *Sheiltot de-Rav Ahai Gaon*: Yitro, no. 56, ed. Kenig, 45a, where it is asserted that the mother is the source of the child's "flesh and blood," whereas the father supplies the more subsequent structural elements of "tendons and bones."

When asking God to order our actions in the world, we tend to use father language, but we tend to use mother language at the primal level of elementary need, which long precedes our sense of ourselves as truly acting persons.[43] In the personal intimacy of prayer, God is seen as either mother or father. One cannot cry to the neutered God of the philosophers. God is more than any male or female or any other limitations to be sure, but God must be seen as possessing motherly and fatherly strengths if there is to be any mutual relationship between God and humans. And at the most elementary human level, we sense those strengths as motherly. Every child feels his or her most basic claim is on mother. From her life the little girl or little boy expects her or his life and nurture to be forthcoming. Indeed, in Judaism, one's most basic identity is determined by the mother before the subsequent identity is determined by the father.[44]

And, finally, not only is the experience of the object of prayer essentially female, but our own experience in prayer is just as essentially female. As pointed out shortly above, even the formal etiquette of prayer as public worship is learned from Hannah's spontaneous prayer in the sanctuary at Shilo.[45] How much more is to be learned from her about preformal desire! The fervor of Hannah's prayer is very much connected to the content of her prayer: "See the suffering of Your maidservant; remember me and do not forget your maidservant, but give your maidservant a child (*zera*)" (I Samuel 1:11). What impudence is it to implore God to be the cocreator of his own image! And, yet, is not her cry the archetype of all human claims made to God? Is not the depth of our desire for our mother in direct proportion to our sense of her desire to bear us and nurture us? Could any human desire be greater; could any personal need that inspired such desire be greater? How much deeper was Hannah's need than that of her husband, Elkanah, who could not see the difference between the spouse who comes to her body and the child who comes forth from her body: "Am I not better for you than ten sons?" (I Samuel 1:8). Hence it is from our mothers that we all learn both what it means to be weak and dependent on God and what God's strength, upon which we are so dependent, means. Human rights are rooted in natural needs long before they are the subject matter of covenantal negotiation. The covenant realizes natural possibilities in unpredictable ways, but it presupposes them nonetheless.[46]

GOD'S COMMANDMENTS AS HUMAN RIGHTS

It would seem that when it comes to our active life, which for Jews is the life of the practice of the commandments (*mitsvot*), we move from the level of

---

[43] See, e.g., Isa. 64:7–8; I Chron. 29:10–12.

[44] Regarding general Jewish identity following the mother, see B. Kiddushin 68b and parallels re Deut. 7:4. Regarding specific Jewish identity following the father, see M. Kiddushin 3.12.

[45] For the value of such spontaneity, see II Chron. 29:36.

[46] See D. Novak, *Natural Law in Judaism* (Cambridge: Cambridge University Press, 1998), 142ff.

rights to the level of duties.[47] At this level, we seem to experience what God claims from us rather than what we claim from God. It seems to be a total transition from the passive experience of the child we always remain to a certain extent, to the activity filled life of the adult we usually want to be. Ontologically, there is much truth in this phenomenological observation. There is certainly a priority of the active over the passive life. And for us, duties do have a priority over rights inasmuch as God's claims on us are prior and more complete than any claims we have on him. As we have seen above, we can only claim that God listen to what we desire, not that he is in any way obligated to do as we desire. But God has a claim that we both listen to what he commands and do it. Nevertheless, there is also a strong assumption that we do have the right to ask God to give us commandments by which to live. "I am a stranger on earth, do not hide your commandments from me" (Psalms 119:19).[48]

We can see the connection between God's right to command us and our right to be commanded by God as follows: "He [Moses] took the book of the covenant and read it into the ears of the people. And they said, 'everything that the Lord speaks, we shall do and we shall hear' " (Exodus 24:7). There are a number of significant interpretations of why the people at Mount Sinai mention their doing before their hearing.[49] The best known is the talmudic one that sees this order of precedence in the acceptance of the covenant, which indicates that the people committed themselves to practice the commandments of the Torah even before they could understand them.[50] Now, this understanding cannot mean understanding *how* to do *what* the commandments require. Lack of that type of understanding could very well lead to invalid practice altogether.[51] "An ignorant person (*am ha'arets*) cannot be pious," as the Mishnah puts it.[52] So, instead, it seems to mean more an understanding of the deeper meaning of the commandments. And the deepest possible meaning they could have is to answer the question of *why* they were commanded. The Rabbis called this inquiry "the reasons of the commandments" (*ta'amei ha-mitsvot*).[53] It is the theology of the law over and above the pragmatics of the law. And in this theology, there are two ways to understand the reasons of the commandments, both of which assume that the reasons of the commandments are their proper ends.

---

[47] In fact, death is defined as the stage when one is "free of the commandments" (*patur min ha-mitsvot*). See Niddah 61b re Ps. 88:6.

[48] See Y. Berakhot 9.5/14d re Ps. 34:8.

[49] E.g., Rashbam in his *Commentary on the Torah* thereon interprets "we shall hear (*nishma*) as a request for further revelation" (cf. B. Gittin 60a re Ps. 40:8).

[50] B. Shabbat 88a.

[51] See, e.g., M. Pesahim 10.5. That is why the study of the Torah (*talmud*) is seen as the necessary precondition for proper practice (*ma'aseh*). See B. Kiddushin 40b and parallels.

[52] M. Avot 2.5.

[53] See Novak, *Natural Law in Judaism*, 64ff.

First, we can see the ends of the commandments as being identical with the source of all the commandments, who is God himself. In other words, God has given us all the commandments that we might fulfill his purposes for the world, the highest of which is a relationship with himself. As the prophet put it, "Everything that is called by my name, I created it, I formed it, I made it for My glory" (Isaiah 43:7). This is, of course, true, and it is a theological concern of the first order. Everyone comes from God and desires God, beyond whom there is nothing. "Like the hind panting (*ta'arog*) for brooks of water, so do I myself (*nafshi*) pant for you O' God. I myself thirst for God, the living God; when will I come to be seen by the present God (*pnei elohim*)?" (Psalms 42:2–3). The question is, however, whether it is the only theological concern. For the kabbalists it was, and their theology becomes to a very large extent a speculation about the commandments as they symbolize the inner relations of the divine life. In their theology, the relation between source and end becomes one, so that even what transpires between them is also divine. That is because when God is taken to be all encompassing, even what seems to us to be a separate human reality cannot in truth be taken as anything more than a mere appearance, whose ultimate validity is its ability to point to what some philosophers have called "panentheistic" reality, namely, that all reality is contained within the only reality that is not an appearance: the Godhead (*elohut*).[54]

Secondly, though, the reasons of the commandments can be seen on a penultimate level, one that is more specifically human in its meaning. In contrast to kabbalistic panentheism, it can see human reality as related *to* God but not actually *within* God; hence, human reality is something apart *from* God as well, even though ever dependent *on* God. In this type of theology, there is room for a phenomenology of the commandments that can see them operating within what Husserl called the human "lifeworld" (*Lebenswelt*).[55] At this level, we can begin to see the function of many of the commandments, even most of the commandments, which is to fulfill human needs. If that is so, then we can see the meaning of many of the commandments being God's response to human needs. If these needs are sufficiently understood, then, can they not be seen as our rights, which is expressed in our desire for God to direct us in paths that lead us to our own true ends?[56]

---

[54] See J. Ben-Shlomoh, *Torat ha'Elohut shel Rabbi Mosheh Cordovero* (Jerusalem: Mosad Bialik, 1965), 294f.; Gershom Scholem, *The Messianic Idea in Judaism* (New York: Schocken, 1971), 223ff.; *On the Kabbalah and Its Symbolism*, trans. R. Manheim (New York: Schocken, 1969) 122ff.; also, C. Hartshorne and W. L. Reese, *Philosophers Speak of God* (Chicago: University of Chicago Press, 1953), 166.

[55] See *The Crisis of European Sciences and Transcendental Phenomenology*, trans. D. Carr (Evanston, Ill.: Northwestern University Press, 1970), pt. 3, 103ff.

[56] See Deut. 6:24–25; Ps. 119:62, 65, 73, 93.

One can see all of the specific reasons of the commandments as being the fulfillment of specific human needs. (Whether all of the commandments have such specifically human reasons, however, is a different matter. One could well argue that at least some of the commandments are simply God's exercise of his own primary right to command any of his creatures in any matter he wills.)[57] And when we claim the fulfillment of those needs from either the divine or the human lawgiver, we can be said to be exercising our rights. Nevertheless, in the case of the revealed law of the Torah, the determination of these originating rights as reasons of the commandments is a matter of highly speculative inference a posteriori.[58] What we need to see is whether any of the divine legislation in the Written Torah itself, when being formulated, is in response to the explicit exercise of human rights by rights holders themselves a priori.

If rights are most easily recognizable when they are willingly and explicitly exercised by those who hold them, one can see agency as a basic legal right. In agency (*shelihut*), persons are able to extend their claims beyond their actual presence before the object of any such claim. As the Mishnah puts it, "One's agent is like oneself (*kemoto*)."[59] Thus one can be held responsible only for the acts of an agent he or she has willingly and explicitly appointed. And the act of the agent is invalid if it violates what the principal had specified.[60] Moreover, it is invalid if it violates the law itself, inasmuch as violation of the law is not a right, hence it cannot be delegated.[61]

At Mount Sinai, one sees the dynamics of agency at work in the constitution of the covenant between God and Israel. There Moses has the unique function of being both the agent of God and the agent of the people of Israel. As God's agent, Moses has a specific mission to Israel. God tells him, "[T]hese (*eleh*) are the words you shall speak to the children of Israel . . . and he placed all these words that the Lord had commanded before them" (Exodus 19:6–7).[62] As such he is acting on behalf of God's right to command the people whom God has elected for the covenant.[63] Once the commandments have been issued, it is clear that Moses is to literally state them to the people; in their specifics the commandment are not subject to any negotiation with the people.[64] But Moses is also just as much the agent of the people, who want him to be their intermediary to receive for them what they themselves think they cannot bear to receive directly from God. "And they said to Moses: 'you speak with us and we shall hear, but let not God speak with us lest we die' " (Exodus 20:16).

[57] See Novak, *The Election of Israel*, 251f.

[58] See Novak, *Natural Law in Judaism*, 74f.

[59] M. Berakhot 5.5. See M. Rosh Hashanah 4.9.

[60] See, e.g., M. Kiddushin 2.4.

[61] B. Kiddushin 42b and parallels. See B. Baba Metsia 10b and Rashi, s.v. "bar hiyyuva hu." Cf. B. Kiddushin 42a re II Sam. 12:9; B. Baba Kama 71a re Exod. 21:37.

[62] See *Mekhilta*: Yitro, ed. Horovitz-Rabin, 246 re Deut. 4:35.

[63] See ibid., 209f. re Exod. 19:8.

[64] See Nahmanides, *Commentary on the Torah*: Exod. 19:7.

Now the question is whether Moses' role as the people's agent is passive or active. That is, is he only to receive for them whatever God specifically commands them, or can he also actively claim from God what the people think they need? In other words, is at least part of his function as the agent of the people to express to God what they think are their rights, which they hope that God will acknowledge and respond to? One can answer this question by pointing to a number of rabbinic texts which assert that Moses' claims were subsequently validated by God. That is, the impetus of what is finally accorded the status of a divine decree originally is taken to come from Moses, not just to him.[65] But, of course, any human must always be aware that God is the final judge of whether these rights are valid or spurious, that is, whether they are real or only apparent. That is because the rights of all creatures are entitlements from God, the original holder of all rights. Nevertheless, as we shall see in chapter 4, these entitlements can be taken as irrevocable when they come from God's promises.

This more active role for Moses on behalf of the people can perhaps be seen in the words describing the speech situation between God and Moses at Sinai: "Moses speaks and God answers him vocally (*ya'anennu be-qol*)" (Exodus 19:19). Now, it would seem that if revelation is the passive acceptance of what God commands, it would have been more appropriate to say, "God speaks and Moses answers." Is that not what the people did when first approached at Mount Sinai, namely, "And all the people answered (*va-ya'anu*) together saying: 'all that the Lord speaks, we shall do' " (Exodus 19:8)? So, it seems another point is being made. Could we not say that revelation, at least in part, consists of Moses presenting before God what he thought were the legitimate needs of the people to be claimed from God?[66] And God's answer would seem to be either yes, no, or otherwise. Indeed, we have at least two explicit examples in the Written Torah itself of such a negotiation between God and the people being handled by Moses as the agent of both parties.

In the second year of the Exodus from Egypt, Passover was observed for the first time as the celebration of a past event. Now, one could not be in a state of physical impurity (*tum'ah*) due to contact with a dead body and still be able to participate in the main aspect of the celebration: the eating of the pashcal lamb. Some of those who found themselves in this state of impurity complained to Moses (and Aaron along with him): "Why should we be prevented (*niggara*) from offering the Lord's sacrifice in its appointed season in the midst of the children of Israel?" (Numbers 9:7). Moses agreed to present their case before God, which meant he would voice their claim for them. God's answer was to command them to observe what came to be called the "Second

---

[65] See, e.g., B. Berakhot 32a re Num. 14:20; *Bemidbar Rabbah* 19.33; also, Abraham Joshua Heschel, *Torah min ha-Shamayim be'Ispaqlarya shel ha-Dorot* 2 (London: Soncino, 1965), 280ff.

[66] See *Midrash Tehillim*, chap. 18, ed. Buber, re I Sam. 22:36; Ibn Ezra, *Commentary on the Torah*: Exod. 19:19.

Passover" (*pesah sheni*), which enabled such persons and those who could not physically be present on the "First Passover" to celebrate the eating of the paschal lamb one month later.[67] In other words, God validated their right, through Moses, to the celebration of Passover as the defining national event. Moses, as it were, won their case for them. And their case became the basis of a law that applied to everyone else in their situation thereafter.[68]

In another case won by Moses, the five daughters of Zelophehad, a man who died without leaving male heirs, came before Moses (and Eleazar the High Priest) and asked to be made their father's heirs. "Why should the name of our father be deleted (*yiggara*) from the midst of his family just because he had no son?" (Numbers 27:4). Moses agreed to take their case before God. And God's answer was favorable to their cause too: "The daughters of Zelophehad have spoken correctly (*ken*); give them an inheritance (*ahuzat nahalah*) in the midst of the brothers of their father; transfer their father's portion to them" (Numbers 27:7). Here again, Moses won the case of human claimants; and here again, the verdict in their case became the basis of a general law.[69] Furthermore, in both of these cases, Moses could not very well have been the advocate of the people unless he believed that their case was valid. It is just that he himself was not authorized to rule in these cases.[70] Unlike in other situations, he could not make the law here.[71]

Of course, there is no guarantee that God will answer in anyone's favor. God is the final judge, and since revelation is at this time still in process, God's judgment is made according to often mysterious criteria. Moreover, the outcome is not always favorable by the claimants' criteria anyway. Thus, Korah's claim for more democratic levitical leadership in place of the seeming oligarchical authority of Moses and Aaron is refused by God. In fact, the very exercise of the claim itself is judged to be unjust. Thus, when God says to Moses and to Aaron, "[S]eparate yourselves from this company," Moses interprets that as a judgment for everyone to separate from "these wicked (*resha'im*) men" (Numbers 16:21, 26). It would seem that Moses' role as the people's agent is also to advise claimants on God whether they are entitled even to make any such claim, irrespective of what the outcome from God might be. He functions like a modern lawyer. So, even though the Passover petitioners and the daughters of Zelophehad could have had their cases judged negatively

---

[67] See Num. 9:9–14; M. Pesahim 9.1–3.

[68] See B. Pesahim 95a–b.

[69] See *Sifre*: Bemidbar, no. 134 re Num. 27:8.

[70] See B. Baba Batra 119b re Deut. 25:5 for an imaginary scenario depicting how intelligently the daughters of Zelophehad argued their case before Moses and his court in what might be seen as their preliminary hearing.

[71] Regarding Moses' own legislative authority, see Y. Megillah 4.1/75a; Maimonides, *Mishneh Torah*: Tefillah, 12.1; and Karo, *Kesef Mishneh* thereon re B. Baba Kama 82a; also, Josephus, *Contra Apionem*, 2.175.

by God, Moses clearly thought that they already had the right to at least request what they did nonetheless. But in the case of Korah, where Moses himself is being challenged, God had to show that Korah and his followers even making the claim was illicit, let alone the claim's actual content. And in this case, since Moses was being named as a defendant, as it were, he was obviously in no position to be the judge (functioning like a grand jury today) of whether or not Korah and his company were justified in making their claim at all.[72] What we see from all of this is that the right to make a claim on God, although limited, is still greater than the right to have one's claim affirmatively answered.

THE HUMAN RIGHT TO GOD'S JUSTICE

One can locate three types of rights humans have in relation to God, that is, three types of claims we have on God. The first is the claim on God to listen to our cry for an answer to our needs. The second is our claim on God to give us commandments whereby we can live in the world with him and fulfill at least some of our worldly needs by our own acts. And, third, there is our claim on God to finally judge our acts in the world. That means that we should be responsible for the final consequences of our acts, both good and bad. Thus one can see rights of the first type being emotive, that is, they are the primary expression of our felt needs in desire. One can see rights of the second type being cognitive, that is, they are the subsequent awareness of what it is for us to do in order to fulfill our needs. Finally, one can see rights of the third type being effective, that is, the hope that our acts will be more than just present experiences but that they will have a lasting outcome in the future.

What we see in this scheme are three types of intention. In our emotive rights we passively intend the source of our fulfillment. "I lift up my eyes towards the mountains, where will my help (*ezri*) come from? My help is from the Lord, maker of heaven and earth" (Psalms 121:1–2). In our cognitive rights we actively intend the objects of our fulfillment. "Keeping the commandments and statutes of the Lord your God, which I command you this day, is what is good for you (*le-tov lakh*)" (Deuteronomy 10:13).[73] And in our effective rights we intend the final outcome of our acts. "I know my redeemer lives, even if he be the last to arise on earth" (Job 19:25).[74]

There is a good deal of confusion about the doctrine of divine justice as retribution. As "reward and punishment" (*sekhar v'onesh*), it is often criticized as being the intention of ends extrinsic to the acts themselves.[75] In other words,

---

[72] See B. Ketubot 105b; B. Sanhedrin 29a re Num. 35:23.

[73] See Nahmanides, *Commentary on the Torah* thereon.

[74] See Rashi, *Commentary on the Hagiographa* thereon (perhaps alluding to Dan. 12:2).

[75] See B. Avodah Zarah 19a re Ps. 112:1 and M. Avot 1.3; B. Sotah 22b; Y. Berakhot 9.5/14b; Y. Kiddushin 1.7/61b re Prov. 5:6; Maimonides, *Mishneh Torah*: Teshuvah, 10.4. And, in fact,

emphasis of divine justice as reward and punishment is often seen as turning the commandments into the means for the fulfillment of simply selfish ends. It seems to turn the higher into the lower, that is, God's will is taken to be for the sake of human will. Should one have to be promised future payment for doing what is God's right in the present? Should our deeds in the present for God be instrumental in essence, namely, deeds done for a future payment to ourselves? Nevertheless, when two of the students of the ancient Sage, Antignos of Socho, inferred from his criticism of "those who serve the master for the sake of (*al menat*) of receiving payment (*pras*)" that there is no ultimate reckoning for good or bad acts therefore, they were seen as having founded heretical movements in Judaism thereby.[76] Perhaps a phenomenological analysis of how these three intentions function in an apodictic order will indicate a more cogent way theologically to understand the anticipation of divine justice as retribution. Accordingly, all three intentions must be seen working in a consecutive order. The effective intention becomes distorted, however, when it is taken as primary, thus jumping over the emotive and cognitive intentions.

Our primary experience of our dependence on God directly leads into our acceptance of God's right to command us. It is like our being taught by our mother how to cooperate with her response to our needs. As the most immediately experienced source of our life and nurture, she has the right to command us. But we are still only becoming aware of how this is done, but not yet why. We accept that even before we have any understanding of just how our cooperation with her commands actually does fulfill our needs. So far, we are still at the emotive level alone. However, as we become more active in the world, we begin to learn why we have been commanded as we have. Without that designation of the objects of our acts, we can never achieve any active independence.[77] That often requires our father's teaching inasmuch as our bond with him is never as emotively dependent on his body as is our dependence on our mother's body.[78] Hence our father is often experienced as the one who transfers us from the passivity of the cradle to the activity of the public square, and that is so even though father plays a domestic role too and mother often plays a public role too.[79] At this point, we are now at the cognitive level. Here the ends of our acts are intrinsic to the acts themselves. Thus we are not to

---

intending one's own doing of the *mitsvot* for selfish ends (*ha-na'ah*) does not change the essentially transcendent intentionality of the *mitsvot* themselves (see B. Rosh Hashanah 28a; cf. B. Sotah 17a). But for the permissibility of including selfish ends within the larger intentionality of the *mitsvot*, however, see B. Pesahim 8a–b and parallels, and Rashi, s.v. "harei zeh tsaddiq gamur" and Tos., s.v. "she-yizkeh."

[76] *Avot de-Rabbi Nathan* A, chap. 5, ed. Schechter, 13b re M. Avot 1.3.

[77] See *Beresheet Rabbah* 30.10 re Gen. 6:9.

[78] See B. Eruvin 82a–b; B. Ketubot 65b; *Teshuvot ha-Geonim*, ed. Harkavy, no. 212; R. David ibn Abi Zimra, *Teshuvot ha-Radbaz* 1, nos. 123, 429.

[79] See M. Kiddushin 1.7; T. Kiddushin 1.11; B. Kiddushin 29a.

harm others because others have a right not to be harmed; they have a claim on our restraining our own aggressive desires. We are thus restrained for their sake alone. And so we are to help others when they need us because they have a right to our aid, they have a claim on our concern. We are thus concerned for them alone. However, if this is the case, then why do our acts require the intention of extrinsic results over and above the intention of their intrinsic ends or purposes? Should doing well not be its own reward?[80]

It would seem that the reason for this extrinsic requirement is because our commanded acts are ultimately for the sake of cooperation with God's purposes for his created cosmos. Maximally, this means that our good acts, our acts that respond to God's creative rights, should share in the lasting effects of what God has created and *for what* he has created it. The fulfillment of their intentions should be more than initially cognitive but subsequently effective as well. Our acts should be more than just statements of truth; they should also be the effective agents of the active truth they only cognitively intend in the beginning. They should bring about good in the world: this world or the world-to-come. Their effect should go far beyond our immediate experience. As such, our first active intention is a priori: it intends the end *for* our acts (*telos*); and our second active intention is a posteriori: it intends the end coming *from* our acts.[81] That last end (*eschaton*) should be so even when our acts seem to be failures in terms of their present effects, which is quite often the case in this unredeemed world.[82] Minimally, this means that the one who does what is right should not suffer bad in the end because of the good act he or she has now done, and the one who does what is wrong should not enjoy good in the end because of the bad act he or she has now done.[83] We believe that minimally God has commanded us to do what is good for ourselves—and because of our communal nature, along with others in our world.

Much of this comes out in the following text in the Talmud:

> Rabbi Jacob said that there is no commandment in the Torah which does not have its rewards connected to it (*she-mattan sekharah be-tsidah*) and from which the resurrection of the dead is not connected (*teluyah bah*). Thus about honor of father and mother it is written, "in order that (*le-ma'an*) your days be long and in order that it be good for you" (Deuteronomy 5:16); [and] about sending the mother bird away before taking the baby birds (*be-shiluah ha-qan*) it is written, "in order that

---

[80] See M. Avot 4.2 and Maimonides, *Commentary on the Mishneh* thereon. Cf. Spinoza, *Ethics*, 5, prop. 42.

[81] See R. Joseph Albo, *Iqqarim*, 3.28; R. Isaiah ha-Levi Horowitz, *Shnei Luhot ha-Berit*, pt. 3, ed. Amsterdam, 82b–83a re B. Kiddushin 40b.

[82] See B. Kiddushin 39b (the view of R. Jacob—cf. Tos., s.v. "matnitin"). Cf. M. Peah 1.1; M. Kiddushin 1.10.

[83] This is expressed in the general principle "that the sinner not be rewarded for his or her sin" (*hoṭē niskar*). See M. Hallah 2.7; B. Yevamot 92b and parallels.

(*le-ma'an*) it be good for you and you have length of days" (Deuteronomy 22:7). Now it happened that a father said to his son, "go up on this building and bring me baby birds." So he [the son] went up and sent away the mother and took the offspring, but during his return down he fell and died. Where is his "length of days" (*arikhut yamav*)? Where is his "good" (*tovato*)? Nevertheless (*ela*) . . . [it is] in a world without end (*she-kulo arokh*) . . . in a world all good (*she-kulo tov*).[84]

This seminal text indicates how the Jewish tradition refused to accept an ultimately absurd outcome from the properly intended keeping of God's commandments. The son diligently kept the commandment to honor his father's request just as he diligently kept the commandment to send the mother bird away. (Both commandments, interestingly enough, are concerned with the feelings of parents in relation to their children.) Was this his reward?[85] Since there was no way to avoid that conclusion of absurdity in many cases in the history of this world, the tradition had to speculate on how God has the power to enable our acts to reach their ultimate effectiveness in a world-to-come (*olam ha-ba*), namely, a world radically beyond the ordinary processes of history as we know them.[86]

There are two injustices that seem to emerge from the story of the dutiful yet tragic son. First, the son is deprived of the normal life span on earth in which to accomplish his rightful goals like a family of his own, a career of his own. Second, his father is deprived of such a virtuous son, who a father should be able to hope will care for him in his old age and survive him on earth to carry on the family legacy. It would seem, then, that the resurrection of the son would also include the resurrection of his father with him, indeed, the resurrection of all the righteous with him.[87] How could one conceive of an embodied human life without its own community along with it? And, the rectification of these injustices must come about in a world only God could so radically transform. It will have to be "the new heaven and the new earth which I am making" (Isaiah 66:22).

[84] Hullin 142a. See *Ruth Rabbah* 6.6; B. Pesahim 50a.
[85] See Menahot 29b; Y. Hagigah 2.1/77b.
[86] See B. Berakhot 34b re Isa. 64:3. Even Kant, who insisted that moral acts be done for their own sake and not for the sake of an extrinsic end, nevertheless had to postulate God's effecting a real and permanent result of our moral acts in this world. Otherwise we would be intending what we knew is futile in advance; hence our intention would be absurd. See *Critique of Practical Reason*, 1.2.2.1; also Hermann Cohen, *Ethik des reinen Willens*, 4th ed. (Berlin: B. Cassirer, 1923), 470. But the problem for Kant is that this God is subordinate to morality, not to its source; hence, such a God cannot be seriously conceived of as the absolute. Cohen tries to give God a greater role than did Kant, but it is still problematic whether his God is the real source—as distinct from the ideal goal—of the law, hence whether his God too is really the absolute (see Novak, *The Election of Israel*, 54ff.).
[87] See R. Saadiah Gaon, *Emunot ve-Deot*, 7.10 re Ezek. 48:1.

That is why, it seems to me, the early rabbinic texts talk about a general "future" (*l'atid la-vo*), which intermingles talk of the "resurrection of the dead" (*tehiyyat ha-metim*), the "world-to-come" (*olam ha-ba*), and the "messianic days" (*yemot ha-mashiah*).[88] So, when dealing with the soul (*nefesh*) as the restored relational field centered in the human flesh (*basar*), bodily resurrection is invoked. When dealing with time restored for the fulfillment of the human task, the coming world is invoked. And when dealing with the truly fulfilling world community, the messianic kingship is invoked. Moreover, one can see a dialectic at work between these three interrelated doctrines. Without the resurrection, eschatology tends to become talk of a disembodied soul engaged in contemplation of a divine object rather than of an earthly life actively in communion with God.[89] Without the temporality of "the coming-world," eschatology tends to become the absorption of humans into self-contained eternity rather than their engagement in temporal activity both transitive and transactional.[90] And without the messianic kingship, eschatology tends to become the trajectory of lone individuals who no longer need any full earthly community, but who simply enjoy God all for themselves, all by themselves.[91]

In order to be worthy of this finally reckoning, humans do not have to have lived perfect lives. Such an expectation would be beyond all hope. "For there is no one (*adam*) so righteous on earth who has only done good and not sinned" (Ecclesiastes 7:20).[92] What is required of them is that they return to God and regret having offended him by their sins. "Return [at least] one day before the day of your death."[93] Since, of course, we do not know when that day will actually come, we are to return to God every day of our life.[94] And the fact that this regular return is a regular part of the liturgy indicates that it is some-

---

[88] See Novak, *The Election of Israel*, 262f.

[89] But in Maimonides' view, those who merit the world-to-come will be "like ministering angels" (*Mishneh Torah*: Teshuvah, 8.2, re B. Berakhot 17a interpreting Exod. 24:11). Cf. R. Abraham ben David of Posquières, *Hasagot ha-Ravad* thereon, who notes that Maimonides' overly spiritual interpretation of this one rabbinic text seems to flirt with denial of the doctrine of the resurrection of the dead and its greater emphasis on human corporeality. In this critique, he marshals a number of significant rabbinic texts (e.g., B. Sanhedrin 91b re Deut. 32:39).

[90] See Maimonides, *Mishneh Torah*: Teshuvah, 8.8, and R. Abraham ben David of Posquières, *Hasagot ha-Ravad* thereon re B. Sanhedrin 97a interpreting Isa. 2:17. Cf. also Nahmanides, *Commentary on the Torah*: Lev. 26:12; D. Novak, *The Theology of Nahmanides Systematically Presented* (Atlanta, Ga.: Scholars Press, 1992), 126ff.

[91] See Maimonides, *Mishneh Torah*: Teshuvah, 8.6. Cf. *Guide of the Perplexed*, 3.27, where it is emphasized that political life is pluralistic because we are embodied. Hence, it would seem that if *olam ha-ba* is a place of disembodied souls, it cannot be a community in any sense we can understand or even anticipate.

[92] See B. Berakhot 46b. Cf. Tos., s.v. "Mar Zutra" thereon; B. Shabbat 55b and Tos., s.v. "arba'ah."

[93] M. Avot 2.10.

[94] *Avot de-Rabbi Nathan* A, chap. 15, p. 31b; B. Shabbat 153a re Eccl. 9:8.

thing we do together in community. It is not the herculean effort of moral and spiritual virtuosi.[95]

Finally, the forgiveness (*selihah*) we are promised when we do return is taken to be not only a cancellation of the punishing, bad effects of our sins against God, for would that not entail the elimination of much of our lived experience (*Erlebnis*)? Are our sins not part of our very identity as persons? If this were all there is to repentance, would the end result not be a diminishment rather than an enhancement of our overall personal stories? Hence our request for forgiveness has to be much more than just a claim on God to wipe the slate clean (*kapparah*).[96] Indeed, in rabbinic theology it becomes much more audacious. It is a claim on God to actually count our sins heretofore as positive merits (*zekhuyot*) rather than retain them as negative demerits (*hovot*).[97] That is, from the retrospective view of our return to God and his ways (*teshuvah*), all of our past sins are to be now taken as contributions, as it were, to our present state of communion with God. From this perspective, God has not only used our evil deeds for his purposes ultimately, he has also changed their status as regards the record of our own personal lives. We are thus asking God to reverse the very course of history, enabling us to fully retrieve it and not just partially forget it. This, especially, might be the most radical claim any human could possibly make on God. But only such a radical claim can save us from an equally radical despair over the bad outcome of the world, including our own sinful contribution to it.

The claims of God on humans and humans on God begin in person-to-person relationships. But these relationships are secondary to the communal relationships of the covenant, which pertain between God and the people of Israel and the people of Israel and God. And here the rights and duties exercised on both sides, even as they are seen in human interrelationships, are more pronounced and more developed. The remaining chapters of the book are thus devoted to those rights and duties that are more immediately seen as covenantal.

---

[95] See B. Rosh Hashanah 18a re Deut. 4:7; B. Sotah 32b and Rashi, s.v. "mipnei mah taqqnu" re B. Berakhot 31a interpreting I Sam. 1:13; B. Yoma 21a re M. Avot 5.5; Y. Yevamot 8.3/9c re Lev. 6:18.

[96] See M. Yoma 8.8–9.

[97] See B. Yoma 85b re Ezek. 33:19; *Shir ha-Shirim Rabbah* 6.1 re Ps. 45:9; B. Berakhot 34b re Isa. 57:19 (the statement of R. Abahu); and R. Jacob ibn Habib, *Iyyun Yaaqov* in *Ein Yaaqov* thereon. For the notion that God uses destructive human acts for his own punitive purposes, which still leaves them in the status of human sins, however, see *Sifre*: Devarim, no. 229, and B. Shabbat 32a re Deut. 22:8.

CHAPTER III

God and Covenanted Community

THE IMMEDIACY OF THE COMMUNITY

Heretofore, we have examined the relationship between God and human persons in terms of the claims each makes upon the other. Taking rights as primary claims within a normative order, we have seen that all rights are originally God's as creator. The belief that a creator has claims on his creatures is found in many if not all historical cultures.[1] And, moreover, the very fact that humans can recognize their continual dependence on God implies that they have been given the right to implore God's aid as an entitlement from God in creation itself. God's desires to hear from his creatures created in his own image implies that humans have the right to beseech God, that is, to express their needs in desire to him and for him, and also to thank him when their needs are fulfilled. "Before you O Lord is my whole desire (*kol ta'avati*) and my cry is not hidden from you" (Psalms 38:10).[2] The ubiquity of prayer in all historical cultures indicates that the divine-human relationship is not one of strict cause (God) and effect (humans); rather, it is one of primary claims (God on humans) and secondary claims (humans on God) in return.[3] In other words, this relationship is not just a matter of transitive action on God's part; it is even more a transaction between God and humans.

The question to be addressed in this chapter is how the communal nature of human beings, their constant need for interaction with each other, is connected to the personal relationship between God and human individuals we have just examined in the previous two chapters.[4] This book began with that interpersonal relationship because there could be no communal relationship with God unless the persons who make up the community have the capacity for such a relationship individually. The relationship can work in the world only when the persons who comprise the community have the freedom to affirm it or deny

---

[1] See Plato, *Crito*, 54E; *Phaedo*, 62B–C; *Laws*, 716Aff.

[2] Hence this verse can be understood as (1) God knows all of our desires (see Rashi, *Commentary on the Writings* thereon); (2) God is the ultimate object of all human desire (see R. Judah Halevi, "Before Thee Is My Whole Desire," in *Selected Religious Poems of Jehudah Halevi*, ed. H. Brody [Philadelphia: Jewish Publication Society of America, 1924], 87ff.); also, B. Taanit 4a re Hos. 14:6.

[3] See Plato, *Euthyphro*, 12E.

[4] For the recognition of this in rabbinic tradition, see B. Taanit 23a; Zevahim 117a re Lev. 13:46; Maimonides, *Guide of the Perplexed*, 2.40.

it. Only persons are free to act *with* other persons. Accordingly, the acts of any community are ultimately the responsibility of the persons who comprise that community.[5] The question here, however, is whether the locus of the covenant is individual then communal or communal then individual.

In modern times, when society has become so separated from older forms of direct human community, there is an understandable tendency to regard the one-to-one relationship of God and the individual person as primary and the relationship of God and the religious community as being separate from it. This primary relationship, often called "spirituality," is regarded as an inner access to God that each person must develop for himself or herself. The life of the religious community is at best regarded as a supplemental development out of this primary, personal core. At best, "organized religion" is regarded as a coming together of like-minded persons in order to share as much of their inner lives as is possible in a social, institutional setting. This sharing seems to be for the sake of reinforcing outwardly what is essentially always inward. At worst, however, the life of the religious community is regarded as an impediment to the spiritual relationship with God, inevitably turning what is originally the spontaneity of the human I in touch with the divine Thou into a regulated relation of the human I to a impersonal It. As such, the primary claims of God and humans on each other are confined to the individual level: I (*ich*) and Thou (*Du*). At the level of we and Thou though, they are always secondary, even if they function as a supplement rather than as an impediment.[6]

Despite the understandable desire of spiritually sensitive persons today to escape the deadening atmosphere of impersonal social institutions, one cannot understand the covenant as the true locus of all rights and duties if one takes the individual person as the ontological starting point. The core of the covenant is not the relationship between God and the individual human person; it is the relationship between God and the community he has elected for this covenantal relationship. That is certainly clear from the teaching of Scripture itself. Thus the covenant is what lies between God and *us*. But to cogently retrieve the covenant at this point in history, we must be able to intelligently explain how the covenant is not a diminution of the personal relationship with God but, on

[5] Hence no one can hide behind communal authority when he or she knows what is just, but acts unjustly instead. See B. Kiddushin 43a; Maimonides, *Mishneh Torah*: Rotseah, 2.2–3 re Gen. 9:5; M. Horayot 1.1; B. Horayot 2b re Lev. 4:27.

[6] In *I and Thou* (trans. W. Kaufmann [New York: Scribner's, 1970]), 156, Martin Buber, clearly arguing against Søren Kierkegaard, maintains that the God-human relationship is not with "one who is single, solitary and detached" (see also *Between Man and Man*, trans. R. G. Smith [Boston: Beacon, 1955], 40ff.). But for Buber that relationship does not seem to be one with a historically continuous community inasmuch as it excludes law (see *I and Thou*, 160). Cf. Franz Rosenzweig, "The Builders," in *On Jewish Learning*, ed. N. N. Glatzer, trans. W. Wolf (New York: Schocken, 1955), 72ff.; also, D. Novak, *Jewish-Christian Dialogue* (New York: Oxford University Press, 1989), 80ff.

the contrary, how it is the locus of a personal relationship that far exceeds anything that could possibly transpire between God and any lone individual. But that theological retrieval requires some preliminary philosophical work beforehand.

The difference between an individual relationship with God and a communal one, and the question of which has true priority, largely depends on how one constitutes the relation of language and thought. If one sees language as the outer expression of thought, which itself is essentially inner, then language becomes a concession to other humans with whom one has to live most of his or her time. But, with careful preparation, one can arrange for more and more of his or her time away from other humans and their mundane speech. That is a fundamentally contemplative move and it can be done only by an individual person.[7] Nevertheless, it is not a turn to isolation per se. Indeed, it is only sustainable if there is someone better to think about than oneself or any other human with whom one can engage in mundane discourse. Human thought, like speech, cannot be essentially self-referential without descending into madness. So, this inner contemplation inevitably intends God.[8] After all, is anything less than the Absolute worthy of such a consequential personal retreat inward?[9] Much of modern spirituality, even when it lacks the metaphysical intensity of the classical contemplative commitment, is based on this assumption of the primacy of thought over language. And at the level of greatest metaphysical achievement, human thought that has risen above language intends divine thought that has never had to descend to language.[10]

The whole picture radically changes, however, when thought is regarded as a secondary *internalization* of language. That is, the primary locus of our human life, including our relationship with God, is within language.[11] Thought is our periodic retreat inward, not in order to rise above language and its essential communality, but in order to periodically prepare ourselves to better understand what we have heard from others, and thus to be able to speak more intelligently in response. Thought is imaginary discourse, where the two interlocutors are projected within one's minds. As such, it is always transitional.[12] Thought is the imaginative rehearsal of words heard and spoken and can thus

---

[7] See Plato, *Republic*, 518C–D.

[8] Even Descartes, who constituted knowledge as beginning in the consciousness of one's own thinking (*cogito ergo sum*), soon moves on to God as the highest object of one's thought. See *Meditations*, no. 3. This had to be done to avoid the solipsism the cogito itself would lead to if ever taken as noetically sufficient.

[9] See Aristotle, *Nicomachean Ethics*, 1177b25ff.

[10] See Aristotle, *Metaphysics*, 1074b15ff.

[11] See Novak, *Jewish-Christian Dialogue*, 148ff.; D. Novak, *The Election of Israel* (Cambridge: Cambridge University Press, 1995), 202f., n. 10.

[12] See Jürgen Habermas, *The Theory of Communicative Action*, trans. T. McCarthy (Boston: Beacon, 1984), 1:116.

be seen as one's meditation on the intent of what has been heard and is yet to be spoken. In this sense, meditation is a means, not an end; it is for the world, not an escape from it. Human thought, unlike God's thought, is thus only deliberative, not creative.[13] "For my thoughts are not your thoughts and your ways are not my ways, says the Lord. . . . [S]o shall my word that goes forth from my mouth not return empty to me, but it shall do what I desire, and what I have sent shall succeed" (Isaiah 55:8, 11). The power of human thought— unlike God's thought—is catalytic, not substantive. "For He spoke and it came to be; He commanded and it endured. The Lord annulled the project of the nations (*atsat goyyim*); He made the plans (*mahshavot*) of the peoples ineffective" (Psalms 33:9–10). Thought enables human speech to be more than talking and human action to be more than behavior, even if it is not effective per se. It enables us to hear and speak intentionally. The very freedom of intentionality, inherent in all genuine speech and action, requires periodic thought.[14] The freedom of individual persons is for the sake of the speech and the action that they alone can truly *mean*. This freedom is *for* or *against* an other: either human or divine. But we do not have the freedom to put any other person who has spoken to us permanently behind us. Language is the very limit of our world.[15]

The full force of the rabbinic teaching that "the Torah speaks according to human language" (*dibbrah torah ke-lashon bnei adam*) is that God addresses us as the essentially communal beings we are by nature.[16] That is, there is no higher relationship with God possible than the relation of the word. Any word in order to be intelligible, let alone normative, must be addressed to a discursive being. And a discursive being is not one who only remembers language but, rather, one who is presently engaged in language and anticipates it. One never speaks to one person alone, for the very employment of language makes

---

[13] As such, one could say that all thought (even what God has revealed to us of his thoughts) is what Aristotle termed "practical reason" (*phrōnesis*) because it is done *sub specie durationis* for the sake of an act (see *Nicomachean Ethics*, 1139b25ff.). For deliberation (*boulēsis*) as transitional thought, see 1112a15ff. Even our contemplation of the acts of God is ultimately practical reason inasmuch as it is contemplation of transitive divine action for the sake of either our imitation of it or our praise of it. For the goal of imitation, see B. Shabbat 133b re Exod. 15:2; Solomon Schechter, *Some Aspects of Rabbinic Theology* (New York: Behrman, 1936), 199ff. For the goal of praise (*shevah*), see Maimonides, *Sefer ha-Mitsvot*: positive precepts, no. 3.

[14] See B. Berakhot 5.1 and Maimonides, *Commentary on the Mishnah*, thereon; Y. Yoma 3.2/ 40b re II Sam. 7:18.

[15] See Ludwig Wittgenstein, *Tractatus Logico-Philosophicus*, trans. D. F. Pears and B. F. McGuiness (London: Routledge and Kegan Paul, 1961), 5.6–5.61. In his later writing, Wittgenstein emphasized how ordinary language is the limit of a wider world than is the more logically constrained language of formal reason (see *Philosophical Investigations*, 2nd ed., trans. G. E. M. Anscombe [New York: Macmillan, 1958]), 1.18, 105–9). I mean language here in the later Wittgensteinian sense.

[16] See D. Novak, *Natural Law in Judaism* (Cambridge: Cambridge University Press, 1998), 146, n. 69.

any conversation, no matter how privately conducted, a public matter.[17] The locus of living language is no place other than a community itself engaged in the discourse necessary for human life here and now, and then into the future. Anyone not participating in such a living, discursive community is not living a fully human life.[18] And God's word can be addressed to humans only in their personal fullness in the world. "The end of the matter, everything to be heard: fear God and keep his commandments for this is the whole human person (*kol ha'adam*)" (Ecclesiastes 12:13). Even our silence before God is a silence for the sake of speech, either God's or our own. It is either our preparation to better hear what he has to say to us or our preparation to truly intend what we have to say to him. "Be silent (*has*) all flesh before the Lord, for he has been roused from his holy abode" (Zechariah 2:17).[19]

That is why law is so central to the covenant. Law as the most immediately normative function of language is thus an essentially communal matter. Law, then, is integral to the covenant as a communal entity. It is the practical universal.[20] Indeed, it is the priority of this practical universal that enables us to group things into categories theoretically, for when we speak of these things, we have already grouped ourselves into a community capable of including them by our words (*devarim*). We have already constituted ourselves together as a universe discursively. Categories of nonhuman things are in essence constituted by analogy to our own human universe of discourse. They follow the way we constitute our own community by the analogies between the persons who inhabit it, that is, our interrelationships with each other. That is why we speak of natural patterns as "laws of nature."[21] Law is the formal component of that grouping

[17] See Wittgenstein, *Philosophical Investigations*, 1.243–48.

[18] See Aristotle, *Politics*, 1253a25–30, where it is asserted that only beasts or gods can live outside discursive community. But Aristotle does admit of the fact, at least in principle, that one can transcend ordinary human community by becoming godlike through contemplation of God (see *Nicomachean Ethics*, 1177b25–30). From our point of view, however, that is impossible. Such a god is an ideal, not a *telos*, i.e., he is made, not discovered, by humans.

[19] Cf. Isa. 6:5–9.

[20] See Aristotle, *Nicomachean Ethics*, 1135a5. But, unlike Aristotle, the practical universal is, in my view, prior to the theoretical universal ontologically (cf. 1141a21).

[21] See Novak, *Natural Law in Judaism*, 124, n. 3. In his critique of the ontology and epistemology that come out of the Judeo-Christian tradition, Martin Heidegger insightfully noted about the whole theory of correspondence: "*Veritas* as *adaequatio rei ad intellectum* . . . implies the Christian theological belief that, with respect to what it is and whether it is, a matter, as created (*ens creatum*), is only insofar as it corresponds to the idea preconceived in the *intellectus divinus*, i.e., in the mind of God, and thus measures up to the idea (is correct) and in this sense is 'true.' The *intellectus humanus* too is an *ens creatum*. As a capacity bestowed upon man by God, it must satisfy its *idea*. . . . *Veritas* as *adaequatio rei* (*creandae*) *ad intellectum* (*divinum*) guarantees *veritas* as *adaequatio intellectus* (*humani*) *ad rem* (*creatum*). Throughout, *veritas* essentially implies *convenientia*, the coming of beings themselves as created, an 'accord' with regard to the way they are determined in the order of creation" ("On the Essence of Truth," trans. J. Sallis, in *Martin Heidegger: Basic Writings*, ed. D. F. Krell [New York: Harper and Row, 1977]), 120f. Heidegger's

together. It is the first manifestation of reason with its logic of the one and the many. Our ability to speak *to* each other and interact *with* each other formally is what admits things into our discourse by assigning words to them so that we can speak *about* them, by surrounding them, as it were, even if we can never fully penetrate them.

If law can be seen as the most evident expression of rights and duties, then rights and duties involve all the members of the covenant, even God, who is its chief member, its self-appointed king and lawgiver. Law, then, is not subsequent to covenantal theology; it is the inherent concern of that theology. That is why covenantal theology is a form of *political* theory, taking "polity" in its fullest possible sense. As such, the deepest religious concerns are public before they are private.

Even the prophets, when addressed by God individually, are recipients of messages that are to and for the people. Thus, Elijah, who could very well be considered the most private of all the prophets, desires death when he is convinced that his tie to the people of Israel has been broken. "And he went into the wilderness, a day's journey, and he sat under a broom tree, and he asked that he might die. He said, 'Lord, it is too much now, take my life for I am no better than my fathers' " (I Kings 19:4). God finally restores his desire to live with "a still small voice" (*qol demamah daqqah*—I Kings 19:12) rather than with the impersonal noises of God's power in wind, storm, and fire. Only the voice addresses him in the same way he is to address the people, and so that the word can be communicated among them. Immediately thereafter, renewed from his solitary sojourn in the wilderness, Elijah is sent back to the world, where his main task is to prepare his successor Elisha as the prophet the people of Israel will need in the near future.[22]

The community only mediates this personal relationship with God, thereby diluting it to the point of extinction, when the community has lost its primary role as the place for interpersonal speech. That happens when the institutions of society become more than just the outer political periphery of the discursive community needed to protect it from dissolution. It happens when the institutions of society no longer facilitate true communal discourse but attempt to replace it with what could be described as words without transcendent intent. These words are designed to perpetuate the human authority who uttered them for their effect.[23] But these words are not designed to persuade their hearers

---

view of this Christian belief (which is an even earlier Jewish belief) is based on a Platonized formulation of that basically theological notion of truth, especially as constituted by Augustine (see *De Civitate Dei*, 11.29). The non-Platonized Jewish view of truth might formulate its definition of truth as *veritas est adaequatio intellectus humani ad verbum Dei efficacem* (see *Beresheet Rabbah* 1.1 re Prov. 8:22, 30). Thus, all knowledge is grounded in the exercise of God's practical intelligence. See D. Novak, *Jewish Social Ethics* (New York, 1992), 76ff.

[22] I Kings 19:15ff.

[23] For a rabbinic treatment of this type of abuse of authority, see B. Berakhot 27b and its allusions to M. Rosh Hashanah 2.9 and Bekhorot 36a.

by any true recognition of the claims of these hearers as persons themselves. They are designed for manipulation. Today that is what we call propaganda. These words are only transitive, not transactional: a monologue, not a dialogue. "And the Lord said that because this people has approached with its mouth and its lips honoring me, but its heart is far from me, and their fear of me is a commandment of men learned by rote (*mitsvat anashim melummadah*), therefore will I increase doing wonders with this people, wonders upon wonders (*haflē ve-fele*), so that the wisdom of its wise will be lost and the understanding of its savants be concealed" (Isaiah 29:13–14).

Indeed, because Jewish society is often far less than the covenanted community God's election has meant it to be, the Rabbis call the true covenanted community *keneset yisrael*, "the congregation of Israel."[24] This notion can be seen to stem from the prophetic notion of the "remnant of Israel" (*sh'erit yisrael*—Ezekiel 11:13), except that for the Rabbis it refers to the spiritually intact core of the larger people rather than to the minority of Jews who have escaped physical extermination. Now, particular Jewish communities do have a right to regard themselves as this "remnant," this little "congregation." However, they are in great danger of becoming the hollow society they have rejected whenever they see themselves not as the core *within* the people Israel but as the replacement *of* this people instead.[25] Individual Jews may choose to come together for particular covenantal purposes, but they may never forget that God has elected the whole people Israel for the covenant. To forget that is to commit the basic modern distortion of the covenant, which has asserted in one way or another that it is not God who elects Israel but Israel who elects God.[26] But since the last full unanimity of the people Israel was at Mount Sinai, any Jewish response to God's election of Israel can only be the decision of a group of individuals who are often a small minority of the people as a whole.[27]

Because of the primary necessity of community and the simultaneous (now more than ever) political fragmentation of the Jewish people, an individual Jew must seek and join *a* Jewish community which for him or her best instantiates *the* true covenantal community. But to regard any such grouping as communally sufficient is pseudomessianism of the most dangerous kind. It assumes that the people—in one particular grouping, that is—has already been

[24] See B. Berakhot 53b re Ps. 68:14 and parallels; B. Pesahim 87a and B. Baba Batra 8a re Cant. 8:10 (the statement of Rava); B. Pesahim 118b re Ps. 113:9 and 116:1; *Shir ha-Shirim Rabbah* 2.1 re Cant. 2:1.

[25] Thus even the members of the Pharisaic communities (*havurot*), who took upon themselves additional structures pertaining to purity (see T. Demai 2.2–3), are still required to interact with lesser observant Jews for the sake of overall community (see M. Gittin 5.9; B. Gittin 61a; also, B. Yevamot 14a re Deut. 14:1).

[26] See Novak, *The Election of Israel*, 22ff.

[27] See *Mekhilta*: Yitro, ed. Horovitz-Rabin, 206 re Exod. 19:2.

redeemed.[28] When this happens, the rights and duties of the covenant are distorted, especially the primary rights of God, his claims on the whole covenanted community.

ELECTION AND COVENANT

In the scriptural narrative, the original hope for a united humankind under the rule of God, for one human city on earth, is dashed by the arrogant attempt of the builders of the Tower of Babel to unite humankind against God.[29] According to one ancient tradition, this grandiose attempt to solve the problem of political insecurity in the world also resulted in the neglect of individual human claims for justice to be done.[30] This teaches quite well how denial of God's kingship always leads to injustices against those created in God's image, and how these injustices lead to denial of God's kingship. Creation in the image of God means that every human being is capable of a direct relationship with God, and that relationship is the basis of the dignity of each and every human person, a dignity that (as we shall see in chapter 7) any human society is obligated to respect and enhance.

The result of all this is that humankind is now considered to be permanently fragmented and incapable of ever reuniting by its own power. "The Lord has scattered them over all the earth" (Genesis 11:9). And this is to be the permanent human situation until the coming of the Messiah, "when kingdom is the Lord's" (Obadiah 1:21); "when the Lord will become king over all the earth" (Zechariah 14:9); when the Messiah will be God's agent, who because "the knowledge of the Lord will fill the earth as the water covers the sea" will be "a banner of the peoples, whom the nations will seek" (Isaiah 11:9–10). At that time, and not before, God "will turn to the peoples with a clear message (*safah berurah*), summoning all of them in the name of the Lord to serve him with one accord" (Zephaniah 3:9).[31]

Because of the inherent fragmentation of humankind in this world, the scriptural narrative quickly turns to God's relationship with one distinct community. In God's choice of Abraham and his descendants, his direct covenant with at least some humans, however few they are within humankind as a whole, is now Scripture's primary concern. The more indirect covenant with the earth and its natural order, which came with Noah and humankind that survived the Flood, now becomes the background for the prime divine-human reality in the

---

[28] See Novak, *The Election of Israel*, 254.

[29] See *Beresheet Rabbah* 38.8 re Gen. 11:4.

[30] See Louis Ginzberg, *The Legends of the Jews* (Philadelphia: Jewish Publication Society of America, 1909), 1:179.

[31] See Maimonides, *Mishneh Torah*: Melakhim, chap. 11 (uncensored version), ed. M. D. Rabinowitz (Jerusalem: Mosad ha-Rav Kook, 1962), 416.

world. The Noahide covenant and its law are the minimal conditions for the emergence and development of this more specific covenant. They are not, however, rich enough in detail or direct enough in intensity to suffice for the fuller life with God on earth required by the concrete historicity of the human condition. The Noahide covenant is the precondition of the new covenant with Abraham and his people.[32]

Like creation itself, one cannot know why God elected this people in any a priori sense. God's primary claim on this people, like his primary claim on the world itself, is justified because God is God. "Our God is beyond (*ba-sha-mayim*); anything he desires he does" (Psalms 115:2).[33] In each case, one can accept the divine claim and live well or reject it and live badly. But just as no creature can either create or destroy the world, so the covenanted people, collectively and individually, can neither create nor destroy the covenant. Like the very substance of creation itself, the substance of the covenant—this people Israel—is always in the foreground. To be sure, unlike creation, the covenant does have historical antecedents, but like creation, its existence comes from nowhere (*ex nihilo*). In the covenant as in creation, all God's claims are understandable only a posteriori, that is, we can sometimes discern their form—what they are meant to accomplish—but we cannot determine why their very subject matter had to be at all. We can sometimes determine their essence, but we can never determine their existence: why there is something rather than nothing.[34] The covenant, like creation, is the result of God's unfathomable command. And just as humans are created to be communal beings, so are the Jews elected as a people. In both cases, the locus of the person is within the authentic community.

The historicity of the human condition requires singular events and their celebration, which can only be the subject of the living memory of a singular community among others in the world. The Noahide covenant involves the generality of nature; it does not supply historical content. It presents negative limits but not the positive claims that can only be presented in a community by persons with a historical identity. Nevertheless, no matter how singular this covenant appears here and now, it is ultimately meant for all humankind, when all the separate histories have run their course. It is not parochial in essence. Thus God informs Abraham at the very moment of his initial call that "all the families of the earth shall be blessed through you" (Genesis 12:3). The covenant is of universal significance, even if that significance is for a radically transformed future world. At present, though, the covenant is still a matter of local experience and practice. Being situated between nature in the background and the End of Days in the foreground, the covenant must be respectful of the

---

[32] See Novak, *Natural Law in Judaism*, 156ff.

[33] See *Tanhuma*: V'era, ed. Buber, 17b re Exod. 19:20.

[34] See Novak, *The Election of Israel*, 125f.

rights discerned from nature as its past. But it must not regard them as in any way sufficient for it own immediate life in the present, let alone the life of the completed human community in the future that its present life intends. As such, the covenant presents both general and specific rights, which are the natural claims of God on all people and God's historical claims on Israel, his covenanted people.[35]

At the beginning of the covenant, which is with Abraham the progenitor of the covenanted people, both general and specific claims are made on the people by God. The most strikingly specific claim made on the people is circumcision. "This is my covenant (*briti*) that you shall keep between Me and you, and between your progeny after you: circumcise all of your males ... and the uncircumcised male (*v'arel zakhar*) who will not circumcise the flesh of his foreskin, that person shall be cut off from its people; he has broken (*hefar*) My covenant" (Genesis 17:10, 14). Circumcision is to be something that separates the people of Israel from her neighbors. So, even if the neighbors themselves practice circumcision, if any one of them is converted to Judaism, the covenantal blood (*dam berit*) must be drawn from the place on the male organ where the foreskin had been, which is also to be done for any Jewish male who happens to be born without a foreskin.[36] It is the experience of the covenantal event that is unique, not its actual physical distinctiveness.[37] Circumcision is the first of a number of commandments that entail a separation between the covenanted community and the world.[38]

Nevertheless, that separation from the world does not entail a separation from the justice that God requires of the human world, a requirement that is voiced through natural rights, which are the just claims of human persons and communities. The general claims on that world, which the rabbinic tradition sees going back to Noah, even to Adam and Eve, are not overcome by the covenant (*aufgehoben*); instead, they are subsumed into the covenant intact.[39]

GENERAL COVENANTAL CLAIMS ON THE COMMUNITY: JUSTICE

It is important to remember that in the scriptural narrative telling how the covenant was established with Abraham as the chieftan of his clan, a key point is when Abraham is visited by the three angels disguised as men. "And the Lord appeared to Abraham at the oaks of Mamre while he was sitting at the door of his tent in the heat of the day. Then he lifted up his eyes and he saw

---

[35] See B. Yoma 67b re Lev. 18:4.

[36] See B. Shabbat 135a; Maimonides, *Mishneh Torah*: Isurei Biah, 14.5.

[37] For the rabbinic recognition that the physical practice of circumcision is not uniquely Jewish, see M. Nedarim 3.11; also, Josephus, *Contra Apionem*, 1.168–71.

[38] See *Pesiqta Rabbati*, chap. 15, ed. Friedmann, 69b–70a.

[39] B. Sanhedrin 59a and Tos., s.v. "leeka"; B. Yevamot 22a. Following the contrast made with a Hegelian *Aufhebung*, one could say this is an *Erhebung*.

three men (*anashim*) standing directly over him" (Genesis 18:1–2). In rabbinic tradition, each of these three angels can have only one task, one mission. So, it is imagined that the first angel came to tell Sarah of the birth of Isaac, the second angel came to destroy the evil cities of Sodom and Gomorrah, and the third angel came to heal Abraham from the wound of his recent circumcision.[40] In looking at each of these respective functions, one sees that one of them is specifically covenantal: the birth of Isaac as the continuation of the line of Abraham. It pertains primarily to the direct relationships between God and the elected community. The other two, though, primarily pertain to the relationships between humans themselves. The first such function—the destruction of Sodom and Gomorrah—is about justice (*din*). The second such function— attending the needs of the sick—is about compassion (*rahamim*). Furthermore, in rabbinic tradition, each of these functions is a matter of *imitatio Dei*, that is, each is an exemplary norm, even before it is turned into an actual prescription.[41] The three respective functions correspond to the famous prophetic dictum: "It has been told to you humans what is good, and what the Lord requires of you: but to act justly (*mishpat*), love kindness (*hesed*), and walk humbly with your God" (Micah 6:8). That is, justice and kindness have human objects, and humility has a divine object. Since justice is more general than compassion, it might be best to begin with justice as the most evident covenantal claim God makes on the community.

In the scriptural narrative, Abraham is presented with God's plan to destroy the evil cities of Sodom and Gomorrah himself. It is presented as a proposal about which Abraham is invited to be a consultant. This invitation is more for Abraham's sake than it is for God's. Thus God says,

> How can I hide from Abraham what I am going to do? Abraham is to be a great and important nation, through whom all the nations of the earth are to be blessed. For I know him intimately (*yeda 'tiv*) and this is to lead (*le-ma 'an*) to his commanding his children and his household after him, that they might keep the way of the Lord to practice righteous judgment (*tsedaqah u-mishpat*). This is to lead (*le-ma 'an*) to the Lord's bringingabout all that he has spoken concerning him. (Genesis 19:17–19)[42]

First, there is the question of why God thinks he has to inform Abraham of what he plans to do with these two cities. The answer seems to be that unless Abraham and the community around him and from him (at that time, beginning

---

[40] B. Baba Metsia 86b.

[41] Regarding effecting justice as *imitatio Dei*, see B. Shabbat 10a; *Midrash ha-Gadol*: Beresheet, ed. Margulies, 307 re Gen. 18:19. Regarding attending the sick (*biqur holim*) as *imitatio Dei*, see B. Sotah 14a re Gen. 18:1. Regarding the precept to effect justice, see Deut. 16:20 and *Sifre*: Devarim, no. 144. Regarding the precept to attend the sick as *imitatio Dei*, see B. Baba Kama 100a re Exod. 18:20; Maimonides, *Mishneh Torah*: Evel, 14.1 re Lev. 19:18.

[42] For *le-ma 'an* as indicating an effect rather than an end, see Nahmanides, *Commentary on the Torah*: Deut. 29:18.

with his own domestic circle) have actually been assured of God's most elementary justice, they could not possibly model their own practice of justice on
it. For justice to be more than a human pursuit, it must be connected to "the
way of the Lord." Whereas in creation alone the justice God demands is inferred from the voices of just human claims, in the covenant justice is to be
directly taught by God archetypically. In the covenant, justice is not only what
God has decreed *for* the world, it is what God does *in* the world as well.[43] And
for the way of the Lord to be a model for human practice by imitation, it must
be minimally consistent in its application. That is, the innocent and the guilty
must not be confused, and any punishment must be appropriate to the crime.

Second, this demonstration of ultimate divine justice functions as an antidote
to the despair that so often comes when the quest for justice, which is the
response to legitimate human rights, is based on human idealism. The futility
of the finite and mortal human situation taken in and of itself belies any idealism in the end.[44] Indeed, total human efforts to bring about justice in the world
have inevitably led to far more injustice than they purported to cure. One need
only think of the colossal fiasco of the utopian promises of Marxism in this
century. The pursuit of justice for the sake of human rights can be maintained
in good faith only when those who seek it see themselves in a cosmic reality
whose final outcome transcends their own fragile efforts. The final victory of
true justice belongs to God alone. For this reason, human prayer for God to
do justice in this world is a vital affirmation that there is any justice at all. "I
said that you were divine (*elohim*), that all of you were sons of the Most High;
but you are surely like mortal men (*k'adam temutun*), and like any of the
princes who will fall. Arise O' God and judge the earth for all the nations are
your possession (*tinhal*)" (Psalms 82:6–8). This prayer is as important as
human efforts to effect justice in our own little domain of activity in the world.
For Jews, that little domain is the covenanted community. It is the primary
locus where the general command "justice justice you shall pursue" (Deuteronomy 16:20) is to be fulfilled. Justice is always social justice. But such a
prayerful claim on God to do justice in the world, which is such a central
feature of the communal liturgy (*avodah*), is not meant to be a substitute for
human efforts that will themselves be judged in the end.[45] Instead, God's justice
is the paradigm for increased human efforts to practice justice in his world.
Human imitation is entailed by any praise of God for what he does for us in
the world.[46]

Third, the scriptural text describing the sublime dialogue on justice between
Abraham and God indicates that the greatness and importance of the Abrahamic

---

[43] See B. Sanhedrin 7a re Ps. 82:1.

[44] See Novak, *Jewish Social Ethics*, 163ff.

[45] See Isa. 1:10–17; M. Yoma 8.9 re Lev. 16:30.

[46] See B. Shabbat 133b re Exod. 15:2; also, Maimonides, *Guide of the Perplexed*, 3.54 re Jer.
9:23.

nation is not to be a matter of material or military might. Its greatness in the eyes of the world is to be moral. "Not by power (*hayil*) and not by strength (*koah*), but by my spirit says the Lord" (Zechariah 4:6). Minimally, that would mean that God's relationship with this community results in a system of law in which concern for human rights would impress anyone truly concerned with social justice. Thus Moses tells the people of Israel poised to enter the Promised Land of the universal significance of the law God has given them.

> For it is your wisdom and understanding in the eyes of the nations who will hear all these statutes and will say, "surely this nation is a wise and discerning people." For what great nation has God so close to them as we do when we call upon the Lord our God? And what great nation has such righteous statutes and ordinances (*huqqim u-mishpatim tsaddiqim*) as this whole Torah. (Deuteronomy 4:6–8)

Indeed, an important part of the messianic vision is that the nations of the world will eventually come to Jerusalem for their claims to be justly adjudicated. They will say, "[L]et us go up to the mountain of the Lord, to the house of the God of Jacob, and he will direct us from his ways and we shall walk in his paths. . . . [H]e will judge between nations and instruct many peoples" (Isaiah 2:3–4). Indeed, this divine justice might be the reason for the attraction to the worship of God, which even in King Solomon's day attracted "the stranger (*ha-nokhri*) who is not of the people of Israel, coming from a far off land, for the sake of Your name" (I Kings 8:41), and which in the end of days will make the Temple in Jerusalem "a house of prayer for all peoples" (Isaiah 56:7).[47]

Because God's claim on his covenanted community is that they exercise their duty to deal justly with everyone, communally as well as individually, the greatest indictment of this community and its institutions by the prophets was their condemnation of the perversion of the rights of the most helpless members of the community by those with the societal power to do otherwise. Political destruction is promised unless "you seek justice (*mishpat*); rectify oppression; champion (*shiftu*) the orphan and plead the cause of the widow" (Isaiah 1:17). And frequently, the non-Jewish members of the overall polity are the most vulnerable to injustice. Thus the prophet says in the name of the Lord that "I will pour my wrath upon them" (Ezekiel 22:31), namely, "the people of the land who defraud (*ashqu*) and rob, cheating (*honu*) the poor and the destitute, and defrauding the sojourner (*ha-ger*) unjustly (*be-lo mishpat—* 22:29)."[48] Because the covenant is with an all-seeing God, no perversion of rights can hide behind the anonymity of faceless institutions. God's concern for the welfare of everyone whose life is touched by the covenanted community gives every such person the right to demand proportional concern from that community. They are to imitate God in his role as "father of orphans and

---

[47] See T. Sotah 8.6 re Deut. 27:8; Y. Sotah 7.5/21d; B. Sotah 32a.
[48] See B. Yevamot 79a re I Kings 5:29.

judge for widows, God in his holy abode, who settles the lonely (*yehidim*) in a home and who brings forth those bound in chains" (Psalms 68:6–7).

That concern for justice in its widest extent is to include just dealings with those who are outside the covenanted community altogether, who are not even sojourners (*gerim*) therein. Injustice toward any gentile, for the Rabbis, entails the sin of "profanation of God's name" (*hillul ha-shem*).[49] Any such injustice prevents the gentiles from appreciating the inherent justice of the Torah and praising God for it, as well as stifling any desire on their part to appropriate the teachings of the Torah into their own systems of law.[50] Any such injustice would not inspire them to come to Jerusalem, literally or figuratively, for a just solution to their moral and legal dilemmas.

God's rights and God's championing the rights of those he has entitled to these rights creates numerous duties for the community in its social, institutional role. But the issue of just adjudication of claims is something that transcends the actual political institutions of the covenanted community. Thus, in rabbinic jurisprudence, when the Jewish authorities are unable to properly adjudicate the rights of persons in their own domain, even Jews, individually or collectively, are allowed to go to gentile authorities with their claims for justice.[51] Of course, they are not to go to any gentile authority, but only to those operating within a political-legal system where the due process of law is practiced.[52] This judicial impotence of the covenanted community itself is to be regarded as a tragedy when it is beyond communal control due to external political limitations.[53] But it is to be regarded as a moral indictment of the covenanted community when this judicial impotence is due to the moral cowardice of the Jewish authorities.[54]

SPECIFIC COVENANTAL CLAIMS
ON THE COMMUNITY: COMPASSION

As we shall see in chapter 5, compassion is immediately the claim of the weaker on the stronger members of the community for help and, indeed, on the community itself, as we shall see in chapter 7. Nevertheless, compassion

---

[49] See B. Baba Kama 113b re Deut. 22:3; Hullin 94a; *Teshuvot Rav Sar Shalom Gaon*, ed. Weinberg (Jerusalem: Mosad ha-Rav Kook, 1975), no. 137.

[50] See B. Baba Kama 38a; also, Novak, *Natural Law in Judaism*, 77ff.

[51] See B. Baba Batra 54b and parallels. Cf. *Mekhilta*: Mishpatim, 246; B. Gittin 88b re Exod. 21:1.

[52] See Maimonides, *Mishneh Torah*: Gezelah, 5.13, 17–18, and R. Vidal of Tolosa, *Magid Mishneh* thereon.

[53] See M. Gittin 9.8.

[54] See D. Novak, *Halakhah in a Theological Dimension* (Chico, Calif.: Scholars Press, 1985), 29ff.; "Parental Rights in the Marriage of a Minor," in *Jewish Law Association Studies*, ed. E. A. Goldman (Atlanta, Ga.: Scholars Press, 1997), 9:131ff.

is also a claim God makes on the community. It is a claim on the community to imitate God's more specific kindness to the people of Israel. And this kindness must be seen as something above and beyond the justice that God requires of every human being, even over and above God's own justice that Israel is to imitate as much as she can understand and do. A good example of such a compassionate claim on the community is the prohibition of usury (*ribbit*).

The scriptural proscription reads as follows:

> When your brother becomes impoverished, his means among you having descended, you shall support (*ve-hehezaqta*) him; he shall live with you as a sojourner and tenant (*ger ve-toshav*). Do not take interest (*neshekh*) or profit (*tarbit*) from him. Your money you shall not lend to him on interest, and for profit you shall not give him your food. I am the Lord your God who has brought you out of the land of Egypt to give you the land of Canaan in order to be your God. (Leviticus 25:35–38)

This is clearly meant as to be an intercovenantal norm. Thus a related scriptural text states: "You may take interest from the stranger (*la-nokhri*), but not from your brother" (Deuteronomy 23:21).[55]

This is not only the type of personal interaction that the Torah mandates within the covenant and that the covenanted community largely enables. It is, primarily, a matter of economic policy that God requires from the community itself precisely because she is covenanted to him. Accordingly, the prohibition also extends to those representatives of the community such as witnesses and guarantors, whose very presence makes a financial transaction involving interest a public matter.[56] What we have here, then, is a granting of special privilege to members of the covenant in cases of economic hardship. As one commentator pointed out: "The basis of this commandment is that the good God wanted true community for his people (*yishuv ammo*) whom he has chosen, hence he commanded [them] to remove an impediment (*mikhshol*) from their path so that one not swallow up the goods (*hail*) of his fellow without feeling anything himself."[57]

This type of covenantal privilege, however, does not contradict the more general justice that is actually precovenantal in that it is required of all humans even before the election of Israel, beginning with Abraham. As we saw above, Abraham had to have a developed sense of justice toward all humans in order to be able to enter into the covenant with God in the first place. The covenanted

---

[55] See B. Baba Metsia 70b. Cf. R. Joseph Albo, *Iqqarim*, 3.25, and R. Isaac Abrabanel, *Commentary on the Torah*: Deut. 23:20, who exclude gentile monotheists (implying Christians and Muslims) from the class of those with whom one may engage in interest giving and taking. This is not, however, the actual halakhic practice (see R. Joseph Karo, *Shulhan Arukh*: Yoreh Deah, 159.1, and note of R. Moses Isserles [Rema] thereon).

[56] M. Baba Metsia 5.11; B. Baba Metsia 75b.

[57] *Sefer ha-Hinukh*, no. 68. But note ibid., no. 34, where he explains the prohibition of murder on the basis of human community per se (cf. Maimonides, *Mishneh Torah*: Rotseah, 4.9).

community itself provides a context for the further development of this sense of justice, but that development is a matter of greater specification of the general principles of justice already in place. Nothing really new is added onto these universal principles, which are themselves taken to be rational.

The prohibition of usury, however, is not based on any such rational principle because the taking of interest is not unjust per se. Hence there is nothing universal about it.[58] If there is nothing wrong in making a profit on the sale of one's own possessions, what is wrong with one profiting from renting his or her possessions, as it were, including one's money?[59] Moreover, what is most important to bear in mind at this point is that Jews are required to pay to their non-Jewish lenders what has been stipulated in the loan contract with them just as they take interest from non-Jewish borrowers by the same type of financial transaction.[60] Hence the specific release from paying and taking interest within the covenant is not any special privilege Jews are asking from the world. It is a special privilege granted only when all the parties are within the covenant itself.

Even in those societies where the payment of interest is permitted, a difference is usually made between "usury," which is usually seen as a ruthless way of taking advantage of those in need, and "interest," which is usually seen as rightful recompense for the risk involved in lending to someone in financial straits and the loss of the use of one's possessions while they are being used by someone else. It seems to be akin to the right of a society to regulate prices, rents, and wages for the sake of its common good.[61] There are good reasons why a society must maintain some control over economic transactions (a point discussed in chapter 6), permitting some, regulating others, and prohibiting still others. But what these controls are and what their extent is to be is largely a local matter. It is, as the Mishnah states about wage standards, something governed by "societal policy" (*minhag ha-medinah*).[62] In the covenanted polity, any taking of interest is considered to be contrary to the common covenantal good.

The meaning of the inter-Jewish prohibition of financial transactions involving interest seems to be that the members of the covenant are all to regard

---

[58] See B. Baba Metsia 70b–71a and Tos., s.v. "tasheekh."

[59] This was the position of John Calvin, who challenged older Christian prohibitions of usury (whatever the percentage of the principle taken) that saw it as *malum in se*. See B. Nelson, *The Idea of Usury*, 2nd ed. (Chicago: University of Chicago Press, 1969), 73ff.

[60] The arguments against a Jew getting involved in matters of interest with gentiles were not based on any animus against the practice itself but, rather, on the fear that such commercial involvement would lead to assimilation. See B. Baba Metsia 71a.

[61] See, e.g., B. Baba Batra 89a (cf. Rabbenu Gershom and Rashbam, s.v. "le-sha'arim" thereon); Maimonides, *Mishneh Torah*: Geneivah, 8.20.

[62] See M. Baba Metsia 7.1; Maimonides, *Mishneh Torah*: Mekhirah, 26.7–8, 27.11.

themselves as partners in a joint, unending enterprise.[63] That enterprise as a truly communal matter began when God took the people of Israel out of Egypt. The exodus is thus an enterprise in which God is the senior partner and the people are all junior partners together equally. The equality among the human members of the covenant is directly because of the superiority of the divine member, the founder and sustainer of the covenant to whom they are all equally related.[64] Short of societal ownership of all property, which itself would generate greater bureaucratic inequality and personal arrogance and resentment than would the uncertainties of an open market economy, economic policy must emphasize partnership as much as possible nonetheless.[65] In fact, when the economic survival of the community required by competition in a larger economy itself requires that Jewish loans be the same as non-Jewish loans de facto, a legal fiction called *heter isqa* has been devised to make these loans assume the form of being the sharing of partnered gains and losses, at least de jure.[66]

This is to be contrasted with a situation of either buying or renting, where the relationship between the parties ends when the debt has been paid. The parties share nothing more in common because their relationship is contractual, not covenantal.[67] But where the prohibition of giving and taking interest is operative, the situation is like arbitration, where nobody wins and nobody loses, but each person takes less than would be rightly required of him or her. And that is the case because persons are involved in an unending covenantal relationship. In the case of the lender, he or she takes less from the fellow covenantal partner/borrower than could be gotten on the open market. In the case of the borrower, more is given back to the covenantal partner/lender than would be the case if he or she were destitute and the object of straight charity. All of this means that the covenant requires more compassion from its members than the exercise of their own, individual rights. And that is doing more, not less, than universal justice.[68] It is the result of the covenant, not its presupposition.

---

[63] See B. Shevuot 39a and B. Sanhedrin 27b re Lev. 26:37; R. Hayyim ibn Attar, *Or ha-Hayyim*: Exod. 39:32; also, Y. Eruvin 3.2/20d re Prov. 3:17.

[64] Even Spinoza, who regarded the biblical covenant to be passé, was impressed by the fact that in that covenant every member of it was directly related to the divine sovereign. This, he believed, was a powerful prophylactic against human authorities becoming tyrants. See *Tractatus Theologico-Politicus*, trans. S. Shirley (Leiden: E. J. Brill, 1989), chap. 17, 255f.

[65] See Novak, *Jewish Social Ethics*, 208ff.

[66] See ibid., 223f., endnote.

[67] See Novak, *The Election of Israel*, 150f.

[68] In this sense, it is like the principle of *lifnim me-shurat ha-din* (not taking full advantage of a legal right). Here the precovenantal rights of an individual are to be waived for the sake of this higher communal end (see B. Baba Kama 100a re Exod. 18:20 and parallels). The only difference between them is that the prohibition of interest is a generally applicable norm, whereas *lifnim me-shurat ha-din* is only an ad hoc procedure.

SPECIFIC COVENANTAL CLAIMS
ON THE COMMUNITY: PUBLIC WORSHIP

In the previous chapter, we saw how prayer, as the way humans essentially beseech God for the fulfillment of their needs, is a claim that humans are entitled to make on God. That is, they have a right to have God listen to their pleas, even though they have no right to determine how God is to actually answer them. We also saw that prayer (*tefillah*) can be part of public worship (*avodah*), but that it is not identical with it. Prayer per se is a matter of the heart, and that makes it primarily an individual, spontaneous matter.[69] Nevertheless, even though public worship would be a hollow exercise if its participants did not also use it as an occasion to offer their personal prayers, it is primarily concerned with other matters. These matters are twofold.

First, public worship is concerned with the covenantal claims the community has to make on God. Here, as we shall see in the next chapter, these claims are more a matter of justice than the mercy from God prayer beseeches. That is, not only does the community have a right to call upon God as a community, but it has a right to expect that God keep his covenantal commitments to the community justly.

Second, public worship is concerned with the assertion of proper doctrine about God, which is addressed to the community itself as much as it is directed to God.[70] On this level, worship can be seen as a specifically covenantal claim God makes on the community, which is that the community express the truth about God that has been revealed to them, most prominently in Scripture. The reason, it seems to me, that this theological exercise is a matter of worship rather than philosophical-type discourse is that the truth about God is best uttered when God himself is experienced as present. Personal presence requires a direct address rather than the absent object a description merely calls to mind after its appearance. To merely describe God's acts when he is present is like talking about a person as if he or she were not here. And from the human side of worship, how can one talk about God without immediate consideration of our dependence on God? Without awareness of that dependence, we are not personally present before God. Prayer is a response to God's phenomenality; it is not our mental construction of an epiphenomenon.[71]

---

[69] See *Sifre*: Devarim, no. 41, and B. Taanit 2a re Deut. 11:13; Maimonides, *Mishneh Torah*: Tefillah, 1.1–2. Cf. B. Baba Metsia 107b re Exod. 23:25.

[70] Maimonides emphasized how precision in liturgical language is for the sake of theological precision. See *Mishneh Torah*: Tefillah, 1.4, 6.3; *Teshuvot ha-Rambam*, vol. 2, ed. Blau (Jerusalem, 1960), no. 261.

[71] Cf. Plato, *Republic*, 524B, where knowledge is a "second look" (*episkepsis*) at an object after it has appeared/been present and is thus already absent. In the case of God, though, we may never publicly speak of him as if he were absent. See Ps. 139:7–13; B. Rosh Hashanah 18a and B. Yevamot 49b re Deut. 4:7.

That public worship is more the acknowledgment of God's acts (*hoda'ah*) than our requests of God is seen in the fact that the centerpiece of the liturgy is not a prayer at all in the usual sense, that is, it is not our words to God. Instead, the heart of the liturgy is the twice daily recitation of the *shema*, which consists of the recognition of God's unique kingship over us, then God's claim on our love, then God's reminder that our acts will be judged with good or bad consequences as their ultimate effects, then God's claim that we remember all his commandments, and finally the requirement that we repeatedly proclaim the founding covenantal event: the exodus from Egypt.[72] The theological necessity of the proper order of the liturgy, especially the *shema* as the centerpiece of the liturgy is brought out by the Mishnah.

> Rabbi Joshua ben Qorhah asked why the *shema* ("Hear O Israel, the Lord is our God, the Lord alone"—Deuteronomy 6:4) precedes the *ve-hayah im shamo'a* ("If you will surely to my commandments . . ."—Deuteronomy 11:13). It is because one should first accept the yoke of the kingship of God (*ol malkhut shamayim*) and then, afterward, accept the yoke of the comandments (*ol mitsvot*).[73]

All this is brought out by the fact that the next most important part of the liturgy, the *Shemonah Esrē*, the "Eighteen [actually nineteen] Benedictions," which is said three times daily is considered to be a doctrinal statement, basically worked out by the "Men of the Great Assembly" (*anshei keneset ha-gedolah*) sometime after the return of the Jews from Babylonian Exile in the sixth century B.C.E.[74] And whereas the sections of the liturgy that express petitions to God may be supplemented, as needs and the perception of needs do change often, the sections of the liturgy that express praise and thanksgiving of God are not to be changed at all.[75] The integrity of these words is taken to be almost as sacred as the integrity of the words of Scripture (*torah she-bi-khtav*).[76] The truth, especially the truth about God, requires that it be spoken, and that its speech take precedence over all other forms of speech. Thus the *shema* ends with the words, "It is true (*emet*), the Lord is your God" (Jeremiah 10:10)—and then the verse itself continues, "[H]e is the living God, the everlasting king (*melekh olam*)."[77] For that reason, it seems, the public teaching of the Torah takes precedence over public worship in most cases. The words of the Torah are still the most direct forms of divine self-description, even sur-

---

[72] This scriptural collation is: Deut. 6:4–9, 11:13–21; Num. 15:37–41; Jer. 10:10. For the temporal ordering of this recitation, see M. Berakhot 1.3 re Deut. 6:7.

[73] M. Berakhot 2.2.

[74] See B. Megillah 17b; B. Berakhot 33a; Maimonides, *Mishneh Torah*: Tefillah, 1.4–7.

[75] B. Berakhot 34a.

[76] See Y. Berakhot 6.2/10b.

[77] In other words, it expresses a relationship that does not absorb God's transcendence. See R. Hayyim ibn Attar, *Or ha-Hayyim*: Deut. 6:4.

passing the reworked words of the humanly composed liturgy.[78] Hence they
are *the* primary expression of the highest truth available to any human community. That is also why the liturgy is constructed to reflect the sacrificial system
in the Temple, which itself is a matter of direct divine decree in the Torah.[79]
And even though verbal worship was already a structured institution by the
time of the Second Temple, and hence not a replacement for the sacrificial
system but an accompaniment to it, verbal worship is still regarded as incomplete until the more primary sacrificial system is restored in the messianic
future.[80] Its present status as being the sole form of public worship is thus
considered to be temporary and partial. It will not be replaced by the sacrificial
system anymore than it replaced the sacrificial system, but it will be re-placed
in its proper context within the full exercise of the covenant.[81]

THE MOST SPECIFIC COVENANTAL CLAIM
ON THE COMMUNITY: MARTYRDOM

The greatest claim that God makes on the covenanted community is that they
die as martyrs rather than substitute the covenantal worship of God with anything or anyone else. Indeed, martyrdom itself (*qiddush ha-shem*) could well
be regarded as the supreme act of Jewish worship.[82] It is more than just the
right of the community to call upon its members to die for its life or liberty.

---

[78] Thus, e.g., when one is reading the Torah as study (*talmud torah*), he or she must change the
character of the act from intent to study to intent to recite the *shema* liturgically if he or she is to
be accounted as having recited the *shema* as an act of worship (M. Berakhot 2.1). In other words,
one moves from a higher level of piety to one beneath it, as it were. For the notion that Torah
study (albeit for rare persons who are totally absorbed in it) is not to be interrupted even for
worship, see Y. Berakhot 1.5/3b. For the ruling that places of Torah study have even greater
sanctity than places of worship, see B. Megillah 26b–27a; Maimonides, *Mishneh Torah*: Tefillah,
11.14 re B. Berakhot 28a and parallels.

[79] See B. Berakhot 26b (the view of R. Joshua ben Levi); Maimonides, *Mishneh Torah*: Tefillah,
1.5, and R. Joseph Karo, *Kesef Mishneh* thereon. The other view presented in the Talmud there is
that of R. Yose, son of R. Hanina, viz., the liturgical order reflects the times of the spontaneous
prayers of the patriarchs. It seems that the first view sees worship as essentially communal ab
initio. The second view seems to view worship as initially individual and subsequently communal.

[80] See M. Tamid 5.1. The hope for the restoration of the Temple with its sacrificial worship
(*qorbanot*) permeates the traditional Jewish liturgy. Those forms of liberal Judaism which have
eliminated this element from their liturgies have thereby eliminated a major connection to the
traditional Jewish institution of worship itself. Worship ultimately reflects our desire to do everything that the Lord has commanded us—even those things which are far from our contemporary
experience and sentiments. It is not our construction of what we would like God to be like.

[81] See Maimonides, *Mishneh Torah*: Melakhim, 11.1.

[82] Thus the same verse, "and I shall be sanctified (*ve-niqdashti*) in the midst of the children of
Israel" (Lev. 22:32) is used to designate the quorum of ten (*minyan*) required for public worship
(B. Berakhot 21b) and the requirement of martyrdom (B. Sanhedrin 74b).

During the darkest days of the Roman persecution of the Jews and Judaism in the second century C.E., the criteria of martyrdom were set down.

> [The Rabbis] concluded and determined (*nimnu ve-gamru*) in the attic of the house of Nitzeh in Lydda that for the transgression of all the prohibitions in the Torah, if one is told to transgress or be killed, one should transgress and not be killed (*ya'avor ve'al yehareg*). That is, except for the transgression of the prohibitions of idolatry (*avodah zarah*), sexual sins (*gilui arayot*) and murder (*shefikhut damim*). If one is told to transgress them or be killed, one should be killed and not transgress (*yehareg v'al ya'avor*).[83]

A key point here, one that has been amazingly overlooked by virtually all the commentators, is that these three cardinal, inviolable sins, are identical with the core of the Noahide laws, which are the laws the Rabbis determined are binding on all humankind.[84] Although as many as thirty such laws are proposed by some, and the later tradition settled for seven (*sheva mitsvot bnei Noah*), these three laws (actually categories of laws) seem to be the indisputable core of the Noahide law.[85] So, it turns out that what is the absolutely minimal sine qua non for the gentiles is the same for the Jews. Furthermore, since the gentiles are considered to be liable for the death penalty—at least in theory—by their violation of any of these norms, it would seem that they should let themselves be killed rather than violate them;[86] if they violated them by their own volition, they would be criminals deserving of death, but if they died rather than violate them, they would be moral heroes—moral heroes yes, but literal martyrs no. That is because martyrdom is dying for the sake of the Lord God of Israel rather than willingly performing acts that are inherently incompatible with his kingship. It is more than just resisting what is inherently evil. Maryrdom has a much more transcendent intent.

When such a willing death is accepted by a Jew, he or she is upholding the command that the Lord "be sanctified in the midst of the children of Israel" (Leviticus 22:32).[87] That is most likely to occur when the sin to be avoided by

[83] B. Sanhedrin 74a. See Y. Sanhedrin 3.6/21b; also, *Sifra*: Aharei-Mot, ed. Weiss, 86a re Lev. 18:5.

[84] See D. Novak, *The Image of the Non-Jew in Judaism* (New York: Edwin Mellen Press, 1983), 28ff.

[85] See B. Sanhedrin 57a. Cf. 56a; Hullin 92a–b.

[86] For the ruling that the violation of any of the Noahide laws is a capital crime, see B. Sanhedrin 57a. Because a Noahide is not commanded to die as a martyr—that being only a Jewish requirement—Maimonides infers that a person may violate the three cardinal sins under the duress of a death threat (*Mishneh Torah*: Melakhim, 10.2 re B. Sanhedrin 74b). However, since the reason for allowing oneself to be murdered rather becoming a murderer oneself is presented as being a "rational matter" (*sevara*—B. Sanhedrin 74a and B. Pesahim 25b), would that not apply to any human being as a moral obligation, even if not a theological one? Cf. B. Kiddushin 43a re II Sam. 12:9; R. Isaac Abrabanel, *Commentary on the Former Prophets*: II Sam. 12:9.

[87] See Maimonides, *Sefer ha-Mitsvot*: positive precepts, no. 9.

death is idolatry. And that martyrdom is to be suffered even if the lifesaving option presented is to convert to another monotheistic religion like Christianity or Islam.[88] Rabbi Akibah, who himself died as a martyr, saw the source of the demand of martyrdom in the verse in Scripture—and saw it reiterated in the *shema*—"you shall love the Lord your God . . . with all your soul" (*be-khol nafshekha*—Deuteronomy 6:5), which he interpreted, first for himself and then for all Jews, to mean "even when he takes your life breath (*nishmatekha*) away."[89] At this level, then, this is a claim that God can make on each and every Jew personally, but as a member of the covenanted community, not just as a lone individual. Hence it has a far deeper significance even than the notion of having to return my life to God my creator at the time of my own death.[90]

We are now ready to examine what the covenanted community, elected by God, can claim from God in return.

[88] See Maimonides, *Mishneh Torah*: Yesodei ha-Torah, 5.1ff.; R. Abraham Gumbiner, *Magen Avraham* on *Shulhan Arukh*: Orah Hayyim, 128.37; also, Novak, *The Election of Israel*, 195.

[89] *Sifre*: Devarim, no. 41; B. Berakhot 61b.

[90] See Ps. 31:6, which is to be said by one on his or her deathbed (see Nahmanides, *Torat ha'Adam*: Inyan Vidui, in *Kitvei Ramban*, ed. C. B. Chavel [Jerusalem: Mosad ha-Rav Kook, 1963], 2:47; cf. B. Berakhot 5a). Although it is a Jewishly mandated prayer, it could be said by anyone who accepts God as her or her creator. In other words, there is nothing uniquely covenantal about it.

CHAPTER IV

Covenanted Community and God

COVENANTAL FAITHFULNESS

As is the case in the relationship between God and persons, where initial divine claims on humans lead to subsequent human claims on God, so do God's claims on the covenanted human community lead to the claims this community can make on God. That is, from the underived rights of God come the derived rights of his creatures, which are entitlements (*zekhuyot*). These entitled rights of human creatures are most easily justifiable when exercised in the interhuman realm itself. Accordingly, at the universal level, since being "made in the image of God" (Genesis 9:6) means that every human being is capable of a direct relationship with God, every human being is, therefore, very much "an end in himself or herself" and is to be treated with proper respect by every other human being and every human community in the world.[1] And, accordingly, at the specifically historical level, since "every man of Israel, your children, your wives, and the sojourners in the midst of your camp" (Deuteronomy 29:9–10) are direct parties to the covenant with God, every member of the covenanted community has a direct claim on the specific, historically constituted concern of every other member of that community and on the community herself.[2] (Chapters 5, 6, and 7 deal with these interhuman rights.) But in an ontologically prior sense, humans even have rights in their relationship with God, although these rights are less obvious than interhuman rights, simply because we are not accustomed to using rights talk when speaking of the relationships between God and humans.

The notion that humans have rights in their relationship with God is rooted in the two most basic truths about God known to us from Scripture and Tradition. First, God is the creator of the entire universe, of all that is, and this act of creation is totally free, neither determined by any prior grounds nor even limited by any external conditions. "When I act, who can challenge it (*mi yeshivennah*)?" (Isaiah 43:13). Second, God assumes responsibility for what he has chosen to create. God chooses not only to create but to be continually

---

[1] See D. Novak, *Natural Law in Judaism* (Cambridge: Cambridge University Press, 1998), 167ff.

[2] Thus, when the covenant is to be renewed every seven years at the public reading of the Torah by the king in the Temple in Jerusalem (see M. Sotah 7.8), the event was to be as inclusive as possible (see B. Hagigah 3a re Deut. 31:12).

involved in his creation as "king of all the earth . . . God who rules over the nations" (Psalms 47:8–9). But a king "sustains his throne by kind concern (*hesed*)" (Proverbs 20:28).[3] Thus God's autonomous exercise of his responsibility *for* what he has created thereby enables his creatures to claim his response *to* their own creaturely needs in return. In this sense, God's underived rights as creator institute self-imposed duties derived *from* his being a *responsible* creator. Even though creation is not limited by any external conditions, it does involve an internal limiting condition, one that God has placed in it initially: by becoming creator, God also makes himself an object of response from his creatures. The very way God makes his claims on us as our creator enables us to make our claims on him as his human creatures, precisely because we are made aware of our own creaturely uniqueness by God. "What a man (*mah enosh*)! It is because (*ki*) You take notice of him. What a human being! It is because (*ki*) You assign him!" (Psalms 8:5).[4] By the very admission of that type of reciprocity, which is irrevocable as we shall soon see, God limits his own claim to be the sole rights holder in the cosmic order. Without that reciprocity, asymmetrical to be sure, the relation with God would be one way only: from God *to* humans. It would strictly be a relation of cause and effect, transitive action from a subject to an object rather than a full transaction between persons. It would not be what is *between* God and humans *together*, and it would thus not be a covenant. To be able to respond to God as creator is thus already a covenantal act.

A covenant is initiated and sustained by divine election.[5] In the case of human persons per se, God elects his human creatures from all his other creatures for a conscious and reciprocal relationship with himself. As we have seen in the previous chapter, being made aware of our creaturely dependence on God, we assume there is a right to call upon God to fulfill our needs, even if we cannot determine exactly how that is to be done by God. But here is where the communal rights of the covenanted community in relation to God are far greater than the rights of an individual in relation to God: the community elected by God is told more of what God is to do for her in the covenant than individual persons have been told about what God is to do for them in the world.[6] In the case of individuals, they can only assume that God governs the

---

[3] That is why God's transcendent "might" (*gevurato*) is to be associated with his immanent "concern" (*intvetanuto*—literally, "humility"). See B. Megillah 31a re Deut. 10:17–18.

[4] The usual translations of the verse assume *mah* functions interrogatively as a rhetorical question, viz., "What is man that Thou art mindful of him?" And the answer is to be then supplied by the hearer or reader, who is to refer to some human property or other. However, *mah* seems to function vocatively, viz., expressing amazement because God is mindful of humans. In other words, that divine mindfulness itself is what makes humans so unique and so attractive. For the vocative use of *mah*, see, e.g., Num. 23:3; Ps. 92:6.

[5] See D. Novak, *The Election of Israel* (Cambridge: Cambridge University Press, 1995), 115ff.

[6] As such, what can be said about God is determined by what has been revealed to the community and by what the community has determined may be publicly said about God in the liturgy.

universe by a just order in which they too participate, and that God listens to
their cries and responds mercifully. But the covenanted community is given
more specific assurances.[7] As such, they have the right to hold God to his
specific promises to them because these promises are integral to their being
God's people.

All other peoples, conversely, seem to be related to God by creaturely necessity. They are dependent on the moral authority of God's cosmic law. Thus the
people of Nineveh, to whom the Israelite prophet Jonah is sent to call them to
repentance for their sins, do repent and are saved from destruction. "And God
saw their deeds whereby they had turned away (*ki shavu*) from their evil way,
so God then changed his mind (*vayinnahem*) about the bad things he said he
would do to them and did not do so" (Jonah 3:10). Clearly, the people of
Nineveh are morally related to God.[8] Nevertheless, there is no indication at all
that this relation is the result of their being elected by God for a covenantal
relationship.[9] As such, they are under the general order of justice at work in
the universe. This is brought out by the identification of their sin as "violence"
(*he-hamas*—3:8), which is the very same sin that led to the destruction of the
generation of the Flood, and which is a sin known by human reason. It is
something humans do not require covenantal revelation in order to be culpable
for.[10]

In the case of individual persons, there is no permanent claim on God because humans are mortal by nature. Ultimately, every human being has to
accept God's decree of his or her death, however much he or she might have
rightfully begged God for life or anything less than life. At this level, everything belongs to God by right. "All lives, they are mine" (Ezekiel 18:4). "For
everything is from You, and what is from your own hand do we give back to
You" (I Chronicles 29:14). To indict God for what he has done to us as persons
is blasphemy, which is to make ourselves morally superior to God. Thus when
Job's wife says to him in his agony, "[C]urse God and die" (Job 1:9), he replies,
"[D]o we only take the good from God, but we do not take the bad?" (1:10).

However, whereas in the case of individual persons, the life of the world
will transcend their own deaths, in the case of the people of Israel, we will
survive at least as long as the earth herself. "Just as I promised that the waters
of Noah will no longer pass over the earth [to destroy it], so have I promised
. . . that my kindness shall not depart from you and my covenant of peace will

---

See B. Berakhot 33b and B. Megillah 25a; Y. Berakhot 7.3/11c; Y. Megillah 3.7/74d; B. Yoma
69b.

    [7] See, e.g., B. Rosh Hashanah 18a B; Yevamot 49b re Deut. 4:7.

    [8] Cf. Jer. 46:1ff.; Amos 1:3ff.

    [9] This might well explain why Jonah, who was one of the nationalistic court prophets of Israel
(see II Kings 14:25) was so reluctant to prophesy for the benefit of a gentile nation (Jon. 1:2–3).

    [10] See Nahmanides, *Commentary on the Torah*: Gen. 6:13.

not be moved; so says the Lord who loves you" (Isaiah 54:9–10).[11] God's promise of the permanence of his covenant with Israel is the basis of her extraordinary claim on God that God not allow her to die as a people, that God grant her perpetual life even in this world. "I shall not die but live, for I shall declare the works of the Lord" (Psalms 118:17)[12] Clearly, that is a statement that only the covenanted community of Israel can properly make here and now. Jewish survival is an immediate claim on God, one that is justified by Jewish affirmation of the purposes of the covenant. Thus when Jews praise God for giving them the Torah, they affirm that God "has placed everlasting life (*hayyei olam*) in our midst."[13] As for individual humans, even when they are members of the covenanted community, about them it is said, "[S]hall he live forever, never seeing destruction? . . . Their grave is their home forever, their dwelling places from one generation to the next" (Psalms 49:10, 12).[14] "Naked did I come out from my mother's womb, and there will I return naked. The Lord has given and the Lord has taken away; blessed be the name of the Lord" (Job 1:21).

This Jewish claim on God for survival is even more extraordinary in that it is not contingent on the virtue of the Jews. Israel's right to life, her claim on God to save her from death in the world, is to be exercised even when she has turned against God. "Although she has sinned, Israel is still Israel," as the Talmud firmly put it.[15] The covenant is indelible, which means Israel is indestructible. Thus, even when Israel is rightfully punished by God for her sins, that punishment is never to be permanent. She is always to survive it. "The Lord has certainly punished me, but he did not turn me over to death" (Psalms 118:18).

All of this can be seen in the way Scripture and the Rabbis treat Moses' reconfirmation of the covenant after Israel rejects God by worshiping the Golden Calf. Even after God relents from his threat to destroy the people for their great sin, Moses still insists that the covenant requires that God maintain his direct relationship with Israel. When God accepts this requirement, Moses then says, "If your presence does not go [with us], do not bring us up out from this place" (Exodus 33:15). By this assertion, Israel claims God's perpetual

---

[11] See B. Sanhedrin 99a.

[12] Thus, Israel's life is guaranteed by God in this world and into the world-to-come. Only a rebellious minority is excluded in the world-to-come. See M. Sanhedrin 10.1 re Isa. 60:21; also 6.2 re Josh. 7:25.

[13] See R. Jacob ben Asher, *Tur*: Orah Hayyim, 139 re Eccl. 12:11, who argues that this "everlasting life" does not refer to the world-to-come but to the ongoing tradition of the Jewish people (*torah she-b'al peh*), which is in this world.

[14] For the connection between this assertion of human mortality and the rabbinic doctrine of the resurrection of the dead (*tehiyyat ha-metim*); see Novak, *The Election of Israel*, 262f.

[15] B. Sanhedrin 44a re Josh. 7:11. This text speaks of the indelibility of the people of Israel. Later tradition extended its meaning to include the indelibility of the election of every individual Jew. See Novak, *The Election of Israel*, 189ff.

presence as her right. To best appreciate the deeper meaning of this covenantal negotiation, we must now look at one of the most theologically charged passages in the entire Talmud.

> "And Moses implored the presence of the Lord" (Exodus 32:11). . . . Rava said that this means until he released Him from His vow (*nidro*). . . . "Remember Abraham, Isaac, and Israel your servants to whom You took an oath (*nishba'ta*) by Your own self (*bakh*)" (32:13). What does "by Your own self" mean? Rabbi Eleazar said that Moses said to the Holy-One-blessed-be-He: "Master-of-the-universe, if you had taken an oath for them [Israel] by heaven and earth, I would have said that just as heaven and earth will be destroyed (*betelim*), so will your oath be destroyed. But now that you took an oath for them by your great name, just as your great name lives and endures forever and ever, so does your oath endure forever and ever."[16]

This passage is based on the legal institution of vows and oaths, which is the closest thing to autonomy that is allowed by Jewish law, as we shall see in chapter 7. In a vow or an oath, an individual person creates an obligation for himself or herself. In the case of human beings, a vow or an oath may be annulled retroactively by a higher authority if it can be shown that the fulfillment of that vow or oath is contrary to the common good or even contrary to the good of the person who made it in the first place. But the power of annulment presupposes that the one making the vow or oath is subordinate to someone greater than himself or herself, thus making it a matter of very much qualified autonomy. In the case of God, however, there is no such greater person. God's autonomy is absolute. Indeed, because of God's exclusive autonomy, the freedom of any of his creatures is limited by it.[17] As such, when God makes the strongest personal commitment possible, which is to promise in the form of an oath in his own name alone, and thus that oath is not contingent on any external factors, then God cannot annul that oath without destroying his own moral authority. The basis for God's claim on the people to be faithful to the covenant is that God himself is faithful to the covenant. Indeed, the covenant is the criterion of truth (*emet*) for Israel precisely because God is true (*ne'eman*) to it.[18] Thus, when the prophet Hosea teaches the people that they may not abandon God because God has not abandoned them, he says in the name of God: "I have betrothed you forever (*l'olam*). . . . I have betrothed you in faithfulness (*b'emunah*)" (Hosea 2:21–22).[19]

---

[16] B. Berakhot 32a. Also, see D. Novak, *Halakhah in a Theological Dimension* (Chico, Calif.: Scholars Press, 1985), 126ff.

[17] Thus even the free acts of evildoers are used by God for his own purposes. See *Sifre: Devarim*, no. 329, and B. Shabbat 32a re Deut. 22:8.

[18] See Novak, *The Election of Israel*, 126f.

[19] See B. Pesahim 87b.

Much of Jewish communal prayer in the form of collective requests (*baqashah*) is the claim on God to perpetually remember just who his people is. Thus at the heart of the New Year service of Rosh Hashanah in the synagogue, where the liturgy expresses a cosmic trial of Israel before God, God is implored to "forever remember his covenant" (Psalms 111:5).[20] Although Israel is for the most part obliged to recognize her own difficulties as stemming from unfaithfulness to the covenant and thus praise God (*hoda'ah*) for his ready forgiveness of her sins, there are times when Israel has the right to express her anger with God for what seems to be unjustified harshness. "See O' Lord and look at whom you have done this, women even eat their own children!" (Lamentations 2:20)[21]. In fact, the only limit on this expression of anger is the prohibition of blasphemy, the curse that wishes God to be dead.[22] Justified anger with God must also include the patience to wait for God's answer to our desperate complaints. Otherwise, such anger would lead to the conclusion of our own moral superiority to God, a superiority of which blasphemy is the most acute expression.[23] We may not draw any final conclusions, even from our very understandable anger, "because judgment (*mishpat*), it is God's" (Deuteronomy 1:17). We have the much harder task of living with it until the very endtime. "My soul is terrified, and you O Lord, how long!" (Psalms 6:4).

The right of the covenanted community to be angry with the presently unjustified ways of God assumes very special importance for the Jewish people after the Holocaust. There is the great temptation to turn away from God for not rescuing so many of his people from the Nazi murderers and their cohorts.[24] Part of that turning away from God concludes that there is no justice at all, anywhere and anytime. But if there is no cosmic justice at all, then to pursue justice in the human world seems futile when that world is a tiny island in a sea of absurdity.[25] Thus Jewish abandonment of the universal God because of the experience of gross injustice can quickly lead (and for too many has already led) to the conclusion that justice is not to be done because it cannot be done. Having no real effect, justice has nothing in which to endure. At this point, survival itself becomes the sole task. But survival per se is always in extremis where there are no moral restraints. But could that not also mean individual survival at the expense of the covenant, namely, assimilation?[26] Only survival

---

[20] See B. Rosh Hashanah 32b.

[21] For a classic statement of rabbinic anger with God over God's seeming indifference to the persecution of the Jews by their enemies, see B. Gittin 56b re Exod. 15:11; also, Y. Berakhot 7.3/11d; Y. Megillah 3.7/74d; B. Yoma 69b re Jer. 32:18; B. Eruvin 18b re Ps. 150:6.

[22] See B. Sanhedrin 56a re Exod. 22:26; M. Sanhedrin 7.5; B. Megillah 24b re Isa. 8:17.

[23] See B. Baba Batra 16a re Job 9:24 (the view of Rava). Cf. Job 27:6.

[24] The best known proponent of this view has been Richard L. Rubenstein in *After Auschwitz*, 2nd ed. (Baltimore: Johns Hopkins University Press 1992).

[25] See D. Novak, *Jewish Social Ethics* (New York: Oxford University Press, 1992), 163ff.

[26] Along these lines, note the case of Miriam bat Bilgah, who during the Maccabean period, when the Hellenized Syrians were persecuting the Jews, is reported to have struck the altar of the

for the sake of the covenant includes inviolable moral restraints, even in extremis. "Teach me to do your will, for you are my God . . . for the sake of your name O'Lord let me live!" (Psalms 143:10–11).[27] Jews cannot cogently claim God's covenantal protection without reaffirming our own covenantal duties simultaneously.

The total abandonment of God by some Jews is their desperate attempt to transcend our anger with God by drawing a conclusion from it that permanently eliminates God from the world and so from our life as well. This abandonment is a moral judgment, but it tragically deprives those who make it of any real basis for resisting the temptation to act unjustly, a temptation especially acute to those who have themselves suffered very real injustice in the world. And even those Jews who still want to cling to the ancient Jewish tradition of God talk, but without the affirmation of the cosmic justice of the universal God, also have no real basis upon which to resist the great temptation to act unjustly, for often the "god" they affirm is for all intents and purposes a tribal deity, one who is incapable of judging us but who only endorses our hatred of our enemies. Such a god is a projection of ourselves and our own power. Such a god is not the source or the protector either of human rights or of Jewish rights. However, the God we serve is not confined to Israel; both his rule and his judgment extend over all the nations throughout the world—including Israel—at all times. He is the "Master of the universe" (*ribbono shel olam*), which is the name most often used when God's judgment of Israel as well as of the nations is called to mind.[28]

SPECIFIC JEWISH COVENANTAL CLAIMS

In Scripture, it seems that the people of Israel have specific claims on God to reward them for their observance of the commandments. Thus in a scriptural selection that is included in the most important part of the Jewish liturgy, the twice daily affirmation of the kingship of God (*shema*), we read: "And it will come to pass that if you shall carefully listen to My commandments . . . I shall make it rain in your land" (Deuteronomy 11:13–14). But there are at least

---

Temple as a blasphemous gesture, decrying God as "a wolf . . . who did not stand by them [the Jews] in their time of trouble" (T. Sukkah 4.28; Y. Sukkah 5.8/55d; B. Sukkah 56b; cf. *Avot de-Rabbi Nathan* A, chap. 1, ed. Schechter, 2b). But the great irony of her anger is that she herself had already removed herself from the covenant by marrying one of the officers of the Hellenized persecutors, a violation of the law under any circumstances (see Deut. 7:3; B. Kiddushin 68b; B. Avodah Zarah 36b).

[27] Hence, even though when there is danger to life, most of the commandments are to be violated (see B. Yoma 85a–b), not all of them are to be violated (see B. Sanhedrin 74a and parallels).

[28] See, e.g., B. Berakhot 4a re Ps. 27:13.

two great theological problems with drawing this easy conclusion from such scriptural passages.

The first problem emerges when we see the logic of such passages as being consequential, that is, when we see worldly goods as the necessary *effect* of keeping God's commandments. This problem is specifically epistemological, namely, we sometimes know from bitter experience that not only is righteousness not rewarded in this world, but that it is often the righteous who suffer most and the wicked who suffer least. Indeed, the wicked often seem to enjoy life the most. As the Rabbis sometimes put it, "[T]he sinner is rewarded."[29] Is that not a direct contradiction of the divine promises? Indeed, in Scripture itself we see the prophets complaining about this to God. "You are just (*tsaddiq*) O' Lord and because of that I will contend with you, even making a case (*mishpatim*) against you: Why does the way of the guilty (*resha'im*) prosper; why are the treacherous at ease?" (Jeremiah 12:1). More often than not, one can only conclude from experience that "the same thing happens (*miqreh ehad*) to the innocent and the guilty" (Ecclesiastes 9:2). But, as we saw in chapter 2, the rabbinic answer to this problem of theological epistemology is to assert that we cannot draw any conclusions from experience because the experience of the endtime is not yet at hand. As such, God has *not yet* brought about the full effects of the acts of the righteous or the acts of the wicked in this world (*olam ha-zeh*), this "vale of tears" (Psalms 84:7). That will have to wait for the world-to-come (*olam ha-ba*), which still lies even beyond the historical horizon. As we might say today, "The jury is still out." At this level, both individual persons and the people of Israel have not yet been answered by God. The redeemer has yet to come. Without this answer, the claims of the Torah would be falsified by its own criteria, that is, God could not deliver on his own promises.

The second problem with such passages emerges when we see their logic as being teleological, that is, when we see the enjoyment of worldly goods as the desired *purpose* of keeping God's commandments. This problem is specifically ethical: Should the relationship with God involved in the keeping of the commandments be a means to a selfish end that does not seem to intend God at all? Is this not a subordination of what is higher to what is lower, of the transcendent to the immanent? The rabbinic approach to this problem is to emphasize in many places that the true overall purpose of keeping the commandments is to love God who has so commanded us, who has so enabled us to include him in our lives and even more so to be included in his own life. And it is in the world-to-come where that mutual inclusion will be fully realized. There God will be the true *telos*: both the object of our desire in the beginning and the consummation of our desire in the end. "I am the first and I am the last, besides me there is no god" (Isaiah 44:6).

---

[29] B. Avodah Zarah 2b and parallels.

From this type of theology, it seems that the mention of extraneous rewards and punishments is for the sake of those unreflective, selfish people who would not keep the commandments unless motivated by such gross instrumentalism. Yet this theology still does not adequately deal with the reason why Scripture is so explicit, repeatedly, in its connection of the commandments with physical realities in this world. What are our claims on God as regards them? The answer, I think, had to wait for the theological insight of Maimonides. He asked:

> Since it is known that the reward (*sekharan*) of the commandments and the good we merit when we keep the way of the Lord written in the Torah is the world-to-come . . . why is it written throughout the whole Torah that if you listen, such and such will befall you (*yagia lakhem*), and if you do not listen, such will happen (*yiqreh*) to you? All of these things are in this world![30]

In other words, the whole order of ethical priorities seems to be reversed. Then Maimonides answers his own question as follows:

> God assured us in the Torah that if we practice it with joy and personal pleasure (*u-ve-tovat nefesh*) and we enjoy its wisdom continually, then God will remove from us all those things that prevent (*ha-mon'im*) us from practicing it, such as sickness, war, and famine, and the like. And he will extend to us all the good things that strengthen our ability to practice the Torah, such as physical satisfaction, and peace, and the increase of silver and gold. This is so we do not have to devote all our days to bodily needs. . . . For at a time when one is wearied (*tarud*) in this world by sickness, and by war, and by famine, he does not engage in wisdom or the commandments whereby he merits the world-to-come.[31]

Maimonides has solved the ethical problem of the physical rewards and punishments promised in the Torah. Instead of the commandments being for the sake of gaining physical benefits and avoiding physical detriments, these physical benefits (and the avoidance of their opposites) are now to be seen as preconditions for the keeping of the commandments. That is, the full practice of the commandments requires the best means to that end.[32] Thus we either need the materials necessary for the observance of the commandment itself, like sufficient food to be able to feed the hungry in the community, or we need not to be distracted from such commandments as the study of the Torah by the type of poverty that leaves us little if any time or energy for anything more than mere physical survival. In this way, the keeping of the commandments is the bridge between the things of this world, which are beneath us, and the

---

[30] *Mishneh Torah*: Teshuvah, 9.1.

[31] Ibid. See ibid.: Melakhim, 12.4.

[32] For an astute presentation of this whole point, see L. E. Goodman, *On Justice* (New Haven: Yale University Press, 1991), 142ff.

world-to-come, which, as the fullest community with God and each other, is the final intention of God in creation and which is still beyond us.

But has Maimonides not actually exacerbated the epistemological problem of reward and punishment by seeming to say that we can really assume the wherewithal to practice the commandments *whenever* we are but prepared to practice them with full and proper intention? Does not at least our present and past experience seem to falsify any such judgment? Nevertheless, perhaps we can interpret Maimonides' theological point here as follows: It is not that Jews can be assured in advance that their keeping of the commandments *necessarily* entails the satisfaction of their bodily needs. Instead, Jews are assured that they are justified in claiming from God, in prayer, that he *should* provide them with the wherewithal to keep the commandments fully. In other words, Jews have the right to ask for the fulfillment of these needs when and only when they want them to be fulfilled for the sake of the covenant. Ultimately, of course, it is for God to decide if and when these needs are to be fulfilled, be that in this world or the world-to-come. We are always subject to God's judgment in the end. But the covenant enables Jews to approach God with more than just a general plea from a creature for mercy from his or her creator.

If the commandments are given to us by God for the sake of the covenant, and if the whole existence of the Jewish people is for the sake of the covenant, then the commandments themselves tell us what our justified needs are. That is, from what we need to fully keep the commandments we learn what needs we have the right to ask God to help us fulfill—hopefully in this world. Thus, for example, our need for food is so that we may thank God for it and share it with the hungry, or our erotic need is so that we may build a lasting and creative union: a man with a woman and a woman with a man, and thus build up the families of Israel. (Note how all our needs are essentially communal, hence all the more so covenantal.) Indeed, it would even seem that we have the right to ask God why these needs were not fulfilled in this world at those times when we are convinced that our intention in serving God was pure. Looking at the Jewish liturgy, especially the vast majority of it that speaks collectively in the name of Israel, we see that Jewish tradition has not been at all reticent in its precise designation of what it claims from God. And that turns out to be a good deal more than any individual person would even know how to beseech God for.[33]

LEGAL AUTHORITY AS A COMMUNAL RIGHT

One of the most important events in the history of Jewish theology was when the authors of the Septuagint translation of the Torah into Greek, which was

---

[33] See B. Megillah 17b–18a.

the first translation of the Torah into another language, rendered the word *torah* as *nomos*.[34] By this choice of words, they affirmed that God's primary relationship with the world, and especially with his covenanted people, is one of governance.[35] The Torah as law, in the fullest sense of that word, is considered to be God's greatest achievement. Indeed, the editors of the Babylonian Talmud chose to conclude that greatest compendium of Jewish thought with a midrash on the verse "the everlasting ways (*halikhot olam*) are His" (Habakkuk 3:6)— "Do not say 'the everlasting ways' but, rather, 'the traditional laws' (*halakhot*)."[36] In other words, our connection with God is keeping his law on earth, which was not the case until Moses brought the law of the cosmos itself directly from heaven down to earth.[37] Even that aspect of the Torah which is immediately *theōria*, not *praxis*, is ultimately *praxis* inasmuch as it is for the sake of what is to be done—passionately and intelligently to be sure.[38]

Since the Torah is given over to humans on earth to be their law, they are obviously obligated to interpret it and apply it. Without that ongoing interpretation and application, the Torah would "be left in a corner," as the Talmud puts it, a museum piece rather than the normative force in the covenanted community that it is meant to be.[39] Thus immediately after the giving of the Decalogue, Moses is told: "these are the laws (*mishpatim*) you shall place before them" (Exodus 21:1), which the Rabbis say are "to be placed before them like a set table (*ke-shulhan arukh*)."[40] The laws do not present themselves. Nevertheless, the question arises as to how much of the Torah is divine law and how much of it is human law phenomenologically. Even though it is affirmed that the law of the Torah is *from God* in the sense of God being its first cause, does not the fact that the Torah is "no longer in heaven" (*lo ba-shamayim hi*), which means its entire interpretation and application is a matter of human authority—does that not make our experience of the law a human phenomenon?[41] But if that is

---

[34] This is closely akin to, if not the basis of, the rabbinic notion that the Torah is not just law for humans but, rather, the law of the cosmos. See *Beresheet Rabbah* 1.1 re Prov. 3.14; M. Avot 4.2.

[35] See Novak, *Natural Law in Judaism*, 146ff.

[36] Niddah 73a and parallels. However, contrary to much popular misunderstanding, this passage is not deriving the etymology of the word *halakhah* from the verb "to walk" (*halokh*). Rather, it is connecting the concept of earthly law with the concept of heavenly law. Thus what seems mundane is really sublime, not vice versa. For the Babylonian etymology of *halakhah* as "statutory law," see Saul Lieberman, *Hellenism in Jewish Palestine*, 2nd ed. (New York: Jewish Theological Seminary of America, 1962), 83, n. 3.

[37] For the theological problem in asserting the originally heavenly status of the Torah, see *Shir ha-Shirim Rabbah* 8.13 re Num. 19:14.

[38] See, e.g., B. Berakhot 17a re Ps. 111:10.

[39] B. Kiddushin 66a.

[40] *Mekhilta*: Mishpatim, ed. Horovitz-Rabin, 246. For the notion that the normative presentation is human actualization of divinely given potential, see Maimonides, *Teshuvot ha-Rambam*, ed. Y. Y. Blau (Jerusalem: Megitsei Nirdamim, 1960), vol. 2, no. 182, re B. Berakhot 11b.

[41] Cf. B. Kiddushin 32b re Ps. 1:2; B. Makkot 22b re Deut. 25:3; Temurah 16a re Josh. 15:17.

the case, in what sense is the Torah still covenantal, that is, in what sense is it not only something *from* God but, even more so, something shared *with* God? In other words, does the finality of revelation entail the right of the Jews to take the Torah *away from* God?[42]

This fundamental theological question is dealt with in one of the most famous passages in the Talmud. The passage talks about a debate between two first-century C.E. Rabbis, Rabbi Eliezer ben Hyrkanus and Rabbi Joshua ben Hananiah, over a legal question of the purity of a certain type of oven. Rabbi Eliezer declares it to be pure (*tahor*), which means that food cooked in it may be eaten by those having particular dietary restrictions according to the Temple cult. But Rabbi Joshua, expressing the view of the majority of the Sages, declares it to be impure (*tamē*) and thus food cooked in it may be eaten by anyone.[43] After the legal facts are set forth, the Talmud records the following dramatic scene:

> Rabbi Eliezer said to them [the Sages] again, "If the law is according to my view, God will so attest." Thus a heavenly echo (*bat qol*) came forth and declared, "Why do you hold a view against that of Rabbi Eliezer? The law is according to him." Rabbi Joshua then stood up on his feet and said, "It is not in heaven!" (Deuteronomy 30:12). . . . Rabbi Jeremiah said that the Torah has already been given from Mount Sinai and we do not, therefore, regard a heavenly echo as being authoritative, for You already wrote at Mount Sinai, "Incline after the majority" (Exodus 23:2). Rabbi Nathan happened to meet Elijah. He said to him, "What did the holy-One-blessed-be-he do at this time?" He said to him that He smiled and said, "My children have vanquished me indeed (*nitshuni*)!"[44]

This "vanquishment" does not mean that God's law has been taken over from God by humans to such an extent that the law has lost its connection to God. Moses is not Prometheus.[45] Instead, this means that because of the duty humans have to interpret and apply the law of the Torah, they also have a claim on God's endorsement of what they have sincerely discerned to be the intent and the scope of that law.[46] Thus normative interpretation (*derash*) is not only God's claim on Israel, but it is also Israel's claim on God for the sake of the covenant. That is, in order for the law to be a transaction between God and

---

[42] See Y. Taanit 4.5/68c re Deut. 9:17.

[43] M. Kelim 5.10.

[44] B. Baba Metsia 59b. See Novak, *Halakhah in a Theological Dimension*, 124f. Re the authority of the opinion of the majority of the Sages, see B. Berakhot 9a and parallels; Hullin 11a re Exod. 23:2; cf. M. Peah 4.1; M. Eduyot 1.5 and R. Abraham ben David of Posquières (Ravad), *Commentary on the Mishnah* thereon.

[45] Nevertheless, for the notion that God complied with a number of Moses' autonomous innovations, see *Avot de-Rabbi Nathan* A, chap. 2, pp. 5a–b; B. Shabbat 87a and B. Yevamot 62a; Y. Taaniyot 4.5/68c.

[46] See *Shemot Rabbah* 15.3 re Exod. 12:2.

Israel rather than a transfer from God to Israel, Israel must claim God's endorsement of what she has decided about the law. That means Israel herself has the right to determine the original normative intent of the divine lawgiver, so that the law will still be considered "the intact (*temimah*) Torah of the Lord" (Psalms 19:8), a bridge connecting humans and God and not a barrier separating them; in rabbinic theology, it is emphasized that God is so committed to the covenant with Israel that he submits himself to the law that governs their mutual covenant.[47] Thus the law is not only from God, it is also *for* God as well. Human interpretation begins in God's claim on the scholars of the Torah in the covenanted community to make his law normative de facto, but it immediately leads into the community's claim on God to accept their interpretation of the law as God's own original intent, retroactively de jure.

This is most easily seen in the early (tannaitic) rabbinic texts in which normative Jewish practice is derived (*nidrash*) from the revealed words of Scripture. Much of this task was not so much to show that new law could be inferred from the ancient text but, rather, to show that ancient Jewish practice had always been based on the words of Scripture.[48] To be sure, this had to wait for the correct exegesis to be properly shown. Thus the Rabbis noted that "anything a venerable student teaches . . . was said to Moses at Sinai."[49] In this period, rabbinic exegesis (*midrash*) flowered and the most minute details of traditional Jewish practice were consistently shown to be derived from the words, even the letters, of Scripture. At this level, we see normative teaching to be primarily a process of exegetical retrieval of lost or latent connections between the traditional life of the Jews and the words of Scripture, both of which were seen as having always been with them.[50] The claim of these scholars on God was always to be guided in their interpretation of the words of Scripture so that it might truly reflect what God had initially willed the Torah to teach. Thus Rabbi Nehunya ben ha-Qanah used to pray when entering the rabbinic academy, where questions of the law were decided, "that no harmful error (*teqalah*) happen because of me."[51] In other words, he realized the great responsibility his right to call upon divine approval of normative rabbinic teaching involved.

Nevertheless, the Rabbis also recognized that everything they taught normatively could not be specifically traced back to a text or to a practice already there. There are times when there are new situations facing the people for which there are no traditional precedents and no words of Scripture to be

---

[47] See Y. Rosh Hashanah 1.3/57a–b re Lev. 22:9.
[48] See David Weiss Halivni, *Revelation Restored* (Boulder, Colo.: Westview Press, 1997), 47ff.
[49] Y. Peah 2.4/17a re Eccl. 1:10.
[50] See, e.g., *Sifre*: Bemidbar, no. 75; Y. Megillah 1.10/72b.
[51] M. Berakhot 4.2.

convincingly mined for a suitable answer. Does that mean that humans are left to either normative silence or to their own normative invention? Either course of action would seem to divert necessary Jewish practice from the revealed law of the Torah.

The problems associated with attempting to find scriptural or traditional sources in order to respond adequately to a new situation in Jewish life can be seen in the way the Rabbis struggled with the holiday of Purim. Purim celebrates the downfall of the Persian prime minister Haman and the frustration of his plan to exterminate all of the Jews in the Persian empire, which was where virtually all the Jews lived after the Babylonian Exile in 586 B.C.E. Certainly, such an event requires celebration of the fact that God saved his people when they were at the very brink of destruction. Not to do so would lead to a secular celebration of a great event in Jewish history, and it would seriously suggest that God does not act in history on behalf of his people.[52] But where is the scriptural basis for initiating such a celebration? If there is none, then did not the Torah rule that "you shall not add onto what I have commanded or detract from it" (Deuteronomy 4:2)?[53] And, yet, as one of the Rabbis put it: "If when we were brought from slavery to freedom [at Passover] we sang a song, should it not be all the more so when we were brought from death to life?"[54]

The reasoning employed in this last point is what is called *qal va-homer*, that is, the inference of a major point from a minor point (what logicians call a fortiori).[55] In the Talmud, it is recognized that to employ such reasoning, one need not have a specific traditional warrant, which is not the case with the inferences based on the presence of a common word in two different contexts (*gezerah shavah*).[56] What this means is that the Rabbis recognized that more basic principles than are found in the text of Scripture itself might very well lie beneath the surface of the text, and that they can be discovered by the exercise of human reason. However, even with this type of exegetical reasoning, there has to be some more specific point of scriptural reference from which to at least begin the process of exegesis. It too has its definite limits.[57] And there seems to be no place in the Torah per se to even begin this process of logical inference regarding Purim.[58]

The third-century Babylonian Sage, Samuel of Nehardea, expresses impatience with what he considers the earlier, inadequate attempts to infer the cele-

[52] See Novak, *The Election of Israel*, 174.

[53] See B. Megillah 14a; Y. Megillah 1.5/70d.

[54] B. Megillah 14a.

[55] See D. Novak, "Maimonides and the Science of the Law," *Jewish Law Association Studies*, ed. B. S. Jackson (Atlanta, Ga.: Scholars Press, 1990), 4:108ff.

[56] See Y. Pesahim 6.1/33a.

[57] See B. Shabbat 87a and Tos., s.v. "u-mah."

[58] For the permanent place of Purim in the Jewish tradition, see Y. Megillah 1.5/70d re Est. 9:28.

bration of Purim from various scriptural verses. He finds the basis for the celebration of the new holiday in the book of Esther's description of the popular acceptance of the rabbinically enacted holiday, namely, "they upheld it and accepted it" (*qiyyemu ve-qibblu*—Esther 9:27), which he interprets to mean: "in heaven (*le-ma'alah*) was upheld what they had accepted on earth (*le-mattah*)."[59] About a century later, another Babylonian Sage, Rava, said that only Samuel's explanation stands up to critical examination.[60] But the question to ask here is just *why* the ruling of the human court of Mordecai was accepted in heaven. Could one infer from this that Jews have the right to assume divine approval of any institution their authorities happen to make and they happen to accept?

The answer to this question can perhaps be seen in the fact that this same verse, "they upheld it and accepted it," is also employed by Rava elsewhere in the Talmud to explain the covenant itself.[61] There it mentions how God forced the Torah on the people of Israel at Mount Sinai. Even though this affirms that in principle the authority of the Torah as God's word is not contingent on human approval, nevertheless, in order for the covenant to be practically operative, the Torah does have to be accepted willingly by the people herself. Without that willing acceptance, there would be no one to either interpret or apply the words of the Torah. There "they upheld and they accepted" is taken to mean: They willingly upheld during the days of Mordecai and Esther what they had to accept in the days of Moses. Thus a verse that more narrowly refers to the celebration of Purim is now taken to refer to the whole covenant itself.

Yet, as one of the medieval commentators pointed out, there is room for both interpretations of the verse from Esther; they do not contradict each other.[62] In fact, not only do they not contradict each other, they are in conceptual harmony, for what we learn from the broader use of the verse is that the Jewish people during the time of the Persian Exile, when they lacked political sovereignty, still accepted the Torah in a new way. That is, instead of accepting it in fear just because of its divine source, they were now accepting it more in love because of its divine purpose. They accepted it because they now wanted to be in covenant with God, which is a desire that can be fulfilled only in intelligent freedom. But one of the results of this new commitment to the covenant, which was its historical renewal, is the justification of Purim as a celebration in harmony with the Torah and not as an anti-Torah or even para-Torah institution.

Because of this new commitment, the people actualized a right that was only a potential when they were simply living under direct divine rule through the prophets: the right to interpret and apply the law for the sake of its pur-

---

[59] B. Megillah 7a.
[60] Ibid.
[61] B. Shabbat 88a. Also, see Novak, *Jewish Social Ethics*, 28f.
[62] B. Megillah 7a and Tos. s.v. "le-khulhu."

poses.[63] One of the purposes of the Torah is to recognize and glorify God's saving acts, and that is what justifies an institution like the celebration of Purim. That right of interpretation and application is actualized by the full exercise of human reason, for it is human reason that discovers the purposes of the Torah and understands how they correspond to authentic human desires. The exercise of that reason is rooted in the people's desire to be in covenant with God, and it leads to their assurance that God desires to be in covenant with the people. The purposes of God and the purposes of the people are now taken to be quite similar, if not identical. Thus the Torah had at long last become truly covenantal inasmuch as the purposes of the Torah were now seen to be at least as important as the source of the Torah.[64] Upon the knowledge of these purposes much could be justifiably built. This unleashed a tremendous reservoir of Jewish creativity, which became quite apparent during the rabbinic period, the period that produced the Talmud. It was during this period that many new institutions (*taqqanot*) were introduced, which were justified by their being for the sake of the overall purposes of the Torah, even without ascertainable connection to any of the specific verses or words of the Torah text itself.[65]

The purposes of the Torah are twofold: they are either for the sake of God directly (*bein adam le-maqom*) or for the sake of God indirectly through humans (*bein adam le-havero*). In the case of those commandments directly pertaining to God, they are considered so much a part of the divine law that before their performance one actually utters the blessing that contains the words "Who has sanctified us by His commandments and commanded us to do such and such."[66] But how one can say that a commandment is commanded by God when it is really the result of human legislation? The Talmud answers this question by invoking the scriptural commandment to listen to the words of the Sages, "not to deviate (*lo tasur*) from them either to the right or to the left" (Deuteronomy 17:11).[67] However, that verse itself simply says that the legal rulings of the properly appointed legal authorities, which are about the law that has already been revealed and written in the Torah, are to be followed. Even when one expands the meaning of this authority to include laws made by these authorities themselves, that only indicates that the ultimate source of

---

[63] Because of this, the role of the Sage (*talmid hakham*) took on greater importance than that of the prophet (*navi*) inasmuch as the work of the Sages is more creative than the work of the prophets. See B. Baba Batra 12a; R. Judah Loewe of Prague (Maharal), *Gevurot ha-Shem*, ed. Krakow, intro., 2a; Hullin 5a and note of R. Zvi Hirsch Chajes (Maharats Chajes) thereon.

[64] See Maimonides, *Guide of the Perplexed*, 2.40.

[65] See David Weiss Halivni, *Peshat and Derash* (New York: Oxford University Press, 1991), 16ff.

[66] See Maimonides, *Mishneh Torah*: Berakhot, 11.2, and R. Joseph Karo, *Kesef Mishneh* thereon.

[67] B. Shabbat 23a.

their lawmaking power is in the revealed law of God.[68] But if that is the case, then the blessing should be a general blessing about being commanded to hearken to the commandment of the Elders (*mitsvat zeqenim*)—in general, as indeed one rabbinic source suggests.[69]

However, the reason, it seems to me, that the blessing is specific, designating the specific act as the law of God, is because the act is perceived to be what God himself *would have commanded* had he not left certain areas of the law to the constructions of human reason. Nevertheless, these constructions are not arbitrary in essence; rather, they are justified teleologically. They are designed either to protect the more general law from specific infringements of its scope (*gezerot*) or to give the purposes of the Torah the fullest possible reign.[70] As such, they make a claim on God to justify what has been legislated by human authorities *as if it were his own explicit law.*

In the area of interhuman relations we see the widest possible role for human reason. That is because so much of interhuman legislation requires natural-law-type reasoning, namely, reasoning based on considerations of human nature perceived by those with legislative and juridical authority.[71] Although there are specifically covenantal reasons for some of the interhuman legislation by the Rabbis, the natural law factor is never very far in the background.[72] For even here, it is an area where something originally interhuman becomes a factor in the God-human relationship without, however, its own interhuman quality being distorted in the process. That is the case because so much of what is dealt with in this area does not assume that the phenomena at hand are uniquely Jewish.

To see the ultimately covenantal character of this interhuman reality (which is the topic of the next three chapters), it has been important to see that its covenantal character would be lost unless we see how it fits into the base of the covenant, which is the relationship between God and humans, especially the relationship between God and the people of Israel. Without the constitution of that prior dimension, one could not very well appreciate how human rights, in the fullest sense, are best understood in the context of the covenant. The covenant is the highest purpose of created human existence.[73] And even those who cannot appropriate the whole covenant for themselves should, nevertheless, not lose sight of the fact that to discuss the rights of humans among themselves is always a partial view of a much larger reality. This now leads us into the second part of this book, which deals with interhuman relationships,

[68] See B. Berakhot 19b re Deut. 17:11.

[69] Y. Sukkah 3.4/53d. See B. Yevamot 20a and parallels.

[70] See Novak, *Natural Law in Judaism*, 105ff.

[71] See Nahmanides, *Commentary on the Torah*: Deut. 6:18; R. Vidal of Tolosa, *Magid Mishneh* on Maimonides, *Mishneh Torah*: Shekhenim, 14.5.

[72] See Novak, *Natural Law in Judaism*, 76ff.

[73] See Maimonides, *Mishneh Torah*: Isurei Biah, 14.2–4.

both those involving relationships of individual persons and the relationship between individual persons and the covenanted community. This is the area of Judaism of most interest to general political theory. But it must be remembered that, ultimately if not always immediately, political theory must become political theology to be authentically Jewish.[74] That does not mean that political/ ethical theory needs to be deduced from revelation, however. If that were the case, there would be no room for the idea of natural law in Judaism. And, as we shall see in the following chapters, natural law is an important component of the interhuman aspects of the covenant. Nevertheless, the fullness of human rights, for Jews, must be finally seen in the ontologically prior covenantal relationship between God and Israel, which makes even interhuman rights a matter of cosmic significance. Ethics must be finally grounded in ontology.

[74] The great French Jewish philosopher Emmanuel Levinas (d. 1995) asserted about human rights that they are "perhaps . . . God's original coming to the mind of man" ("The Rights of Man and the Rights of the Other," in *Outside the Subject*, translated by M. B. Smith [Stanford, Calif.: Stanford University Press, 1994], 117). But Levinas seems to confine the relationship with God to its ethical function. "This is the trace of God in man, or, more precisely, the point in reality at which the idea of God comes only to man . . . which is not the equivalent of some deduction of the rights of man on the basis of a prior Revelation. . . . The respect for those rights *does not proceed* from 'truths about God' already acquired elsewhere . . . recognized as supernatural" (118). Moreover, Levinas seems to accept Kant's notion of true, ethical, community as "a kingdom of ends" (122), differing with Kant only on the role of freedom. But without an ontological grounding (such as the one provided by covenantal theology), how does Levinas's God function as anything more than the postulate of pure practical reason that is God's function in Kantian ethics? (See Novak, *Natural Law in Judaism*, 82ff., for a critique of Levinas and other liberal Jewish thinkers on this point.)

CHAPTER V

Between Human Persons

PERSONAL MUTUALITY

Throughout the history of Judaism, two basic norms have been invoked in discussions of the rights and duties involved in relationships between individual persons. These basic norms are: (1) What is hateful to yourself, do not do to someone else; (2) You shall love your neighbor as yourself. The specific difference between the two norms is that the former is a negative precept and the latter a positive one. Their generic commonality is that they both prescribe a situation of mutuality: I am not to do to others what is not to be done to me by them, or I am to love others as I want to be loved by them. Each norm prescribes the right I want others to dutifully fulfill for me, which in turn is the duty others want me to rightfully fulfill for them.

In order to develop a coherent theory to cover the whole area of the claims individual persons may justly make on each other, at the outset two questions must be asked about the two basic norms cited above: (1) Are these norms essentially the same, that is, is the positive norm automatically deduced from the negative one and vice versa? (2) Are both norms based on an extension of fundamental self-interest, that is, is my concern for my own protection or my own welfare the basis from which my concern for the protection or welfare of others is to follow? How these two questions are answered will largely determine just how one develops a theory of interpersonal relationships within Judaism.

Maimonides seems to address these two questions with the matchless conceptual clarity he always brings to every question of law and theology. In distinguishing between duties humans owe to God and duties humans owe to one another, he writes:

> Some of the commandments pertain to the ordering of relationships of humans one with the other. For example . . . the commandment to love one another and not to harm one another. . . . If a person upholds the commandments that pertain to the ordering of relationships of humans one with the other, . . . he will attain as an end (*to'elet*) in this world good rapport (*hitnahagut tovah*) with humans. So, if he goes in this way and somebody else likewise, then he too will benefit (*yeheneh gam hu*) from that same end. . . . Note how Hillel the Elder, when the gentile said to him: "Teach me the Torah while [I am] standing on one foot," replied to him: "What is hateful to you, do not do to someone else."[1]

---

[1] *Commentary on the Mishnah*: Peah, 1.1, ed. Kafih, 55. Regarding human mutuality involving reciprocity, see B. Yevamot 117a re Prov. 27:17 and Rashi, s.v. "ve-rabbanan."

The generic mutuality that Maimonides sees governing the realm of the interhuman is distinguished from the lack of mutuality governing the realm of the divine-human relationship. The difference between the two realms is that in the interhuman realm both parties are essentially equal participants in the world they share in common, whereas in the divine-human relationship God and humans are essentially participants in the transcendent "world-to-come" (*olam ha-ba*), a world whose reality is now beyond us. Even though humans can practice the commandments that directly pertain to God, they are still doing so in this world nonetheless; hence, they are largely ignorant of what these commandments truly intend.[2] Moreover, even when humans do attain this transcendent realm, to which they have directed their action in this world, they will still be very much unequal to God.[3] They will only be living much closer to the knowledge of God than they could possibly have lived in this world. Human mutuality, then, can be seen in greater focus when it is shown in sharp contrast to the essential inequality between humans and God.

This human mutuality, for Maimonides, seems to consist of two things. One, it involves the avoidance of mutual harm coupled with the pursuit of mutual benefit. Two, it involves one projecting his or her own need for self-fulfillment onto other humans, what we would call "empathy" today. That empathy, then, is a requirement of self-fulfillment because one cannot fulfill oneself without being related to other humans. They too are striving to achieve the same thing for themselves, which they too cannot do alone. This mutual striving and mutual lack of self-sufficiency constitute the most immediate world for humans.[4]

It would seem that Maimonides does not essentially distinguish between the negative and the positive precepts we saw above, and that he regards love of self as being the foundation from which love of the human other is to follow. After all, Maimonides advocates a virtue-based ethic, one that sees "good" as the basic moral term. It designates what we all seek.[5] But that seeking begins with *me* seeking *my* good.[6] Nevertheless, despite the respect any opinion of Maimonides deserves, I think a more phenomenological investigation of the interhuman realm, both in general and especially in Judaism, might well have to take a different approach than that of Maimonides. Although one can very much appreciate his emphasis of the essential mutuality endemic in this realm,

---

[2] See *Mishneh Torah*: Teshuvah, 8.7 re B. Berakhot 34b on Isa. 64:3.

[3] *Mishneh Torah*: Teshurah, see 8.2 re B. Berakhot 17a on Exod. 24:11, where Maimonides states that humans who have attained the world-to-come are "like ministering angels" (*ke-mala'akhei ha-sharet*), i.e., they are still subordinate to God. See *Mishneh Torah*: Yesodei ha-Torah, 2.7, and *Guide of the Perplexed*, 2.6.

[4] See T. Megillah 3.16 and T. Ketubot 7.5–6 re Eccl. 7:2; M. Ketubot 7.5; Y. Ketubot 7.5/31b; B. Ketubot 71b–72a and parallels; Maimonides, *Mishneh Torah*: Ishut, 13.11.

[5] See Aristotle, *Nicomachean Ethics*, 1094a1.

[6] For the primacy of virtue in Maimonides' ethics, see *Commentary on the Mishnah*: Avot, intro. (*Shemonah Perqaqim*), chap. 4, p. 252. See *Mishneh Torah*: Teshuvah, 8.1, 7 re Ps. 27:13. Cf. *Guide of the Perplexed*, 1.2.

one might constitute it quite differently than he did. This will lead us to make a greater distinction than did Maimonides between the negative precept not to harm another and the positive precept to love one another. It will also lead to an argument against any primacy of self-love at all.

WHAT IS HATEFUL TO YOU

The first presentation of the norm "what is hateful to yourself, do not do to another" is found in one of the most famous narratives in the Talmud.[7] The overall purpose of the narrative is to contrast the open, accepting personality of the first century C.E. Sage, Hillel the Elder, with the rigid, rejecting personality of his contemporary colleague, Shammai. A number of anecdotes are told to illustrate this point. In one of them, a certain gentile comes to Shammai with the request: "Convert me on the condition that you teach me the whole Torah while I stand on one foot." The impatient Shammai, sensing the absurdity of this request, angrily drives the impudent gentile away. But Hillel does convert him by responding to his challenge as follows: "What is hateful (*sani*) to yourself, do not do to another (*le-haverakh*). This is the whole Torah; the rest is its commentary (*pirushah*). Go and learn."

Now, the obvious problem with this terse response is that it does not seem to be true. Surely, Judaism contains many other norms, all of which are no less important than this one. In fact, giving a random sampling of this very multiplicity of norms is itself a requirement for those instructing candidates for conversion to Judaism.[8] Furthermore, why pick a norm that is by no means unique to Judaism for someone proposing to make the most radical change possible by Jewish standards, that is, "being reborn"?[9] It only seems to be the most evident norm of a universal morality, its barest minimum: Do no harm.[10] Would it not have been far more correct to have responded to this gentile with the norm "you shall love the Lord your God . . . with your whole life" (Deuteronomy 6:5), which is taken to be the covenantal requirement to die as a martyr rather than personally give up the Torah?[11] Certainly, this is a demand that could only be made of a Jew; hence it indicates most clearly what being a Jew entails.[12]

---

[7] B. Shabbat 31a.

[8] See B. Yevamot 47a.

[9] See B. Yevamot 22a and parallels.

[10] Thus the *Corpus Juris Civilis* of Justinian speaks of the basis of all law as "to live honorably: not to harm another (*alterum non laedere*); to give each his own (*summ cuique tribuere*)" (1.1.3). Cf. Plato, *Republic*, 331C; Thomas Aquinas, *Summa Theologiae*, 2/1, q. 95, a. 3.

[11] B. Berakhot 61b re Deut. 6:5.

[12] See Maimonides, *Mishneh Torah*: Yesodei ha-Torah, 5.1, and Melakhim, 10.2 (and Radbaz thereon) re B. Sanhedrin 74a–b on Lev. 22:32.

Nevertheless, what Hillel seems to be saying is that the very moral impetus to respond to the most evident presence of the human other standing before yourself logically leads to the impetus to respond to the less evident call of the divine presence speaking in the Torah.[13] The latter is the "commentary" on the former. Concern for the claim of the human other upon oneself ultimately leads to the supreme divine claim on all humans. At first, the human claim mediates the divine claim. In authentic Pharisaic-Rabbinic teaching, the commentary is not what supplements the text but, rather, what grounds it.[14] Only in the commentary does one truly hear what the text essentially means to say. In the case at hand, I think the precise determination of the text of what might be called "the norm of human mutuality" chosen by Hillel is important.

Following our assumption that every right has its correlative duty and every duty its correlative right, and that rights generate the duties that are to respond to their personal claims, where is the originating right in the case of the norm of human mutuality? It would seem that the originating right lies in my claim on others not to harm me.[15] Originally, I come into the world crying. I come into the world not so much requesting what is good *for* me but, rather, protesting the harm that others can easily do *to* me. Before I have even learned what is good for me, I intuitively know what can harm me. (Indeed, the very touch of another person is feared as harmful until I learn that it can also be beneficial.) Initially, I can only receive from others; I cannot as yet give them anything. I am still basically a terminal of experience rather than the source of any action yet. And experience is initially negative; fear is its most primary response. Action is primarily positive; love is its most primary motive, as we shall see later. What happens to me comes before what I can do anything to anyone else. I fear before I love.[16]

Because of this order, I first learn of my own capacity to act upon others when I learn that the harm I fear for myself I myself can also inflict upon others. I not only cry, but I now can hear their cry as well.[17] Being able to do more entails more demands upon me. I am becoming a participant in a common world, a participation that will be complete only when I can do as much as I can experience, when I can give as much as I can take. Thus the claim I make upon others not to harm me is now heard as their claim upon me not to harm them. To be able to act upon others, which means to be able to engage in a

---

[13] See B. Shabbat 31a, Rashi, s.v. "d'alakh" re Prov. 27:10.

[14] See David Weiss Halivni, *Peshat and Derash* (New York: Oxford University Press, 1991), 3ff.

[15] See Emmanuel Levinas, *Totality and Infinity*, trans. A. Lingis (Pittsburgh: Duquesne University Press, 1969), 232ff.

[16] For the phenomenological priority of fear over love, see Maimonides, *Mishneh Torah*: Teshuvah, 10.5.

[17] See Gen. 4:10 for the first moral protest in the world, which is "the voice of your brother's blood crying (*tso'aqim*) to me."

transaction *with* them, now signifies that the initial right I exercise upon others, calling for their dutiful response *to* me, must reverberate as a dutiful response *from* me to their right. In other words, only when becoming aware of others being the experiencing subject I am, am I capable of doing to them what I have already requested from them. At the most primary level, that means not doing to them what I cry that they not do to me. This personal transaction is well described by the contemporary French Protestant philosopher Paul Ricoeur in his analysis of what many have called the Golden Rule.

> Acting and suffering then seem to be distributed between two different protagonists: the agent and the patient, the latter appearing as the potential victim of the former. But because of the reversibility of the roles, each agent is the patient of the other. Inasmuch as one is affected by the power over one exerted by the other, the agent is invested under the rule of reciprocity, which the rule of justice will transform into a rule of equality.[18]

RETALIATION

The reciprocity that becomes equality comes out in what many have seen as the elementary right of retaliation, namely, the right to respond to harm that has been done to me in equal measure. As we shall see in the next chapter, society in its judicial function largely insists that it fulfill this right for me rather than my doing so for myself. Here it is assumed that because of my personal trauma, I will be unable to retaliate in equal measure, that I will inevitably overreact. Thus the injustice committed against me will inevitably lead to another injustice being committed against my erstwhile persecutor instead of to just retribution as a true resolution of the original crime. But even though the enforcement of this right has been transferred from an individual to society, the right itself remains intact in essence.

If I claim a right of retaliation, so that the one who has harmed me will "not get away with it," and so that the consequences of such an act will be as harmful to the one who has perpetuated it as it has been to me who has suffered it, then it follows that someone else has the very same right under similar circumstances. It seems that I learn not to harm others from the warning that when I do so, I have just forfeited my own right to protection from their harming me.[19] I cannot claim protection from those others whom I have not protected from my own aggression. Thus Cain, the first murderer, bemoans the fact that "whoever finds me will slay me" (Genesis 4:14). Because he is pun-

---

[18] *Oneself as Another*, trans. K. Blamey (Chicago: University of Chicago Press, 1992), 330. See also his *Fallible Man*, trans. C. Kelbley (Chicago: Henry Regnery, 1967), 30.

[19] See *Sifre*: Devarim, no. 293, ed. Finkelstein, 312 and n. 1 thereon; Maimonides, *Mishneh Torah*: Rotseah, 1.7 re B. Sanhedrin 49a.

ished for his crime, it can be assumed that he knew in advance that what he did was wrong.[20] But because he did not know in advance what the exact punishment for his crime would be could be the reason why the punishment he does receive from God is not commensurate with the crime he committed: exile rather than death.[21] After that, though, the commensurate punishment is something that is now evident to everyone. "Whosoever sheds human blood, by humans shall his blood be shed" (Genesis 9:6).[22]

The right to retaliation can also be seen as underlying the right to self-defense. The norm here is expressed in rabbinic sources as: "If someone comes to kill you, kill him first."[23] This norm is not based on the primacy of self-interest, however, for everyone has the duty to prevent an imminent assault on anyone else.[24] If it can be done by maiming the assailant, that is always to be the first recourse. But if the only way to save the would-be victim is to kill the assailant, then killing him or her is mandated.[25] This is inferred from the right to retaliate in the sense that it is better to prevent an assault before it actually occurs, even by the very same means intended by the assailant, than to retaliate after the assault has already taken place,[26] For after the assault has taken place, the retaliation cannot bring about any restitution of what the victim has lost. The right to protection can thus be derived a fortiori from the right to retaliation. In the case of a would-be assailant, the one who is physically prepared to commit his or her assault imminently has thereby forfeited any right to protection. In this situation, that right now belongs solely to the innocent would-be victim of the assault about to begin.

SELF-INTEREST AND SELF-LOVE

Most political theories that see rights as basic assume that the fundamental motive for all action is self-interest. And at the bottom of this self-interest is the irreducible fact of self-love.[27] It is because I love myself that I act on my own behalf. Others are taken into consideration to the extent that my self-love

[20] See D. Novak, *Natural Law in Judaism* (Cambridge: Cambridge University Press, 1998), 31ff.

[21] Along these lines, see B. Sanhedrin 41a re Deut. 17:6; Hullin 41a and Rashi, s.v. "m'ai"; Maimonides, *Mishneh Torah*: Sanhedrin, 12.2.

[22] See *Mekhilta*: Yitro, ed. Horovitz-Rabin, 232.

[23] B. Sanhedrin 72a. For the more difficult question of determining an imminent danger to the life and liberty of the community, see B. Sotah 44b.

[24] B. Sanhedrin 73a re Lev. 19:16; Maimonides, *Mishneh Torah*: Rotseah, 1.6.

[25] B. Sanhedrin 49a.

[26] Along these lines, cf. M. Makkot 1.6 re Deut. 19:19.

[27] See, e.g., John Rawls, *A Theory of Justice* (Cambridge: Harvard University Press, 1971), 190, 463.

can include them.[28] Narcissism, then, would be the only type of self-love that could not include anyone else in its orbit. It differs from a more "healthy" self-love only in degree, not in kind. It is because of self-love that I exercise my rights. Others do the same. Because we share a common world, we all have to negotiate our rights so that minimally we do not harm one another and maximally we help one another get what each of us wants for himself or herself.

But self-love contains a problem so elementary as to question its very logic. The problem is that of reflexive action. The general fallacy was best exposed by Plato when he wrote: "Now the phrase 'master of himself' (*kreittō hauton*) is an absurdity, is it not? For he who is master of himself would also be subject to himself, and he who is subject to himself would be master ... the same person (*ho autos*)."[29] In other words, in any relation of the self to itself, have we not excluded the separation of subject and object that is necessary in any transitive act? And that is all the more so in any transaction, where one person is acting with another person. Moreover, if the subject is by definition not-the-object, and the object not-the-subject, then does any such reflexive act not finally entail the violation of the law of contradiction by falling into the fallacy of the "excluded middle" ($A = {\sim}A$)?[30] Plato himself solves the problem by seeing a fundamental division within the soul: the better, rational part is what is to rule the lesser, nonrational parts. As for love, that is not a relation within the soul but one between its better part and the Good beyond itself toward which it aspires.[31] Therefore, for Plato, there is no self-love. The best part of the soul loves what is the source and end of all goodness, its own included.[32] But my *self* can only be my consciousness here and now; it can only be a subject, never an object.

From a Jewish point of view, one could certainly differ with Plato's division of the person into better and worse parts. And one could differ with him as to who or what is the ultimate object of our love.[33] But one could certainly agree

---

[28] Thus even David Hume, who condemns self-love as morally inadequate, does so only when it is at the level of immediate (therefore "selfish") gratification, i.e., when it is exclusive and not extensive. Nevertheless, it is still the starting point of all affection. See *An Inquiry Concerning the Principles of Morals* ed. C. W. Hendel (New York: Liberal Arts Press, 1957), app. 2. 113; cf. 47; also, *A Treatise of Human Nature*, ed. L. A. Selby-Bigge (Oxford: Clarendon Press, 1888), 3.2.2, p. 487.

[29] *Republic*, trans. P. Shorey (Cambridge: Harvard University Press 1930), 431A, 1:358–59. See *Laws*, 731E. Cf. Aristotle, *Nicomachean Ethics*, 1133b6, 1166a1, 30–35, 1168b34.

[30] See Aristotle, *Prior Analytics*, 66a25ff., cf. *Metaphysics*, 1072b 20–30.

[31] See *Republic*, 490A–B.

[32] See *Symposium*, 211C–D.

[33] The difference seems to be as follows: When the object of our love is unresponsive, then we do not relate with it as another person. As such, our desire becomes the desire for union with that object, what has been called *unio mystica*. But when God's love for us is not only original but responsive to our love for God, i.e., covenantal, then any *unio mystica* would destroy both persons in the covenantal relationship. Here two can never become one. As such, Pascal was right when

with him on logical, ontological, and anthropological grounds that oneself is not the object of one's love, and that love is the most profound act of which any person is capable. Yet one does not act on his or her own behalf all the time. And, as we have seen, we initially exercise our rights/claims on our own behalf. How, then, do we separate self-interest from self-love?

Self-interest lies at the beginning of the exercise of rights. It is, indeed, the self as a whole acting on behalf of a part, like, for example, when I act on behalf of the advancement of my career. My career is an important part of me, but I am certainly more than my career. But self-love by its total rather than partial claims seems to be literally absurd. The only solution to that absurdity is to dissolve the self into differing, antithetical parts. But that involves the philosophical problem of dualism, and the theological problem of the dispensability of the body (which we shall examine in the next section).

The question now to be asked is: For whose benefit do I act when exercising my right to anything? It must be assumed that ultimately everything I do is for the sake of those I love. And it must be assumed that love as an act is motivated by the desire to benefit its own object. Indeed, as we have seen in the previous two chapters, love is a relationship where both persons involved in it desire each other's love. Hence, when I make a claim on someone else I am doing so for the sake of that person or some other person whom I love. Whatever benefit to myself I do experience is my pleasure in doing what is right. It is a secondary effect. It is reflexive, but not the primary intention of the act itself. It is an "accompaniment," as Plato and Aristotle point out in their powerful arguments against pleasure being a prime moral motive.[34] Pleasure is an immanent reverberation of the primary thrust of the act, which is transcendent.[35] In the case of love, which is certainly more than the pleasure it sometimes (but not always) brings, I claim love from someone else and he or she claims love from me. Unrequited love is tragic. In loving someone else, I always risk that my love might not entice his or her desire. At times of authentic love, which makes total claims, both lovers are involved in a transaction that is simultaneously giving and taking for both of them and that they hope will never end. That is unlike a commercial type exchange with someone I do not love, for that involves a tertium quid: a giving of something and a taking of something else by both sides. And it also involves a terminus ad quem: there is a definite

---

he famously wrote that the God of Abraham, Isaac, and Jacob is not the God of the philosophers. Along the lines of the nontransactional God of the philosophers, see, e.g., Plato, *Symposium*, 201B; Aristotle, *Metaphysics*, 1072a25–35; H. A. Wolfson, *The Philosophy of Spinoza* (Cambridge: Harvard University Press, 1934), 2:285ff. In all of the above, the lower loves the higher, but the higher does not love the lower.

[34] See Plato, *Philebus*, 60Dff.; Aristotle, *Nicomachean Ethics*, 1172b25ff.

[35] See M. Avot 1.3 and *Avot de-Rabbi Nathan*, A, chap. 5, ed. Schechter, 13b; also, Menahot 99b and Tos., s.v. "lo."

conclusion to the exchange desired by both parties in advance.[36] It is a contract, not the open-ended covenant that originates in and is sustained by love.[37]

Furthermore, when I make a claim on someone for something less than their love, as would be the case, let us say, in a claim on someone for material assistance, I am still not making that claim for myself. Instead, I am making it for the sake of those whom I love. And even when I make such a claim for myself alone prima facie, when it is my stomach I need to fill, this claim is ultimately so that I might have life and health for the sake of serving those whom I love. As we have seen in the previous chapters, the final and most complete object of my love is God, for whom both my life and my death are to be a sacrifice. Indeed, it could well be said that those who have no one else to love have no real reason to live either. Thus self-interest is essentially instrumental. Its purpose is to enable the person to give himself or herself to those who justly claim his or her love. Self-interest is always to be a penultimate end. So, the most famous Jewish expression of self-interest should be read as follows: "If I am not for me (*ani li*) who is for me?" (I must first exercise my own claims on others as a subject) "But when I am for myself (*l'atsmi*), what am I?" (As the object of all that I do, I lose my own coherent identity.)[38]

The above distinction between self-interest and self-love, and the necessary connection of self-interest and authentically transactional love, might enable us to interpret a famous case in rabbinic literature differently from the way it is usually interpreted.

Two people were traveling in the wilderness, and only one of them had a flask of water in hand. If that one would drink the water, he would be able to reach a human settlement (*le-yishuv*); but if both of them would drink the water, both of them would die [before reaching the settlement]. Ben Peturi concluded from the meaning of the verse (*darash*) the following: Let both of them drink the water and die because Scripture states "and your brother shall live with you (*imakh*)" (Leviticus 25:36). But Rabbi Akibah said to him: "and your brother shall live with you" [means]: your life takes precedence (*qodmim*) over the life of someone else (*haverakh*).[39]

There are two basic versions of this case in rabbinic literature, and they should be examined together to get a fuller theoretical grasp on the same moral problem each presents respectively. The version quoted above is from the earlier text, *Sifra*. In the later version in the Babylonian Talmud, only

---

[36] See Aristotle, *Nicomachean Ethics*, 1156a15ff.

[37] See D. Novak, *Jewish Social Ethics* (New York: Oxford University Press, 1992), 33ff.; *The Election of Israel* (Cambridge: Cambridge University Press, 1995), 138ff.

[38] M. Avot 1.14.

[39] *Sifra*: Behar, ed. Weiss, 109c. See E. E. Urbach, *Halakhah* (Jerusalem: Yad le-Talmud, 1984), 138.

Rabbi Akibah's opinion is seen as being derived from the interpretation of Leviticus 25:36. Ben Peturi's opinion there is based on conceptual reasoning, namely, "it is better (*mutav*) that they both drink the water and die than one should see the death of his colleague (*havero*)."[40] Thus combining the two versions, we now have both an exegetical reason and a conceptual reason for the practical conclusion of Ben Peturi.[41] And, it would seem that we also have a conceptual reason for the conclusion of Rabbi Akibah in addition to his exegetical reason: my life takes precedence over the life of anyone else. Indeed, this conceptual reason is even more important for Rabbi Akibah's conclusion than is that of Ben Peturi for his conclusion inasmuch as "with you" (*imakh*) seems to imply equality between the two parties rather than the priority of one over the other.[42]

Ben Peturi's conceptual position is the clearer of the two: One life, even my own life, is not to be saved at the expense of another life. All lives are absolutely equal. But what is Rabbi Akibah's reason? One could say that it is based on the priority of self-love. Thus a medieval French exegete, Rabbi Joseph Bekhor Shor, commenting on the verse "You shall love your neighbor as yourself" (Leviticus 19:18), connected its meaning to Rabbi Akibah's interpretation of "with you" here. He writes: "It does not say that one should love another (*aher*) like himself (*kemo atsmo*), . . . for if that were so, 'your neighbor' should have been preceded by the word *et* [which designates the direct object]."[43] He then points out that the term "your neighbor" is preceded by a preposition designating the indirect object—literally, "to your neighbor" (*le-re'akha*). Hence its meaning seems to be: Extend your love of yourself to subsequently include others beside yourself.

Bekhor Shor's interpretation is certainly plausible both exegetically and conceptually. Nevertheless, it is problematic theologically. How could I move up from the love of myself to the love of God that is to be greater than the love of myself? Thus, for example, if I die for myself—even when convinced that this is an act of self-love—that suicide is still in essence an act of pro-

---

[40] B. Baba Metsia 62a. Of course, if both persons could safely share the water, i.e., there is enough to enable both of them to reach a human settlement, then the water must be shared by its owner, even by force. The owner of the water may claim payment, however, for whatever loss he incurs after both persons have reached safety. See T. Baba Kama 10.28; Y. Baba Kama 10.4/7c; my late revered teacher R. Saul Lieberman, *Tosefta Kifshuta*: Nezikin (New York: Jewish Theological Seminary of America, 1988), 128; B. Baba Kama 60b and Tos., s.v. "mahu"; B. Baba Kama 117b; B. Sanhedrin 74a; Maimonides, *Mishneh Torah*: Hovel u-Maziq, 8.2.

[41] This combination is presented in a medieval Yemenite midrash, *Midrash ha-Gadol*: Leviticus, ed. Rabinowitz, 638.

[42] See Malbim, *Commentary on the Torah*: Leviticus—Qedoshim, no. 32; Behar, no. 75; also, B. Berakhot 45a re Ps. 34:4.

[43] *Commentary on the Torah*: Lev. 19:18, ed. Nevo, 214. The same connection is also made in the respective Torah commentaries of Hizquni, Nahmanides, and Gersonides (Ralbag, ed. Venice, 162a). See also R. Samuel Edels (Maharsha), *Hiddushei Aggadot*: B. Shabbat 31a.

scribed homicide; if I die as a martyr for God because I love him, that is an act of the greatest holiness (*qiddush ha-shem*).[44] So too when I live for myself. In other words, when love of self is foundational, it not only does not lead up to the love of God, it turns one away from the love of God to the idolatrous worship of the ideal self I have created for myself. Therefore, it would seem that it is sounder theology to assume that all human lives are equal as equal creatures made in the image of God, and that this equality is highlighted by our mutual human inequality with God.[45] It is when I accept my essential equality with other persons on earth that I am more profoundly moved to look toward heaven for the One who is greater than the world and anyone in it: my finite, mortal self or others like me.

I think that this theological insight enables us to interpret the ethical debate between Ben Peturi and Rabbi Akibah as follows: Both Sages agree in general that all human lives are equal; they disagree when that equality leads to mutual death. For Rabbi Akibah, the priority is the saving of a human life, even if an unintended result of saving *this* life is to abandon *that* other life to death. The criterion for whose life is to be saved is not "my life over your life" but, rather, *the person whose life is most proximate to the person who can save but one life*. As such, the key term in Rabbi Akibah's opinion is not "your life" but, rather, "takes precedence" (*qodmim*). It is similar to the phrase, "whoever comes first (*kol ha-qodem*) . . . is entitled (*zakhah*) to benefit first."[46] It is not that self-love is the basis for the priority insisted upon by Rabbi Akibah. On this point he and Ben Peturi can be seen to agree. But in the case at hand, the closest life to be saved *happens to be my own*. That closest life must be saved no matter what. As the great modern Hebrew essayist Ahad Ha'Am (d. 1927) argued in an insightful analysis of this text: "Justice says that whoever is able should save himself because every person's life is a deposit (*piqadon*) given to him to guard, and guarding what has been deposited with you takes precedence over what has been deposited with someone else."[47] However, if this

---

[44] See *Beresheet Rabbah* 34.13; also, D. Novak, *Law and Theology in Judaism* (New York: KTAV, 1974), 1:80ff.

[45] R. Samuel Edels (Maharsha), in *Hiddushei Aggadot*: B. Baba Kama 30a, divides the objects of obligation into three: (1) God, (2) other humans, and (3) self. Elsewhere (*Hiddushei Aggadot*: B. Sanhedrin 6b), the order is: (1) God, (2) self, (3) other humans. However, Israel Schepansky, in *Ha-Taqqanot be-Yisrael* (Jerusalem: Mosad ha-Rav Kook, 1992), 2:318f., rightly notes that in the rabbinic and medieval (*rish'onim*) sources, there is no real distinction made between obligations to other humans and obligations to oneself, citing M. Avot 4.1 especially. Schepansky takes issue with the comment of R. Elijah of Vilna (Gra), on Isa. 1:2 (who seems to be following the earlier view of R. Edels on B. Baba Kama 30a).—What distinguishes the view of R. Edels, R. Elijah, et al. from modern liberal views of self-love, however, is that in their view, self-love is not foundational. The love for God is always primary.

[46] M. Sanhedrin 1.4; also, M. Baba Kama 3.3.

[47] "Al Shtei ha-Se'ipim" (1910), *Kol Kitvei Ahad Ha'Am*, 2nd ed. (Tel Aviv: Dvir, 1949), 373. Of course, the idea of a "deposit" presupposes a "depositor" (*mafqeed*—see, e.g., Isa. 62:6; *Bere-*

priority of the self would be the moral conclusion in every case, then self-love would seem to be the simpler explanation for Rabbi Akibah's position, following Bekhor Shor's theory. To avoid that conclusion, we must discover at least one similar life-and-death case where self-love is clearly not the determining principle, and then see how another principle more adequately explains *both* this case *and* the flask of water case.

Such a case would be where someone else's life is more proximate to my own rescuing capacity than my own life is. If so, it would take precedence even over my own life. Along these lines, the Talmud presents a case where a powerful official commanded someone to kill somebody else, and if he would not do so, then this official would kill him. Self-love would indicate that his life takes precedence over the life of this potential victim. But the talmudic conclusion is that the person so commanded is to die rather than comply with this lethal command. The reason given, which is conceptual and not exegetical, is stated in the form of a rhetorical question: "How could you possibly think that your blood is redder, perhaps that man's blood is redder!"[48] What this means theoretically is that I am not to regard myself as superior to anyone else in a life-threatening situation. As Ahad Ha'Am put it quite well: "Saving your life (*piquah nefesh*) does not entitle you to violate the prohibition 'you shall not murder' [Exodus 20:13]; go and be killed rather than become a killer yourself."[49]

The principle of proximity to the means of rescue, just presented above as the theory behind Rabbi Akibah's ruling in the flask of water case, works in the case of the lethal command as well; disobedience of this command by passive resistance rather than obeying it actively is the more proximate option. It is like the talmudic preference of omission: "sitting and doing nothing" (*shev ve'al ta'aseh*)—to commission: "getting up and doing something" (*qoom aseh*) in cases of wrongdoing.[50] As such, the life of the would-be victim takes precedence over the life of the would-be murderer. In Jewish law, this proximity principle is widely operative.[51]

Understanding how the proximity principle operates could well save us from a widely held misinterpretation of the locus classicus in rabbinic literature on abortion. "When a woman is in hard labor, the fetus is to be cut up inside her and extracted limb by limb. That is because her life takes precedence (*qodmin*) over its life. But if most of his body is already outside her body, then he is not to be harmed. That is because one life (*nefesh*) is not to be pushed away (*dohin*)

---

sheet Rabbah 53.5 re Gen. 21:1; *Yalqut Shimoni*: Proverbs, no. 964), which is a point the nontheistic Ahad Ha'Am assiduously avoided. It shows that Jewish ethics cannot be fully separated from its roots in Jewish theology.

[48] B. Pesahim 25b (see Rashi, s.v. "m'ai hazit" thereon) and B. Sanhedrin 74a.

[49] "Al Shtei ha-Se'ipim," 373. Along these lines, see *Vayiqra Rabbah* 27.5 re Eccl. 3:15.

[50] For the use of these terms, see B. Yevamot 90a–b; B. Sanhedrin 58b–59a. See also B. Sanhedrin 74b and Tos., s.v. "ve-ha"; B. Pesahim 25b and Tos., s.v. "af."

[51] See, e.g., M. Baba Metsia 2.11, where it is assumed that my gaining the world-to-come through Torah study is more proximate than my having gained this world through my birth.

for the sake of another life."[52] The misinterpretation of this text is usually based on a comment on the first half of the text by the medieval French exegete Rashi, who stated that the fetus in utero is "not a life" (*l'av nefesh hu*).[53] Most of the recent moral debate over abortion has centered around the question of whether or not the fetus is a "person." Assuming that the Hebrew word *nefesh* functions like the English word *person*, it is inferred from this text and Rashi's comment on it that, according to Jewish law, the fetus is not a person.[54] Therefore, it is concluded: abortion is not murder. That in general is the logic of those who want to invoke Judaism in favor of what is now called the "pro-choice" position. For them, the fetus does not have what is now called a "right to life." Only the mother has the right to either let it live or kill it.

However, this logic is dangerous because the basic premise is false. The fact is that the fetus is a person with a right to life. For example, a pregnant woman's duty to fast on the Day of Atonement (*yom kippur*) is set aside if she has a strong desire to eat.[55] The same Rashi, whose view above is invoked as a categorical definition of personhood, comments here that this desire is the desire of the fetus (*ve-hu mit'aveh*), which its mother's body expresses for it, as it were.[56] Thus her desire to eat is on behalf of both their lives.[57] So, the

---

[52] M. Ohalot 7.6.

[53] B. Sanhedrin 72b, s.v. "yatsa ro'sho."

[54] See, e.g., R. Isaac Klein, "Teshuvah on Abortion," in *Conservative Judaism and Jewish Law*, ed. S. Siegel with E. B. Gertel (New York: Rabbinical Assembly, 1977), 259, who makes that assumption, even though finally affirming the traditional ban on nontherapeutic abortions (263). However, Jewish ethicists, unlike R. Klein (d. 1979), who are not committed to the authority of the Halakhah, have used this comment of Rashi to argue for the permissibility of elective abortion.—On this point, Maimonides' designation of the fetus threatening its mother's life "like a pursuer after her" (*ke-rodef ahareha*—*Mishneh Torah*: Rotseah, 1.9 re B. Sanhedrin 72b) adds an important conceptual development: The fetus only loses its "personal" right to life—as does any other pursuer (as we saw earlier)—when it puts its host (its mother's body) in imminent danger. This right, like any other human right, is never totally absolute. The definition of personhood (*nefesh*) is functional, not substantial. Furthermore, even if the fetus is taken to be part of its mother's body (B. Sanhedrin 80b; cf. Tos., s.v. "ubar" thereon), one is not allowed to amputate a part of her body unless that amputation is required to save her life (see Maimonides, *Mishneh Torah*: Mamrim, 2.4). Anything less than that is prohibited mutilation, either by oneself or by someone else (B. Baba Kama 91b).

[55] M. Yoma 8.5.

[56] B. Yoma 82a, s.v. "ubrah." See also T. Taaniyot 2.14; Y. Taanit 1.5/64c; Maimonides, *Mishneh Torah*: Taaniyot, 3.5. A counterexample that is sometimes cited is from M. Arakhin 1.4, which deals with the execution of a pregnant woman guilty of a capital crime, where the fetus's life is not taken to be a mitigating factor unless it is already moving down the birth canal. Rashi (Arakhin 7a, s.v. "she-teled") explains that this is not a concern because the mother and the fetus are still "one body" (*de-had gufa hu*). However, earlier, Rashi points out (6b, s.v. "peturin") that this applies only to Jewish capital punishment, which implies that one may not use it by analogy to decide any other normative issue. There is a general talmudic principle that inferences are not to be drawn from laws of punishment (*ein onshin min ha-din*—B. Sanhedrin 54a and parallels). See R. Jacob Reischer, *Teshuvot Shevut Yaaqov*: Yoreh Deah, 2, no. 82.

[57] Along these lines of the interdependence of two bodies having a common need, see B. Yevamot 80a–b and Rashi (80b), s.v. "mipnei ha-sakkanah"; also, Y. Yoma 8.4/45a re Ps. 58:4.

point is that *only* when the fetus is a mortal threat to its mother is its right to life set aside in order to save her life. Thus our primary intent is not to kill the fetus but to save the mother. And here the reason is seen in the term "takes precedence" (*qodmin*). The mother's life takes precedence when the fetus is still in utero because here and now her body is the more proximate one to be saved when only one endangered body can be saved.[58] Her body is revealed; its body is concealed. But when both bodies are equally revealed to us, then as Maimonides put it, "this is the nature of the world" (*tiv'o shel olam*), which is like our saying, "let nature take its course."[59] That is, we are not to prefer one life over the other; both are to be left alone, as it were, because there is no basis for preferring one over the other. When both bodies are equally before us, as the Palestinian Talmud puts it, "we do not know who is killing (*horeg*) whom."[60]

The principle of proximity has been formulated here in order to dispel the notion that the cases in which one is allowed to act in his or her self-interest are based on a principle of self-love. This is especially pertinent in the proscription of elective abortion as bloodshed (which is a somewhat wider legal category than legally prosecutable murder).[61] Any case where it is permitted is where it is mandated to save the mother. The only real debate among traditional authorities is how widely or narrowly to interpret the condition of maternal threat.[62] It is a dispensation, and like all dispensations from the normal rule, the burden of proof is on the accuser, that is, the one who proposes an exception to the normal rule.[63] There is no right to abortion. There is only the right to save a human life, whether one's own life or the life of another. That right is exercised as a duty to save one's own life when one is disinclined to do so, and it is exercised as a duty on behalf of someone else, who is either unable or unwilling to exercise it for himself or herself.[64] Abortion is permitted only

[58] See Novak, *Law and Theology in Judaism* 1:114ff. For a thorough overview of the rabbinic response on abortion, see J. D. Bleich, "Abortion in Halakhic Literature," in *Jewish Bioethics*, ed. J. D. Bleich and F. Rosner (New York: Hebrew Publishing Co., 1979), 134ff.

[59] *Mishneh Torah*: Rotseah, 1.9.

[60] Y. Shabbat 14.4/14d.

[61] See B. Sanhedrin 57b re Gen. 9:6 for the notion of "bloodshed" (*shefikhut damim*). However, there are cases where someone who committed intentional murder cannot be executed, e.g., when the victim is already suffering from a fatal wound (B. Sanhedrin, 78a and Tos., s.v. "be-goses"). In this case, one cannot be sure which wound was the actual cause of death (see B. Makkot 7a). The benefit of the doubt is to be in favor of the life before us, which is that of the perpetuator (see B. Sanhedrin 79a and parallels). Nevertheless, there is no doubt that the one intending to shed innocent human blood is guilty, even if he or she can escape capital punishment through what is, in effect, a legal loophole (see M. Shabbat 23.5; B. Shabbat 151b; Maimonides, *Mishneh Torah*: Rotseah, 1.1, 4.6–9).

[62] See D. M. Feldman, *Birth Control in Jewish Law* (New York: New York University Press, 1968), 275ff.

[63] See B. Baba Kama 46a–b (re Exod. 24:14) and parallels.

[64] See M. Eruvin 7.11; B. Ketubot 11a.

as a right or mandated as a duty in cases where only one life out of two lives can be saved.

In the end, the emphasis of self-love as *the* moral foundation leads to abuses of any other person who does not contribute to my self-interest—and that includes abuses not only of the rights of other individual persons, but also abuses of the rights of the community as a collective person, as we shall see in the next chapter. And it ultimately leads all the way up to abuses of the rights of God, the prime person in whose image all lesser persons are created. Inevitably, when self-love is taken as foundational, there are more persons who are a threat to it than there are persons who are useful for it.[65]

RIGHTS AND SELF-INTEREST ALONE

Now that we have separated self-interest from self-love, we are in a better position to understand the truly legitimate role of self-interest as *an* exercise of my rights as an individual person. We can now address the issue of the right of *either* exercising *or* waiving a right, that is, to make a claim or not to make a claim on others. For some liberals, that right becomes *the* right from which all other rights flow.[66] It is the right to make claims based only on one's own autonomous will. That always entails the right of refusal. This, of course, hearkens back to the problem of self-love.

The right of refusal being inherent in every right per se cannot be cogently asserted in a normative Jewish context, for refusal is rooted in my will, which is my capacity to possess or dispossess property: to keep what I own or to release it. But my most basic claims, which I exercise as rights by myself for myself or, if need be, others exercise as rights for me, are made by the very presence of my whole person in the world. That personhood is greater than anything I can possibly project out of myself by my will. I can neither possess myself nor dispossess myself by any act of will. In the great insight of the French Catholic philosopher, Gabriel Marcel, being is prior to having.[67]

The most important rights I exercise as a whole person before someone else, are rooted in duties to others, which when we fulfill them are good for us as well. The most basic right of a person, the right to life, is exercised because the community of which I am a participant claims that life for its own life and

---

[65] Self-love is often seen as the beginning of self-deification. See, e.g., Ezek. 29:1–12.

[66] On this point, see the Jewishly based critique of rights talk by Martin P. Golding, "The Primacy of Welfare Rights," in *Human Rights*, ed. E. F. Paul, J. Paul, and F. D. Miller, Jr. (Oxford: Blackwell, 1984), 129. Because Golding sees rights as being essentially waivable, he seems to conclude that rights talk is, therefore, irrelevant to Jewish normative discourse. My friend Professor Golding has made that point to me in our many conversations on this whole question.

[67] See *Being and Having*, trans. K. Farrer (New York: Harper and Row, 1965), 82.

because God claims "all lives are mine" (Ezekiel 18:4).[68] Ultimately, such a right is my claim upon others to let me fulfill my duty to my community and to my God, that is, to answer their claims on me.

My right is a means to a dutiful end. That is why these rights are to be exercised for us when, for whatever reason, we are unable or unwilling to do so by ourselves. They may not be waived. The best example of this would be fulfilling the duty to rescue a suicidal person from self-destruction. "You shall not stand idly by the blood of your neighbor" (Leviticus 19:16).[69] Here one is required to exercise the right to life of a suicidal person, even though that person is in a state of mind where, as Maimonides put it in another context, "his bad tendency has overcome him," and he (or she) does not want to live anymore.[70] The lack of willingness to exercise a legitimate right is to be taken as a temporary lapse and it is understood that one's underlying human desire, one's natural inclination, is to do what is just and to be part of the law-abiding human community.[71]

Here, though, one might well ask: If these basic human rights are rooted in prior duties, why use rights language at all? I would answer as follows: First of all, all duties in the covenant are still based on God's primordial right as the Creator, which is a right that is absolutely original with no duty of any kind underlying it. It creates duties; duties do not create this right. When God is absolute, it would be an absurd, infinite regress to say that God has a duty to command duties Furthermore, even though human rights are ultimately rooted in duties to God, it is still very important to see them as rights/claims of the human members of the covenant themselves. Thus they are entitlements from God. Seeing the rights of God as primary not only does not eliminate our own rights; instead, it properly grounds them and orders them, be they individual or communal rights.

God's claims on us are covenantal: God asks us to respond to him so that he may respond to us. Part of that response on God's part is dignifying our needs, allowing us to claim their fulfillment from other members of the covenanted community. Although the general source of all these duties is God's will, they are specifically given for the sake of fulfilling the needs of those persons who benefit from their performance. Politically legitimized needs are rights. Desire gives voice to those needs so that they can be recognized as rights by others.[72] However, the only desires that can be recognized by others

---

[68] See B. Berakhot 5a re Ps. 31:6.

[69] See B. Sanhedrin 73a.

[70] *Mishneh Torah*: Gerushin, 2.20.

[71] See D. Novak, "Privacy," in *Natural Law and Contemporary Public Policy*, ed. D. F. Forte (Washington, D.C.: Georgetown University Press, 1998),13ff.

[72] However, only those desiring voices that express needs that are consistent with the overall covenant are to be heard. The voice itself is not its own claim. See, e.g., B. Sukkah 31a and Rabbenu Hananel and Rashi, s.v. "pa'ita."

are those that can be justified as rights within a community. For Jews, that political legitimacy is made within the covenant. As this book is trying to argue, liberals have not so co-opted rights talk that adherents of Judaism cannot direct this talk back to earlier, nonliberal ways of thinking, even when they agree with liberals about a number of individual rights and even about their precise content.

However, not all rights are specifically rooted in previous duties. Some rights are rooted in the autonomous will of the individual person, which is the projection of his or her power. In this area, there is only the general duty that "all your deeds be for the sake of God."[73] Aside from that overall consideration, one may determine just how that is to be done by himself or herself autonomously, as we shall see in more detail in chapter 7. In talmudic nomenclature, this is the area of the "optionally permitted" (*reshut*), which is epitomized by the notion of private property.[74] Here, indeed, one may either exercise or waive his or her rights. The issues here involve one's taking or leaving property to which one is justly entitled.

Let us begin by looking at marriage, which is the most important matter of status possible between two persons—and between them and their community. Because marriage involves a certain amount of freedom of will, especially at its inception, its initial legal terms are borrowed from commerce: the permitted transfer of property.[75] Marital status results from the exercise of autonomy. That was always the case for men; for women, though, the recognition of their autonomy itself has been a developing process.

If one were to look at Scripture alone, it would seem that marriage is a right exercised by a man and that the woman he marries is simply there for his use. In fact, in the Written Torah, the act of initiating marriage is specifically mentioned only in the context of a man's right to divorce his wife "because he found in her something disgusting (*ervat davar*)" (Deuteronomy 24:1). There the initiation of marriage is described as "he takes (*yiqah*) a woman and masters her (*u-vo'alah*)," the latter by all accounts meaning his having coitus with her.[76] In fact, looking at such sources alone prompted the thirteenth-century Provençal exegete Rabbi Menahem ha-Meiri to note that if this is all there were to Jewish marriage, no woman would want to remain "a daughter of Abraham our father."[77] It was in the rabbinic tradition, however, that the most

---

[73] M. Avot 2.12. See Prov. 3:6; T. Berakhot 6.7 re Ps. 35:10; B. Berakhot 61b and parallels re Deut. 6:5; B. Betsah 16a re Ps. 68:20; B. Kiddushin 82a.

[74] See, e.g., M. Baba Kama 1.2 and 5.2–3; B. Baba Kama 13b; Maimonides, *Mishneh Torah*: Nizqei Mammon, 1.7 re Exod. 22:4 (cf. *Mekhilta*: Mishpatim, 296).

[75] M. Kiddushin 1.1; B. Kiddushin 2a–b (see Tos., s.v. "ve-kesef" on 2a).

[76] See *Sifre*: Devarim, no. 268; Y. Kiddushin 1.1/58b; B. Kiddushin 4b.

[77] *Bet ha-Behirah*: Kiddushin, ed. Sofer, 8. Cf. B. Ketubot 72b and 82b, wherefrom Meiri took this phrase, adapting it to a more radical meaning here.

significant marital rights of women were discovered, especially her autonomy to marry or remain single.[78]

The most basic right so discovered by the Rabbis is that a woman's consent is a necessary condition for any marriage to be valid. That is, if it can be shown that a marriage was initiated when the woman was under duress, the marriage is annulled automatically. Nevertheless, the explicit enunciation of this right and the legal fact its denial creates did not actually come about until shortly after the official publication of the Babylonian Talmud, although this enunciation found its way into subsequent texts of that main source of Jewish law.[79] Before that time, the best that could be done was to annul a forced marriage by a formal procedure. That is, the marriage was taken to be valid initially, but terminated thereafter by a specific rabbinical ruling post factum.[80] The later form of annulment is more radical. It declares that there never had been a marriage at all ab initio.

The reason for this development might be that in earlier times, most marriages were initiated, at least formally but not physically, when the bride was a minor. Scripture speaks of the normal procedure of a man declaring, "I gave my daughter to this man" (Deuteronomy 22:16), and the daughter is called "a girl" (*na'arah*). In fact, the Rabbis derive the right of a father to initiate a marriage for his daughter from this very verse.[81] However, as the age of marriage for women seemed to have become older, the growing independence of women that came with their greater maturity had to be taken into account. This is so much the case that by the third century C.E., the Babylonian authority Rav was able to rule: "It is forbidden (*asur*) for a man to initiate (*she-yiqadesh*) a marriage for his daughter when she is a minor (*qetanah*), namely, until she is grown up enough (*she-tigadel*) to say 'I want (*rotsah*) this man.' "[82] In other words, rabbinical authority removed a right the father had from Scripture and, in effect, designated a new right for his daughter. Even though such a child marriage would have to be taken as valid ex post facto, undoubtedly because it seemed to be explicitly mentioned in the Written Torah, a father who initiated one would be held in contempt of rabbinical authority and would be subject to penalties for his violation of that authority.[83] (We will see more about this

---

[78] The greatest rabbinic entitlement to women is usually considered to be the marriage contract (*ketubah*), whereby a woman is guaranteed a minimum financial settlement in the event of being divorced or widowed, to which increments can be negotiated. See B. Yevamot 89a; B. Ketubot 10a and Tos., s.v. "amar," 101a; ibid., 82b; Maimonides, *Mishneh Torah*: Ishut, 24.3.

[79] B. Kiddushin 2b. The source of the view that the first section of this tractate (2a-3b/top) is actually post-talmudic (saboraic) is *Igeret Rav Sherira Gaon*, 2.4, ed. Hyman, 60.

[80] See B. Baba Batra 48b; Maimonides, *Mishneh Torah*: Ishut, 4.1 and *Hagahot Maimoniyot*, n. 1 thereon; also D. Novak, *Halakhah in a Theological Dimension* (Chico, Calif.: Scholars Press, 1985), 29ff.

[81] B. Ketubot 46b.

[82] B. Kiddushin 41a. See Tos., s.v. "asur" thereon.

[83] See R. Isaac Lampronti, *Pahad Yitshaq*, ed. Livorno, 4:119b, s.v. "makkat mardut."

overall communal right in the next chapter.) The father by so doing had now violated the right of his daughter. In other words, looking back at what seemed to be the case in scriptural times, the tables now seem to be turned 180 degrees when it comes to the issue of rights to the initiation of marriage. Now all women, at least ab initio, have the right to either accept or reject any marriage proposed to them. As Maimonides put it in a different context, "[A] woman is not like a captive (ke-shevuyah) to be forced to have intercourse (she-tiba'el) by and with someone hateful to her."[84]

It could actually be argued after a certain point in the history of the Halakhah that women have even greater autonomy at the initiation of marriage than men have, that is, they have more rights. This point comes out when looking at the following debate in the Mishnah: "A man is commanded to procreate but not a woman. Rabbi Yohanan ben Beroqah says that Scripture is speaking about both of them [men and women] when it states, 'God blessed them (otam) and said to them . . . be fruitful and multiply' " (Genesis 1:25).[85] The law follows the former opinion, which is seen as being based on the notion that marriage as a social institution mirrors the natural act of intercourse, whose initiation is when the man penetrates the woman.[86] Now on the surface, this seems to place a woman at a disadvantage. The man and not the woman has the merit of fulfilling this primary duty. And it is usually asserted that "greater is the person who acts because of being commanded (metsuveh ve'oseh) than one who acts without being commanded."[87] Is it not the man who is fulfilling a duty, which is taken to be more important than the mere exercise of a right? If so, is a woman then merely a means for the fulfillment of his end; may she at best refuse him? One could answer "no" in two different ways.

First, it could be said that men need to be commanded to marry and raise a family—which is what "be fruitful and multiply means"—whereas the Rabbis assume that women have a more natural desire for the married state.[88] Women are assumed to be the primary home builders; hence they might not need a commandment to act in this area.[89] One need only look at the aggressiveness of all the matriarchs on the home front: Sarah, Rebekah, Rachel, and Leah.[90]

Second, however, it could be more a matter of will than of natural inclination. Excluded from the commandment, women now actually have more power

---

[84] *Mishneh Torah*: Ishut, 14.8. Cf. B. Ketubot 63b–64a and Tos., s.v. "aval." That is why even in the levirate, where it would seem the marriage of this specific couple is mandated, the couple are to be persuaded by rabbinical authorities to legally release each other from such a marriage (*halitsah*) when personal incompatibility seems likely. See M. Yevamot 12.6; B. Yevamot 44a and 101b; Y. Yevamot 12.6/12d; cf. B. Yevamot 39b.

[85] M. Yevamot 6.6.

[86] B. Yevamot 65b re Gen. 1:28. See also B. Kiddushin 2b re Deut. 24:1 and Niddah 31b.

[87] B. Kiddushin 31a and parallels.

[88] Ibid., 41a and parallels.

[89] See B. Shabbat 118b; B. Yevamot 77a re Gen. 18:9; B. Baba Metsia 59a.

[90] See Gen. 21:9–12; 27:13; 29:32; 30:1.

than men in the initiation of marriage. A man must marry; only the particular woman he is to marry is left to his own discretion. But a woman does not have to marry at all; she has no specific duty to do so. As the fourteenth-century Spanish exegete Nissim Gerondi (Ran) put it: "Even though a woman is not commanded to procreate (*be-piryah ve-rivyah*), she has an obligation (*mitsvah*) to do so in order to help her husband fulfill his duty (*le-qayyem mitsvato*)."[91] Now, the word *mitsvah* has several meanings in rabbinic literature: primarily it means "a commandment" specified by either Scripture or the Rabbis, the violation of which entails penalties; secondarily it means "something that ought to be done," but for which there are no penalties when not done.[92] In this case, then, it is a moral duty rather than a legally enforced norm.

From this point, the right of a woman—but not of a man—to limit and space the number of her offspring is derived.[93] In other words, not having a duty can imply having a greater right. Thus it would seem that the success of the marital union could depend even more on a woman's exercise of her right than on a man's fulfillment of his duty. And if a right is a justified desire of one person for another, then the duty of a man to initiate marriage is a legitimate response to the prior right of a woman to be married; it is, as the Palestinian Talmud puts it, "her claim to be married" (*tova'at le-hinasē*).[94] Adam is seduced by Eve, even before he pursues her. "And she gave the fruit to her husband along with her, then he ate (*va-yyokhal*)" (Genesis 3:6). As such, the communal claim on men to start families, which we shall explore in the next chapter, is fundamentally asserted by women making their domestic claims upon men. (At a time when the whole issue of the respective rights of both men and women is under intense discussion, the subtleties of the Jewish marital relationship should be examined with greater scrutiny, especially for their far-reaching implications.)

The issue of which rights may be waived and which rights must be exercised can be seen in the responsibilities of a husband and a wife for each other within their marriage. According to the rabbinic interpretation of Scripture, a man is obligated to provide his wife with food, clothing, and sexual intercourse.[95] In fact, "food and clothing" include all that constitutes normal material support. A woman, in turn, is obligated to keep house and turn over to her husband whatever she might earn or find.[96] Thus she has claims on him and he has

[91] *Commentary on Alfasi*: B. Kiddushin, chap. 2, ed. Vilna, 16b. See B. Baba Batra 119b; R. Yom Tov ben Abraham Ishbili, *Hiddushei ha-Ritva*: Yevamot 62a; Gersonides, *Commentary on the Torah*: Gen., chap. 1, shoresh 1, p. 13a.

[92] See B. Sukkah 33a re Exod. 15:2, B. Baba Batra 120a re Num. 36:6.

[93] See Feldman, *Birth Control in Jewish Law*, 53ff.

[94] Y. Taaniyot 4.6/69c and Y. Megillah 1.4/70c and R. David Fraenkel, *Qorban ha'Edah*, s.v. "tova'at le-hinase," who distinguishes this from the male duty to procreate re B. Yevamot 65b.

[95] B. Yevamot 47b re Exod. 21:10.

[96] Ibid., 47b and parallels. See Maimonides, *Mishneh Torah*: Ishut, 12.1–5.

claims on her. Are any of these claims negotiable, that is, may one waive any of these rights based on an individual assessment of his or her own self-interest? Can a private agreement be worked out that is publicly valid? The following text deals with this question:

> If a man says to a woman: "You be married (*mequdeshet*) to me on the condition (*al menat*) that I am not responsible for providing [you] food, clothing, and sexual intercourse (*onah*)," she is married (*mequdeshet*). The condition, however, is null and void (*u-tena'o batel*), in the opinion of Rabbi Meir. Rabbi Judah says that in the monetary matters (*be-davar she-be-mammon*),the condition is valid (*qayyam*).[97]

Of course, this text assumes that the woman to whom such a proposal has been made is willing to accept it. According to Rabbi Meir, she may not accept it because it makes a condition that is contrary to what the Torah has stipulated as the minimal rights of a woman in marriage.[98] In his view, she may no more waive her rights than the man may waive his duties. According to Rabbi Judah, however, the monetary rights of the marriage may be negotiated and waived by mutual agreement. Thus a woman may waive her right to material support by negotiating with her prospective husband that he waive his right to her earnings and findings.[99] And the subsequent law follows Rabbi Judah on this point.[100] Maimonides insightfully noted that this is an area where one is neither evading an obligation mandated by the Torah nor claiming something from which one has been barred by the Torah.[101]

In his Talmud commentary, Rashi explains the difference between sexual intercourse, on the one hand, and material support, on the other: "Money, by definition, may be waived (*de-nitan le-mehilah*); hence conditions may be made concerning it. But precluding sexual intercourse is personally painful (*de-tsa'ara de-gufa*) and is not something that may be waived."[102] In other words, it is assumed that a normal woman wants the sexual attention of her husband. Without it, their relationship does not partake of what is a uniquely marital right and duty. Sexual intercourse is legitimate only between spouses. Outside of marriage, it is neither a right nor a duty; indeed, according to most of the sources, outside of marriage it is a transgression.[103] In a normative Jewish

---

[97] B. Kiddushin 19b and parallels. See Maimonides, *Mishneh Torah*: Ishut, 12.9.

[98] M. Ketubot 9.1; M. Baba Metsia 7.11; M. Baba Batra 8.5.

[99] B. Ketubot 58b. See ibid. 83a and Gittin 77a–b.

[100] See B. Eruvin 46b.

[101] *Mishneh Torah*: Ishut, 6.9.

[102] B. Kiddushin 19b, s.v. "be-davar she-be-mammon." For the notion of *mehilah* in monetary matters, see B. Ketubot 85b; B. Sanhedrin 57a and 59a. *Mehilah* is used by analogy to describe God's right to forgive sinners by waiving the punishment they deserve (see M. Sotah 7.6).

[103] *Sifre*: Devarim, no. 260, ed. Finkelstein, 283 (see n. 8 thereon); Maimonides, *Mishneh Torah*: Ishut, 1.4, and R. Vidal of Tolosa, *Magid Mishneh* thereon re B. Yevamot 61b; R. Jacob ben Asher,

context, a woman or a man who does not want to engage in sexual intimacy in essence does not really want to be married, and should not marry if that is a precondition of the marriage, as we have seen. What that person wants, it seems, is a friend, and friends need not be married to each other; in fact, most friends may not be married to each other.[104] Furthermore, since the marriage proposal is a public matter inasmuch as it requires witnesses, who are the surrogates for the community as a whole, the community has an interest in it.[105] As we shall see in the next chapter, marriage lies at the core of Jewish community. As such, the community has an interest in not allowing private conditions to be upheld in marriage that make the relationship between the parties no real marriage at all. Such conditions, in effect, ridicule the whole communal institution of marriage by confusing it with other, more general, human relationships.

The distinction between the monetary and the bodily is that one's body is endemic to who the person himself or herself really is. Our bodies are the physical locus of our selves and the point from which we enter our various personal relationships in the world. They are not our property precisely because we cannot separate ourselves from our bodies.[106] Indeed, we can only imagine what is beyond their sensitive range. (Mathematics is the prime instance of such imaginative construction.) In fact, one can see the scriptural term *nefesh*, which is usually translated as "soul," as meaning "the capacity of a conscious body to engage in a range of relations." The center of that relational range is not designated by the term "body" (*guf*), which after all could refer to inanimate "bodies" as well, but by the term "flesh" (*basar*).[107] Hence, "soul" is not a distinct entity, which transcends the body both before birth and after death, as Plato and his followers (including his Jewish followers) have maintained.[108] Instead, the soul is the function of the fleshly self in the world as man or as woman. When the body totally loses that functional presence in the

---

Tur: Even ha'Ezer, 26; R. Joseph Karo, *Shulhan Arukh*: Even ha'Ezer, 26.1 and n. of R. Moses Isserles (Rema) thereon.

[104] It is significant, though, that whereas friendship is much wider than marriage, marriage is considered the deepest form of friendship. Thus in the seven nuptual benedictions (*sheva berakhot*), the fifth one refers to the bride and groom as "loving friends." See B. Ketubot 8a and Rashi, s.v. "re'im ha'ahuvim"; also, B. Kiddushin 41a and Niddah 17a re Lev. 19:18.

[105] See B. Kiddushin 65b; also, Novak, *Halakhah in a Theological Dimension*, 30ff.

[106] See Gabriel Marcel, *The Mystery of Being*, trans. G. S. Fraser (Chicago: Henry Regnery, 1960), 1:114ff.; Maurice Merleau-Ponty, *Phenomenology of Perception*, trans. C. Smith (London: Routledge and Kegan Paul, 1962), 90ff.

[107] See, e.g., Gen. 6:3. Re *guf* not being limited to humans or even sentient creatures, see Maimonides, *Commentary on the Mishnah*: Sanhedrin, chap. 10 (Heleq), introduction: principle 10, ed. Kafih, 141; *Mishneh Torah*: Yesodei ha-Torah, 1.7–8; *Guide of the Perplexed*, 2.19.

[108] See Maimonides, *Mishneh Torah*: Yesodei ha-Torah, 4.9; Teshuvah, 8.3. Cf. Plato, *Phaedo*, 70Bff.

world—minimally, its breathe—death is the result.[109] Death is the loss of the soul, not its release to resume its own independent life. At that point the human body becomes a rotting piece of flesh that contaminates all who come into contact with it.[110] But being the former locus of a personal life, that flesh deserves the dignity of being returned to the earth whence the human person (*adam*), male and female, originally came.[111] Thus the doctrine of resurrection (*tehiyyat ha-metim*) teaches us that if there is to be a restoration to life after death, it will be the resurrection of our bodies and their range of relations.[112] For all of these reasons, then, our bodies are not our projects; they are not objects with which we may negotiate, from which we may ever depart ourselves. Our bodies are not to be primarily under the control of our will.

Our possessions, however, are parts of our personal projection into the realm of things.[113] We may, therefore, use them as our right as long as we do not violate the rights of other persons. As we have seen, this comes under the norm "what is hateful to you, do not do to someone else." But we must also be subordinate to what the community considers its interest in the monetary relations of individuals, such as the observance of its particular commercial customs;[114] without a communal context, there would not be enough trust among individual persons for them to be able to agree on anything of any duration. And without societal structure, monetary interaction would never advance beyond the crudest form of barter. Jews must also avoid projects that violate the rights of God, the best example being doing business on the Sabbath. By the Sabbath, at least for the time being, all of our projects are to be already completed.[115] Another example is destroying for no constructive reason even something we ourselves own, which is considered a violation of the earth, which is the Lord's and which has been but lent to us for good use only.[116]

As long as monetary relations do not overstep these boundaries, they are left to the voluntary discretion of individual persons. Human will is illegitimate only when it denies any inherent limits on its own projection. Although the classical Jewish sources are far more committed to the real authority of the community than is laissez-faire capitalism, I know of no basis in these sources for making individuals, either as economic suppliers or consumers, simply

[109] See B. Yoma 85a re Gen. 7:22.

[110] See *Shir ha-Shirim Rabbah* 8.13 re Num. 19:14.

[111] See B. Eruvin 17a–b.

[112] See D. Novak, *The Election of Israel* (Cambridge: Cambridge University Press, 1995), 262f.

[113] Thus property is the projection of our hand's ability to make things and demarcate areas of its control. See *Sifre*: Devarim, no. 269, and Y. Gittin 8.1/49b re Deut. 24:1; B. Baba Metsia 57b re Num. 21:26 and Exod. 22:3; also, B. Kiddushin 26a re Jer. 40:10.

[114] See M. Ketubot 6.4; M. Baba Metsia 7.1; B. Baba Metsia 87a; R. Israel Isserlein, *Terumat ha-Deshen* 1, no. 342.

[115] See *Mekhilta*: Yitro, 230 re Exod. 20:9; also, Novak, *Jewish Social Ethics*, 143ff.

[116] See B. Shabbat 129a re Deut. 20:19; also, Novak, *Jewish Social Ethics*, 118ff.

parts of society. In other words, there is no basis there for socialism, even a socialism that is not based on the atheism essential to Marxism.[117] As we shall see in chapter 7, the privacy that private property presupposes is legitimate per se and something that prevents society from taking itself to be totally sufficient for all human needs. It is one of the ways society is prevented from any self-divinization, any apotheosis.

In some cases, status that is seen as one's right, one's claim on others to respect, may also be waived as if it were disposable property. But since this is permitted only in some cases but not in others, we must now ask what distinguishes one kind of status from the other. The Talmud makes the following distinctions:

> Rav Isaac bar Sheila said in the name of Rav Mattnah who said in the name of Rav Hisda: When a father waives his right to be honored (*she-mahal al kevodo*), that honor may be so waived. When a rabbinic master (*ha-rav*) waived his right to honor, that honor may not be so waived. But Rav Joseph said that even when a rabbinic master waived his right to be honored, that honor may be so waived.[118]

Later on in this discussion of the right to be honored, it is recorded that "Rav said that even the authority who holds that when a prince waives his right to be honored, his honor may be waived, nevertheless holds when a king waives his right to be honored, his honor may not be waived."[119]

It would seem that the reason that Rav Hisda would not permit a rabbinic master to do what a father is permitted to do is that the master is the conduit of the Torah for his students. Since the Torah's honor may not be waived, so the honor of the one who has the power to transmit the Torah may not be waived either.[120] It would also seem that this is the reason why a king may not waive the honor due him, for he is the personification of the whole national community, and the honor of the community should not be waived at the discretion of any individual, even its leader.[121] However, Rav Joseph's view is explained a generation later by another Babylonian scholar, Rava, who regards the status of the master to be more his own hard-earned possession, and thus something he may waive voluntarily.[122] And the subsequent law follows Rav

---

[117] See Novak, *Jewish Social Ethics*, 181, n. 13.

[118] B. Kiddushin 32a. For another example of the right to waive a right, see *Tur*: Yoreh Deah, 374, and R. Joseph Karo, *Bet Yosef*, s.v. "katav" re B. Moed Qatan 26b.

[119] B. Kiddushin 32b.

[120] See, e.g., B. Moed Qatan 21b re Ps. 37:31; B. Baba Kama 41b re Deut. 6:13 and Edels (Maharsha), *Hiddushei Aggadot* thereon.

[121] B. Sotah 25a and Maimonides, *Mishneh Torah*: Mamrim, 3.4, where defiance of public authority is not to be overlooked. Cf. B. Sanhedrin 47a, where for the honor of the Torah, the public may waive its own honor, in this case not honoring its own king, who himself despised the Torah, even at his own funeral. For the king's duty to set the honor of the Torah above his own, see B. Sotah 41b re Deut. 17:15 and Tos., s.v. "mitsvah."

[122] B. Kiddushin 32a–b re Ps. 1:2.

Joseph.[123] But what is it exactly that the master is waiving, and why would he want to do so, and why would the law permit him to do so?

Maimonides points out that even when a master waives his right to be honored, his pupils must still "show him respect" (le-hadro).[124] If that is correct, then it is only some of his honor that is being waived. If that can be more precisely determined, then we might see why he would want to do so, and why that voluntary refusal is permitted.

The term "honor" (kavod) used here also covers what is designated by the term "fearful respect" (mora).[125] Now, one of the main aspects of this respect is not to contradict one's master. However, when that is the case, there is much less chance that the pupils will internalize for themselves the dialectic method of the Talmud, which consists primarily in asking hard—even embarrassing—questions of those more learned than oneself.[126] Thus in order for a master to truly fulfill his function, which is to finally enable his students to no longer be dependent on him but to become his colleagues instead, it would seem that he would have to develop a more informal relationship with them (or at least with the best of them).[127] That means he would have to waive his right to the "fearful respect" normally due him for the sake of that end. And that is left to his individual discretion. Yet to do so for any other reason, it seems to me, would be an irresponsible compromise of the honor due the Torah, which in its primarily oral character becomes embodied in the persons of her rabbinic masters.[128] It would also seem that this informality is necessary if the pupils are to learn the Torah in the best possible way: by loving their master. Love can not be induced but only enticed. The enticement of love would seem to be the reason why a father should "let up" on the strict respect due from his children.[129] But all this is a matter of persuasion, not mandate; example, not precept.

So we might finally say that the right to waive claims of property or status pertains when there is no immediately contradicting duty. These are the areas

---

[123] Karo, *Shulhan Arukh*: Yoreh Deah, 242.32.

[124] *Mishneh Torah*: Talmud Torah, 5.11. See R. Isaac bar Sheshet Parfat, *Teshuvot ha-Rivash*, no. 220.

[125] *Sifra*: Qedoshim, 87a re Lev. 19:3; Y. Peah 1.1/15c; B. Kiddushin 31b.

[126] See, e.g., B. Nazir 49b and B. Kiddushin 52b; B. Avodah Zarah 29b. In a long responsum on the subject of rabbinic honor, R. Hayyim Lazar Spira begins by quoting M. Avot 2.5 ("the bashful do not learn") in bringing a full range of talmudic sources for the necessity of less formality between master and pupil. See *Teshuvot Minhat Eleazar* (Bratislava: n.p., 1922), vol. 4, no. 6. For the opportunity of a father to waive his right to the attention of his son so as to free the son for fuller Torah study, see T. Bekhorot 6.11; B. Nedarim 38a and R. Nissim Gerondi (Ran), s.v. "ha-madir"; Y. Bikkurim 3.6/65d.

[127] The goal of the master (*rav*) is to enable as many of his students as possible to eventually become his colleagues (*talmid-haver*). See, e.g., B. Berakhot 27b.

[128] See B. Makkot 22b; Y. Sotah 7.6/22a.

[129] See Maimonides, *Mishneh Torah*: Mamrim, 6.8 re B. Kiddushin 32a.

that are left to individual discretion. There are times, as we shall see in the next chapter, when certain individual rights had to be removed by communal authorities because their continued exercise had proven to be detrimental to the common good. But the common good itself is often well served by encouraging the responsible exercise of individual autonomy, autonomy that is neither morally foundational nor to be obliterated by overbearing communal authority that encourages mindless conformism.

THE LOVE OF NEIGHBOR

As noted at the beginning of this chapter, the two basic norms determining the various rights and duties involved in interpersonal relationships are the norm not to harm another and the norm to love one's neighbor. There have been those who have seen these norms as essentially one norm, which is either expressed negatively as in "do no harm" or positively as in "do love." Thus Maimonides paraphrases the commandment to "love your neighbor as yourself" (Leviticus 19:18) as "everything you want others to do for you, you do to your brother."[130] In other words, the positive is is taken to be the direct obverse of the negative and vice versa. However, one can well question the cogency of this simple equation for two reasons. One, the desire to be loved is certainly deeper than the desire not to be harmed.[131] Two, the range of no harm is wider than the range of love. Along these lines, the great modern Jewish theologian Franz Rosenzweig (d. 1929) noted that the prohibition of harm is "only the lowest negative limit" and thus better stated in the negative form in order to distinguish it from the fuller affirmation of love.[132] At best, one can say that love presupposes no harm in the sense that love cannot be practiced unless harm has been proscribed. But a presupposition does not engender what presupposes it.[133] There can certainly be no harm without any

---

[130] *Mishneh Torah*: Evel, 14.1. Cf. *Mishneh Torah*: Deot, 6.3 re M. Avot 2.10, 4.1 and 12. There he states: "It is a commandment for everyone to love every other Jew like his own self (*ke-gufo*)." See also *Sefer ha-Mitsvot*: positive commandments, no. 206. In *Avot de-Rabbi Nathan* B, ed. Schechter, 27a, Hillel's dictum is placed in the mouth of R. Akibah, the Sage who said that "love your neighbor as yourself" is "the most all inclusive principle (*kelal gadol*) in the Torah" (Y. Nedarim 9.3/41c). The early Christian sources also use both the positive and negative forms of the commandment. For the positive form, see Matt. 7:12 and Luke 6:31; for the negative form, see *Didache*, 1.2.

[131] See Canticles 8:6–7.

[132] *The Star of Redemption*, trans. W. W. Hallo (New York: Holt, Rinehart and Winston, 1970), 239. The more abstract character of the negative formulation was also emphasized by Ahad Ha'Am ("Al Shtei ha-Se'ipim," 374). However, he saw the negative rule as being superior to the positive rule precisely because of its more abstract, impersonal conceptualization. This is the opposite of what Rosenzweig meant by his distinction.

[133] See D. Novak, *Jewish-Christian Dialogue* (New York: Oxford University Press, 1989), 129ff.

necessity at all for love to follow from it or even after it. There are numerous people, I am reasonably assured, who would not harm me, but I am just as assured that they would not love me nor would I love them either.

We have examined the question of love somewhat when rejecting self-love as a moral motive. Love is not only transitive; it is essentially transactional. It requires personal mutuality to be effective. Here we need to examine love of neighbor more carefully in order to interpret the meaning of a commandment and the claims it makes for its objects. It is certainly a commandment that is concerned with the most intense relationship possible between persons. A phenomenology of love, especially love in the covenant, is what we need in order to better understand this commandment and the rights and duties it involves.

The first question to be addressed is: How can an emotion, especially one like love, be commanded? Love seems to be involuntary: I can either love someone else or I cannot. It seems that I can no more start love than I can stop it.[134] Unrequited love is the subject of tragedy, but one cannot morally fault someone who honestly cannot respond to the offer of love from someone else. And why cannot one respond to *any* offer of love? It would seem that is because we can respond to love only when that love is what we truly need. That is why children inevitably respond to the love of their parents (when authentic, that is). Without it, children have no place in the world. With it, they have been welcomed into the world.[135] Thus love inherently makes claims upon those whom it intends, and they make claims in return upon those who have loved them first. It is a gift given at a definite time at a definite place. It is specific, not general. Accordingly, love must always originate in human time, which is history. It is not a universal presupposition of historical continuity like the prohibition of harming others. We need not know who in particular could harm us like we need to know who in particular does love us. So, for example, one can think about avoiding the harm of death without having died. But one cannot think about the joy of being loved unless one has already experienced love personally. One must always be aware of the source of his or her being loved. Only then can one truly respond with his or her own love. Love is always extended in desire, not projected at will. It is remembered, not invented. But with whose desire does it begin? It always seems to precede us.

For Jews, love in the covenant begins with God's desire for Israel. Indeed, that desire is what founds the covenant. We are continually reminded of how God showed his love to his people Israel; the point constantly emphasized is that its beginning is the exodus from Egypt. "Not because of your being numerous did the Lord desire you (*hashaq bakhem*). . . . Because of the Lord's love

---

[134] See Immanuel Kant, *Critique of Practical Reason*, trans. L. W. Beck (Indianapolis, Ind.: Bobbs-Merrill, 1956), 1.1.3, p. 85f.

[135] See Novak, *Jewish-Christian Dialogue*, 144ff.

(*me'ahavat ha-Shem*) for you and his keeping the promise he made to your ancestors, did the Lord with a strong hand bring you out and rescue you from the house of slaves, from the hand of Pharaoh king of Egypt" (Deuteronomy 7:7–8). Initially, the exodus was experienced as an act of divine coercion, like parents coercing, as it were, the conception and birth of their children. "I had to overpower (*heheziqi*) them to be brought out of the land of Egypt. . . . I forced (*ba'alti*) them, says the Lord" (Jeremiah 31:31).[136] However, whereas the prophet Jeremiah seems to have seen the loving and accepting response to God's love by the people as an eschatological event, the Rabbis saw the loving response of the people beginning in the Persian exile when at long last they confirmed the covenant with God out of their love of God.[137] Rabbinic Judaism itself can well be seen as the unfolding of the loving response of the Jewish people to the covenant initiated in God's love for them.[138] And it is Rabbinic Judaism that gave much of the structure and content to the covenant and its teaching (*torah*) and practice (*mitsvot*).

How are the people to respond to God's love of them? Optimally, the response should begin in feeling and then find expression in action. Love originates in need that expresses itself in desire. In rabbinic psychology, that is seeing an act as being a result of the proper intention (*kavvanah*) of the actor.[139] But there are times when one's feelings are still confused or inchoate. In such cases, the action should proceed and the actor should hope that the proper feelings will arise from within the act already being done. Optimally, love should originate in desire, but when that is not yet possible, then it must originate in willful obedience. To cite some helpful scriptural examples, "Jacob loved Rachel" (Genesis 29:18) before he married her, whereas his father, Isaac, first married his wife, Rebekah, and then "he loved her" (Genesis 24:67).[140] Because desire preceded action in the case of Jacob marrying Rachel, their relationship showed more intense passion than did the relationship between Isaac and Rebekah. Yet both marriages were loving. Nevertheless, the act is what is primary inasmuch as love is manifest in what we do for the object of our love. Action can be formally commanded, whereas feeling can only be enticed. But feeling love without a tangible transaction with the one I love— doing something for that person—is in effect loving myself by loving some fantasy within myself. Love must show itself in action *for* the beloved. Not feeling love for a proper object of love—especially and primarily for God— is when my desire and my need are not yet in harmony. As regards other

---

[136] See M. Avot 4.22; also, Novak, *Jewish Social Ethics*, 27ff.

[137] See B. Shabbat 88a–b re Prov. 11:3 and Rashi, s.v. "de-saginan be-shlemuta" thereon.

[138] See Novak, *The Election of Israel*, 170ff.

[139] See M. Rosh Hashanah 3.7.

[140] In his *Commentary on the Torah* thereon, Nahmanides points outs that Isaac's love for Rebekah was because of her "righteousness and virtuous acts" (ed. Chavel, 140). That is something that comes from subsequent experience, not spontaneous passion.

persons, need without desire is unconscious; desire without understanding of need inevitably misses the object it truly intends.

In the most immediate covenantal sense, Jews are to respond to God's love by engaging in acts that express their love for God in return. Thus when Jews are commanded to "love the Lord your God with all your heart, with all your life, and with all your strength" (Deuteronomy 6:5), that love is to find its expression in such acts as our learning the Torah, wearing *tefillin* on arm and head, and affixing *mezuzot* to the doorposts of our houses. Indeed, as the early rabbinic work *Sifre* points out in its comment here: "Act out of love (*aseh me'ahavah*)," which is distinguished from fear, where one is simply restrained and feels no need to do anything for the one he or she fears.[141] It also emphasizes that those we love need us and have a right to our attention to them. The need and the attendant right are mutual. In this sense, all love between persons is *eros*, of which sexual love is but one part. That might be termed the "vertical" dimension of covenantal love. It is best expressed in the most erotic of all books, Song of Songs.[142]

But there is also what might be termed the "horizontal" dimension of covenantal love. That is the love that is to pertain between the members of the covenant. Maimonides, who I noted above equated love of neighbor with "doing unto others what we want others to do for us," places it in the context of "your brother in the Torah and the commandments."[143] That is, he designates this love as an intercovenantal matter. In that context, he points out what this general norm of love of neighbor includes:

> It is a positive commandment of the Rabbis (*shel divreihem*) to attend the sick, to comfort the mourners, to provide a funeral for the dead, the dower the bride, to escort guests, and to engage in all the matters of burial . . . and also to rejoice with the bride and the groom by providing them with all their [wedding] needs. These are "acts of personal kindness" (*gemilut hasadim*), which are to be enacted in person (*she-be-gufo*). Even though these are all rabbinic commandments, they are under the general norm of "you shall love your neighbor as yourself." (Leviticus 19:18)[144]

Thus the formal legal status of these acts is rabbinic, not scriptural. However, the overall impetus for their enactment as norms is the scriptural commandment to love your neighbor. And, not only is the general norm of which they are more specific applications scriptural, the very authority of the Rabbis to enact such norms is also seen as scriptural: "You may not deviate from what they [the Rabbis] tell you" (Deuteronomy 17:11).[145]

---

[141] *Sifre*: Devarim, no. 32, p. 54. See Y. Berakhot 9.7/14b.
[142] See *Shir ha-Shirim Rabbah* 1.11.
[143] *Mishneh Torah*: Evel, 14.1.
[144] Ibid. See *Commentary on the Mishnah*: Peah 1.1.
[145] B. Shabbat 23a. See *Sifre*: Devarim, no. 154.

Moreover, although one could see the enactment of these specific noms as being required by general human decency, the Rabbis see most of them as being originally learned from covenantal acts of God in intimate relationship with his people. These acts are not learned from nature but from revelation.

> Rabbi Hama son of Rabbi Hanina queried why Scripture states "You shall walk after the way of the Lord your God" (Deuteronomy 13:5). Is it possible for a human to walk after the divine presence (*shekhinah*)? Does it not say earlier "for the Lord your God, he is a consuming fire" (Deuteronomy 4:24)? Nevertheless, it means to walk after the personal qualities (*middotav*) of God.[146]

Then examples are bought: God attending Abraham when he was sick; God comforting Isaac at the time of his mother's death; God burying Moses. All of these are set forth as the paradigms for "acts of personal kindness." In other words, the Rabbis derived how and what to enact in this interpersonal area from sacred history. This should be contrasted with much of their legislation in civil and criminal matters that seems to be based on their reflections on what human nature in its sociality truly requires.[147]

When one looks at all of this, it seems that the people of the covenant (*bnei berit*) are to do for each other that which imitates what God does for them as the chosen people.[148] They are thus to be God's partners both in their relationship with God and in their relationship with each other.[149] And, of course, although the general character of these personal acts can be seen as decent human concern in general, the specific content takes on a uniquely Jewish character. Thus attending the sick not only involves physical attention to generally human maladies, it also involves specifically Jewish forms of prayer to God, whose healing powers as "the Lord your physician" (Exodus 15:26) are learned from how he saved his people from the diseases of Egypt.[150] And burying the dead involves burying them in a specifically Jewish way that leaves the body intact, which is very much connected to the specifically Jewish doctrine of the resurrection of the dead.[151]

Love is maximal justice in that it makes the greatest of all claims and engenders the greatest of all duties. Its specificity should be contrasted with the generality of minimal justice.[152] Thus the duty not to harm anyone and the duty

---

[146] B. Sotah 14a. See also *Beresheet Rabbah* 8.13, ed. Theodor-Albeck, p. 67, and nn. thereon.

[147] See M. Baba Batra 10.8 and R. Israel Lifschitz, *Tiferet Yisrael* thereon: Yakhin, n. 84.

[148] For the term *bnei berit*, see M. Baba Kama 1.3.

[149] See B. Shabbat 119b; B. Shevuot 39a–b; B. Rosh Hashanah 29a and Rashi, s.v. "af-al-pi."

[150] *Bemidbar Rabbah* 7.1; Nahmanides, *Commentary on the Torah*: Exod. 21:19; B. Shabbat 12a–b.

[151] See B. Moed Qatan 25a and Nahmanides (Ramban) quoted in R. Abraham ben Yom Tov Ishbili, *Hiddushei ha-Ritva* thereon, and in R. David ibn Abi Zimra, *Teshuvot ha-Radbaz* 3, no. 988; B. Baba Batra 154a.

[152] To use legal language, one could say that not to harm one another is the primary case of *ius in rem*, i.e., a claim on everyone and anyone, whereas love is the primary case of *ius in personam*,

to save anyone from harm are stated in general terms of "the world," as for example, "whoever destroys one human life (*nefesh ahat*), it is as if (*k'ilu*) he destroyed an entire world (*olam malē*); and whoever saves one human life, it is as if he saved a whole world."[153] Love, conversely, is much more selective, both by God and by his covenanted people. Its depth, however, is limitless.[154]

The connection between the vertical and horizontal dimensions of covenantal love can be seen in a rabbinic discussion based on the scriptural verse "This is my God and I shall glorify him (*ve'anvehu*)" (Exodus 15:2). One Sage sees it as designating that the worship of God be aesthetically pleasing: a beautiful *sukkah*, a beautiful Torah scroll. Another Sage, though, sees it as designating *imitatio Dei*, namely, doing as we have learned from our sacred history about how God treats his people: as he is gracious and compassionate, so you be gracious and compassionate.[155] The first opinion speaks of the direct response to God's love in the covenant. The second opinion speaks of an interhuman relationship to be connected to the relationship with God. It is directed to the other human members of the covenant, and it enables us to be the instruments of God's love, whereas the former, which is directed immediately to God, enables us to be the direct recipients of God's love. The relation between the two might well be seen as dialectical. Thus an act of personal kindness could very well be enabling another Jew to practice a commandment directed to God, such as the observance of a holy day (*yom tov*); and the practice of the holy day could very well require that I include another Jew with me in its celebration, such as having him or her as a guest in my home on that day.[156]

WHO IS YOUR NEIGHBOR?

All of this leads us to the question of neighbor love that has been of especial concern to many modern Jewish thinkers: Is my "neighbor" my fellow human

---

i.e., a claim on a designated person, hence one that presupposes a direct relationship between the two persons. See Wesley N. Hohfeld, *Fundamental Legal Conceptions*, ed. W. W. Cook (Westport, Conn.: Greenwood Press, 1964), 72f. In early modern natural law theory, this distinction is made between "imperfect" duties to everyone and anyone and "perfect" duties to someone. See J. B. Schneewind, *The Invention of Autonomy* (Cambridge: Cambridge University Press, 1998), 132ff.

[153] M. Sanhedrin 4.5. See *Avot de-Rabbi Nathan* A, chap. 31, ed. Schechter, pp. 45b–46a and n. 2 thereon; Louis Ginzberg, *The Legends of the Jews* (Philadelphia: Jewish Publication Society of America, 1925), 5:67, n. 8.

[154] Hence "acts of personal kindness" (*gemilut hasadim*) as the expression of love are to be done "without measure" (M. Peah 1.1). Regarding the limits on monetary expenditure (*tsedaqah*), however, cf. B. Ketubot 50a; B. Sotah 49b; *Mekhilta*: Mishpatim, 329–30 re Exod. 23:11; Nahmanides, *Commentary on the Torah*: Lev. 25:5.

[155] B. Shabbat 133b. See Maimonides, *Mishneh Torah*: Avadim, 9.5 and Melakhim, 10.12 re Ps. 145:9; *Guide of the Perplexed*, 3.54.

[156] See Maimonides, *Mishneh Torah*: Yom Tov, 6.18 re Hos. 9:4.

being in general or my fellow Jew specifically?[157] There are classical Jewish sources for both of these alternatives.[158] Theological judgment is required, therefore, to emphasize and develop that alternative most appropriate for dealing with covenantal questions facing us here and now.

The general alternative seems to be what is involved in the following rabbinic discussion:

> "You shall love your neighbor as yourself" (Leviticus 19:18). Rabbi Akibah says that this is the most all inclusive principle (*kelal gadol*) in the Torah. Ben Azzai says that "This is the book of the human generations" (Genesis 5:1) is an even more inclusive principle.[159]

The first thing to note here is that Rabbi Akibah is citing a rule *of what is to be done*, whereas Ben Azzai is citing a statement *about what is the case*. That is, it seems that Ben Azzai is alluding to the conclusion of the verse from Genesis 5:1, namely, "in the likeness (*demut*) of God He made him [the first human]." Accordingly, one could say that Ben Azzai is not disagreeing with Rabbi Akibah's designation of the most all inclusive commandment, but he is only providing it with a reason. A reason is always more general than what is ruled on its behalf. Furthermore, if the reason for the commandment is because of the general nature of human beings, then the commandment must minimally cover all those included in that same reason.[160] This connection of a rule with its reason would mean that in fact there is really no real dispute here at all; instead, Ben Azzai's statement deepens the meaning of Rabbi Akibah's statement. Using our right-duty correlation, one could say that every human being has a right to my love (following Ben Azzai), and that I therefore have a duty to love him or her (following Rabbi Akibah). This is why, no doubt, this discussion became such a favorite of Jewish theologians influenced by Kantian notions of universal moral obligation.[161]

However, is that what Rabbi Akibah really meant by his famous dictum? Although he also teaches "beloved is the human being (*haviv adam*) who is created in the image (*be-tselem*)," he concludes that statement by saying, "as an additional act of love (*hibbah yeterah*) it is made known to him that he is created in the image, as Scripture teaches, 'in the image of God He made humans (*ha'adam*—Genesis 9:6).' "[162] But this "making known" is due to the

---

[157] See Ernst Simon, "The Neighbor (*Re'a*) Whom We Shall Love," in *Modern Jewish Ethics*, ed. M. Fox (Columbus: Ohio University Press, 1975), 29ff.

[158] See Novak, *Jewish Social Ethics*, 182, n. 30; Louis Jacobs, *Religion and the Individual* (Cambridge: Cambridge University Press, 1992), 25ff.

[159] Y. Nedarim 9.3/14c; also, *Sifra*: Qedoshim, 89b.

[160] See Novak, *Natural Law in Judaism*, 69ff.

[161] See Hermann Cohen, *Religion of Reason Out of the Sources of Judaism*, trans. S. Kaplan (New York: Frederick Ungar, 1972), 119.

[162] M. Avot 4.14.

revelation of the Torah. And it could be said that it is also the revelation of the Torah to the covenanted community that spells out exactly how this love is to be put into practice. In other words, the commandment of neighbor love is intercovenantal, not universal at all. But if that is the case, then we would have to say that Ben Azzai is not just providing a reason for Rabbi Akibah's dictum about neighbor love, but that he is disputing the narrowness of its range. Moreover, for him too, scriptural statements about humans as the image of God are normative even if not literally prescriptive. What they say is that the very uniqueness of human existence claims love as its proper recognition wherever it presents himself or herself. Contrary to Hume, who most famously asserted that no moral conclusion can be made from any statement of fact, the greater immediacy of human objects over things in our experienced world means that their very "is" functions as an "ought" to us.[163] Unlike things, we may not detach ourselves as spectators from the presence of any human being there before us. The fact (the "is") about all of us is our primordial engagement one with the other, our claims ("ought") on each other. There is much more to truth than to facticity, which itself is an abstraction from the fullness of truth.[164]

Getting back to Rabbi's Akibah's view (being distinct from that of Ben Azzai), though, it avoids the imperialistic implications of universal love, which Jews have so rightly resented when expressed by Christians to us, for example.[165] That is its greater theological and ethical attraction. If I am to love everyone because God's love is to extend to everyone in the world through me, in what does that love consist? Inevitably, it means including that other person into the love of God that I have experienced. (For Christians, that has meant bringing these others "to Christ.") In effect, it means my trying to make everyone else just like me. I elect them as God has elected me in love. And, of course, when any of those others refuse the specific content of that love— as Jews have continually refused Christian claims on them—the anger of unrequited love is frequently the result. Thus it seems better to take our obligation to those outside of the covenant to be more one of minimal justice than of unclaimed love. Accordingly, much of the impressive theological reassessment of relations with Jews and Judaism, undertaken after the Holocaust by important segments of Christianity (who have accepted that fact of how easily Christian anti-Judaism lent itself to modern, racist anti-Semitism), has begun to face the great injustice that proselytizing efforts aimed at Jews have entailed,[166] for they have frequently led to the view that Jewish "stubbornness"

---

[163] See Novak, *Jewish Social Ethics*, 49ff; also, G. E. M. Anscombe, "Modern Moral Philosophy" (1958) in *The Is-Ought Question*, ed. W. D. Hudson (London: Macmillan, 1969), 175ff. Cf. Hume, *A Treatise of Human Nature* 1.1.1, 4; 2.3.3, 9; 3, 1.1.

[164] See Novak, *Jewish Social Ethics*, 16f.

[165] See Novak, *The Election of Israel*, 161f.

[166] See, e.g., Paul van Buren, *A Theology of the Jewish-Christian Reality* 1 (San Francisco: Harper and Row, 1987), 1:64f.

in refusing to convert is the result of a moral fault, and that political discrimination should be a response to it.

That does not mean, however, that others are to be excluded from intercovenantal love. Intercovenantal love not only does not entail hatred of others (a favorite charge of anti-Semites); it does not even entail automatic exclusion of others either. This inclusion into Jewish neighbor love occurs in one of two ways.

First and foremost, non-Jews who want to be included in the covenant, and thus in the love of and for Jews it entails, can always present themselves as candidates to become full converts to Judaism and the Jewish people (*gerei tsedeq*).[167] Thus the Torah states: "When a sojourner (*ger*) dwells with you (*itekha*) you may not persecute him. The sojourner shall be to you like one of your native born (*k'ezrah*); you shall love him like yourself (*kamokha*) because you were sojourners in the land of Egypt—I am the Lord your God" (Leviticus 19:33–34). Of course, this statement could easily refer to the non-Jewish resident-alien living *among* the Jewish people, but not literally being one *with* them. As such, it could mean: do not oppress foreigners living among you as you were persecuted as foreigners by the Egyptians.[168] The commandment, then, is based on a negative analogy, not a strict identification. It could be a specification of the norm "what is hateful to you, do not do to someone else." However, in the rabbinic tradition, this commandment is taken to refer to the full convert, he or she who is one *with* us.[169] A medieval anthology of rabbinic dicta, which in one section gathers and summarizes the mostly positive attitudes toward converts of the earlier Rabbis, comments as follows: "Just as it says about Jews, 'you shall love your neighbor as yourself,' so does it say about converts 'you shall love him as yourself.' "[170]

But how does the fact of being a sojourner in Egypt fit into this interpretation? After all, as much as Israel did not want to be a persecuted sojourner in Egypt, so does a convert want to be accepted as a member of the people of Israel. Perhaps, though, the comparison might be as follows: Just as you were sojourners in the land of Egypt and *I the Lord your God brought you out of the land of Egypt* (Leviticus 19:36), so did I bring the converts out of their gentile status.[171] That is why, in the text cited above, it states just before the comparison of the two verses from the same section of Leviticus, "[D]o not disparage your own blemish (*moom*) in someone else."[172] That means that both

---

[167] See Novak, *The Election of Israel*, 177ff.

[168] See B. A. Levine, *The JPS Torah Commentary: Leviticus* (Philadelphia Jerusalem: Jewish Publication Society, 1989), Lev. 19:33, p. 134.

[169] See B. Yevamot 46b–47a; also, B. Megillah 17b.

[170] *Mishnat Rabbi Eliezer*, chap. 16, ed. Enelow, 302f.

[171] See B. Pesahim 116a.

[172] *Mishnat Rabbi Eliezer*, chap. 16, p. 302. See *Mekhilta*: Mishpatim, 311 re Exod. 22:20; B. Baba Metsia 59b.

of you—native born and converts—are not "aboriginals"; both were originally outside the covenant, and included in it only because of divine grace; hence the justification of this mutual love for each other.[173] In rabbinic tradition, any disparagement of converts, especially pertaining to their origins, is considered a violation of a number of negative commandments.[174] The more recent convert is to remind us Jews of our more remote origins.

Furthermore, one need not become a full member of the covenant to be the object of intercovenantal love. In the days of the First Temple, the resident-alien (*ger toshav*) was someone who lived among the people of Israel. And that was to be taken as his or her choice, demonstrated by the rabbinic assumption of public acceptance of at least certain minimal laws pertaining to general interhuman relations.[175] On the positive side, the "acts of personal kindness" (*gemilut hasadim*) that we saw as being the content of intercovenantal love are to be practiced for resident-aliens, for these "sojourners," as well.[176]

The actual status of "resident-alien" most immediately applied to the right to domicile in the land of Israel.[177] The Rabbis saw this formal legal institution as operating only when all of the tribes of Israel were themselves domiciled in the land of Israel. That meant that this legal institution per se operated only during the days of the First Temple. (In the days of the Second Temple, already only two of the twelve tribes—Judah and Benjamin—could be found living in the land of Israel.)[178] Nevertheless, this did not seem to affect the issue of neighbor love in the covenant. Indeed, in terms of rights of domicile, the Jews did not now have their own original rights anymore than the gentiles living among them ever had. All the other covenantal benefits that resident-aliens had, gentiles willing to live among the Jews and respect Judaism (yet not having to ever convert to Judaism) still had too.

This can be seen in the chief covenantal benefit: *shalom*. Although usually translated as "peace," *shalom* means more than its usual connotation in English: the cessation of hostility. It is a positive presence, not just an absence of harm.[179] In the rabbinic tradition, it is one of two principles taken to govern the way Jews are to treat non-Jews with whom they come into contact. The first principle is what is to done "to avoid enmity" (*mipnei eivah*).[180] That is roughly the equivalent of "what is hateful to you, do not do to someone else." It is basic human decency. The second principle is what is to be done "for

---

[173] See Lev. 25:23 and *Sifra*: Behar, 108a–b re I Chron. 29:15 and Ps. 39:13.

[174] B. Baba Metsia 59b.

[175] B. Avodah Zarah 64b.

[176] See Maimonides, *Mishneh Torah*: Melakhim, 10.12.

[177] See *Mishneh Torah*: Avodah Zarah, 10.6 and Isurei Biah, 14.7.

[178] Arakhin 29a re Deut. 23:16. See B. Gittin 45a.

[179] See *Bemidbar Rabbah* 11.16 re Num. 6:26.

[180] See B. Avodah Zarah 26a–b and Tos. (26b), s.v. "l'afuqei"; also, B. Gittin 70a and Tos., s.v. "Rav Shimi."

the sake of the ways of peace" (*mipnei darkhei shalom*). That is roughly the equivalent of "love your neighbor as yourself."[181] So, that commandment can now be taken to mean: Love your fellow Jews—and whoever happens to be among them—when they are both in need of your personal concern. Thus we learn:

> In a city where there are Jews and gentiles: the [Jewish] welfare officials (*parnasim*) are to collect charity funds from both Jews and gentiles because of the ways of peace. The gentile poor are to be supported (*mefarnesim*) along with (*im*) the Jewish poor because of the ways of peace. The gentile dead are to be provided with a funeral (*maspidin*) and buried because of the ways of peace. The gentile mourners are to be comforted because of the ways of peace.[182]

Clearly, the "ways of peace," as a theologically grounded principle, is far deeper than the goodwill and tolerance that comes from social contract type thinking. *Shalom* is of cosmic significance; it is considered to be one of the names of God.[183]

All of this indicates that there is no overt exclusion from intercovenantal love of any outsider, and at the same time no overt inclusion of any outside either. Thus the former precludes xenophobia, and the latter precludes imperialism.

Based on all of the above, one could say that the commandment of neighbor love should be interpreted as follows: Extend God's love for his people to his people as you yourself want to be loved by that same love—and never leave out anyone who is among God's people, however partially, however temporarily, however involuntarily.[184] And the verse in Leviticus 19:18 ends with the words: "I am the Lord." That is the true ground of the commandment: Because the Lord loves Israel, individual Jews are able to share that love with others in the covenant. As Rabbi Akibah emphasized, surely that is the most inclusive aspect of the Torah.

---

[181] See M. Gittin 5.8; M. Sheviit 4.3; Y. Sheviit 4.3/35b.

[182] T. Gittin, 3.13–14, ed. Lieberman, 259; Y. Gittin 5.9/47c and parallels; B. Gittin 61a.

[183] See B. Shabbat 10b re Judg. 6:23; B. Sotah 10a and Tos., s.v. "ela"; R. David ibn Abi Zimra, *Teshuvot ha-Radbaz* 1, no. 220.

[184] For inclusion of gentiles in covenantal celebrations when they are living in proximity to Jews, see B. Betsah 21b (regarding the practice of Mremar and Mar Zutra).

CHAPTER VI

Covenanted Community and Human Persons

THE COVENANTED COMMUNITY

In the Jewish tradition, it seems that the community makes four types of claims on her individual members. (1) At the most necessary level, the community requires her members not to harm one another. She does that by threatening penalties to anyone who could do so. Communal life cannot function if the members of the community feel they will not be protected from aggression by others.[1] (2) The community adjudicates conflicting interests when humanly culpable harm has been done to persons or their property. Communal life cannot function if there is no social institution for settling interpersonal disputes. (3) Based on notions of what she needs to function well for the largest possible number of her members, the community engages in the redistribution of status or wealth. (4) The community at times requires her members to live for her or to die for her. The first two types of claims are made judicially, the third is made legislatively, and the fourth is made existentially. As we shall see, only the fourth type of claim is a truly original right.

Were the community to function only in the realm of the first three types of claims, the judicial and the legislative, it would be instrumental in essence. At this overall level, the community (*Gemeinschaft*) is a society (*Gesellschaft*), functioning impersonally through its formal political and legal institutions. When only engaging in the prevention of harm, the rectification of personal disputes, or the redistribution of status or wealth, the community has no original rights. Only persons have original rights. All institutions, conversely, are instruments for ends outside themselves.[2] At the level of prevention, adjudication, and redistribution, the community is still only a society. *It* functions abstractly as indeed befits the abstraction that society per se is. Society functions on behalf of its "citizens." That is quite different from, let us say, the relationship between "Israel" and her "sons and daughters," which is the language of full community. Hence, in order to be a complete covenanted polity, the Jewish people must function both as a community in the existential sense and as a society in the judicial and legislative sense. But it is also to be emphasized that whereas the society of Israel is part of the community of Israel, the com-

---

[1] See M. Avot 3.2; B. Avodah Zarah 4a re Hab. 1:14.

[2] For the distinction between intrinsic/inherent and extrinsic/instrumental ends, see Aristotle, *Nicomachean Ethics*, 1094a1–10.

munity of Israel is not part of the society. Society is a function of community; it is a communal construct. The task of this chapter is to show how the covenanted polity makes both social and communal claims on her members, and how these claims are interrelated. We need to look at the derivative rights of society before we look at the original rights of the community. Because of our experience of living in modern nation-states, which define themselves as societies, we are more familiar with social claims than with the more original communal claims that in truth precede them.

Even in the case of the redistribution of wealth, as in taxation for example, the justification is ultimately that this is for the sake of most of the individuals in the society. In other words, what society takes *from* its citizens initially, it finally gives *back* to them—if and when they need it. As John Rawls has argued most famously in recent years, society's redistribution of wealth is justified when one posits an "original position" into which everyone could imagine themselves.[3] That position might be characterized as follows: what is being done *to* you now by society (taking what you can still live without) is what would be done *for* you later by society (giving you what you cannot live without). It functions much like an insurance policy: one pays less in the present for what one might need more of in the future.[4] At this level, society has some immediate claims, but they are not original rights inasmuch as the justification of the claims society makes upon its individual members is that these responsive duties are for the sake of originally individual rights. In other words, these rights are not those of the community but those of someone else. They are social duties, and like all duties, they are generated by someone else's rights. In the next chapter, we shall see more fully how in these areas the original claim is that of the person upon the community, not vice versa.

The only explanation for the expansion of the claims of the community beyond being the direct, social instrument for the enforcement of individual rights is to see the plural life of the community herself as having her own original claims upon her individual members.[5] These claims are not the inverse of individual claims upon the community. Individual persons are never to be the instruments of the community in the same way that the community is at times to be the instrument of individual persons. In this century, especially, we have seen the havoc wreaked by collectivist ideologies, whose adherents have gained enough political power to claim individual persons as their instruments:

---

[3] *A Theory of Justice* (Cambridge: Harvard University Press, 1971), 126ff.

[4] According to Jewish law, the community has the right to tax her members (1) for social welfare redistribution and (2) to pay the price the Jewish community was assessed by the gentile host societies for the privilege of living in them as, in effect, *imperium in imperio*. For (1), see B. Ketubot 49b and Tos., s.v. "akfeih"; B. Baba Batra 8b and Tos., s.v. "akfeih" For (2), see B. Baba Batra 54b and Rashbam, s.v. "dina."

[5] For the notion that the human need for community transcends mere individual need, see Aristotle, *Politics*, 1278b20; also, *Nicomachean Ethics*, 1155a5.

to be used or discarded at will. Since Jews have frequently been the most abused victims of such collectivist societies, it would be a ghastly irony if our own tradition had the same instrumental view of persons as social creatures. Our historical experience should be at least of some help in our selective appropriation of our tradition, an appropriation that is necessarily selective because it is an act of finite moral judgment, which is conducted for the needs of a definite time (*sub specie durationis*). The tradition certainly affirms our fundamental sociality, but with the proviso that it is God and not any society who creates humans as the social creatures they are in truth. For Judaism, it is God who has placed human persons in those communities worthy of their human allegiance. In the case of the Jews, that placement is the election by God for the covenant with God.[6]

One must avoid the tyrannical implications of the idea of a community that is more than the mere enforcer of individual rights. The best way to do that, it seems, is to see the community as the fulfillment of the definite need of her members for her, but not to see the community as the fulfillment of all human needs.[7] In other words, human needs are both communal and individual. The individual needs of human persons can be subsumed under the category of privacy (*bonum sibi*). At one level of privacy, some internally conceived self-project is to be the object of the person as a rational agent. But at the level of what might be termed "existential privacy," or the level of the soul rather than just the self, human persons have the need for the presence of each other on a truly plural basis (*bonum commune*).[8] Here, others are the external objects of an act of the whole person. In a community in which we desire to live, as opposed to a society in which we have to survive, these objects are those persons *with* whom and not just *among* whom we exist. Hence our human needs are both proprietary and participatory, both immanent and transcendent.

Our transcendent need for community, which alone explains why individual persons can affirm the original authority of their own community, is both a function of our past and a function of our future, both a recollection and an anticipation. As a function of our past, our most primary community is the family into which we are born. It makes its claims upon us even before we are aware of our own personal need for it. As a function of our future, we are

---

[6] See D. Novak, *The Election of Israel* (Cambridge: Cambridge University Press, 1995), 115ff.

[7] Cf. Plato, *Republic*, 434Dff., who attempts to constitute a society that does fulfill all human needs. For a critique of the tyranny such a view entails, see Karl Popper, *The Open Society and Its Enemies*, 5th ed. (Princeton: Princeton University Press, 1966), 1:86ff.

[8] In the most celebrated presentation of liberal political theory in the last half century, Rawls's *A Theory of Justice*, there is no real transition from *bonum sibi* to *bonum commune*. Note: "Public goods consist of those instrumentalities and conditions maintained by the state for everyone to use for his own purposes as his means permit, in the same manner that each has his own destination when traveling along the highways" (521).

called upon by our community to perpetuate her identity. That claim too is first made by our family, as we shall soon see in greater detail.

In order for the community to truly fulfill our transcendent needs, however, she must intend her own transcendence. That is, the very life of the community must be *for the One who* is beyond her own grasp. If that is not the case, if the community is taken to be the last rather than the first realm beyond the individual soul, then her own life becomes the final end. When this happens, she does not overcome the very selfishness whose personal inadequacy leads individual persons not only to desire their community's heritage, but to desire their community's perpetuation as well. What collectivism does is merely transfer immanence from individuals to a collective. That is the error of any kind of socialism in claiming to have overcome the loneliness of the soul. In the case of individual selfishness, the immanent projects of oneself are disproportionately emphasized at the expense of the greater needs of the whole person, thus resulting in individual spiritual pathology. So in collective selfishness, immanent social projects are emphasized over the greater need of the whole community, thus resulting in social pathology.

In the case of the community, this usually translates into the dominance of those persons whose existence coincides with the collective project or ideal, over those persons seen as farther removed from it. Indeed, those privileged members of the society are usually the very same people who propose these projects or ideals in the first place—for their own selfish benefit. Also, it usually translates into hatred of those outside the community; the communal need for transcendence, having been twisted by the pathology of collective selfishness, becomes a negative rather than a positive intention, one that identifies itself *against* rather than *for* the other.[9] In the case of the Jewish people, its collective life must always be more for the sake of God than it is for the sake of being different from the other peoples in the world. "And you shall be holy for me (*li*) because I the Lord am holy; and I shall separate you from the peoples to be for me (*le-hiyot li*)" (Leviticus 20:26).[10]

---

[9] Along these lines, note Jacques Maritain, *The Rights of Man and the Natural Law*, trans. D. Anson (San Francisco: Ignatius Press, 1986), 122–23: "Nor in the racial type of community . . . is there an object, a common task to perform. . . . It is not for an objective purpose that they assemble, but rather for the subjective pleasure of being together, of *marching together* (*zusammenmarschieren*). . . . Fusion within the community thus becomes a compensation for an abnormal feeling of loneliness and distress. Nothing is more dangerous than such a community: deprived of a determining objective, political communion will carry its demands to the infinite, will absorb and regiment people, swallow up in itself the religious energies of the human being. Because it is not defined by a work to be done, it will only be able to define itself by its opposition to other human groups. Therefore, it will have essential need of an *enemy against whom* it will build itself; it is by recognizing and hating its enemies that the political body will find its own common consciousness."

[10] See *Sifra*: Qedoshim, ed. Weiss, 93d and comment of R. Abraham ben David of Posquières (Ravad) thereon; also, Rashi, *Commentary on the Torah*: Lev. 20:26. Spinoza, conversely, saw

Such social pathology is quite possible even in a covenantal community. This is especially the case now since those who have voluntarily defected from the covenant in modern times have most often done so based on individualistic criteria, which can be summarized in the phrase (or something like it) "it is not meaningful for me." Hence it is an easy temptation simply to opt for collectivism as the ready antidote to the individualistic myopia of most of the defectors from the tradition who live in democratic societies. But collectivism is both a practical and a theoretical error. When it does appear in the guise of practical injustice against "outsiders" or even dissenting "insiders," insightful jurists (which are what rabbis as halakhic authorities are in essence) are morally obligated to refute it on legal grounds. And when it is proposed rhetorically in the guise of a faulty ethnocentric or conformist imagination, insightful theorists (beginning with those who regularly preach the Torah in public) have a moral obligation to refute it on theological grounds. The covenant as theonomy is more than the autonomy of individualism or the heteronomy of collectivism.[11]

There is little doubt that in the Jewish tradition, the authentic communal needs of the human person do take precedence over his or her individual needs. (But it should be remembered, as we shall see in the next chapter, this precedence over individual needs is quite distinct from the denial of them.) Communal needs are greater. Indeed, as we have already seen in the first four chapters, even the relationship between God and individual persons is still one between God and the members of the covenanted community. We can be whole persons before God only when we stand together with those others, without whom we would be less than fully human ourselves. Our privacy is, in effect, an abstraction from our full communal selves, although an abstraction that is required for the community to be a true communion of free persons.

This social priority means that the authority of the community is its power to *generalize*, that is, to make rules for the common interest that require the inhibition of the full exercise of many individual interests. Thus a principle of rabbinic legislation is that the Rabbis made rules only based on what is common, that is, usual (*milta de-shekhiha*), and not on what is individual, that is, unusual (*milta de-la shekhiha*).[12] Moreover, unlike essentially individualistic social contract theory, this compromise is not instrumental. It is not a sacrifice of some individual interests in return for the social protection of others. Protection is only what lies on the surface of our authentic communal desire. Instead, it is not a necessary burden (although it appears to be one at times), but the

---

Jewish separateness as a pure negation, i.e., separation for its own sake motivated by hatred of the other. See *Tractatus Theologico-Politicus*, chap. 1 (following Tacitus, *Histories*, 5.5).

[11] See D. Novak, *Jewish Social Ethics* (New York: Oxford University Press, 1992), 46ff.

[12] See B. Eruvin 63b and parallels; Y. Yoma 1.1/38d; Maimonides, *Guide of the Perplexed*, 3.34.

just claim of the community for its very generality, which itself is a partial fulfillment of the fully human need for self-transcendence. Only an unjustly constituted society is in essential conflict with that most basic human need, for it demands either too much as in the case of tyranny, or it demands too little as in the case of that type of liberalism that advocates a normative minimalism, which can only be taken to be antinomian in essence. As communal persons we are less than Marx's "species beings" (*Gattungswesen*) and more than John Stuart Mill's "sovereign individuals."[13]

It is not that we come to society as already self-formed individuals, with our own bundle of selfish interests in hand, ready to bargain some of the less important ones away so that we can safely keep the more important ones. Instead, it is only after having been socialized that we come to realize that some of our individual needs can be justified as human rights, which are distinct from our social duties. It is, then, our task and that of the political authorities themselves to protect these human rights of ours, which can be justified only when they do not conflict with our prior social duties, duties that themselves are rationally correlated with our deeper need for community herself. Nevertheless, in order for individual rights to be able to truly limit communal duties by denying them any totalizing, collectivist pretensions, they must only not contradict any prior communal duties. They do not have to be justified as being for the sake of collective good, as many utilitarians would have it.[14] That is so even though a respect for individual rights is itself an important function of a just society. "Learn to do good; seek justice (*mishpat*); strengthen the oppressed; uphold the rights of the orphan; defend the widow" (Isaiah 1:17).

COMMUNITY AND NORMATIVE GENERALITY

The need for normative generality is the claim that the community makes upon us to act more as communal persons than as lone individuals.[15] As the Talmud puts it when discussing the process of generalization needed for the making of effective norms, "[O]ne's individual preference is annulled (*batlah da'ato*) in relation to that of everyone else (*kol adam*)."[16] (What distinguishes this approach from that of modern collectivism, as we shall see in the next chapter, is that there are definite areas where one's private preferences are protected. Being a communal person does not mean that the presence of the community is to be ubiquitous.) This comes out in both formal legislation, which

---

[13] See Marx, "Zur Judenfrage," in *Werke* (Berlin: Dietz, 1964), 1:370; Mill, *On Liberty*, in *Utilitarianism, Liberty, and Representative government* (London: Everyman Library, 1993), 78.

[14] See Mill, *On Liberty* (London: Everyman Library, 1993), 79.

[15] Along these lines, see Jacques Maritain, *The Person and the Common Good*, trans. J. J. Fitzgerald (Notre Dame, Ind.: University of Notre Dame Press, 1966), 31ff.

[16] B. Berakhot 35b and parallels.

society can enforce, and in moral exhortation, which elicits more voluntary compliance.

At the legal level, the Rabbis saw it to be the right of justly appointed and properly functioning communal authorities to actually remove certain rights from individual persons, even if they were seen as being scripturally authorized.[17] (In the case of removing individual duties for the sake of the common good, the Rabbis were much more circumspect and conservative, however.)[18] Such removal is always justified by considerations of the common good that override the private need the fulfillment of which an individual's right intends. What we have, in effect, is a transfer of rights.

Following our scheme of seeing the first three of the four areas of communal rights being (1) preventive, (2) rectifying or adjudicative, and (3) distributive or legislative, let us now see how this transfer of rights is effected.

At the level of prevention, one can see this transfer in the striking scriptural case of the "rebellious son" (*ben sorer u-moreh*) and its interpretation by the Rabbis. Scripture states:

> when a man has a rebellious son, who does not listen to his father's voice and his mother's voice, and whom they chastise, but he still does not listen to them, his father and mother shall seize him and take him out to the elders of his city. And they shall declare to them [the elders]: "This rebellious son of ours does not listen to our voice; he is a glutton and a drunkard." (Deuteronomy 21:18–19)

The section concludes with the prescription of the death penalty for this wayward youth.

According to the Mishnah, this is a preventive measure because such a youth is very likely to commit more serious crimes in the future (*nidon al shem sofo*), crimes that go beyond his own family circle and that endanger the whole community.[19] Now, of course, this raises the very serious moral question of whether it is just to punish a person for crimes he or she might commit, even probably will commit, but that have not yet been committed. Furthermore, it seems that this criminal is but a child himself. On the surface, it also seems to provide legal cover, as it were, for homicidal parents to kill a troublesome child with impunity. For these reasons and others, it seems, there is an opinion in the Talmud that this law was never and will never be put into actual practice. If so, why was it written in the first place? The answer is: "for meritorious speculation" (*darosh ve-qabbel sekhar*).[20] This answer seems to be saying that even though the rules here are in fact inapplicable, there are principles that can

---

[17] See, e.g., B. Yevamot 89b; B. Kiddushin 12b; Y. Yevamot 5.2/6d.

[18] See, e.g., B. Yevamot 90b re Deut. 18:15; B. Nazir 43b and Tos., s.v. "ve-hai."

[19] M. Sanhedrin 8.5. For further discussion of this institution, see D. Novak, *Law and Theology in Judaism* (New York: KTAV, 1976), 2:56ff.; Novak, *Jewish Social Ethics*, 167f.

[20] B. Sanhedrin 71a.

be discerned behind them, and these principles do have moral significance and even legal implications.

One such principle I discern is that there are times when a family cannot care for one of their own members by themselves. This is especially so when they feel helpless to prevent an emotionally disturbed member from effecting great harm in the community. What they are doing here is transferring their right of preventive discipline, which is not the same as retributive punishment, to the institution of society. Indeed, they might now have the duty to do so for the sake of the community as a whole, however embarrassing that might be to them.

At the level of rectification, we can see the transfer of individual rights into communal duties in the case of revenge. Revenge is basically the right of a person to return harm, in equal measure, to one who has harmed him or her initially. Now, of course, there is a long history of opposition to revenge, especially by philosophers, because it is seen to be fundamentally irrational: What good is accomplished by adding harm to harm?[21] Yet the only alternative responses to being harmed are either doing nothing or attempting to reform rather than punish the criminal. However, victims suffering in silence only encourage criminals by removing any negative consequences of their crimes. And attempting to reform the criminal, although meritorious in and of itself, presupposes that we really know what makes criminals do what they do. Moreover, it seems to be more concerned with the welfare of the criminal than with the plight of the victim of his or her crime.

Revenge is a corollary of the basic interpersonal norm we examined in the preceding chapter: What is hateful to you, do not do to your fellow human. Revenge means: What is hateful to you will be done to you if you do it to your fellow human.[22] What is important to see here is that revenge accomplishes two things. One, it is an aspect of the prevention of crime: crime should not pay. Without revenge, criminals would always benefit from their crimes.[23] Two, revenge gives us our moral idea of "measure for measure" (*middah ke-neged middah*) in criminal justice.[24] Unlike doing nothing in return or seeing the reform of the criminal as our primary response, revenge intends equality.[25] Doing nothing, however, suggests that the response to the crime be in a lesser amount than the amount of the crime itself. An attempt to reform the criminal as our response to the crime itself could mean that our response is either in a

---

[21] See Plato, *Crito*, 49D; *Republic*, 410A (cf. *Laws*, 735E); also, more recently, L. E. Goodman, *On Justice* (New Haven: Yale University Press, 1991), 44ff.

[22] See Deut.19:19, where even a conspiracy to convict someone of a crime he or she did not commit is punished as if it has been done. See B. Baba Kama 5a; Maimonides, *Mishneh Torah: Edut*, 20.2.

[23] See, e.g., B. Yevamot 92a and parallels.

[24] See M. Sotah 1.7.

[25] See Maimonides, *Guide of the Perplexed*, 3.41.

lesser amount or a greater amount than the amount of the crime itself. It would be in a lesser amount if compassion for the criminal prevented us from penalizing him or her altogether; and it would be in a greater amount if that same compassion for the criminal led to his or her indefinite stay in a mental hospital until he or she seemed to psychological experts to be "cured." But such a sentence, in the case of anyone not thoroughly psychotic, lacks the essential justice that even criminals are entitled to, namely, knowing in advance the legal consequences of their crime.[26]

The moral problem with revenge is not the principle underlying it but, rather, the fact that individual victims of crime are usually too emotionally distraught to be able to rationally effect revenge equal to the crime itself. They will inevitably overreact, thus setting in motion counterreactions, what we now would call a vendetta.[27] As is well known from such modern societies as Sicily, such an unending atmosphere of violence is an enormous impediment to the common good. That is why society has to remove the right of revenge from individuals and turn it into a social duty to be exercised by the authorized representatives of society, who are much more likely to operate in a cooler, more rational manner. In addition, with the exception of capital punishment for murderers, society is able to make retribution be more permanently beneficial to the victims of crime themselves by changing it to monetary restitution instead of leaving it at the momentary level of emotional satisfaction in seeing one's victimizer physically suffer as he or she did.[28]

This comes out in the rabbinic interpretation of the *lex talionis*: "an eye for an eye" (Exodus 21:24). As is well known, the Rabbis interpreted the retribution to be monetary compensation for the loss of economic function by the victim of the mutilation instead of actual mutilation in kind.[29] A number of reasons are proposed for this interpretation, but to my mind the best one given in the Talmud is that money can be equalized in a way bodily parts cannot be. Thus one can abstract from the victim's body its monetary worth as a wage earner and demand its equivalent in money from the mutilator in a way that one cannot equalize, let us say, the eye of a two-eyed victim with the eye of a one-eyed mutilator. The victim will still have sight if revenge is bodily, but the mutilator will be blinded.[30] The heart of the argument, though, is that the more abstract character of money enables a more precise, a more just form of

---

[26] Thus the forewarning of a criminal (*hatra'ah*) is to express the prohibition of the crime (*azharah*) and the punishment (*onesh*) for it. See T. Sanhedrin 11.1; Maimonides, *Mishneh Torah*: Sanhedrin, 12.2.

[27] See Maimonides, *Guide of the Perplexed*, 3.40.

[28] For the refusal of monetary restitution in cases of murder or manslaughter, see Num. 35:31 and B. Ketubot 37b. Cf. B. Yevamot 118a and 120a re Judg. 16:30.

[29] M. Baba Kama 8.1.

[30] B. Baba Kama 83b re Lev. 24:22. For a fuller discussion of this issue, see Novak, *Jewish Social Ethics*, 169ff.

retribution than the literal "eye for an eye." And money is such an abstraction because it is a social invention, a construct rather than a natural entity like the body.[31] Thus the right to individual revenge, which is a relation between two bodies, now made into a monetary matter requires the more abstract formality of third-party adjudication. Society, in its judicial institution of the court, is that third party. In the end, revenge becomes the duty to submit one's grievances against a fellow human, whether because of harm to body or property, to the social institution now having authority over both parties in any dispute.

At the level of distribution, we need to see how society is empowered to transfer property for the sake of the common good. A good example of this rights transfer is the following:

> Ulla said that the literal law of Scripture is that a debtor may pay his debt with the poorest quality produce (*zeburiyot*), as it says: "you [the claimant] are to stand outside [the dwelling of the debtor] and the man whose debt you are claiming shall bring the pledge out to you" (Deuteronomy 24:11). Now, what does one usually bring out; is it not the least valuable stuff among his things (*pahot she-ba-kelim*)? Therefore, what is the reason (*u-mah ta'am*) the Sages rule that a debtor is to be paid with at least minimum quality produce (*beinonit*); is it not so that (*kedei*) the door will not be closed in the face of borrowers?[32]

This is one of several rabbinic rulings that, in effect, removed a scripturally recognized individual right in the sake of the overall economy of the community.[33] The assumption is that the full exercise of the right of debtors to basically unload merchandise, which is difficult to sell in their own locality, as repayment of their debts will in the end stifle the easy lending of money or goods. (Actually, in the context of the scriptural passage cited in the quotation above, the issue is more one of affirming a person's right to have the sanctity of his or her home—namely, the locus of one's privacy—respected, a right that the rabbinic ruling does not remove.[34] That aspect of the earlier law is not changed inasmuch as the old right of privacy is still confirmed in the method of payment; it is the choice of the means of payment that is removed.[35]) Such a breakdown of communal responsibility on the part of borrowers is envisioned to have bad consequences for the entire community.

Furthermore, such an exchange of an individual right into a social duty can be seen when the community has limited resources at her disposal for social welfare, which of course is the usual state of affairs. As such, there must be

---

[31] See Aristotle, *Nicomachean Ethics*, 1133a30.

[32] B. Baba Kama 8a. Cf. B. Gittin 49b.

[33] See M. Gittin 4.3; B. Gittin 36a–b; also, Novak, *Jewish Social Ethics*, 212ff.

[34] See B. Baba Metsia 115a re Deut. 24:10.

[35] For the difference between payment in movables and payment in real estate as regards this rabbinic ruling, see B. Baba Kama 8a, Tos., s.v. "le-hotsee."

limits on what she can spend on any one person so that funds not be depleted that could help many more persons in distress. In other words, some sort of rationing of resources is required by the common good. This is best seen in the right of any member of the community to be ransomed when captured by an enemy. The original right here is that one not be abandoned by his or her community. Indeed, some have seen this as the most basic claim a person can make on the community.[36] This right is expressed in the rabbinic rule that "one captive is not to be ransomed (*podeen*) by money designated for any other captive."[37] However, even in expressing this rule, the proviso is made that the public authorities, with due discretion, to be sure, may do just that.[38] Based on that type of reasoning, the Mishnah notes that "captives are not to be ransomed for more than the going rate because of the common good (*tiqqun ha'olam*)."[39] In other words, spending too much on any one captive could quickly deplete public resources for ransoming many other captives, and that is so whether there are really other captives to be ransomed here and now or only possible captives in the future. Also, spending too much money on any one captive might very well encourage enemies of the Jews to take even more captives in the future because this would become more and more profitable once it is known that the Jews will pay any price to redeem one of their own.[40] Hence the right to be ransomed is changed into the duty not to be ransomed if this will decrease the danger, both monetary and physical, to the community as a whole.

This type of exchange of rights is not limited to the economic realm. It is sometimes authorized for the sake of the overall sexual propriety of the community. Here the community is concerned with the virtue of her members. Thus, according to scriptural law, a man has the right to initiate his marriage to a woman by means of a specified act of intercourse.[41] That is, he may arrange for two bona fide witnesses to see him sequester himself with a designated woman and then hear him make a statement to her that this act is for the sake of initiating a marriage with her to be his wife, here and now.[42] But there is the probability that such a public event could quite easily have a pornographic effect on the community because of the likeliness of lewd speech and action (*peritsuta*) among the onlookers there. Because of this, the third-century Babylonian authority Rav prohibited this practice and ordered anyone engaging in it to be publicly punished.[43] Thus he turned the original positive right of the

---

[36] B. Baba Batra 8a–b; Maimonides, *Mishneh Torah*: Mattnot Aniyyim, 8.10.

[37] T. Sheqalim 1.12.

[38] See Y. Sheqalim 2.5/47a and R. Mosheh Margolis, *Pnei Mosheh* thereon.

[39] M. Gittin 4.6.

[40] B. Gittin 45a; Maimonides, *Mishneh Torah*: Mattnot Aniyyim, 8.12.

[41] M. Kiddushin 1.1; T. Kiddushin 1.3; also, *Sifre*: Devarim, no. 268; Y. Kiddushin 1.1/58b; and B. Kiddushin 9b re Deut. 24:1.

[42] See Maimonides, *Mishneh Torah*: Ishut, 3.5.

[43] B. Kiddushin 12a. See Y. Yevamot 5.2/6d.

man (and the consenting woman) into a negative duty for the sake of the moral climate of the community, which pornography with its especial degradation of women threatens.[44] This whole approach also has profound implications for the rectification of abuses in Jewish marriage law that enable unscrupulous men and women to impede the finalization of a divorce when the marriage is no longer a true interpersonal relationship. As in the days of Rav, it is the social obligation of halakhic authorities to rectify abuses that result from the immoral exercise of an individual right, abuses that have a bad effect on the community as a whole because of the degradation of the central communal institution of marriage upon which the family is based.[45] Here too, the common good takes precedence over the exercise of an individual right.

There are also cases where the transfer of an individual right is not legislated but only publicly encouraged. Sometimes, the distinction between formal legislation and moral exhortation is just a matter of time, that is, eventually the moral exhortation becomes a legal norm.[46] However, there is also a sense that the common good can be better achieved when persons are encouraged to contribute to it more voluntarily.[47]

The following is a good example of how this works:

> Rabbi Eliezer the son of Rabbi Yose the Galilean says that it is forbidden to submit one's civil case to arbitration (*asur li-vetsoa*) and whoever does so is a sinner. . . . [B]ut let the legal ruling (*ha-din*) pierce the mountain. . . . Rabbi Joshua ben Qorhah says that it is meritorious (*mitsvah*) to submit one's case to arbitration as Scripture says, "True and peaceful justice (*mishpat shalom*) you shall adjudicate in your gates" (Zechariah 8:16). But is it not so that when there is justice there is no peace, and when there is peace there is no justice? So what kind of justice contains peace? That is arbitration.[48]

The phrase used in the first opinion—"let the legal ruling pierce the mountain"—means that whereas it is easier to go around a mountain, the most direct way to get beyond it is to go through it. The experience the metaphor invokes is that of something being accomplished immediately. In other words, the law is to be upheld without regard for social consequences. It is like the Latin proverb, "Let justice be done, even if the world is destroyed" (*fiat iustitia*

---

[44] See B. Ketubot 8b; also, B. Sanhedrin 75a; Maimonides, *Teshuvot ha-Rambam*, ed. Y. Blau (Jerusalem: Miqitsei Nirdamim, 1960), vol. 2, no. 207, p. 366.

[45] See D. Novak, *Halakhah in a Theological Dimension* (Chico, Calif.: Scholars Press, 1985), 29ff.

[46] See, e.g., M. Baba Metsia 4.2; B. Baba Metsia 48b re Exod. 22:27.

[47] For the role of autonomy in the covenantal system, see chapter 6 above.

[48] B. Sanhedrin 6b (cf. Y. Taaniyot 4.2/68a and Y. Megillah 3.6/74b). *Mitsvah* here does not mean a positive commandment, whose nonobservance would comprise a sin but, rather, an optimal act (as distinct from a merely optional act [*reshut*]; see B. Sanhedrin, 7a), but not one entailing any legal opprobrium for its nonobservance (see, e.g., B. Yevamot 106b).

pereat mundus). In this case, the law is for the sake of the rights of the litigant who is judged by the authorities to be the innocent party in the case. In the end, he benefits, but the litigant who is judged by the same authorities to be the guilty party suffers because of his or her legal defeat. Following the metaphor of "piercing," this "loser" is "stabbed" by the law.

In the second opinion, there is the political issue of the peace of the community over and above the legal issue of whose individual claims are to be enforced and whose are not. In this opinion, the authorities must combine concern for individual claims (*mishpat*) with concern for the public weal (*shalom*). The only way this can be done with legal integrity is if before any decision is made in an interpersonal monetary dispute, both parties themselves agree to waive their respective rights to the possibility of total legal victory and, therefore, agree that neither of them will either win or lose.[49] Both are willing to compromise (*pesharah*) for the sake of the common good, from which they and everyone else as communal beings will benefit,[50] for after the trial is over, both litigants will still be living together as members of the same community. The achievement of that communal peace is less direct than strict justice and takes more time.[51] That is finally more important than the literal accomplishment of justice for one individual at the expense of the other, both in terms of his or her property or his or her embarrassment. Furthermore, even though no one is literally obligated by the law to agree to arbitration in lieu of a formal trial, legal authorities are to persuade litigants to do so.[52] The authorities should convince the opposing parties that there is good reason for naturally social beings to rise above the level of even legitimate private interest for the sake of *their* community, which should be more important to them and every other member of the community in the end.[53] That such a procedure is to be persuasive rather than coercive means that the community is to be as much as possible a communion *of* free, rational persons working together instead of an external force standing *over* these same persons and, in effect, throwing them together or tearing them apart.

---

[49] See T. Baba Kama 2.10; Y. Baba Kama 3.5/3d; B. Sanhedrin 32b re Deut. 16:20 (as distinct from Lev. 19:15).

[50] See R. Samuel Edels (Maharsha), *Hiddushei Aggadot*: B. Sanhedrin 6b.

[51] It is very much a matter of not insisting on the full measure of one's own rights (*lifnim me-shurat ha-din*). See B. Baba Kama 99b–100a re Exod. 18:20 and Tos., s.v. "lifnim."

[52] See Maimonides, *Mishneh Torah*: Sanhedrin, 22.4, 6; *Tur*: Hoshen Mishpat, 12 and R. Joseph Karo, *Bet Yosef*, s.v. "u-mitsvah" re B. Sanhderin 7a and Rashi, s.v. "mitsvah;" R. Joseph Karo, *Shulhan Arukh*: Hoshen Mishpat, 12.2 and R. Shabbtai ha-Kohen (Shakh), *Siftei Kohen*, n. 6 thereon; I. Schepansky, *Ha-Taqqanot be-Yisrael* (Jersualem: Mosad ha-Rav Kook, 1993), 4:36.

[53] This point is especially emphasized by R. Joseph Boaz, *Shiltei ha-Gibborim*, n. 1 on *Alfasi*: Sanhedrin, chap. 1, ed. Vilna, 1b. He makes the important distinction between judicial imposition (*tsad hekhreh*) and judicial informative persuasion (*piyusim*), the latter always being preferable in the interest of communal peace. See, also Maimonides *Commentary on the Mishnah*: intro., ed. Kafih, 1:16f., who likens *pesharah* to preventive medicine and *din* to therapy after illness has already occurred. In other words, *pesharah* operates as if there has been no rupture of the *bonum commune* at all. It is retroactive.

FAMILIAL DUTY

Too much political theory has ignored the significance of family to human polity. That comes into conflict with the Jewish tradition (and other traditions), which sees a continuum from family to community and from community to family. This divergence must be understood in order to better understand how a Jewish theory of community constitutes the correlation of communal claims/ rights and personal responses/duties in a distinct way. This issue is central to the idea that the community does, indeed, have original rights, and that they are more than instrumental duties for the sake of individual rights. We must discover the exact locus of communal claims that are more than institutions of preventive, rectifiying, or even distributive justice, all of which are ultimately based on what persons can claim from the community.

Most liberalism ignores the political significance of family by seeing the main political relationship as being between individuals and the state.[54] But it is also the case with the political theory that inspires many conservatives today (that is, those who are not, in effect the most radical liberals themselves: libertarians), that of Aristotle. Now, it is true that Aristotle is quite critical of Plato's suggestion that at the highest level of political leadership, for whom his optimal polity (his "Republic") is founded, familial ties of husband and wife and parents and children are to be abolished.[55] He rightfully notes that persons who have no attachment to their biological-historical roots are more likely to have no real attachment to anyone in the society rather than to everyone in it, which Plato presents as the reason for his proposed social transcendence of the limits of family attachment.[56] Nevertheless, even for Aristotle, despite the fact that those who govern the polity are not to abolish their family attachments, these attachments, with their inherently permanent hierarchy, are essentially bracketed when it comes to the inherent equality among themselves that is essential for the ruling, enlightened class to rule intelligently.[57]

This more conservative separation of family and polity, as distinct from Plato's more radical displacement of family by polity, is still inadequate to deal with sexuality as the necessary link between family and polity in a way that can constitute a truly integrated view of it. And by "sexuality," I mean the

---

[54] See Rawls, *A Theory of Justice*, 511. For the continuing breakdown in modern Western law of the communal dimension of marriage, which is so connected to birth and care of children, stemming from Enlightenment emphasis of the absolute primacy of individuals (especially from the influential views of John Stuart Mill on marriage as essentially a contract between private parties), see John Witte, Jr., *From Sacrament to Contract* (Louisville, Ky.: Westminster Knox Press, 1997), 194ff.

[55] *Politics*, 1262a5ff.

[56] *Republic*, 463Dff.

[57] See *Nicomachean Ethics*, 1158b12ff., where friendship (*philia*) as the true bond between political equals is precluded from any familial relationships. See also *Politics*, 1253a20.

relationship between men and women, the most basic biological difference within the human species, a relationship that involves more than just genital acts. Surely, our familial relationships with mother and father, sisters and brothers, and beyond extend into our polity rather than being bracketed for it or overcome by it. At times of great political crisis, especially a military threat from outside, it is almost inevitable that the familial character of the community will be invoked to rally her sons and daughters to her aid.[58]

This separation of familial sexuality and political sexuality has the effect of making familial sexuality too far removed from political equality. There are issues of justice in the family itself that only society can properly handle. If not, the family is insufficiently regulated and supported by society. And it has the effect of making political duty too far removed from the sexual order of family. Indeed, the very matrix of communal duties, which are more than just the instruments of individual rights, a matrix that is found in our familial attachments, is thereby lost. In other words, without a beginning in distinctively familial duty, it is questionable whether a true understanding of uniquely communal duty can be attained.

Much of what I have been discussing more theoretically heretofore comes out more practically in current public debates about the nature of family and about whether or not sexual unions should be limited to women with men and men with women, as they have been traditionally. The public recognition of the permissibility of homosexual unions, let alone the public endorsement of them by the institution of same-sex marriages, calls into question traditional views of family. Virtually everyone on either side of this great political issue would agree that it is tradition that is on trial here. Thus the debate necessarily involves the question of exactly what original right, if any, a community can just exercise as a claim upon her members, a claim the response to which is their duty. And, as Maimonides saw so well, the hardest duties for humans to fulfill are the duties that involve the limitation and direction of libido.[59] Furthermore, if Western civilization is viewed as a continuum between the poles of Athens and Jerusalem, then whatever else can be more directly traced back to Athens, the ideas of sexuality and family and their attendant duties, which have been reflected in that civilization, especially in its systems of law, can certainly be most directly traced back to Jerusalem, to Hebraic rather than to Hellenic sources. Hence it is Jewish tradition that is on trial, and it is that aspect of the Jewish tradition which traditional Christian moral teaching has adopted knowingly and willingly, with virtually no alterations.[60]

---

[58] See Judg. 4:7 and the comment of R. David Kimhi, *Commentary on the Former Prophets*, thereon.

[59] *Mishneh Torah*: Isurei Biah, 22.18. See R. Joseph Karo, *Kesef Mishneh* thereon re *Sifre*: Bemidbar, no. 90 and B. Yoma 75a re Numb. 11:10.

[60] See, e.g., Thomas Aquinas, *Summa Theologiae*, 2/1, q. 98, a. 5 and q. 100, a. 2.

Human sexuality is inseparable from family. Even in our most intimate, supposedly private sexual contacts, our families are always there too—at least psychically.[61] And in the case of marital sex, family is present in the flesh. All of this must be examined in some detail, not only historically but dialectically as well, in the light of current debates over what has come to be called "sexual politics."

The centrality of family relationships in Judaism and the unequivocal prohibition of homoerotic acts in Jewish law are facts that are irrefutable.[62] Any deviation from them would require a reconstruction of Judaism so radical that its continuity with the normative Jewish tradition would no longer be recognizable. Nevertheless, since the pioneering investigations of Freud at the beginning of this century, most of the old conventions concerning sexuality have been called into question during the rest of this century. That has required both those who advocate these originally Hebraic norms be changed and those who advocate they remain in force to devise new arguments for their respective positions. The current debate over homosexuality, especially, has called for such new arguments because the case at hand seems so radical when made by those who advocate change and so lacking in rational persuasion when made by those who advocate tradition. They concern, as we shall soon see, the very heart of what a community fundamentally is and what her rights are. For this reason, it is appropriate to engage in a somewhat lengthy discussion of it at this point in our inquiry. Furthermore, such discussion relates the theory being presented here to one of the most significant normative debates of our time: the role of society in regulating sexual behavior.

The essential question to be discussed is that of deciding just what human sexuality intends, that is, just what its purpose truly is. Now, at the prima facie level, there seem to be three purposes of human sexuality: one, pleasure; two, personal communion; three, procreation. Thus human persons engage in sexual activities because they desire (1) the unique enjoyment of bodily union; (2) the transcendence of personal loneliness; and (3) generational continuity,

---

[61] See B. Sotah 36b re Gen. 39:12; Y. Horayot 2.5/46d re Gen. 49:24.

[62] Even though one could argue that the original prohibition in Lev. 18:22 ("With a male you shall not lie as with a female") refers to anal intercourse between two males only (see *Sifra*: Qedoshim, ed. Weiss, 92a re Lev. 18:22 and Deut. 23:18; M. Sanhedrin 7.4; B. Sanhedrin 54a–b; Y. Sanhedrin 7.7/24d–25a), the subsequent Jewish tradition saw the prohibition as including all sexual acts between males. Hence the generic term *mishkav zakhur* ("male intercourse") includes even sex play among very young children, where actual anal penetration by a penis is most unlikely (see B. Shabbat 17b). For the general prohibition of any sexual contact between males, see M. Kiddushin 4.14; B. Pesahim 51a; B. Berakhot 43b; Maimonides, *Commentary on the Mishnah*: Sanhedrin 7.4; and *Mishneh Torah*: Isurei Biah, 22.2; *Sefer ha-Hinukh*, no. 209; *Tur*: Even Ha'Ezer, 24; Karo, *Bet Yosef*, and R. Joel Sirkes, *Bayit Hadash* thereon; Karo, *Shulhan Arukh*: Even Ha'Ezer, 24.1; R. Samuel Phoebus, *Bet Shmuel* thereon. As for female homosexuality, see B. Yevamot 76a and Tos., s.v. "mesolelot"; B. Shabbat 65a; Maimonides, *Mishneh Torah*: Isurei Biah, 21.8 re Lev. 18:3. Cf. Niddah 61a and Tos., s.v. "amar R. Ami."

namely, what has traditionally been called "family." Some theorists have attempted to affirm all three of these purposes as three separate, albeit related, ends.[63] Others have attempted to emphasize one of them at the expense of the others.[64] However, I think the best case can be made that all three purposes are essentially one, with procreation being "first among equals" (*primus inter pares*).

The way to see all these purposes in unison is to assert that the purpose of sexuality is to initiate and maintain a family as a primarily intergenerational community. In the full sense of the term, "family life" means the intended permanent union of a man and a woman, which therewith intends the conception, birth, and parenting of children. As Scripture puts it, "A man shall leave his father and his mother and cleave unto his wife, and they shall become one flesh" (Genesis 2:24). In traditional Jewish exegesis, "one flesh" refers to the heterosexual couple themselves, who intend to conceive a child by their union, and the child himself or herself who issues from their permanent, sustained union.[65] And from this passage, the Rabbis see all the universal (and rational) sexual prohibitions, that is, from a positive commandment they infer these negative ones, these prohibitions (*isurim*).[66]

Now, the argument against this traditional definition of family life is that it is too exclusive. Specifically, it seems to exclude homosexuals, sterile persons, and celibate persons from familial fulfillment. In current moral debate, into which this Jewish perspective is being entered, the charge of homosexual exclusion is the one most intensely debated. The charge is most serious for a religious tradition like Judaism (from which the moral rejection of homosexual acts is derived by Christianity and, hence, passed on to Western civilization virtually intact) that presents itself as a primarily communal relationship with God. It is against Judaism, originally, that the charge is made that homosexuals are being denied their participation in the most basic aspect of that community: marriage as the foundation of family. Have homosexuals, then, been denied a justifiable right by the Jewish tradition? And has the community made an unjust claim on them by not enabling them to fulfill their sexual desire?

The reason that the definition of family cannot be stretched to include homosexual unions is that by design they preclude procreation. Homosexual unions do not produce children, nor do they intend to produce them. Even the insemination of a lesbian woman, who with along with her female partner intends to raise the children she has given birth to, is not the intention of that lesbian union itself. It is not *their* union that has produced *her* child, however much

---

[63] See John M. Finnis, "Law, Morality, and 'Sexual Orientation,' " *Notre Dame Journal of Law, Ethics, and Public Policy* 9 (1995): 27ff.

[64] See Augustine, *De Bono Coniugali*, 9.9.

[65] See B. Sanhedrin 58a and Rashi, s.v. "ve-davaq"; Rashi, *Commentary on the Torah*: Gen. 2:24; also, Y. Kiddushin 1.1/58c.

[66] B. Sanhedrin 58a re Gen. 2:24.

they might wish it to be so. That is why the minimal contribution of a male, in the form of his sperm, is still needed in this situation. But such an abstraction of a generative substance from its source in a human person is itself an immoral use of something *personal* (unlike waste fluids) as a means to an end extrinsic to that of the *person* himself.[67] The same is also the case with a gay man inseminating a woman in order that she give birth to a child whom he and his male partner will raise. Both of these cases are essentially unlike a heterosexual marital union in which two persons conceive and raise children *together*, and remain *their* parents forever, however impermanent their own mutual relationship might possibly be. Donated sperm is not the father a child can honor, and a donated womb is not the mother a child can honor.[68]

A family, in the full sense of the term as it is traditionally used, is a miniature community including men, women, and children. So it would seem that like the community at large, there has to be a division of responsible authority between the adult members, who alone are capable of it, as well as the education of children to assume such responsible authority when they are ready to exercise it, minimally in the families they will perpetuate in the future. Accordingly, we cannot very well avoid the proportional equality that pertains between fatherly authority (patriarchy) and motherly authority (matriarchy). Literal equality, on the other hand, is an abstraction that applies only to the juridical function of rectifying improper gains and losses (like the restoration of misappropriated property by equivalent restitution) or a reality before God alone (like our equally human status as the image of God).[69] In full communal relationships, there is always hierarchy, however proportional.[70] Without it there could be no effective division of labor and responsibility in the community. Rather than ignoring it or presuming it can be willed away, as most egalitarians do, in an idealistic, utopian fashion, it is far better to properly order it so that justice be practiced by all and for all in the community.

In Judaism, marriage for the sake of procreation is a positive duty.[71] But to whom do we owe this duty? Who has a right to it? Of course, the most generic answer is that this duty is owed to God, that it is God's original right. Ultimately, that is true; as we have seen in the earlier chapters, God is "the first

[67] See B. Hagigah 15a and Rashi, s.v. "b'ambati," where the situation of artificial insemination from a nonspouse is taken to be a grotesque accident. For the rabbinic notion that one's sexuality and all that it entails is not a commodity, see B. Kiddushin 19b and Rashi, s.v. "b-davar she-be-mammon." For the inherently personal status of semen, see Niddah 31a.

[68] Hence both parents of a child are considered to be God's personal partners in his or her creation (Niddah 31b and B. Kiddushin 30b). For the designation of honor of natural parents as a natural human need of their children, see Saadiah Gaon, *Book of Beliefs and Opinions*, 3.2.

[69] See M. Sanhedrin 4.5.

[70] See Aristotle, *Politics*, 1277b15ff.

[71] See M. Yevamot 6.6; B. Yevamot 65b and Tos., s.v. "ve-la" re Gen. 1:28. For further details and developments, see D. M. Feldman, *Birth Control in Jewish Law* (New York: New York University Press, 1968), 46ff.

and the last" (Isaiah 44:6). However, unlike such divine rights as the right to our communal worship and individual prayer, where God is clearly both the original and the immediate source and end of the commandment, in the case of the commandment "be fruitful and multiply" (*piryah ve-rivyah*), the immediate source and end is the community.[72] We become parents ourselves because the pull to perpetuate our family is usually exercised by our own parents, as was the case with their parents before them. In a Jewish sense, it would be a historically myopic parent who did not want this and who did not communicate that desire to his or her children. And when a Jewish family sees itself being a family in essentially Jewish terms, then both that force and that attraction to have grandchildren is the force and attraction of the whole house of Israel (*bet yisrael*).[73] (Such frequently heard queries of Jewish parents to their grown children as "So, when are you going to get married and give us some grandchildren?" is more than just the subject of delightful ethnic humor; it is folk wisdom deeply rooted in the Jewish tradition.)[74] Like all original human rights, the right of the Jewish community to the procreative duty of all its members (for whom it is possible) is a covenantal entitlement from God. And like any such covenantal entitlement, it is as irrevocable as the very covenant of which it is a part.

If there is no genuine procreative, mutual intent, as we have seen is the case of homosexual unions, why should the community permit, let alone sanction, such unions to take place in her midst? Homosexual unions can be regarded as only unjustified diversions from the fulfillment of communal duty, which they preclude by design. The community, which herself fulfills a natural need of human persons, surely intends her own transmission into the future. The community needs new members, and these new members are best born, cared for, and raised to responsible adulthood in a home founded on a permanently intended heterosexual union. In fact, the community's interest in traditional family life is so strong that to compromise it in any way could only seriously weaken it. This seems to me to be the best argued reason for the traditional

---

[72] That is why a gentile who has been converted to Judaism has fulfilled his duty to procreate only when the children he has fathered while still a gentile are themselves converted to Judaism along with him. See B. Yevamot 62a; Maimonides, *Mishneh Torah*: Ishut, 15.6 and R. Vidal of Tolosa, *Magid Mishneh* thereon; *Tur* and Karo, *Shulhan Arukh*: Even Ha'Ezer, 1.7. Cf. B. Yevamot 62a, Tos., s.v. "R. Yohanan"; Karo, *Bet Yosef* on *Tur*: Even Ha'Ezer, 1, s.v. "hayu" re R. Yom Tov ben Abraham Ishbili, *Hiddushei ha-Ritva*: B. Yevamot 22a quoting Y. Yevamot 2.6/4a; also, B. Hagigah 2b and Tos., s.v. "lo"; R. Judah Ashkenazi, *Beer Heitev* on *Shulhan Arukh*: Even Ha'Ezer, 1.7, n. 11.

[73] Thus a Jewish man who fathers children from a non-Jewish woman has not fulfilled his procreative duty. See B. Kiddushin 68b re Deut. 7:4; Ishbili, *Hiddushei ha-Ritva*: B. Yevamot 22a re B. Yevamot 17a quoting Hos. 5:7. In addition, he has violated a rabbinic prohibition (see B. Avodah Zarah 36b).

[74] Regarding the importance of grandchildren, see B. Yevamot 62b re Gen. 31:43. Regarding folk wisdom as revelation, see B. Pesahim 66a.

Jewish prohibition of all homoerotic acts and homosexual marriages. Sexuality is just too integral a part of authentic human sociality to simply leave it to private desire. As a traditional Jewish matchmaker (*shadkhan*) is reported to have once said, "Marriage is much too important to be left to the whims of children."[75]

ACCORDING TO NATURE

In Jewish tradition, homosexuality has been considered to be inconsistent with human nature and, therefore, to be avoided as humanly inappropriate behavior.[76] That is why it was not regarded as a uniquely Jewish prohibition, but one that applies to humankind per se.[77] But today, arguments that invoke "nature" are often attacked as being based on either faulty generalizations from variable human behavior or as reductions of humanness to physical determinism. Nevertheless, a more careful analysis of what is meant by "nature" might yield some better results. And contrary to some opinions, Jewish tradition, going back as far as Scripture, definitely does have an idea of what could well be called "nature."[78]

Heterosexuality is privileged, indeed exclusively privileged, when we look at the original meaning of our word *nature*, which comes from the Latin *natura*, which itself is derived from the Latin word for being born, *natus*. What is *natural*, then, is what is connected to birth. Its intent includes the desire to procreate in the original way, that is, by an act of heterosexual intercourse. Natality is our connection with the chain of life. Our nature is vital.

On this very point, there is a remarkable congruence of Latin, Greek, and Hebrew terms. (For Jews, that means that a truth of the Torah has also been recognized by some other cultures in the world.) Just as *nature* comes from *natus*, so does the Greek word for nature, *physis*, come from *phyein*, "to grow." As for Hebrew, the most explicit statement of human nature can be seen in this scriptural verse: "This is the book of the generations (*toldot*) of humankind (*adam*), on the day of God's creating humans, in the likeness (*demut*) of God He made him: male and female (*zakhar u-neqevah*) He created them" (Genesis 5:1).[79] This teaches the two essential features of what humanness is to be—what we could certainly call "human nature." They are: one, to be male and

---

[75] I thank my friend Rabbi Yechiel Poupko of Chicago for relating this bon mot to me.

[76] See B. Nedarim 51a re Lev. 18:22.

[77] See D. Novak, *The Image of the Non-Jew in Judaism* (New York: Edwin Mellen Press, 1983), 211ff.

[78] See Novak, *Jewish Social Ethics*, 29ff. contra Leo Strauss, *Natural Right and History* (Chicago: University of Chicago Press, 1953), 81.

[79] See Y. Nedarim 9.3/41c, where the "book" (*sefer*) mentioned in the scriptural verse is interpreted to mean the whole Torah as the truest index to human nature.

female related to each other in fecundity; two, to be ready for a unique relationship with God in the world.[80] These two features of human nature are experienced normatively, that is, as claims made upon us. The claim to be heterosexually fecund in a permanent family comes from the community herself. To be sure, anyone born into a human family is fully human, with all the rights to life and care that this entails.[81] But those incapable of a heterosexual life, procreation, or both because of factors beyond their control are regarded as tragic in much the same way those who are physically or mentally or emotionally handicapped are tragic.[82] And those who choose to avoid full family life and its procreative intent are regarded as being guilty of a sin of omission.[83]

Procreation is not only the act that conceives life; it also includes the joint rearing of children and remaining the parents of these children, minimally for as long as both parents are alive. Heterosexuality is a key factor in making a male-female union permanent, for if sexual acts between the couple were only permitted to physically produce children and then be terminated, their union itself would most likely lose its permanence even ab initio. Thus procreation as the primary end of marriage very much includes the subordinate ends of bodily union and the transcendence of personal loneliness. They too contribute to the permanence of marriage.[84] Indeed, the union is meant to be so permanent that it obtains even after both parents are dead inasmuch as our parents are with us in memory. (That is why in Jewish tradition, the commandments to honor and revere mother and father obtain both when they are alive and after they have died.)[85] What is intended here is not only the claim the family makes upon us when children are physically and emotionally dependent on their parents, but also the claim the family makes upon us for its continuity into the future. That continuum includes more than just the two generations most immediately present in most homes, but also the previous generations in the person or memory of grandparents and beyond into the past, and the coming generations in the person or anticipation of grandchildren and beyond into the future.[86] Most of us want our families to remain intact, even transgenerationally. That is why the divorce of parents is so often extremely painful to their children, whatever their age. Indeed, the children of divorced parents often feel as though a vital connection with their living community has been broken, even when they no longer need their parents for physical support.[87]

---

[80] See D. Novak, *Halakhah in a Theological Dimension* (Chico, Calif.: Scholars Press, 1985), 96ff.

[81] See M. Niddah 5.3.

[82] See Gen. 15:2, 30:1; I Sam. 1:1ff.; Isa. 56:3–5.

[83] See B. Yevamot 63b re Gen. 9:6–7. Cf. 62a and Tos., s.v. "bnei."

[84] For the theological problem of divorce, therefore, see D. Novak, *Law and Theology in Judaism* (New York: KTAV, 1974), 1:1ff.

[85] See B. Kiddushin 31b.

[86] See Ps. 128:6; B. Kiddushin 30a re Deut. 4:9.

[87] Hence they cannot observe the commandment to honor and respect their parents with both parents in tandem. See B. Kiddushin 31a.

In this view of nature, only heterosexual marital intercourse is natural inasmuch as it alone intends the same relationship that minimally gave us life. And, maximally, it gave us our family, our first human community in which we live. Optimally, it gave us a community in which to live well. All valid intercourse, then, reconfirms the origin and purpose of our own lives. Nevertheless, the issue of timing the birth of one's children and limiting their number is a separate issue. There are ample sources in the Jewish tradition that neither of these programs is a denial of the essentially natal character of the marital union. Indeed, this recognizes, as we have seen in the preceding chapter, that when the family is the core of the community, women truly initiate it and determine its membership.[88]

Finally, there is an overall meaning of nature, which is nature as an inherent limit(*peras*) on activity in the world—in our case, human activity.[89] Not only is nature immanent; it is also specific. Each area of human activity in the world has its own inherent boundaries, which experience discovers and reason appropriates *in order to* direct human action to properly attainable ends.[90] In Hebrew, such order is designated by the word *mishpat*. For example, "You shall erect the sanctuary according to its form (*mishpato*), which you were shown on the mountain" (Exodus 26:30).[91] Certainly, human sexual activity is no exception in its specifics. Here, finally, I think heterosexuality and the procreative union it intends do enjoy an exclusive privilege, one entailing both positive and negative norms.

Arguments for the social approval of homosexual acts inevitably turn into arguments for pansexuality, that is, sex as an area of human activity that itself contains no limiting norms. If the choice of sexual activity is determined only by a person's experience of his or her own inclination, what possible moral limits could one inherently impose upon it? However, does our moral experience not begin when we learn to internalize limits on what we may do with our genitals and what we may not do with them? Is repression not a necessary part of our introduction to communal reality, being harmful only when taught in a cruel, irrational manner?[92] Would any parent raising a child, who sent a message either explicitly or implicitly that what he or she does with his or her genitals is a matter of moral indifference, would not such a parent be failing in his or her moral education of that child? What kind of preparation for the

---

[88] Regarding women determining the primary Jewish identity of their children, see B. Kiddushin 68b re Deut. 7:4.

[89] See Aristotle, *Metaphysics*, 1022a14.

[90] See Aristotle, *Nicomachean Ethics*, 1111b20–30.

[91] LXX translates *mishpato* in Exod. 26:30 as *eidos*, which Plato had used to designate the intelligible paradigms underlying all reality, both physical and social, viz., the Forms (see *Republic*, 476Aff.). For further examples of *mishpat* as "form" in this sense, see Josh. 6:15; Isa. 28:17; Eccl. 8:6.

[92] Cf. *Semahot* 2.3.

social world would that be? Are parents not supposed to be the intermediaries between elementary narcissism and human community, and does that not begin in the sexual education of their children?[93] (And that begins simultaneously with an answer to the question "Where do I come from?") Could there be a human community, much less a human society, where there is unrestrained sexual activity? Would not such unrestrained sexuality pose too much of a distraction from the business of physical survival, as well as from the fulfillment of other communal and individual needs? Is that not why family morality begins with the prohibition of incest, from which all other sexual restrictions follow?[94] Does this prohibition not protect us from being devoured by sexuality rather than being able to integrate it into a truly communal life?

Those who would argue for the permission of homosexual activity usually argue that sexual activity per se is an essentially private matter between consenting adults. That, however, is a necessary but not sufficient condition of human sexual acts that are morally justifiable.[95] It is not sufficient because, as I have tried to show above, it does not delve deeply enough into the public significance of sexual acts between these consenting adults,[96] for the only criterion of this minimal condition is that each party intend her or his pleasure in a way approved by the other party with whom one is sexually engaged at present.

However, in the Jewish tradition, pleasure itself is a desirable accompaniment to sexual activity; it is not its essential purpose. At best, it is a *conditio sine qua non* of any sustained sexual relationship.[97] Indeed, Jewish tradition asserts that pleasure is never an end in itself, but its value is dependent on whether the acts it accompanies are right or wrong.[98] Along these lines, let it be said that all acts are transitive, that is, they intend objects outside their own actors. For Judaism it can be maintained, I think, all acts ultimately intend personal objects. They are not only transitive, but transactional. Even nonpersonal objects (things) have to be included in a valid personal relationship in order that their use be justified. The world is to be enjoyed, but that enjoyment is always for the sake of enhancing relationships with those persons who make more primary claims on us.[99] That is the case with the pleasure of the table and all the more so with that of the bed. Sexual pleasure is what most of us

[93] See Hegel, *Phenomenology of Spirit*, trans. A. V. Miller (Oxford: Oxford University Press, 1977), no. 450, p. 268.

[94] See Freud, "The Most Prevalent Form of Degradation in Erotic Life" (1912), in *Collected Papers* trans. J. Strachey (London: Hogarth Press, 1952), 4:205f.

[95] For the necessary condition of mutual consent in sexual relationships, see B. Eruvin 100b; Maimonides, *Mishneh Torah*: Deot, 4.5. See also M. Ketubot 7.9–10; B. Ketubot 63b; Maimonides, *Mishneh Torah*: Ishut, 14.8

[96] See B. Kiddushin 12b; Maimonides, *Mishneh Torah*: Ishut, 1.1, 4.

[97] See B. Sanhedrin 7a.

[98] See Ps. 10:3. Cf. Plato, *Philebus*, 60Dff.; Aristotle, *Nicomachean Ethics*, 1173b30ff.

[99] That is why the pleasures of eating are to be included in both divine-human community (see M. Berakhot 6.1; B. Berakhot 35a; Y. Berakhot 6.1/9d–10a) and interhuman community (see

would regard as the most intense and desirable of bodily delights. It is acceptable when it contributes to my intimate relationship with my wife, who is the matrix of my family life.[100] That intimate relationship involves her being the mother of the children we have either already brought into the world or whom we intend to bring into the world when we can.[101] Furthermore, since the experience of beauty is quite often intentionally erotic, the communal importance of marriage is so important that it determines the public aesthetic judgment of everyone at weddings. Thus every bride is to be called beautiful because she is a daughter of the house of Israel about to answer her call to become a beloved wife and mother in Israel. By definition, therefore, she is desirable.[102]

Since pleasure can be experienced only by a person himself or herself, to make pleasure an end in itself is to make oneself the immediate and ultimate object of his or her own acts. Hedonism, which is pleasure for its own sake, can only be narcissism. Once pleasure is shared by two persons, it is already communal, and thus more than just a bodily sensation. It immediately acquires interhuman meaning.[103] So, in the end, we are left with family life, which includes (but does not annul) personal communion and which is to be accompanied by sexual pleasure (and other pleasures as well). Indeed, those who truly enjoy family life in this generative sense could well argue that it enhances both their personal communion and their bodily pleasure. Homosexual unions, however, even if they include good personal communion and satisfying bodily pleasure that is not compulsive, still do not intend the core of good family life, which is to procreate in both the narrowest and widest senses of that term. And Judaism makes the admittedly severe demand on those who by inclination cannot or do not intend this overall end minimally to refrain from those sexual activities that contradict it. It is recognized that this can be quite painful at times.[104]

EXCEPTIONS TO THE NORM OF PROCREATION

We are still left with the problem of the marriage of sterile persons and those who chose to be celibate. How do they stand in relation to the communal claim of procreation? There are actual restrictions in Jewish law as regards some

---

M. Berakhot 7.1; B. Berakhot 45a re Ps. 34:4 and 59b and Tos., s.v. "ve-Rabbi Yohanan"; B. Kiddush in 31a–b and Rashi, s.v. "u-mevi'o" re Y. Peah 1.1/15c).

[100] See B. Shabbat 118b and B. Gittin 52a.

[101] For the notion that the character of the sexual relationship of the parents influences the character of their children, see B. Nedarim 20a–b.

[102] See B. Ketubot 16b–17a. See also B. Sotah 47a; Y. Yoma 4.1/41b. Nevertheless, public judgments of female beauty at weddings should carefully avoid expressing fantasies of what rightly belongs to the privacy of husband and wife, which is to be respected. See B. Ketubot 8b (cf. B. Kiddushin 12b and Rashi, s.v. "nagdeih").

[103] Thus the initiation of marriage is an occasion of communal celebration. See B. Ketubot 7a–b and Meiri, *Bet ha-Behirah*, ed. Sofer, 73; also, B. Megillah 3b and parallels.

[104] See B. Sanhedrin 75a; Maimonides, *Mishneh Torah*: Yesodei ha-Torah, 5.9.

persons with certain genital deformities from marrying.[105] Nevertheless, most sterile persons, already aware of their physical and emotional capability for sexual intercourse, are unaware of their sterility until they have long been in a marriage. Here again, Jewish law does regard the commandment to procreate to be so important that one may obtain a divorce from a sterile spouse if he or she is determined to fulfill this commandment with a new spouse.[106] However, it seems that the tradition is respectful enough of the integrity of the marital unit, including its privacy, that many authorities do not make divorce mandatory when sterility has not been intended.[107] In fact, such persons are often encouraged to adopt children whose parents cannot or do not want to raise them.[108] These children are, in fact, required to practice the commandment of filial honor and respect for their adoptive parents.[109]

The hardest case is, of course, the marriage of persons who know they are sterile, usually persons who are clearly beyond the age of childbearing. But I would say, using Wittgenstein's theory of "family resemblances," that there are enough similarities to most marriages here to rationally justify the permission of such marriages.[110] Indeed, to distinguish between fertile and infertile couples ab initio would require a judgment to allow or not allow marriage in the case of each and every couple based upon an extensive premarital physical examination and evaluation. However, in the Jewish legal tradition there is ample precedence for simply assuming that *most* heterosexual couples are fertile, and, therefore, *all* heterosexual couples are to be considered as such.[111] At the prima facie level, there is no generally evident difference between fertile and infertile couples. That is quite unlike the very evident difference between heterosexual couples who are fertile and all homosexual couples, who are infertile. Most women and men are capable of conceiving a child, whereas no two women or two men are capable of doing so. Law is made for what is usual (*de minimis non curat lex*); indeed, that is a function of the communal need for generality that law is to fulfill.[112] Furthermore, in the case of most older

---

[105] See Deut. 23:2; M. Yevamot 6.5; B. Yevamot 61a–b and 76a–b; Y. Yevamot 6.5/7c and 8.2/9a–b.

[106] M. Yevamot 6.6; B. Yevamot 64a; Y. Yevamot 6.6/7c.

[107] See B. Yevamot 64a and Tos., s.v. "yotsee"; B. Ketubot 77a, Tos., s.v. "leetnei"; *Hagahot Maimoniyot* on Maimonides, *Mishneh Torah*: Ishut, 15.7, n. 4; R. Isaac bar Sheshet Parfat, *Teshuvot ha-Rivash*, no. 15; R. Moses Isserles (Rema), note on *Shulhan Arukh*: Even Ha'Ezer, 1.3 and 154.10 (and R. Zvi Hirsch Eisenstadt, *Pitehei Teshuvah*, n. 27).

[108] See B. Sanhedrin 19b re Num. 3:1–3.

[109] Although adoption cannot erase the natural bond between birth parents and their children, adoptive parents assume the role of teachers, whose rights are almost identical with those of biological parents. See R. Moses Schreiber, *Teshuvot Hatam Sofer*: Orah Hayyim, no. 164; also, D. Novak, *Law and Theology in Judaism* (New York: KTAV, 1976), 2:60ff.

[110] *Philosophical Investigations*, 2nd ed., trans. G. E. M. Anscombe (New York: Macmillan, 1958), sec. 67, 32.

[111] See M. Yevamot 4.10; B. Yevamot 42b; Maimonides, *Mishneh Torah*: Gerushin, 11.20.

[112] See B. Shabbat 35b and parallels; Hullin 11a.

adults who marry at the time they are already beyond their childbearing years, they are themselves persons who earlier in life did have children or they were persons who could not marry any earlier for reasons beyond their control. In fact, in many such cases, the new spouses figuratively "adopt" the children of their new spouses, for the spouse of one's parent in many ways is functioning like one's parent, especially the spouse of one's widowed parent. Thus they continue the initially heterosexual phenomenon of parenting.

As for celibacy, Judaism obviously recognizes that there are persons who, for a variety of physical and emotional reasons, are of incapable of initiating or sustaining a marriage. Like any disability, this is regarded to be an unfortunate state of affairs, and persons suffering from this disability should not be made to feel any worse than they often do already, especially in a community where natality is so highly regarded. However, voluntary celibacy of heterosexuals physically and emotionally capable of marriage in the full sense is another matter. Jewish tradition does not regard this as an acceptable way to live, and the sources are replete with statements of opprobrium.[113] That is why matchmaking is considered to be no less than an act of *imitatio Dei*: God himself brought Eve to Adam.[114] Nevertheless, although there are social pressures for single persons to marry, no one can force them to do so.[115] That seems to be based on respect for the private, individual aspect of marriage. In fact, a forced marriage can be annulled.[116] Furthermore, there are few social restrictions placed on unmarried persons.[117] My experience in traditional Jewish communities has been that most people there assume quite compassionately that when a person is celibate, it is usually due to some disability (for example, physical or emotional impediments, or simple lack of opportunity) rather than being the result of a real choice. The same is also usually assumed about childless couples in the community. The community cannot demand from some people what is impossible for them to fulfill. The community owes compassion to those who are so unfortunate.

Finally, one could very well argue that the Jewish prohibition of homoerotic acts is stronger than the Christian prohibition of them on theological grounds, even though the legal source for the prohibition in Scripture (at least regarding

---

[113] See M. Yevamot 6.6 and *Bavli* and *Yerushalmi* thereon; also, Novak, *Jewish Social Ethics*, 98, n. 9.

[114] See B. Shabbat 95a re Gen. 2:22.

[115] See B. Kiddushin 2b and Meiri, *Bet ha-Behirah*: Kiddushin, ed. Sofer, 8; R. Moses of Coucy, *Sefer Mitsvot Gadol*, positive commandments, no. 48. Cf. Maimonides, *Mishneh Torah*: Ishut, 4.1 and *Hagahot Maimoniyot* thereon. Also, no one can be forced to marry a particular person or at any particular time. Hence, even though it is a *mitsvah* to marry, one has considerable autonomy (*reshut*) in the performance of that commandment (see M. Betsah 5.2; B.Betsah 36b–37a and Rashi, s.v. "d'eet leih" re B. Yevamot 62b commenting on Eccl. 11:6).

[116] See B. Baba Batra 48b.

[117] But see T. Sanhedrin 7.5; B. Sanhderin 36b and Rashi, s.v. "zaqen"; Maimonides, *Mishneh Torah*: Sanhedrin, 2.3.

male homosexuality) is identical. That is because Judaism does not sanction celibacy, and certainly does not regard it as some higher form of holiness.[118] For if the commandment to procreate (in both its full and narrow sense) is considered to be exceptionless, then any avoidance of it is considered to be wrong.[119] Avoidance by the substitution of some nonfamilial sexuality, which is a positive act, is the more severe wrong. Avoidance of it by, as the Rabbis put it, "sitting and doing nothing" (*shev v'al ta'aseh*), is the lesser wrong.[120] That is, commission of sin is worse than the omission of duty. It is also a lesser wrong because inactivity is usually pursued with much less passion than activity, especially activity accompanied by intense pleasure. Hence, despite a developing public cooperation of Jews and Christians on this moral question (which is one among others), based on a common philosophical approach in both theory and practice, Jewish and Christian theorists involved in this common political undertaking should be aware of this specific theological difference stemming from their different and differing traditions.[121] (The cooperation will be more authentic, anyway, when it does not assume either too little or too much commonality.)

THE LETHAL CLAIMS OF THE COMMUNITY

The community continually asks all of her members to live for her, especially in their family life, as we have just seen. Occasionally, the community asks some of her members to die for her as well. Because of the gravity of any question of human life and death, that claim is made rarely and with the most agonizing, introspective deliberation. Thus, for example, a court that seems to have sentenced too many criminals to die by means of capital punishment is called by the Mishnah a "murderous (*hovlanit*) court."[122] Yet at times the community has to take lives with justification.

The first such justification is the right to practice capital punishment. Already in the universal, Noahide law, in the aspect of it that is explicitly scriptural, we learn that "one who sheds human blood, through humans (*ba'adam*) shall his blood be shed" (Genesis 9:6). Surely "through humans" means hu-

[118] Even Protestants, who have rejected the requirement of clerical celibacy, still have to take into consideration that they believe that God became incarnate in a celibate male body. See I Cor. 7:1ff.

[119] For the distinction between a commandment that can be legitimately avoided (*mitsvah*) and one that can only be illegitimately evaded (*hovah*), see Maimonides, *Mishneh Torah*: Berakhot, 11.2. Procreation is of the latter type of commandment.

[120] See B. Sanhedrin 58b–59a.

[121] For an example of this new cooperation, see "The Homosexual Movement: A Response by the Ramsey Colloquium," *First Things* 41 (March 1994): 15ff.

[122] M. Makkot 1.10. For further discussion, see Novak, *Jewish Social Ethics*, 174ff.

mans who are socially authorized to adjudicate and administer justice in cases of murder, not random vigilantes.[123] The crime for which the community executes a criminal is taken to be a crime against the community herself.[124] Now among the Rabbis, there was a clear difference of opinion about capital punishment (although by the time the actual discussions took place, the right to execute criminals had been removed from the Jews and their authorities by their Roman conquerors).[125] Most famously, in the second century C.E., Rabbi Akibah seemed to have been opposed to the practice in principle.[126] Nevertheless, because capital punishment is scripturally mandated ("you shall remove the evil from your midst"—Deuteronomy 21:21), he could not express his opposition as a principle but, rather, he had to devise a means for making the laws of evidence so stringent that it would be improbable de facto, even though possible de jure, to ever execute anyone legally.[127] In other words, he had to argue not that the law was wrong, but that it was meant to be more of a warning against murder than an actually applicable punishment for murder.[128]

Those Rabbis who disagreed with Rabbi Akibah, however, could express their view in principle inasmuch as they were affirming the scriptural norm and providing a reason for it. Their reason was that without capital punishment, "bloodshed would be increased in Israel."[129] Hence, publicly anyway, the difference of opinion on the issue of capital punishment was essentially one of degree and not one of kind.

Here again, though, the right of the community might well be viewed as being instrumental, for what she is doing is to act on behalf of an individual victim of the crime of another individual. Furthermore, the institution of capital punishment is contingent upon the practice of crimes that are severely prohibited in the first place, and whose prohibition the community loudly proclaims. "Cursed be the one who smites his neighbor in secret" (Deuteronomy 27:24).[130] Obviously, the community demands the very opposite of the precondition for

[123] See B. Sanhedrin 57b; Y. Kiddushin 1.1/58c; *Beresheet Rabbah* 34.14. Cf. *Beresheet Rabbah*, 44.4 re Isa. 33:12; *Tanhuma*: Lekh Lekha, no. 19, ed. Buber, 38b re Gen. 9:6.

[124] Hence at the time of the execution of a criminal, Joshua is reported to have said to him, "As you have troubled us (*akharttanu*) so may the Lord trouble you today" (Josh. 7:25). Nevertheless, after quoting this verse, the Mishnah adds, "today (*ha-yom*) you are troubled, but you will not be troubled in the world-to-come" (M. Sanhedrin 6.2)—i.e., if he or she confesses his or her sin and accepts the death sentence as atonement for this (and all other) sin, then the former criminal will be finally reconciled with the community eschatologically.

[125] See Y. Sanhedrin 1.1/18a and 7.2/24b; B. Sanhedrin 41a; B. Avodah Zarah 8b; also, John 18:31.

[126] M. Makkot 1.10. Cf. B. Makkot 5b re Deut. 19:5; T. Yevamot 8.7; *Beresheet Rabbah* 34.14; *Sifra*: Qedoshim, ed. Weiss, 90a; and B. Sanhedrin 63a re Lev. 19:26.

[127] B. Makkot 7a. Cf. M. Zavim 2.2; Josephus, *Antiquities*, 13.294.

[128] Cf. B. Sanhedrin 71a.

[129] M. Makkot 1.10.

[130] See Malbim, *Commentary on the Torah* thereon.

capital punishment. She calls her members to be righteous, not wicked. "Turn from evil and do good and dwell (*shekhon*) forevermore" (Psalms 37:28). And God himself says through a prophet, "Do I really desire the death of the sinner? . . . Is it not that he return from his way and live?" (Ezekiel 18:23).

In the case of war, the community has the right to call upon her sons and daughters to defend her life or political sovereignty at the risk of their own lives. The main question here that should interest us in this inquiry is to what extent individual rights to be exempt from military service, which are specified in Scripture, obtain in the face of the overall communal claim.[131] At this point, one must note the difference made in the rabbinic sources between "optional war" (*milhemet reshut*) and "obligatory war" (*milhemet mitsvah*).[132] There are several debates in the Talmud as to how exactly one is to distinguish between these two types of war. One distinction suggested is that optional war is a preemptive strike against an enemy poised to attack the community (like, for example, Israel's preemptive attack on the Egyptian army poised in the Sinai desert to attack Israel in June of 1967), and that obligatory war is a war of defense, when the enemy has already begun to attack the community (like the Yom Kippur War of 1973, when the Egyptian army already had mounted its offensive campaign against Israel).[133]

In the case of optional war, a number of exemptions from active military service are allowed. And they include "the man who is afraid and whose heart is tender (*ve-rakh ha-levav*)" (Deuteronomy 20:8). This might be an exemption not only for a coward whose presence in battle would have a bad effect on the morale of his fellow soldiers, but it could also mean what we now call a "conscientious objector," that is, someone whose personal moral sense will simply not allow him to kill any other human being.[134] Conversely though, in the case of a truly defensive war, there are no exemptions. The community's life or liberty demand that everyone who is able-bodied answer the call; in the words of the Mishnah, "even the bridegroom from his chamber and the bride from her pavilion (*huppatah*)."[135] Nevertheless, here too, the community's claim on her sons and daughters is contingent on the aggression of foreigners against Israel. That aggression is something that is not to be in the first place.

---

[131] Deut. 20:5–9.

[132] M. Sotah 8.7.

[133] B. Sotah 44b; Y. Sotah 8.10/23a.

[134] For the view that this refers to a coward, see B. Sotah 44b and Maimonides, *Mishneh Torah*: Melakhim, 7.15. Nevertheless, considering that the opinion that refers to "one who cannot stand in military formation and look at an unsheathed sword" is that of R. Akibah, whose aversion to capital punishment we have just noted, perhaps "cannot stand" (*sh'eino yakhol la'amod*) might refer to moral rather than merely emotional aversion to any bloodshed whatsoever. However, even this view exempts such a person only from active military engagement as a combatant in an offensive (or preemptive) war. He is still required to contribute to the overall interests of the community as a noncombatant (see M. Sotah 8.2).

[135] M. Sotah 8.7.

Thus it was said to Israel's ancient enemy Edom, who had inflicted great loss of life and property on the community, "You will be punished for your iniquity O' daughter Edom; He will expose your sins!" (Lamentations 4:22).[136] Furthermore, war is always to be the last resort in matters of international dispute. Peace negotiations are always to be fully pursued beforehand.[137]

But here, although the defense of the life of the community can be seen to be for the sake of the right to life of her individual members, the question of liberty (*atsma'ut*) is an originally communal claim. Individuals have their personal freedom (*deror*); only communities have national liberty or sovereignty.[138] The question of judging how much life is to be sacrificed or endangered for the sake of national liberty is a question of great debate in both ancient and modern Israel.[139]

Although the community does have the right to call upon her sons and daughters to risk their lives, it does not seem to have the right to call upon them to directly kill themselves or allow themselves to be killed for the sake of the life, much less the liberty, of the community. This comes out in the following rabbinic text:

> A company of people [are approached] by gentiles who say to them: "give us one of your number; if not, we will kill all of you." Let all of them be killed and let them not turn over to them any Jewish life. But if they [the gentiles] themselves designate someone, for example Sheba ben Bichri, then let them [the Jews] give him to them so that all of them not be killed.[140]

The choice of Sheba ben Bichri as an example is because he was somebody already condemned to die for a crime.[141] As such, why should a whole group of people die when his presence in their midst was the cause of their being so endangered? It was him that the gentiles spoken of in the text were after, not the rest of the group. But it is also plausible to assume that were the person so designated not guilty of a crime, the group should not turn him over, even if that led to all of them dying, in effect, for him. Furthermore, in a parallel text, disapproval is expressed for even persuading someone wanted by the gentile

---

[136] This is explained by the rabbinic idea that only the wicked (*hayyav*) are used by God as instruments of punishment (*hovah*). See B. Shabbat 32a re Deut. 22:8.

[137] See Y. Sheviit 6.1/36c; *Devarim Rabbah* 5.13 re Deut. 2:24; B. Gittin 46a and Tos., s.v. "keivan"; Maimonides, *Mishneh Torah*: Melakhim, 6.1.

[138] Interestingly enough, the verse "Proclaim liberty (*deror*) throughout the land unto all the inhabitants thereof" (Lev. 25:10), which appears on the Liberty Bell in Philadelphia, and which was chosen at the time of the declaration of independence of the United States of America from Britain in 1776, in the Jewish tradition does not denote political sovereignty but, rather, the individual right of freedom of domicile anywhere. See *Sifra*: Behar, ed. Weiss, 107a and B. Rosh Hashanah 9b re Lev. 25:10. For the notion of sovereignty, see Aristotle, *Politics*, 1280b11ff.

[139] See Novak, *Jewish Social Ethics*, 191ff.

[140] T. Terumot 7.20, ed. Lieberman, 148–49. Cf. M. Terumot 8.12.

[141] Y. Terumot 8.10/46b. See R. Saul Lieberman, *Tosefta Kifshuta*: Zeraim (New York: Jewish Theological Seminary of America, 1955), 420ff.

authorities to turn himself over to them in order to save the rest of the community.[142] This might well be part of the Jewish aversion to the way their Roman conquerors were so cavalier in their treatment of the sanctity of individual human life.[143] (During the years of the Nazi horror, this moral dilemma, namely, the sacrifice of one life in order to save many others, often faced Jewish officials.)[144] It seems to be based on the widely invoked general principle "one life is not to be set aside (*ein dohin*) for another."[145]

Nevertheless, we are still left with the question of whether one can volunteer himself or herself in order to save the community. In other words, could this be a case of a voluntary act of heroism as distinct from a legal duty? Legally, not only does it seem that the community has no right to insist that an individual die on her behalf but, rather, it seems to be the right of the individual to resist such a sacrifice and live. Yet, can the claim of the community upon an individual be responded to as an act of supererogation? This does seem at least to be suggested by the trajectory of this parallel text, for immediately following the disapproval of persuading a person endangering the life of the community to turn himself into the foreign authorities who want him, the story is told of how Rabbi Simon ben Laqish volunteered to save someone captured on what by all appearances would be a suicide mission for him.[146] The key point in his case seems to be that no command was issued to him to do so; he was not even subjected to any informal social "persuasion" to do so. He did it autonomously.[147] As such, since he was not fulfilling a legally mandated duty, he could have decided not to act so heroically and could have done so with full impunity. We can only praise him for what he did, not fault him for what he might not have done.

This point is later suggested independently by the seventeenth-century Polish talmudist Rabbi Solomon Luria (Maharshal). His suggestion comes in the course of a discussion of the prohibition of suicide. There he has to deal with the fact that it states in Scripture about Saul, the first king of Israel, that "he took the sword and fell upon it" (I Samuel 31:4). Despite this fact, though, several rabbinic texts exonerate Saul of the crime of suicide.[148] The question is why. Luria suggests:

> Perhaps Saul's intention (peace be upon him) was that he thought that if he fell into their hands [the Philistine foes] alive, they would abuse and torture him. And it is to be assumed that the Israelites would not be able to see and hear about the

[142] Y. Terumot 8.10/46b.

[143] See T. Yevamot 14.7; B. Yevamot 25b; Y. Yevamot 2.11/4b; B. Gittin 28b; B. Baba Kama 114a.

[144] See L. Tushnet, *The Pavement of Hell* (New York: St. Martin's Press, 1972).

[145] M. Ohalot 7.6; B. Sanhedrin 72b.

[146] Y. Terumot 8.10/46b. See Novak, *Jewish Social Ethics*, 112.

[147] Thus it was like an oath (*Shevu'ah*). Cf. Num. 30:3ff.

[148] *Beresheet Rabbah* 34.13; also, B. Yevamot 78b; Novak, *Law and Theology in Judaism* 1:82ff.

pain of the king and stand by to save their own lives (*ve-lo ya'amdu al nafsham*). And a large number from Israel would fall in the course of avenging him and saving his life.[149]

And he concludes this suggestion with the words "it is permitted (*muttar*) to kill oneself to save the life of others." Of course, this answer is a rather forced explanation of why Saul killed himself in the scriptural story. (Severe depression, of which there is much evidence in the whole narrative about Saul in Scripture, seems more likely.)[150] Nevertheless, Luria's use of the story is of interest to us here. His speculation makes two key points, it seems to me: one, it is only "permitted" but not mandatory (*hayyav*) to kill oneself to save others; two, the plurality of the "others" (*aherim*) is a determination. In other words, were there only one other person, it might not even be permitted to do so.[151] There is an essential difference between the claim of another person for the sacrifice of my life for his or her life and the claim of the plural community for the sacrifice of my life for their lives.

Here, too, it should be remembered that the lethal claim of the community is contingent. It presupposes immoral aggression against the community to which it would rather not have to respond if it could be avoided. Thus it can well be said that none of the lethal claims of the community are *original* in themselves. Originally, the community can only claim the life not the death of her children.[152] Like the most original commandments, those directly from God, the claims of the community that are truly *imitatio Dei* are ones by that, as the Rabbis put it, "one is to live by them not die by them."[153]

Finally, in seeing this as a question of the right of the community to demand (at least by moral implication of a heroic person) even the sacrifice of the life of one for many, it is enlightening to compare this to a similar discussion in the ethical writings of Kant. He asks the question whether a national leader is justified in being prepared to commit suicide rather than being captured alive by an enemy, which could easily result in great harm to his own nation.[154] For Kant, this is a "casuistical" question, that is, one he cannot definitively answer

[149] *Yam shel Shlomoh*: Baba Kama, 8.59. See B. Taanit 18b and Rashi, s.v. "be-ludqiya"; A. Kohut, *Aruch Completum* (reprint; Tel Aviv: Shilo, 1970), 3:238–39, s.v. "harag."

[150] See II Sam. 1:9 and *Targum Jonathan ben Uzziel* and Rashi thereon.

[151] Cf. *Sifra*: Behar, ed. Weiss, 109c and B. Baba Metsia 62a re Lev. 25:36; also, B. Yevamot 1146 and Tos., s.v. "zimnin."

[152] Cf. Kierkegaard's insight that Agamemnon's sacrifice of his daughter, Iphegenia, for the sake of the community to gain the support of the gods in the battle against Troy is essentially different from Abraham's willingness to sacrifice Isaac in what Kierkegaard (rightly or wrongly) called the "teleological suspension of the ethical." See *Fear and Trembling*, trans. H. V. Hong and E. H. Hong (Princeton: Princeton University Press, 1983), 57ff.

[153] B. Yoma 85b and parallels re Lev. 18:5. Even public martyrdom (*qiddush ha-shem*) is still done for the sake of God *before* but not *for* the community (see B. Sanhedrin 74a–b).

[154] *The Metaphysic of Morals*, 2.1.1, trans. M. J. Gregor (Cambridge: Cambridge University Press, 1996), 177.

based on his own ethical principles. That is because his principles deal only with moral conflicts between a person's basically physical desires, on the one hand, and the moral duty the person owes to other persons as rational, rather than sensuous, beings, on the other hand.[155] But here the conflict is between duty to oneself and duty to others when both are taken as rational beings. For Kant, there is no way of determining *who* takes precedence.

Moral duty is something universal; it is owed to oneself and to all others equally. Kant insists that only such rational persons are the subjects of morality and, thus, only they are always to be considered "ends in themselves" (*Zweck an sich selbst*).[156] Even the ideal society that Kant's calls the "ethical commonwealth" cannot be anything more than the sum total of the moral persons who make it up.[157] That is why he cannot in all honesty (and Kant was the most honest of philosophers) resolve this moral conflict between the lethal claims of the community and the vital claims of the individual person. Here the difference between the one and the many is irrelevant because both one and many are noumenal (moral) rather than phenomenal (sensuous) beings. In his view, the community cannot have any original rights over and above those of its individual members because it cannot be taken to be more than a collection of persons. It is not a personal communion (*koinōnia*). Thus for Kant, as for the liberals, the most humans can accomplish in common is a society (*Gesellschaft*), but never a community (*Gemeinschaft*).

A further problem is that his idea of autonomy is that of a universalized human being, someone who is essentially everyone. Thus the very individuality that liberalism correctly sees at the heart of autonomy is lost. (Liberalism's problem is not the location of autonomy but the existential primacy it gives to it.) It is lost because Kantian autonomy does not allow us enough random freedom to pursue our *own* individual projects (mine but not yours). For a covenantal theology, the individualism that allows us to make a voluntary sacrifice, or an oath and a vow, from myself to God is lost if this Kantian view is adopted or even adapted. (This will be addressed more fully in the next chapter.) As such, Kantian universalism makes the community too much a mere collection of lone individuals, and it makes the individual too much a mere cipher of a universal ideal.

Furthermore, as Hegel objected, Kant's view is too abstract by not taking into serious consideration what we now like to call the "thickness" of traditional community and her norms (*Sittlichkeit*).[158] Yet, on the other hand, so

[155] See D. Novak, *Suicide and Morality* (New York: Scholars Studies Press, 1975), 104ff.

[156] See *Groundwork of the Metaphysic of Morals*, trans. H. J. Paton (New York: Harper and Row, 1964), 95ff.

[157] See *Religion within the Limits of Reason Alone*, trans. T. M. Greene and H. H. Hudson (New York: Harper and Row, 1960), 87ff.

[158] See *Phenomenology of Spirit*, 268ff; also Clifford Geertz, *The Interpretation of Cultures* (New York: Basic Books, 1973), 5ff.

much of what emerges from Hegel's alternative strengthens the hand of (although it is not directly responsible for) the type of tyrannical collectivism that has been *the* great political plague of this century.[159] At this point, we surely have the type of "antinomy" that Kant saw at the heart of most of the problems of theoretical philosophy he inherited, and which he attempted to overcome.[160]

But does not covenantal theonomy overcome the antinomy of Kant and Hegel in the past and liberals and communitarians in the present by holding forth God's relationship with both community and each individual as the only true foundation? And does this covenantal theonomy not accomplish this by seeing God's right as more foundational than either the rights of individuals over communal duty or communal duty over the rights of individuals? Surely, it does that by placing politics in an ontological context and addressing itself to human needs that are far more than the needs for merely immanent procedures. Indeed, it is only in this ontological context that the community and individuals are distinct enough from each other for both to be able to contribute to an integral, nonreductive relationship between them. That could not be the case, though, when either individual rights or communal rights are the starting point for the constitution of morals and law. A coherent balancing of the rights of the community and the rights of individuals is possible only when both sets of rights are relative to the absolute rights of God. At any point of conflict between individual and communal rights, then, the conflict can be finally resolved only by judging the emphasis of whose rights in the circumstance at hand enable God's prior rights to be best fulfilled.[161]

In the following chapter we shall look at this relationship from the standpoint of the rights of individual persons in the face of the community in which they live.

---

[159] Even though Hegel cannot be blamed for the excesses of Marx and the Marxists, he can still be seen as having been easily used by them (and other forms of collectivist tyranny, either Right or Left). See Louis Dupré, *The Philosophical Foundations of Marxism* (New York: Harcourt, Brace and World, 1966), 39ff.

[160] See *Critique of Pure Reason*, B433ff.

[161] Thus, e.g., R. Akibah's individual right to live rather than die for the nonobservance of a positive commandment (see B. Sanhedrin 74a and parallels re Lev. 18:5), viz., not teaching Torah to the Jewish public (see *Sifre*: Devarim, no. 34 re Deut. 6:7), was waived in favor of the community's right to be taught the Torah publicly (see B. Berakhot 61b) *because of God's right* to have his word proclaimed and expounded to his people (see *Sifre*: Devarim, no. 41; B. Kiddushin 40b and Tos., s.v. "talmud"). Conversely, as we saw earlier in this section, the right of the community to have one of her members die to protect her life is waived in favor of the right to life of an individual person randomly called for by an enemy (T. Terumot 7.20) *because of God's right* to have every person be recognized as a unique reflection of God himself (see M. Sanhedrin 4.5).

CHAPTER VII

Human Persons and Covenanted Community

THE CONTEMPORARY IMPORTANCE OF INDIVIDUAL RIGHTS

The question of the rights of an individual person in relation to the duties of the community is the question of what are the just claims that an individual person can make upon the community for fulfillment. There seem to be four kinds of such individual rights: (1) the claims of an individual on the community to protect him or her *from* harm by others; (2) the claims of an individual on the community *for* assistance in fulfilling the needs of human life; (3) the claims of an individual on the community for the means *to* greater participation in public life; and (4) the claims of an individual *against* the community's intrusion into his or her own private affairs.

Theories of modern democracy have a tendency to primarily emphasize the rights of individuals against the intrusion of society into their private lives. Although there is far less emphasis of this type of individual rights than of the other types of individual rights in the classical Jewish sources, these rights are not totally absent from the sources. Hence they need to be located and developed; they do not have to be created de novo. Indeed, there have been other times in the history of the tradition when contemporary moral and political needs required considerable development out of what seemed at the time to be sparse sources. Such development, though, is always possible, and it demonstrates the dynamism of the tradition itself.[1]

Surely, modern political experience has taught us the importance of individual rights against society. Nevertheless, for Jews, these rights must be seen in the larger covenantal context, where other types of rights, even other types of individual rights, are more evident. As such, it might be better first to look at these more evident types of individual rights, which have already been more fully developed in the tradition.

THE RIGHT TO PROTECTION FROM HARM

The notion that the main obligation of society is to protect its citizens from the harm each is capable of inflicting on the other lies at the heart of the version

---

[1] See M. Hagigah 1.8; B. Hagigah 11b; Y. Rosh Hashanah 2.5/58d re Prov. 31:14.

of social contract theory that assigns the fewest rights to the individual, that of Hobbes. For Hobbes, the chief reason why individuals in the state of nature are willing to turn over almost all their power to the state is because they fear the real "war of all against all" (*bellum omnia contra omnes*) more than they fear the possible tyranny of the state in the person of its sovereign.[2]

As we have already seen, though, such a view of the essence of society and its authority is much too minimal to hold the moral allegiance of humans as essentially communal beings and, all the more so, the allegiance of Jews as essentially covenantal participants. That is why in the scheme of rights that I have set up in this book, the rights of the individual person in relation to society are dealt with last. To see the prime duty of society to be the protection of its citizens from harming one another is to see society as a collection of strangers at best and an arena of enemies at worst. If this is the foundation of society itself, where communal ties are essentially coercive, it is hard to see how any need other than the need to be free of undue fear of harm from others has any communal significance. But it would seem that such a state of affairs does not indicate the beginning of society but, rather, its end. If this is all there is to the social bond, then it is probably too late for society to even be able to fulfill this minimal right of its members. And, of course, as we shall see later in this chapter, it does not address the fear of tyranny, which is the fear of the harm of society itself, what it can inflict on its individual members, harm that this century alone has taught us is far worse than the random acts of individual criminals within society. Nevertheless, once we see rights in the larger context of historical communities, and within the even larger context of the covenant, the right to protection from harm is one that society is duty bound to uphold. In terms of our experience of society, protection from harm is its first task on behalf of its members. It is the first thing we want *from* society. One must only remember, however, that it is not the chief business of society, and certainly not the final end of the deeper community of which society is but a part. Once that is understood, we are in the proper position to see the right to protection from harm, without which we could not make any more positive claims on society, much less on the community.

The question of how central the right to protection from harm is comes out in the discussion in the Talmud about the origin and order of the Noahide laws, that is, those laws the Rabbis determined to be binding on all humankind, and which were not even repealed by the revelation of the full Torah to Israel at

---

[2] See *Leviathan*, chaps. 14, 21. Thus Hobbes even denies a right to revoke the covenant between a monarch and his subjects. See chap. 29; and Hobbes, *De Cive*, 4.14. This follows from a too minimal community, where the vacuous state of common life is filled by an exaggerated role for the political potentates. This is the presupposition of all tyranny, be the tyrant as benign as James I in Hobbes's day or as malevolent as Hitler, Stalin, or Mao in our own.

Sinai, but were incorporated into the Torah intact.[3] Since even the full law of the Torah presupposes these laws, the talmudic discussion about their origin and order is, in effect, a discussion of the essence of law itself.[4]

As for the origin of these laws, the Rabbis are unanimous in seeing that origin in the very creation of human persons. Indeed, God's first words to his human creatures in the Garden of Eden are: "And the Lord God commanded (*va-yitsav*) humans (*al ha'adam*) saying . . ." (Genesis 2:16). However, there is a major dispute between two Rabbis as to what the first commandment actually is. Following the presentation in the Tosefta, Rabbi Yohanan thinks that the first commandment is the prohibition of idolatry. Rabbi Isaac, on the other hand, following another earlier source, thinks that the first commandment is the prescription to society to establish courts of law. At the prima facie level, the dispute is over the meaning of the word *va-yitsav*—"he commanded."[5] However, the exegesis is so speculative that upon closer examination it seems the dispute is in essence a conceptual one, and that the connection to the actual scriptural verse itself is subsequent to it (*asmakhta*).[6] Nevertheless, despite the presence of a conceptual dispute between these two Rabbis, just how deep does this dispute go? Are these two respective opinions mutually exclusive?

It would seem that what we have here is basically a disagreement about where our first emphasis of law should be. Rabbi Isaac takes what might be termed an ontological approach. That is, he is primarily concerned with the real origin of the law, which, of course, in a tradition rooted in revelation must be the word of God. Rabbi Yohanan would surely not dispute that theological foundation. This explains why, it seems to me, Maimonides, who was the most theological of halakhists and the most halakhic of theologians, follows Rabbi Isaac, rather than Rabbi Yohanan, in his presentation of the ordering of the Noahide laws.[7] Rabbi Yohanan, conversely, takes what might be termed a phenomenological approach. That is, he is primarily concerned with what our first experience of the force of law is. That experience is not that of the initial revelation of the law, even though the law in its originality is always the revelation of God's will. (And even when the concept of Noahide law is taken to be a concept of natural law, it is still the law of God, which is experienced indirectly through abstract reflection on human social nature. This is in contrast to the Mosaic Torah, which is directly experienced in history as the locus of personal contact. In the case of the latter, the law is explicitly spoken by God to the

---

[3] See D. Novak, *The Image of the Non-Jew in Judaism* (New York: Edwin Mellen Press, 1983), 56ff.; D. Novak, *Natural Law in Judaism* (Cambridge: Cambridge University Press, 1998), 149ff.

[4] This presupposition is seen in the late talmudic principle "There is nothing that is permitted to Israel that is prohibited to the gentiles" (B. Sanhedrin 59a; see Hullin 33a and Tos., s.v. "ehad").

[5] B. Sanhedrin 56b. Cf. T. Avodah Zarah 9.4, and as tranposed on B. Sanhedrin 56a.

[6] Regarding *asmakhta*, see R. Judah Halevi, *Kuzari*, 3.73; also, R. Joseph Karo, *Kesef Mishneh* on Maimonides, *Mishneh Torah*: Melakhim, 9.1.

[7] *Mishneh Torah*: Melakhim, 9.1.

people; in the case of the former, the law is implicitly bespoken by humans themselves.)[8] Instead, that first experience of law is when we go to public authorities to protect us from being harmed by somebody else. For many, it is their childhood experience of going to some adult for protection from the neighborhood bully.

In the context of the creation narrative in Genesis, this phenomenological approach gains added significance when we look at the first crime and trial that is recorded, namely, Cain's murder of his brother Abel and his subsequent trial by God. There it will be recalled, Cain's famous defense of himself before God as judge is "I did not know; am I my brother's keeper (*ha-shomer ahi*)?" (Genesis 4:9). Clearly, his "I did not know" does not refer to the fact that he has just killed his brother, but that he claims not to have known what he did to be wrong. As for his claim "Am I my brother's keeper?" there is much rabbinic speculation about what this actually means. One rabbinic theory put forth is especially appropriate to our inquiry here.

> He said to him, "Am I my brother's keeper? You are the keeper (*shomer*) of all creatures, and you inquire about him from me!" To what may we compare this by a parable? It is comparable to a thief who stole vessels at night and was not caught. In the morning the gatekeeper (*sho'er*) caught him. He said to him, "Why did you steal the vessels?" He said back to him, "I am a thief and I have not neglected my profession, but you, your profession at the gate [in public] is to be a guardian (*li-shmor*). Why have you neglected your profession? And now you speak this way to me!" So it was with Cain. He said, "I killed him, [but] you created the evil inclination (*yetser ha-ra*). You are the guardian of all, yet You let me kill him. You killed him, You who are called 'I' (*anokhi*—Exodus 20:2). For if you had accepted my sacrifice, I would not have envied him.[9]

The force of this imagined conversation between Cain and God is that God is accused of having been derelict in his duty to protect his creatures, especially his human creatures who are made in his own image. For them God should be especially responsible, that is, especially responsive to their right to protection from harm. A creator should take care (*shomer*) of what he has made, especially those whom he has made in and for a special relationship with himself. The very issue of divine responsibility is integrally involved in any covenantal theology, as we have already seen in chapter 6. And, whereas we cannot expect an answer from God in this world about his seeming lack of responsibility for those in his charge, we certainly can expect such an answer from similarly entrusted human authorities in this world. Thus the responsibility of society to

---

[8] See Novak, *Natural Law in Judaism*, 142ff.
[9] *Tanhuma*: Beresheet, 9. For further discussion of the question of "Am I my brother's keeper?" see Novak, *Natural Law in Judaism*, 31ff.

protect its members from harm is their right and its duty, a duty that is very much an act of *imitatio Dei*.[10]

One sees the human locus of the right of individual persons to protection from harm and the communal duty to enforce it in a classic rabbinic discussion of collective guilt. The discussion concerns the rather enigmatic rite that the Torah prescribes in the event of a murder victim being found without public knowledge of who his or her murderer is. When this happens, a young calf that has never known the yoke or been worked in any way is to have its neck broken in a river, and then the elders of the nearest city to the site where the corpse has been found are to wash their hands in the river and say, "[O]ur hands did not shed the blood of this person and our eyes did not see it" (Deuteronomy 21:7). At this point the Mishnah raises the obvious question: "Would we have thought that the elders of the court are murderers (*shofkhei damim hen*)? Rather, [what they are saying] is that he [the victim] did not come into our jurisdiction (*le-yadeinu*) and we sent him away without food, and we did not see him and send him off without escort."[11] What we see here is the assumption that it is the right of every person, especially vulnerable strangers, to have the protection of the local authorities in the dangerous business of travel. In other words, the prevention of crime is the duty of society, which here means the protection of the vulnerable before anything happens to them. The Mishnah's question is rhetorical, which assumes that not only are the elders of the court persons of known virtue, but that they have usually been effective in preventing the crime of murder. But when this is no longer the case, namely, when the murder rate indicates a lack of proper social control of criminal acts, then the society in the persons of its leaders no longer has the privilege of self-exoneration. Thus shortly after this passage, the Mishnah curtly notes that "when murderers increased, the rite of the 'calf with the broken neck' (*eglah arufah*) was abolished."[12]

The text of the Mishnah is speaking of the right to society's protection of the potential victim of attack. But the statement of exoneration prescribed in the Torah could be concerned with the right of potential victims to know that criminals are properly punished by society. That means that these potential victims have reasonable assurance that society has done everything possible (within the limits of justice) to effectively deter the commission of crimes in the first place, as well as the assurance that if they are the victims of crime, then their deaths will be avenged by society. As such, in the Palestinian Talmud it is recorded that although the Babylonian Rabbis interpret the statement of

---

[10] See B. Shabbat 10a re Gen. 1:5; also, B. Sanhedrin 7a re Ps. 82:1.

[11] M. Sotah 9.6. See D. Novak, *Jewish Social Ethics* (New York: Oxford University Press, 1992), 176.

[12] M. Sotah 9.9. For the use of the inability to perform the rite of the *eglah arufah* as a metaphor for official sorrow at not having been able to prevent bloodshed in the community, see B. Yoma 23a–b and Tos., s.v. "ve-yerushalyim"; Y. Yoma 2.1/39d.

exoneration in the Torah as referring to the victims (*ba-neherag*), the Palestinian Rabbis interpret it as referring to the criminals (*ba-horeg*), namely, "he did not come into our jurisdiction and we released him but did not execute him, and we did not see him [as guilty] but let him go because we were not diligent in adjudicating his case."[13] Combining these two versions of the statement, we see that individual persons have the right to society's protection of their bodies and their possessions, and that they have the right to assume that every possible measure is being taken to deter and punish criminals. But this is not where the rights/claims of individual persons on society end, as they do in more libertarian views of rights.[14] Rights are more than what Isaiah Berlin famously called "negative liberty."[15]

THE RIGHT TO PUBLIC ASSISTANCE

The right to assistance in situations where a person is unable to provide basic necessities for himself or herself is essentially a right that entails an individual duty. The basic commandment, "You shall love your neighbor as yourself" (Leviticus 19:18), as we have already seen, is one whose subject, "your self" (*kamokha*), is designated as singular. In fact, the most immediate form of such assistance, such as tending to the needs of the sick, is what the Rabbis call "acts of personal kindness" (*gemilut hasadim*). These acts cannot be delegated to somebody else, but must be performed on a person-to-person basis.[16] Thus at this most basic level, the assistance to a person in need cannot as yet be designated by what today is commonly called "welfare."

Nevertheless, built upon this most immediate right is a right to monetary assistance (*tsedaqah*) when truly needed. The duty that this right entails already moves in a more abstract, less personal direction because it involves money, which is itself an abstract social invention, designed for an efficiency in the transfer of property that is impossible when such transfer is limited to a strictly person-to-person basis.[17] Just as money is a social institution, so the distribution of what could be called "charity" has become a social institution, although it must always be remembered that the institutionalization of the distribution of charity, which becomes of course a welfare system, can never replace the more direct person-to-person relationship that it builds upon. Social institutions are to enhance the more basic personal community that must pre-

---

[13] Y. Sotah 9.6/23d.

[14] See Robert Nozick, *Anarchy, State, and Utopia* (New York: Basic Books, 1974), 33ff.

[15] See "Two Concepts of Liberty," in *Four Essays on Liberty* (Oxford: Oxford University Press, 1969), 121ff.

[16] See Maimonides, *Commentary on the Mishnah*: Peah 1.1.

[17] See Aristotle, *Nicomachean Ethics*, 5.5/1133a20ff.

cede it. When these institutions replace what they are been derived from, the result is that persons cease to be living relational centers and become, instead, parts of a larger, all-encompassing whole that functions like a machine. The parts of a machine are made to be disposable. In and of themselves, they are nothing. Ultimately, when this happens, nobody has any rights left.[18]

When society institutionalizes welfare, however partially that should be, persons in need now have a right to call upon society for its help to alleviate their predicaments. That entails a duty for society, over and above that of its individual members, to respond appropriately. That propriety is negotiated between the needs of the rights-bearing, poor persons and the resources of society that can be allocated without the financial ruin of the society itself. This social institution is so basic to organized Jewish communal life that Maimonides writes, "[W]e have never seen or heard of any Jewish community (*qahal*) that does not have a charity fund (*quppah shel tsedaqah*)."[19] Later on, he speaks of all Israel as brothers, who can only turn to each other for support when in need. Throughout this almost rhapsodic description of the importance of Jewish philanthropy, the emphasis of the duty to provide for the poor is made in the plural, both in terms of its objects and its subjects.[20]

That the poor of the community have a right to this provision is emphasized by the fact that charity is not left to totally individual discretion. Thus the Talmud states about the various types of produce that Scripture decrees are to be left for the poor to come and gather for themselves, that "they are not the largesse (*tovat hana'ah*) of the owners"—that is, the distribution of these items is not something that an individual owner can refuse, or even give to those poor who happen to be his or her personal favorites. It is the right of "any of the poor of Israel to take it from his control (*me-yado*)."[21] Whoever comes first has the prior right to it. To play favorites in the discharge of this duty is to rob the poor of their rights.[22] As Rashi points out in his comment, "they force (*kofeen*) him to give."[23] This "forcing" clearly means the social institution of supervised giving to the poor of their allotted gifts inasmuch as virtually all coercion becomes a social monopoly in order to assure its impartial operation for the sake of the common good. Thus the right of the poor to these gifts is compared to the right of any member of the community to the institution of justice, which is clearly a specific duty of society to perform on behalf of the innocent because it is something to which they have a right.[24] Thus Maimon-

---

[18] See Jacques Maritain, *The Person and the Common Good*, trans. J. J. Fitzgerald (Notre Dame, Ind.: University of Notre Dame Press, 1966), 47ff.

[19] *Mishneh Torah*: Mattnot Aniyyim, 9.3.

[20] Ibid., 10.2.

[21] Hullin 131a–b re Lev. 23:22.

[22] M. Peah 4.9 and 5.6; B. Gittin 11b.

[23] Hullin 131b, s.v. "ein bahen."

[24] Hullin 134a re Ps. 82:3.

ides designates the right of the poor as one that they themselves must exercise on their own behalf (*tov'im*).[25]

The question of the needs of the poor versus the resources of those who are "rich" (that is, those who are above a certain designated poverty line) becomes quite different when we distinguish between personal giving and the institutional allocation of funds.[26] The general standard that applies to both is summarized by Maimonides in this formula: "When the poor person comes and asks for his needs to be fulfilled (*dei mehsaro*), but the giver is unable to supply them, he should give as much as he can afford (*ke-fi hasagat yado*)."[27] However, in the case of person-to-person giving, the measure of the gift is determined by the situation at hand: that of the poor person now making the claim and that of the "rich" person to whom the claim is now being made.[28]

The issue of the rectification of poverty is seen as a restoration to the status quo ante. As Rabbi Akibah put it, "[T]he poor of Israel are to be seen as property holders (*bnei horeen*) who have lost their possessions because they are, after all, the descendants of Abraham, Isaac and Jacob."[29] But in the case of the allocation of communal resources, we are at the more abstract level of distributive justice, which involves the socially instituted process of the transfer of wealth. Here the issues are matters of public policy, and these matters are always to be conditioned by what is perceived by those designated as communal authorities to be in the interests of the common good.[30] Indeed, the greater abstraction of this level of charity means that it is not anymore so much a case of where some poor person is standing before another here and now and whose right is to be immediately fulfilled. Instead, it is a case of how the community weighs its own long-range needs and what rights of which individual members take precedence over those of others when the distribution of funds is determined more by abstract percentages than by real presences.[31] In other words, the community has the right to judge for itself how and when the rights of individual persons are to be fulfilled as its communal duty to them.

---

[25] *Mishneh Torah*: Mattnot Aniyyim, 1.10.

[26] Regarding the poverty line, see M. Peah 8.7–9.

[27] *Mishneh Torah*: Mattnot Aniyyim, 7.5. See M. Peah 8.6; T. Peah 4.10 and B. Ketubot 67b re Deut. 15:8.

[28] See B. Taanit 21a.

[29] M. Baba Kama 8.6.

[30] See B. Ketubot 49b–50a regarding the "decrees of Usha," which were public policy decisions concerning the proper redistribution of wealth for welfare purposes.

[31] See, e.g., B. Baba Metsia 71a re Deut. 15:11; Maimonides, *Mishneh Torah*: Mattnot Aniyyim, 7.13 and note of Radbaz thereon in the name of R. Saadiah Gaon (who elebaorates on the view of R. Akibah on B. Baba Metsia 62a re Lev. 25:36). For the main sources for the wide latitude for public policy rulings, even those that temporarily suspend specific laws, see M. Berakhot 9.5; T. Berakhot 6.30; B. Berakhot 63a re Ps. 119:126; B. Yevamot 90b re Deut. 18:15. Unlike specific laws, especially scriptural ones, these public policy rulings are all essentially tentative and conditional (see Maimonides, *Mishneh Torah*: Mamrim, 2.4).

Furthermore, the situation of charity, be it personal giving or public welfare, is never to be a relationship where all the rights lie on one side and all the duties on the other. Such a situation would involve too radical a social imbalance in the covenant, where the equality of all its members before God is essential.[32] It would make the poor become nothing but passive objects looking up to those who provide for them, who then become nothing but active subjects looking down on them. That is why, it seems, the emphasis is that "even the poor person who is supported by charity is to give charity to an other."[33] Thus the purpose of charity is to give its recipients the chance to once again, or initially, become actively contributing members of the community. That purpose is not to be totally postponed to the future. Even at present there is to be a contribution of the welfare recipient, however symbolic it might be here and now. Along these lines, Maimonides sees the eighth and highest form of charity to be the one where the poor person is given "a gift or a loan or a partnership is made with him or work is found for him to support himself—so that he need no longer ask other human beings [for support]."[34] Hence public welfare programs should be designed to avoid prolonged dependence as much as possible.[35] Indeed, it would seem that society has a duty to formulate policies that enable businesses to be started and work to be made available because the poor have a right to them. But, of course, this requires that the members of the society regard those in poverty to still be fellow participants in their communal life and, for Jews, in our covenant. When that is not the case, however, public welfare usually becomes a way to keep the poor away from communal life, which breeds deep resentment on both sides.

The question of public policy versus personal interrelationship in the giving of charity is especially vivid in the case of the right of captives to be ransomed by the community and the way the community fulfills its duty to them. This is an issue we examined in the previous chapter in terms of how individual captives themselves must not expect the expenditure of the full resources of the community to be spent for their own ransom, which means how they must, in effect, perform a duty *for* the community simultaneous with exercising their claim right *from* her.[36] Here we are more concerned with how the community herself understands her duty as a response to the right of captives to be redeemed.

Concerning the captives, Maimonides writes that their ransom takes precedence over supporting the poor "because they are included among the hungry, the thirsty, and the naked, and they stand in danger of losing their lives (*be-*

---

[32] See Novak, *Jewish Social Ethics*, 210f.

[33] B. Gittin 7a–b, 12a re Lev. 23:22.

[34] *Mishneh Torah*: Mattnot Aniyyim, 10.7.

[35] See B. Shabbat 118a and parallels.

[36] Those who do not consider the prior claims of the community are considered to have abandoned her. See M. Avot 2.4; B. Taanit 11a re Isa. 22:13.

sakkanat nefashot)."[37] Nevertheless, already in the early rabbinic period, it was debated whether the first concern of the community in its rescue operations was to be for the captives here and now or to be for the whole situation of captives in general that the community had to face over a long period of time. Along these lines, the Mishnah speaks of how devoting too much money and effort to ransoming or rescuing captives here and now might very well make matters worse for many more captives in the long run. The former position is that of Rabban Gamliel II, who speaks of "what is to be done to alleviate the condition of the captives (*taqqanat ha-shevuyyin*)." But the other Sages see it as an issue of "alleviating the condition of society (*tiqqun ha'olam*)."[38] Now, in the case of a strictly person-to-person relationship, future considerations are not a determining factor.[39] It seems that Rabban Gamliel II wants the issue of the rescue of captives to be seen in this light. But the view of the other Sages is that in a case of a situation potentially involving a whole class of people over time, the community has the right to take this more abstract issue into consideration in what becomes a vital matter of the distribution of its limited resources of both money and energy. As always, the view of the Sages is the codified law.[40]

The right of the captive to be rescued is the right of the member of the community who is most far removed from its life to be restored to it.[41] That is to be done, as we have just seen, with great diligence, just as long as the exercise of the community's correlative duty does not disrupt the life of the community to such an extent that she will not have the resources to exercise this duty in the future. To rescue captives presupposes that we have maintained an intact community to which they can truly return. What we learn from this extreme situation is useful for our attempt now to understand less dramatic rights to inclusion in the life of the community.

THE RIGHT TO SOCIAL INCLUSION

When individual rights are looked upon as the only kind of rights, society's role is limited to that of service, which is minimally to protect persons from harm to themselves and their property (police work) and maximally to rescue them from extreme deprivation (social work). This, of course, assumes that society is only instrumental, that it has no communal function, that it is not

---

[37] *Mishneh Torah*: Mattnot Aniyyim, 8.10.

[38] M. Gittin 4.6. See B. Gittin 45a and Rashi thereon, s.v. "de-leika." See Y. Moed Qatan 1.2/ 80b, where redeeming captives is designated one of those "public needs" (*tsorkhei rabbim*) so urgent that it overrides the normal restrictions of a festival week (*hol ha-mo'ed*).

[39] See, e.g., *Sifra*: Behar, ed. Weiss, 109c and B. Baba Metsia 62a re Lev. 25:36 (the opinion of R. Akibah).

[40] R. Joseph Karo, *Shulhan Arukh*: Yoreh Deah, 252.5.

[41] Along these lines, see Y. Yevamot 8.4/46b.

the domain in which persons want to participate in order to fulfill their need for one another's presence. However, if one assumes that, as Aristotle put it most famously and accurately, "humans are political beings," then the fullest possible participation in communal life is certainly a desideratum.[42] And when one is dealing with the covenant, then the desideratum is the fullest participation possible in the life with God and fellow Jews expressed in the practice of the commandments of the Torah. That involves a high degree of interpersonal responsibility within the covenant, not only to fulfill basic individual needs, but also to include as many as possible in the social practices of the community. That is why every Jew is considered responsible for every other Jew, both to prevent sin and to enhance the practice of the commandments whenever possible.[43] Since the keeping of the commandments is a privilege, the Mishnah records that "God wanted to privilege (le-zakkot) Israel, therefore he increased the number of commandments for them."[44] And since the covenant applies to both the community and each and every person in it, "Israel" here refers as much to individual Jews as it does to the Jewish people themselves.[45]

The question is to what extent this desideratum is a right that the community is duty bound to uphold. Everything one desires, even what one understandably desires, cannot be taken to be his or her right. A right must be justified in a total scheme of things: initially, the created order of nature and, finally, the covenantal order of the Torah. In liberal theory, conversely, a right is coequal with one's will.[46] Its only limit is the tacit agreement one would make not to harm others as the price to be paid for the necessary (but not inherently desirable) protecting presence of society. However, this reduction of human personhood to will ignores the truth that there is much more to human life than human will can ever effect, let alone accomplish. In the covenantal system, where one is initially a person created in the image of God, has an intelligible nature, and, finally, is a member of God's elect community in the world, one's rights are not self-made; they are irrevocable entitlements (zekhuyot) from God. It is always best when one's justified right and his or her will are coequal, but that is not always the case.[47] Sometimes, one has a right to something, even

---

[42] *Nicomachean Ethics*, 9.9/1169b20; *Politics*, 1253a2. Maimonides in *Guide of the Perplexed*, 2.40, accepts that assertion and interprets all of the social teaching of the Torah accordingly, except for those practices he sees as performing the more theoretical task of acting as a prophylactic against idolatry (see 3.30).

[43] See B. Shevuot 39a–b re Lev. 26:37; B. Sanhedrin 43b–44a re Deut. 29:28. Cf. B. Yevamot 65b re Prov. 9:8 (and Rashi thereon, s.v. "lomar" re Lev. 19:17); B. Baba Batra 60b and Tos., s.v. "mutav." See Maimonides, *Mishneh Torah*: Deot, 6.6–9.

[44] M. Makkot 3.16 re Isa. 42:21.

[45] See B. Sanhedrin 44a re Josh. 7:11; *Teshuvot Rashi*, ed. Elfenbein (New York: n.p., 1943), no. 171; also, D. Novak *The Election of Israel* (Cambridge: Cambridge University Press, 1995), 189ff.

[46] See Locke, *Second Treatise of Government*, chap. 8.

[47] See M. Avot 2.4. Cf. *Sifra*: Qedoshim, ed. Weiss, 93d re Lev. 20:26.

if one cannot claim it or does not want to claim it. For example, one's own life has an inviolate claim on others even when one is mentally incompetent to utter that claim, or even when one wants the opposite, as when he or she wants to die.[48] (Nevertheless, a good case can be made that a person does have the right to determine how much pain he or she can bear in medical treatment, even if that means the cessation of a particular medical procedure, and even when the overall goal of the treatment is to prolong life.)[49]

In the covenant, the different social roles one has are largely dependent on which commandments he or she is either obligated to practice or allowed to practice. Does one have rights to socioreligious roles to which he or she is not traditionally entitled? Or, in other words, does one have a right to assume a new social duty? Unlike in the previous sections, where we examined what one may justifiably claim from the community for himself or herself, here we are examining what one may justifiably claim from the community for its own sake, for the public practice of the commandments has immediate social significance both for those who can practice them and those who cannot.[50]

It seems that one must avoid two extremes to get a better understanding of this important covenantal issue. The one extreme is the type of collectivism that sees all personal roles in the community to be permanently fixed. Any change in communal practice is always initiated by some individual; hence individuals are not seen as having any rights, but only communal duties.[51] The more communal conformity, the more the tradition is protected. The other extreme is the type of individualism that cannot see why the community should not accommodate the desires of individuals as long as the fulfillment of these desires is not evidently harmful to other individuals. Here tradition has no claims at all because the community has no claims other than those which are for the sake of the immediate rectification of harm to persons or private property, or which are needed for the sake of the immediate distribution of necessi-

---

[48] See, e.g., M. Shabbat 23.5; B. Shabbat 151b; M. Yoma 83a; Maimonides, *Mishneh Torah*: Gerushin, 2.20. Even though there is a halakhic view that one may pray for death (one's own or that of someone for whom he or she cares), that is a request from God and clearly not a matter of *imitatio Dei* (see B. Nedarim 40a and Rabbenu Nissim [Ran] thereon, s.v. "ein mevaqesh" re B. Ketubot 104a); also, D. Novak, *Law and Theology in Judaism* (New York: KTAV, 1974–76), 1:80ff., and 2:98ff. For a critique of this view, however, see R. Eliezer Waldenberg, *Ramat Rahel*, sec. 5, appended to *Teshuvot Tsits Eliezer* 4–5 (Jerusalem: n.p., 1985).

[49] For sources for such a view, see B. Yoma 83a re Prov. 14:10; B. Ketubot 33b and note of R. Jacob Emden (Yavets) thereon; B. Baba Metsia 85b; B. Avodah Zarah 18a. In all of these cases, though, the request for relief from pain is to be distinguished from a request to be killed or to be allowed to die.

[50] See B. Kiddushin 31a and parallels.

[51] This attitude was famously enunciated in the slogan of the most important leader of what might be termed the "Jewish Counter Reformation," R. Moses Schreiber of Pressburg (d. 1839), viz., "What is new (*hadash*) is forbidden by the Torah." See *Teshuvot Hatam Sofer*: Orah Hayyim, no. 28.

ties to individual members of society. Society's essential function here is to deliver upon individual request.

However, if we are communal beings, the very historicity of human communities necessitates that the tradition have prima facie authority.[52] Without strong and consistent tradition, no community could endure in time. The exercise of individual rights cannot be allowed to disrupt the communal continuity that the tradition alone provides. All of this is true in general, and it is true even in the special situation of the community covenanted by and with God. However, there is one fundamental difference, and that difference makes the covenantal system much more than the usual collectivism, even though it seems to have more in common with it than it does with modern, liberal individualism. In traditional communities, the individual person's connection to whomever is sovereign is in every way mediated by the collective itself. That mediation is through presently operative social institutions that stretch back into time as traditions. But in the covenant, both the community as a whole and each and every individual person is directly related to God as sovereign.[53] Even that quintessential modern apostate from Judaism, Baruch Spinoza, was favorably impressed by this aspect of the covenant. In fact, he saw it as being the only defense against political tyranny.[54]

The community does not mediate that relationship between God and individual persons any more than these persons themselves create the community as an instrument for the fulfillment of their private needs. Thus the Torah as the constitution of the covenant addresses its commandments both to the community and to the various persons who make up the community.[55] There are many commandments involving intimate matters between humans and God and between humans themselves that the community has no jurisdiction to enforce, however much it should encourage their practice.[56] The question is just how

---

[52] See, e.g., Menahot 89a and parallels.

[53] Louis Jacobs, *Religion and the Individual* (Cambridge: Cambridge University Press, 1992), 42ff.

[54] *Tractatus Theologico-Politicus*, chaps. 16–17.

[55] Note: "Natural rights and natural law are not derived one from the other, but . . . both are derived as correlative doctrines from the same underlying view of human personality" (Brian Tierney, *The Idea of Natural Rights* [Atlanta, Ga.: Scholars Press, 1997], 5). As Tierney shows in this beautifully researched and reasoned book, "natural law" traditionally comprises what I have termed "claims of the community on persons" (see chap. 6). Moreover, this "underlying view of human personality" is more beholden to scripturally based theology than it is to classical political philosophy (see Tierney, *The Idea of Natural Rights*, 343). Yet Tierney recognizes how a doctrine of natural rights is only "implicit" in that theology (46). But that is enough for purposes of the contemporary development of it. Such development should always recognize the correlation of communal natural law and individual natural/human rights (see 77).

[56] For example, the numerous laws that pertain to intimate marital relations are left to the private discretion of the marital partners. See B. Sanhedrin 37a re Cant. 7:3; M. Nedarim 11.12 and Maimonides, *Commentary on the Mishnah* thereon; B. Baba Batra 60a re Num. 24:2 and

one balances the communal need for tradition and the needs of individuals to participate in the covenant in new ways. How then are the right of the community for stability and the right of an individual for enhanced communal participation to be resolved? Do they not inherently conflict? Much of the religious turmoil in modern Judaism between traditionalists and liberals has hinged on this very question.

Judaism, going back to Scripture itself, has provided several opportunities for individuals to, in effect, create new forms of socioreligious participation for themselves. The best example is the institution of the oath (*shevu'ah*), which is the opportunity for a person to autonomously create for himself or herself a new obligation.[57] The only restrictions on such oaths are that they be within the realm of human possibility and that they not prescribe acts that are contrary to the Torah: both Scripture and codified tradition.[58] That is why the taking of an oath or a vow and the cancellation of an oath or vow is to be a public act. No individual is in a position to be an adequate judge of the social significance of his or her acts.[59] Even autonomy is not wholly private because there is really nothing that we do that does not have an effect on other persons and things. That is why the community has the right to annul oaths and vows when necessary.[60]

The essence of an oath is that "which pertains to oneself" (*nafsheih*) in relation to someone or something else. A vow (*neder*) is closely related to an oath, except it pertains to someone or something else (*heftsa*) in relation to oneself.[61] Thus the locus of an oath is more closely related to a person's will, which makes it resemble modern notions of individual rights that led to the

---

Rashbam thereon, s.v. "va-yar." For the ultimate location of the gravest of all sins, idolatry, in the heart of each person, see B. Kiddushin 40a re Ezek. 14:5 (cf. 49b and parallels).

[57] See Num. 30:3ff.

[58] M. Shevuot 3.8; M. Baba Batra 8.5. However, in most voluntary matters, with the important exception of giving and taking interest (*ribbit*—M. Baba Metsia 5.11), individuals may autonomously negotiate their own private agreements (see B. Kiddushin 19b).

[59] See M. Negaim 2.5; Maimonides, *Mishneh Torah*: Shevuot, 2.12 and Nedarim, 2.2.

[60] See B. Nedarim 77b–78a; Bekhorot 36b–37a; Maimonides, *Mishneh Torah*: Shevuot, 6.1–3. For the tragic results of a vow (that of Jephthah—Judg. 11:30ff.) not subjected to communal supervision, see B. Taanit 4a; *Beresheet Rabbah* 60.3; *Vayiqra Rabbah* 37.4.

[61] B. Nedarim 2b and 81b re Num. 30:3. Also, since a vow pertains to an external object, but only a person can be the subject of a commandment, one may vow that such an object be forbidden to himself or herself (Nedarim 2.2; B. Nedarim 16b–17a; Maimonides, *Mishneh Torah*: Nedarim, 3.7–8). That is because one does not literally nullify his or her own personal obligation but only removes an object from it. Needless to say, such vows that lessen one's covenantal participation are discouraged, except, perhaps, when the object so removed from one's ordinary observance of the commandments is dedicated to what is taken to be a higher level of sanctity, viz., dedication to the Temple (see T. Nedarim 1.5 and R. Saul Lieberman, *Tosefta Kifshuta*: Nashim [New York: Jewish Theological Seminary of America, 1967], 405; Y. Nedarim 2.2/37b and R. Moses Margolis, *Pnei Mosheh* thereon re M. Temurah 7.2; Maimonides, *Mishneh Torah*: Nedarim, 13.23–25).

idea of autonomy.[62] Indeed, an oath can also be nullified by one's volition through a procedure whereby a court accepts the person's retroactive regret at having made the oath (or vow) in the first place.[63] At this level, then, society actually enables the exercise of personal autonomy.

Of course, unlike modern notions of autonomy, be they Kantian or liberal, the autonomy of the oath (and vow) is not morally foundational. Thus the oath that Israel took at Mount Sinai to accept the Torah from God was, in effect, imposed on her by God himself. There is nothing in Scripture or the rabbinic tradition that even suggests that any answer but "yes" would have been accepted by God.[64] Nevertheless, there is certainly what we might term "supplemental autonomy." The question is just how far it extends. That is important for our inquiry at this point because the ability to make an oath or a vow seems to be the right of an individual person to augment and thereby alter his or her socioreligious status in the covenanted community. The possibility of taking an oath involves either the initiation of a new motivation for an old act or the initiation of a new act per se.

As regards the initiation of new motivation for an old act, the Talmud records the following discussion:

> Rav Gidal said in the name of Rav, "How do we know that one may take an oath
> to uphold (le-qayyem) a commandment? Scripture states, 'I have taken an oath
> and I uphold your righteous decrees to keep them' (Psalms 119:106)." But is not
> one under the oath already authoritative (mushba v'omed) since Sinai? Neverthe-
> less, what this teaches us is that it is permitted for a person to motivate oneself
> (le-zaruzei nafsheih).[65]

In other words, one is actually permitted to regard all his or her practice of the commandments of the Torah as being autonomously legislated. I would dispute whether this is the best motivation for the practice of the commandments; it seems to me that submission to the will of God and appreciation of God's superior wisdom is the better motivation in the context of the covenant. Ultimately, one's autonomy is going to come into conflict with the covenant inasmuch as it includes practices that seem to be absurd in themselves.[66] And, in fact, the tendency of the tradition is to discourage the taking of oaths and

---

[62] Nevertheless, unlike modern notions of autonomy, an oath or a vow is a promise made to God and is ultimately dependent on the acceptance of God's faithfulness in keeping his promises first. See Nahmanides, Commentary on the Torah: Num. 30:3. Cf. Jürgen Habermas, Between Facts and Norms, trans. W. Rehg (Cambridge: MIT Press, 1996), 82ff.

[63] See Maimonides, Mishneh Torah: Shevuot, 6.5.

[64] See B. Shabbat 88a re Exod. 19:17; also, Novak, The Election of Israel, 138ff.

[65] B. Nedarim 7b–8a and parallels.

[66] See, e.g., Bemidbar Rabbah 19.4 re Zech. 13:2.

vows.[67] Nevertheless, this semiautonomous option is a justified right in the tradition, even if one chooses not to exercise it.[68]

All of this has direct relevance to the issue that has caused more consternation than any other in contemporary Jewish religious life, namely, the issue of the fuller participation of women in public rituals, especially in the synagogue. Here we are faced with the issue of how far individual innovation can go in Judaism. Against the backdrop of what might be termed "traditional autonomy," the inadequacy of the liberal and many of the traditionalist approaches to this whole issue becomes more apparent.

What the liberals (that is, the Reform, Reconstructionist, and Conservative movements in North American Jewry, which have now become theologically indistinguishable) have done is to adopt a simplistic egalitarianism, which is totally at variance with the tradition both generally and specifically. This is presented as the generic solution to the problem raised by the desire of many contemporary Jewish women for an augmented role in public rituals. They have simply told men and women that there are no longer any functional differences between them anymore, thus denying the deep differences of gender that permeate the Jewish tradition from its very beginnings in Scripture and forever after.[69] Since individual rights have meaning only in a communal context anyway, this total disregard for the normative tradition will, sooner or later, make the practice of these new religious rights a hollow exercise, for it quickly calls into question just about everything the tradition has ever bequeathed, including the monopoly of heterosexuality. (And, indeed, such is already the case when one listens to some of the more radical Jewish feminists.) But then the continuity of the community is lost, and a new, ideological vision is substituted for it, one based on neither revelation nor reason.[70]

What many traditionalists have done is to assume that the tradition has decreed once and for all every possible role for individuals in the Jewish public

---

[67] See B. Nedarim 10b re Num. 6:11 and 60b and parallels; Hullin 2a re Eccl. 5:4; Maimonides, *Mishneh Torah*: Shevuot 12.12.

[68] Regarding autonomy as voluntary duty, see B. Kiddushin 30a (cf. Tos., s.v. "gadol"); B. Yoma 34b re Deut. 12:12 and Rashi, s.v. "u-tserikhei"; *Beresheet Rabbah* 30.10 re Cant. 17:1. But it is worth noting that one who does not uphold the *mitsvah* when he or she took an oath to uphold it is not liable for the violation of the oath itself, but only liable for the violation of the commandment (see M. Shevuot 3.6 and B. Shevuot 27a re Lev. 5:4).

[69] The locus classicus for this fundamental distinction seems to be the principle in M. Kiddushin 1.7: "For all positive commandments conditioned by a specific time (*she-ha-zman grama*), men are obligated and women are exempt (*peturot*)." Since one's relation to time is the most basic principle of ordering his or her world, this principle would make situations where men and women are religiously equal the exception rather than the rule (see B. Kiddushin 33bff. and parallels).

[70] See, e.g., Judith Plaskow, *Standing Again at Sinai* (San Francisco: Harper and Row, 1990), 223, who basically sees feminism as a new religion, through which she subjects traditional Judaism to a critique from which it would be unrecognizable—that is, were its adherents willing to accept what she proposes.

religious life. They have chosen to ignore the fact that there is plenty of room for individual inventiveness in halakhically structured Jewish religious life, that is, as long as it does not directly contradict existing traditional, communal norms.[71] Thus the recent movement among Jewish women, who are fully observant and who have explicitly indicated their willingness to be bound by all the codified halakhic norms, to establish women's prayer groups (*huggei tefillah*)—has elicited the vehement condemnation of some traditionalists.[72] Even though these prayer groups are run as parallel "services" to the formal, male-conducted services of the synagogue and are not designed to compete with them, and even though these condemnations have been made on easily refutable halakhic grounds, this has not deterred the opposition of many traditionalist men—and even some women as well. Nevertheless, the institution of what are in effect new forms of public ritual is permitted as a voluntary matter. To use a wonderful metaphor of Wittgenstein, it is like adding suburbs onto an old city, which are valid extensions of it as long as they are kept in their secondary, "suburban" role and do not destroy the order of the old city onto which they have been added.[73] That is why women may pray at the same regular times as men do, individually or in groups, as long as they do not assume the roles originally assigned to men, such as being counted in a male quorum (*minyan*) needed for traditional public worship, or acting as the leader (*sheliah tsibbur*) of any such quorum.[74] Furthermore, if any such practices are taken upon oneself as an oath or a vow, then the practice is no longer a voluntary right (*reshut*) but becomes an obligated duty (*hovah*), one that she can no longer practice on a casual take-it-or-leave-it basis anymore.[75]

What distinguishes the proper exercise of these rights *within* the normative structure of the tradition (going as far as the right to take an oath) from the egalitarianism advocated by liberals is that the exercise of these rights is not based on the liberals' essentially revolutionary agenda. It does not place the autonomy of individuals over the continuity of the community that only the normative structure of the tradition can provide. The tradition represents the majority opinion of the normative Jewish community throughout history, even though that same tradition has not predetermined every possible future prac-

---

[71] For example, one should examine the whole ancient Pharisaic institution of *haverut*, whereby ordinary Jews took upon themselves some of the obligations of Aaronide priests (see T. Demai 2.2–17).

[72] This whole issue, citing views both pro and con, is fully discussed in A. Weiss, *Women at Prayer* (Hoboken, N.J.: KTAV, 1990).

[73] *Philosophical Investigations*, 2nd ed., trans. G. E. M. Anscombe (New York: Macmillan, 1958), 1.18.

[74] For my earlier and fuller discussions of these issues, see D. Novak, *Law and Theology in Judaism* 1: 15ff., 2: 135ff.; *Halakhah in a Theological Dimension* (Chico, Calif.: Scholars Press, 1985), 61ff.

[75] See B. Shevuot 29a–b and Tos., s.v. "ki" re B. Gittin 36a; Maimonides, *Mishneh Torah*: Shevuot, 6.8–9.

tice. Indeed, practices originally introduced by individuals can become developments of the tradition itself if and when they are subsequently adopted by the larger community.[76] But the possibility of such adoption presupposes that the innovation did not originally contradict the authority of the tradition as it had developed theretofore.[77]

Without attempting to analyze the psychology of the traditionalist opposition to this legitimate Jewish feminism, one can see that it is based on a type of authoritarianism that is arbitrarily selective, involving a faulty theology that ignores the legitimate role of individuals in the life of the covenant. In fact, their selectiveness in interpreting the tradition is every bit as arbitrary as that of the liberals these traditionalists are so quick to sharply condemn. Nevertheless, the growing number of these women's prayer groups and the positive religious energies they have enabled to come forth into Jewish public life have already greatly enriched not only these pious (and often very learned) women themselves but, also, the whole Jewish community, for they have activated latent resources in the tradition itself. Their patience and courage in the face of condemnation as radicals by many traditionalists, and as accommodationists to patriarchy by many feminists (and their liberal supporters), is impressive. It teaches us that communal traditions and individual initiatives are consistent and mutually fortifying—when they are both directed toward truly covenantal ends, which always involve bowing to the authority of the law of God as revealed in the Torah and interpreted by Jewish tradition.[78]

INDIVIDUAL RIGHTS AGAINST SOCIETY

Because of the excesses of collective tyrannies in this century, and the unprecedented havoc they have wrought in millions and millions of human lives (for Jews, first and foremost, in the lives of six million Jewish victims of Nazism, and in the lives of all the Jewish survivors), it is obvious why concern for the rights of individual persons against society should be a major topic in any contemporary political theory. Liberal democracies have been the only form of polity in modern times where these rights are truly protected. Democracy is not just the rule of the majority as opposed to an oligarchy. If that were all democracy is, then Iran, or for that matter Nazi Germany, would qualify as a democracy. In both societies, the governing powers clearly have or had the support of the vast majority of the citizens. Instead, democracy combines majority rule with the protection of individual rights, even when those rights are in conflict with the interests and policies of the society, as long as they do not

[76] See, e.g., B. Berakhot 17a; *Tur*: Orah Hayyim, 122.
[77] See M. Eduyot 1.5 and Ravad, *Commentary on the Mishnah* thereon.
[78] See Novak, *Law and Theology in Judaism* 1:16, 32.

pose a clear and immediate danger to the society itself. As Ronald Dworkin has put it, "Individual rights are political trumps held by individuals . . . when a collective goal is not a sufficient justification for denying them what they wish . . . or not a sufficient justification for imposing some loss or injury upon them."[79]

For today's Jews, this insight is anything but arcane. Most Jews today live in democracies that recognize the institution of individual rights. Those Jews who still live under antidemocratic regimes are hardly ever supporters in good faith of these regimes. The question, though, is whether there is such a concept at all in the classical sources of Jewish law and theology.[80] Those who desire a closer connection between the Jewish tradition and the current—and cherished—political situation of most of the Jews alive today ought to be especially motivated to find sources for this concept and elaborate on its philosophical and theological implications. However, this research must always be self-consciously critical, lest it degenerate into mere apologetics.

NABOTH'S VINEYARD

The classical sources of Jewish law are replete with examples of all six types of correlations of duties and rights that we have examined in the previous chapters. In each chapter the procedure had to be what the Talmud calls "teaching some things and leaving others untaught."[81] However, when it comes to the issue of individual rights and the correlative duties of the community, especially one's rights against those of the community, one has to search hard for sources. Strenuous research is required. Indeed, many who are immersed in the classical sources of Halakhah, especially, openly deny that there is anything democratic in them at all.[82] And they hold the whole concept of individual rights in particular contempt. The political overtones of these assertions and counterassertions are obvious at this juncture of Jewish history.

If one looks to the very beginnings of Jewish law, in Scripture itself, one notices that the original prohibition of robbery (*gezel*) is presented in this context: "You shall not exploit your neighbor and you shall not rob (*lo tigzol*); you shall not let the hired laborer's pay remain overnight with you until the morning" (Leviticus 19:13). Note that the juxtaposed prohibitions are all concerned with both individual subjects and individual objects. The "you" who is

[79] *Taking Rights Seriously* (Cambridge: Harvard University Press, 1978), xi.

[80] One of the most important reflections on the relation of theocracy and democracy is that of Simon Federbush, *Mishpat ha-Melukhah be-Yisrael*, 2nd ed. (Jerusalem: Mosad ha-Rav Kook, 1973), esp. 26ff.

[81] B. Baba Kama 10a and parallels.

[82] See, e.g., Meir Kahane, *Uncomfortable Questions for Comfortable Jews* (Seacaucus, N.J.: L. Stuart, 1987), 45ff.

not to exploit, rob, or delay payment of wages is in the singular form. The "neighbor" (*re'akha*) does not refer to any collective object.[83] Here we have the claims of one individual upon another. There is also a prohibition of the individual appropriating the community's sacred property connected with the Temple without adequate compensation.[84] But we have no explicit source for the prohibition (*azharah*) of or the punishment (*onesh*) for the community appropriating the property of an individual. We have no explicit source for individual rights *against* those of the community in the Pentateuch.

When we look to the prophets, however, we come across one of the best known and most dramatic incidents in Scripture, the incident of the vineyard of Naboth that was arbitrarily appropriated by King Ahab. Could this be taken as the starting point we are looking for when it comes to developing a concept of the rights of individual persons against those of the community as a whole, that is, against society as a collective entity?

> And it came to pass after these events: there was a vineyard in Jezreel next to the palace of Ahab king of Samaria belonging to Naboth the Jezreelite. The king spoke to Naboth saying, "give me your vineyard to become a vegetable garden for me since it is near my house, and I shall give you in its stead a better vineyard, or if you please its price in money." But Naboth said, "it is forbidden to me from the Lord himself to give my ancestral inheritance (*nahalat avotei*) to you." (I Kings 21:1–3)

As the story continues, Ahab, in his frustration over Naboth's refusal to sell or exchange what the king wants, relates the problem to his wife, Jezebel. She then takes it upon herself to have Naboth framed on charges of blasphemy, for which he is quickly stoned to death by the elders of the city, who have become the queen's accomplices by doing her bidding in this criminal act. The queen then tells the king that he can now take possession of Naboth's vineyard because Naboth is permanently out of their way. The king follows the bidding of his wife, as usual. In response to this shocking abuse of royal power, the prophet Elijah is sent by God to warn Ahab and Jezebel that they will pay for this crime with their lives, dying a particularly ignominious death.[85]

It would seem from a prima facie look at this fascinating story that we have some sort of precedent for the concept of individual rights. The conflict seems to be between Naboth as a private citizen and society in the person of the king, the queen, and the elders of Israel. Nevertheless, this almost obviously modern approach to the story is not reflected in rabbinic treatments of it. This comes out in discussion of what the rights of the king are in relation to those of his individual subjects. In fact, earlier, at the very inception of the monarchy in

---

[83] M. Baba Kama 4.3; T. Baba Kama 4.1; B. Baba Kama 37b re Exod. 21:35.
[84] Lev. 5:15–16. See *Sifra*: Vayiqra, ed. Weiss, 25b.
[85] I Kings 21:17ff.

Israel, the prophet Samuel had stated that if the people choose a king for themselves, "this will be the practice of the king who will rule over you. . . . [Y]our
best fields and vineyards and olive groves he will take and give them to his
servants" (I Samuel 7:11, 14). The word translated as "practice"—*mishpat*—
can have either a descriptive ("he will") or a prescriptive ("he shall") meaning.
Thus one rabbinic opinion takes the term in its descriptive sense and interprets
the passage to be a warning designed to frighten the people about what is likely
to happen, even though it is not what is to be done by the king lawfully. But
an opposing rabbinic opinion takes the term in its prescriptive sense and thus
interprets the passage as stating an actual norm: what is to be done by the king
(*melekh muttar bo*).[86] At this point, a medieval gloss on the talmudic text raises
the case of Naboth and Ahab.[87] How can this be the actual norm? If it were,
then why would Ahab's appropriation of Naboth's field be considered a crime?
Why did Jezebel have to resort to the crime of framing Naboth for the crime
of blasphemy in order for Ahab to take what was lawfully his to take anyway?
Several answers are proposed in this gloss and they are illuminating not only
for what they say, but also for what they infer from this story.

One answer argues that Ahab's crime was that he took Naboth's vineyard
for his own personal use, but if he had taken it for public use (the public being
"his servants" mentioned in I Samuel 7:14), he would have been justified in
so doing.[88] Another answer argues that Ahab engaged in noblesse oblige by
asking Naboth (I Kings 21:2) to *give* him his vineyard, thereby himself creating
Naboth's right (*reshut*) of refusal. But if he had just taken it outright, there
would have been no crime at all.[89] Yet another answer argues that Ahab would
have had the right to take Naboth's field if it had become Naboth's property
through ordinary commerce (*sdeh miqneh*). The crime was, then, that Ahab
wanted to take a field that Naboth had inherited as his ancestral portion and
that was, therefore, something he was not entitled to permanently dispose of.[90]
This answer reflects the tensions described in Scripture between the earlier
form of tribal government and a loosely organized intertribal confederation

---

[86] T. Sanhedrin 4.5; B. Sanhedrin 20b.

[87] B. Sanhedrin 20b, Tos., s.v. "melekh." For further examples of royal rights, see T. Sanhedrin
4.6 and B. Sanhedrin 48b; B. Kiddushin 43a.

[88] The law is that the king has the right to appropriate land for public use (M. Sanhedrin 2.4;
also, M. Baba Batra 6.7; see B. Baba Batra 100b and Rashbam, s.v. "she-le-melekh porets"). For
discussion of any limits to that right, see B. Baba Kama 60b and Tos., s.v. "mahu"; also, R. Zvi
Hirsch Chajes, *Torat ha-Neviim*, in *Kol Kitvei Maharats Chajes* (Jerusalem: Divrei Hakhamim,
1958), 1:47.

[89] Modern biblical scholarship has shown this to be the procedure of suzerainty treaties in the
ancient Near East, viz., where a king allowed vassals to give their consent to his rule, even though
it was not really necessary. See D. R. Hillers, *Covenant* (Baltimore: Johns Hopkins University
Press, 1969).

[90] See Lev. 25:23; Ezek. 46:16–18; also, B. Baba Metsia 79a; Y. Kiddushin 1.5/60c.

being in conflict with the newer centralized authority of the monarchy.[91] In other words, Naboth is not an individual whose rights have been violated by the king and the political forces of society he controls; rather, he is a representative of the older tribal rights in conflict with the newer monarchial rights. Finally, the last answer presented here is that Ahab did not have monarchial rights to begin with since he was not chosen by God and did not rule over both Israel and Judah. The implication is that if he had been of the divinely chosen Davidic line, he might very well have been able to take Naboth's vineyard with impunity.[92]

In summary, one cannot derive from any of these answers the concept of individual rights against the power of the state. One can only derive from them some notion of minority rights, that is, the rights of a tribe against those of the monarchy that rules the whole society. Naboth's only claim upon the king and society is because of a prior *social* rather than a prior *personal* claim on them. And even if we take Naboth here to be an individual person who has been wronged, he was not wronged by the king as the personification of the state. The king is truly a criminal, but he was not acting as the truly authorized leader of that society in his crime against Naboth. So far, we are still left with the rights of one person being violated by another person—to be sure, another person having greater social status and power.[93] If there is a social crime here, that is, dereliction of public duty to uphold the rights of an individual person, then the crime is that of the elders of Naboth's city who became the willing accomplices of Ahab and Jezebel. Not only did they not uphold the rights of Naboth against the power of the king and queen as they should have done, but they also were their agents in the commission of the crime against Naboth.

The upshot of all of these answers is that the case of Naboth's vineyard is not an example of the rights of a lone individual against his society. The case of Naboth's vineyard is more a case of the individual rights of Naboth against the individual rights of Ahab, irrespective of the fact that Ahab happens to be the king, the personification of the state. Thus Ahab, like Naboth, is only a private citizen in the case at hand. Either Ahab acted illegitimately in his own private interest instead of acting in the public interest, or Ahab reduced himself to the level of a private citizen through an act of noblesse oblige, or Ahab as an illegitimate king was thus legally no more than a private citizen himself.

This does not in any way lessen the gravity of what Ahab did to Naboth. As we have seen in chapter 5, the Jewish tradition is zealous in protecting the

---

[91] See Judg. 8:22–23; I Sam. 10:17ff.; I Kings 4:7.

[92] The Rabbis' concerns with non-Davidic kings seem to reflect the problems their Pharisaic predecessors had with the Hasmonean monarchs and their successors, who often regarded themselves as being above Jewish law. See B. Kiddushin 66a; B. Sanhedrin 19a–b; also, Novak, *The Image of the Non-Jew in Judaism*, 180f.

[93] See R. Isaac Abrabanel, *Commentary on the Former Prophets*: II Sam. 12:9. Cf. B. Kiddushin 43a.

just rights of one individual person against the unjust power of another. But it is important that this case be properly classified according to the scheme I have set up. If it is interpreted as a source for the institution of the rights of an individual person over and against the power of society in the form of the state, and if upon careful analysis of the presentation of the case we discover that the scriptural text itself and the rabbinic tradition take it to be something else, then we might too hastily conclude that we are, in fact, searching for a phantom. Fortunately, though, there seems to be a more adequate source for the concept of individual rights over and against the power of the state in the Talmud.

THE RIGHT OF EMINENT DOMAIN

The right of eminent domain is usually defined as the justified claim of society upon private property if it is needed for the common good. The questions associated with this right are: (1) Is the consent of the individual owner of the property required in advance of the appropriation of his or her property? (2) Does the individual owner have to be compensated as would be the case in a transaction between two individuals as private parties?

The Mishnah states that "whoever has a public road (*derekh rabbim*) passing through his field and he appropriated it and gave them another road off to a side: what he gave the public is considered given, and he may not even take possession of what he took to be his own property."[94] Here we have a case of the interests of the community and the interests of an individual person in conflict. The first question is why this private property owner should be penalized for what amounts to an even exchange with the community. Subsequent discussion of this ruling in the Talmud answers that this is a rabbinic decree (*gezerah*) designed to discourage this sort of practice because inevitably the individual property owner will appropriate public property that is more convenient for everyone else and substitute for it property that is inconvenient for them.[95] Earlier in this same discussion, it was assumed that this ruling implies that the individual owner may not exercise his own property rights against public appropriation even if that appropriation entails monetary loss (*pseida*) for him.[96]

The ensuing discussion in the Talmud tries to show that the author of the above ruling is really Rabbi Eliezer ben Hyrkanus. He is quoted in another source assumed to be contemporaneous with the statement in the Mishnah as

---

[94] M. Baba Batra 6.7.

[95] B. Baba Batra 99b. Nahmanides (*Hiddushei ha-Ramban* thereon) reasons that only public authority can prevent anyone from inconveniencing the public at will.

[96] B. Baba Batra 99b. Cf. B. Baba Kama 27b.

saying, "[W]hen the public (*rabbim*) chose a road for themselves, what they chose is considered to have been lawfully chosen."[97] But the Talmud is shocked by this seemingly total disregard for individual property rights of any kind in the face of public interest. It exclaims, "[A]ccording to Rabbi Eliezer are the public (*rabbim*—literally, "the many") allowed to be robbers (*gazlanim*)?"[98] In order to dispel this presumption, which of course means that the rights of the community are limited in some cases by the rights of individuals (hence the question is rhetorical), the Talmud attempts to contextualize Rabbi Eliezer's ruling in the Mishnah so that we are not forced to connect it to what might be termed his collectivist legal theory.[99] It is now stated that the law is not according to the opinion of Rabbi Eliezer. Instead, the ruling in the Mishnah is now explained by the principle of a later authority that "it is forbidden to upset a field adjoining (*metsar*) private property that the public has taken possession of (*she-hehziku*)."[100] The overall aim of the invocation of this principle seems to be to refute the inference that the public may simply seize private property for itself. Thus, contrary to the view of Rabbi Eliezer, the public may take possession of private property only if (1) they make actual improvements in it and (2) the original owners do not protest what has been done, in effect, to them. This latter condition is acquiescence tantamount to explicit consent, a tacit contract as it were.[101] This is finally taken to be the normative position.

The text of the Talmud itself does not answer the underlying question which is: What right does the individual property owner have against the right of the public to take possession of his or her land? The surprise expressed over the view of Rabbi Eliezer is still only rhetorical. Yet, no explication or justification is given. Why is it so unacceptable? Could it be that the rejection of the view of Rabbi Eliezer is really ad hominem, based on the earlier rabbinic rejection of his authority precisely because he refused to abandon his own legal opinions in the face of the opposition of the majority of his colleagues?[102] In other words, could it be based on the irony that the collectivist views of Rabbi Eliezer are

---

[97] B. Baba Batra 100a.

[98] Ibid. Nahmanides (*Hiddushei ha-Ramban* thereon) argues that R. Eliezer's original view is totally unconcerned with the moral problem of public robbery. He then concludes that this view has been rejected by the Rabbis because it is irrational (*v'ein ta'am ba-davar*). Thus, from this we might see why the Talmud on B. Baba Kama 28a does not even mention R. Eliezer's ruling when discussing the question of the public appropriation of private property.

[99] See B. Batra 100a, Tos., s.v. "ve-Rabbi Eliezer."

[100] For the background of the legal institution of possession (*hazaqah*), see M. Baba Batra 3.1ff. and *Bavli* and *Yerushalmi* thereon; also, *Encyclopedia Talmudit*, 13:453ff.; Boaz Cohen, *Jewish and Roman Law* (New York: Jewish Theological Seminary of America, 1966), 2:465ff.

[101] See B. Yevamot 87b. As in all cases of *hazaqah*, if the original owner of the property claims he or she never gave his permission to others to take possession of the property, the burden of proof is on him or her. See B. Baba Batra 166b and Rashbam, s.v. "teiqu"; R. Yehiel M. Epstein, *Arokh ha-Shulhan*: Hoshen Mishpat, 377.3.

[102] See B. Baba Metsia 59b; B. Shabbat 130b; Niddah 7b.

being rejected because of his own judicial individualism? More needs to be discovered to justify the shock at the views of Rabbi Eliezer, not just ad hominem but primarily ad rem.

The principle underlying the ruling of Rabbi Eliezer in the case of eminent domain we have been examining seems to be that the public interest is always to be upheld over and against any private interest.[103] This principle is enunciated and justified by the twelfth-century French exegete Rabbi Samuel ben Meir (Rashbam) and his younger brother, Rabbenu Tam (even though they could not accept the specific ruling of Rabbi Eliezer because of the undisputed rejection of all his controversial views in the Talmud). This principle is justified by them as follows: (1) The Rabbis were much more concerned with protecting the public interest than with protecting the private interest;[104] (2) an individual may not sue the public because the public is like a court (*ke-vet din damu*). As such, how could the public possibly adjudicate a case in which it itself was one of the litigants?[105] The necessary separation of interest from judgment, which is presupposed by impartial justice, is here precluded.[106] Therefore, we are left with two problems in any attempt to constitute a concept of individual rights: (1) Where do we find the prohibition of, in effect, public robbery of private property (which would not be robbery only if the society had no institution of private property)? (2) Even if there is such a presumed prohibition, how could the rights of the individual property owner be protected if the court system is simply an agency of the state? *Whom* could this person sue? Is not the right of private property when in conflict with even ordinary public interest, in effect, an empty right?

The second question is easier to answer than the first. What it requires is a specific refutation of the assumption of Rashbam that the court is identical with the public about whom the talmudic texts at hand are concerned. This comes out in the treatment of both the talmudic texts and the French interpretation of them by the Spanish exegetes, beginning with Nahmanides in the thirteenth century (who was the first Spanish exegete to appropriate the views of the earlier French scholars).

The key point of difference between the two schools, it seems to me, is over the question of the inability of an individual to sue the public who has appropriated his or her property without his or her consent. Rashbam had ex-

---

[103] Along these lines, see M. Middot 2.2 and Maimonides, *Commentary on the Mishnah* thereon.

[104] Tos., s.v. "gezerah" on B. Baba Batra 99b.

[105] Ibid. 100a, s.v. "ke-she'avdah." The text of Rashbam literally states, "But the public are like a *bet din* inasmuch as any one of them could *subpoena* the owner (*mazmin le-hai le-dina*)." In other words, any one of the defendants could be the agent of the court (see B. Baba Kama 112b and Rashi, s.v. "shaliah de-rabbanan").

[106] See B. Ketubot 105b and Tos., s.v. "la." Cf. Maimonides, *Mishneh Torah*: Sanhedrin, 23.3 and R. Joseph Karo, *Kesef Mishneh* thereon.

plained that the individual "is not able (*eino yakhol*) to sue the public in court."[107] Here "ability" seems to be legal capacity. However, when criticizing Rabbenu Tam, whose views here are identical with those of his older brother, Rashbam, Nahmanides argues that the inability of the individual to sue the public is because "the public" is in effect a mob and "he cannot summon each one of them to court."[108] In other words, the inability here is physical, not legal. Thus Nahmanides assumes that the mention of self-defense of one's own private property from the public, which is also mentioned in the talmudic discussion of this case, is actually being endorsed, not rejected, where an individual has no recourse to protection by the public authorities from what seems to be a lawless mob.

The underlying assumption of Nahmanides' criticism of the French position is that there is a distinction to be made between the public and the judicial system. Only an independent judiciary could possibly adjudicate between the rights of an individual and the rights of the public. Thus Rabbi Solomon ibn Adret (Rashba), the most prominent disciple of Nahmanides, in a case involving the claim of an individual that the community had unfairly taxed him, stated in his responsum that "the argument that the community has the right to make [unfair] laws and rulings in this matter seems to me to be nothing but robbery (*gezel*), and they do not have the right (*v'ein yekholin*) to make stipulations (*le-hatnot*) that are robbery."[109] From this important responsum we see that there are now three parties who are acknowledged in a dispute between an individual and the public: the individual, the public, and the judiciary—which is independent of both litigants. The judiciary here is a rabbinate not under the control of the community and, therefore, is able to objectively adjudicate between the public and private interests. Of course, in most cases the interests of the community will take precedence. The common good (*bonum commune*) does have the benefit of a doubt over what is good for an individual (*bonum sibi*). This is certainly so in a society constituted by the covenant between God and a community.[110] Nevertheless, the existence of an independent judiciary does make the defense of the rights of an individual against the rights of the community possible, when the rights of the individual do not interfere with the common good, as they usually do not.[111] For Ibn Adret, this

---

[107] B. Baba Batra 99b, s.v. "am'ai."

[108] *Hiddushei ha-Ramban*: B. Baba Batra 99b–100a. See also B. Baba Kama 28a and Tos., s.v. "ve-linqot"; R. Solomon ibn Adret, *Hiddushei ha-Rashba*: B. Baba Batra 99b–100a; Rabbenu Nissim (Ran) on *Alfasi*: Baba Batra, ed. Vilna, 49a; R. Yom Tov Lippmann Heller, *Tosfot Yom Tov*: M. Baba Batra 6.7.

[109] *Teshuvot ha-Rashba* 1, no. 178. See, also, 1, no. 788; M. Elon, *Ha-Mishhpat ha-Ivri* 1, 2nd rev. ed. (Jerusalem: Magnes Press, 1978), 617ff.

[110] See Federbush, *Mishpat ha-Melukhah be-Yisrael*, 88ff.

[111] Thus R. Menahem ha-Meiri argues that private property may only be appropriated by the public either by legal right (*ba-din*, implying both pressing public need and fair compensation to the individual owner) or with the consent of the individual owner. He argues, furthermore, that if

is certainly to be so when the rights of the community are based on an arbitrary and unfair favoritism, respecting one party over another.

Along these lines, a somewhat later Spanish authority, Rabbi Isaac bar She-shet Parfat (Rivash) stated that "the community has no right (*ein yekholin*) to make any law or enactment discriminating against any individual (*yahid*) from the community not according to law."[112] Although he explicitly bases his view on the earlier one of Ibn Adret, Parfat's argument adds an important new point. He argues that the community has moral restrictions on its rights against individuals even though stipulations can be made in monetary matters that are not according to the strict letter of the law.[113] In other words, more general standards of justice should prevail even in situations where the legislative power of the community is very broad.[114]

The institutionalization of the real distinction between the public and the judiciary can be seen in the institution of the "Seven Trustees of the City" (*shiva tovei ha'ir*). Although we do not know very much about the origins of this institution, it seems to have been a secular one, not of course in the sense of being independent of the governance of the Torah, but in the sense of being separate from the institution of the rabbinical judiciary.[115] Thus even the "religious" system is not to be reduced to the power of clerics. This secularity is recognized by the sixteenth-century Polish authority Rabbi Moses Isserles (Rema). In a resposum he writes:

> It is evident that the trustees of the city do not have the legal power (*koah*) to enact anything that is not according to law and justice (*ha-mishpat*), to behave with tyrannical force (*be-hazaqah*) with individuals. . . . [T]hey only have the right to make enactments by right of the law, but they may not do whatever suits their fancy (*mah she-ta'aleh al ruham*).[116]

It is clear from this opinion that the only reason that the trustees of the city may not "do whatever suits their fancy" is that they would have to answer to

---

a private property owner substitutes another road for public use, one just as convenient as the first one is, such an exchange is valid (*Bet ha-Behirah*: B. Baba Batra 99b–110a, ed. Menat, 321). For more on the right of an individual to sue a community for unfair treatment, see I. Schepansky, *Ha-Taqqanot be-Yisrael* (Jerusalem: Mosad ha-Rav Kook, 1993), 4:516ff, and 585ff.

[112] *Teshuvot ha-Rivash*, no. 477.

[113] See B. Kiddushin 19b; also, Novak, *Jewish Social Ethics*, 212ff.

[114] See B. Baba Kama 99b–100a re Exod. 18:20; B. Baba Metsia 83a re Prov. 2:19.

[115] See B. Megillah 26a–b; Y. Megillah 3.2/74a; also, T. Megillah 2.16. For the distinction between *tovei ha'ir* and the rabbinate, see R. Solomon ibn Adret, *Teshuvot ha-Rashba* 1, no. 617 (cf., however, Maimonides, *Teshuvot ha-Rambam*, ed. Blau, vol. 2, no. 271). See also *Encyclopedia Talmudit* 19:72ff.; S. W. Baron, *The Jewish Community* (Philadelphia: Jewish Publication Society of America, 1945), 2:55 and 3:27, n. 19, and 3:120–21, n. 4; my late revered teacher Louis Finkelstein, *Jewish Self-Government in the Middle Ages*, 2nd rev. ed. (New York: P. Feldheim, 1964), 52f.; and Schepansky, *Ha-Taqqanot be-Yisrael* 4:68ff.

[116] *Teshuvot ha-Rema*, ed. Ziv, no. 308. Cf. R. Joshua Falk, *Meirat Einayyim* on *Shulhan Arukh*: Hoshen Mishpat, 377.

the individuals they have wronged in a court of law whose authority is separate and distinct from their own.

THE ISSUE OF PUBLIC VIOLENCE

Perhaps the reason why there seems to be no explicit prohibition of the public robbing individual persons of their private property is that this crime is subsumed under a rubric different from that of the crime of robbery per se (*gezel*). Thus when the editors of the Talmud are shocked that Rabbi Eliezer would allow the public to be "robbers" (*gazlanim*), they may have been thinking of a crime less specific than that of robbery in the usual sense.

The crime of public robbery could well be that of "violence" (*hamas*), which was considered to have been the crime of the Generation of the Flood, the crime for which God almost completely destroyed the inhabited world. The gravity of this crime is because it was a collective act rather than an individual one. In speculating about this crime the Talmud presents the following dictums:

> Rabbi Yohanan said, "come and see how serious the crime of violence is. The Generation of the Flood committed every transgression, but judgment against them was not sealed until they extended their hands into robbery as it is said; 'for the earth is filled with violence because of them, and I shall destroy them along with the earth' " (Genesis 6:13). . . . It was taught in the School of Rabbi Ishmael that even Noah was included in their judgment, only he found favor in the eyes of the Lord, as it is said: "I regret that I made them; and Noah found favor in the eyes of the Lord." (Genesis 6:7–8)[117]

The crime of violence is explicitly identified as public robbery of an individual in a midrashic treatment of the sins of the Generation of the Flood. There it is related that when a person came along with a basket of nuts, each one of the people stole a negligible number of them so that no one of them could be individually liable for the crime of robbery.[118] Thus each one of them could

---

[117] B. Sanhedrin 108a. The sense of the interpretation of Gen. 6:7–8 is: "I regret I made *them and Noah*." See R. Samuel Edels (Maharsha), *Hiddushei Aggadot* thereon.

[118] *Beresheet Rabbah* 31.5 (see ed. Theodor-Albeck, 279 and nn. 7–8 for the textual variants, esp. re *gezel* or *hamas*). For the rule that one is not liable in a human court for robbing someone else of less than what was considered to be a negligible amount, see B. Sanhedrin 57a and Rashi, s.v. "tsa'ara" re Lev. 5:23 (cf. B. Yevamot 47b). On Y. Baba Metsia 4.2/9c, mention of this sin of the Generation of the Flood is brought in during a discussion about the passage in the Mishnah (M. Baba Metsia 4.2) regarding the moral, but not legally culpable, sin of backing out of a verbal business commitment before the full exchange of property has been concluded. There, also, the sin of the Sodomites is considered to be the same as this sin of the Generation of the Flood. For the notion of the Sodomites committing moral sins technically within the limits of the law, see M. Avot 5.10; also, B. Baba Batra 12b for the designation of such activity as *middat Sodom* ("characteristic of Sodom").

justify to himself or herself collectively what no one of them could justify on a one-to-one basis. Nahmanides, following earlier sources, saw this crime of the Generation of the Flood as being one that was initiated by the officials and judges of society, whom no one dared restrain. And he considered the crime to be contrary to all reason (*inyan muskal*) and, therefore, one that did not even need a specifically enunciated prohibition.[119] In a related comment he argues that this rational commandment (*mitsvah muskelet*) did not need to be prohibited by prophetic revelation because it is "something evil both toward God and man."[120]

We must now question just why the reason for the sin of public violence is more obvious than the reason for the sin of individual robbery. I would venture the following answer. We can begin to see it when we look at the reason for the sin of individual robbery given in a popular medieval treatise explicating the 613 commandments of the Written Torah and their respective reasons.

> The root of the commandment is evident since it is something required by reason, something from which it keeps us far away, and it is right (*ra'ui*) that we be kept far away from it. For one who robs someone weaker than himself knows that someone stronger than himself will come upon him and that he too will be robbed. This would be the cause of the destruction of civilization (*hurban ha-yishuv*).[121]

In order for this reason to be cogent, one must turn the prohibition of robbery into what Kant designated as the first formulation of the categorical imperative, namely, one should universalize his or her act by asking: What if *everyone* did what I am tempted to do now?[122] Of course, the inner contradiction then becomes apparent. If everyone did what I am tempted to do now, that is, rob someone else of her property, then the institution of private property itself would be obliterated, and it is for the sake of increasing my own private property that I am tempted to rob this other person in the first place.

In the case of public violence against individuals, however, one need not imagine just what would happen if everybody acted this way. In this case it is not *what would be* but *what already is*. Real collective robbery, and not just robbery universalized in one's moral imagination, has now become the actual norm of society. The public policy of robbing individuals of their private property is always one that involves violence. Persons do not easily part with what they have usually worked hard to attain and maintain.[123] One need only look to the numbers of deaths that resulted from Stalin's forced collectivization of

---

[119] *Commentary on the Torah*: Gen. 6:2. See D. Novak, *The Theology of Nahmanides Systematically Presented* (Atlanta, Ga.: Scholars Press, 1992), 107ff.

[120] *Commentary on the Torah*: Gen. 6:11.

[121] *Sefer ha-Hinukh*: precept no. 229.

[122] See *Groundwork of the Metaphysic of Morals*, trans. H. J. Paton (New York: Harper and Row, 1964), 88ff.

[123] See B. Shabbat 117b and parallels; B. Sanhedrin 72a.

the property of the kulaks in Russia in the 1920s. Public robbery of individuals (as opposed to very exceptional cases of eminent domain) means that the most minimal reason for everyone's allegiance to his or her own society has now been removed. The most evident task of society is to protect its members against violence to their persons and to their property, even when that violence comes from society itself.

Participation by individuals in a criminal group enables each member of the group to think that he or she is exempt from any personal responsibility for what the group itself does. Certainly, in this bloody century alone, we have seen how the greatest crimes, which have led to the wholesale destruction of millions of human lives and authentic sociality, have not been committed by lone individuals but by human collectives in which individual persons have been reduced to functioning as the merely dispensable parts of a larger whole.[124] When society is not duty bound to protect the rights of individuals, both from other individuals and—even more importantly—from its own power, then it ceases to be an authentic communion of free, rational persons. And when such personal rights are no longer respected, these persons inevitably lose respect for and allegiance to their society.[125] They realize sooner or later how immediately vulnerable *each and every one of them* really is. It is not that society's only raison d'etre is to protect the rights of individuals, but it is certainly a necessary condition for a society to have moral authority over its members.

The question of individual rights is the question of balancing the claims of individuals and the claims of society. On the prima facie level, the claims of society seem to take precedence inasmuch as society as an institution can certainly survive any ordinary individual, but no ordinary individual can survive, much less flourish, without society.[126] Furthermore, whereas in modern social contract theory the essence of the polity is an agreement between individuals and society, in the covenant the essence of the polity is a relationship between

[124] No modern thinker explored this in greater depth than did Reinhold Niebuhr. See his *Moral Man and Immoral Society* (New York: Scribner's, 1934), esp. chap. 1.

[125] Thus Plato argues that even a group of thieves must be able to assure each other that they will not rob each other in order to successfully rob strangers (*Republic*, 351C). Of course, the members of such criminal groups sooner or later turn against each other too since their allegiance to this standard of "justice" is only immediately utilitarian. As soon as any one of them sees a quicker way of gaining wealth than that required by loyalty to his or her present comrades, he or she will do to them what they have all been doing together to strangers. Hence, for there to be any permanent loyalty in a society, that society must affirm inalienable individual rights per se. See Maimonides, *Mishneh Torah*: Gezelah, 5.18 re B. Baba Batra 54b; also, Jacques Maritain, *Man and the State* (Chicago: University of Chicago Press, 1951), 12ff.

[126] See B. Taanit 23a; also, Aristotle, *Nicomachean Ethics*, 9.9/1169b5ff. Aside from the fact that a person who eschewed human society would be living a life without humanizing human discourse (see Aristotle, *Politics*, 1.1/1253a1ff.), his or her physical survival would still depend on skills learned from earlier social experience.

God and the community, one that is initiated by God's election of the community and fulfilled by the community's positive acceptance of that election and the law from God that gives it both structure and content. Even when individuals act alone, they are still very much communal beings in covenant with God. Nevertheless, individuals have just claims upon society in those ordinary circumstances when society's survival is not at all threatened by the exercise of these personal rights. It is only when society itself attempts to become a superperson rather than a communion of separate persons that these individual rights are violated. Indeed, one can see individual rights as a limit on the power of society because the life of the human person as the image of God points to a transcendent dimension beyond the grasp and thus beyond the authority of any human society.

In the case of Jews as members of the covenant between God and Israel (*bnei beit*), the present manifestation of the covenant in any Jewish community is incomplete; hence it does not totally satisfy every need in the lives of its members. Only in the messianic community, promised as the final human redemption on earth, will the needs of every individual person and those of the community itself be so completely fulfilled that neither will have to be kept separate from the other.[127] At present, every society and every individual person is incomplete; hence all their respective claims on each other can be only partial. Therefore, full membership in that redeemed community of the future limits the claims of any community here and now in the same way that citizenship in a nation-state limits the claims that can be made on any citizen by one of its provinces. Without the constant acknowledgment of that transcendent dimension, both of the individual person as the image of God and of the individual Jew as a member of the kingdom of God, society has no reason not to represent its own authority as divine by presenting its own claims as absolute. So, the only way there can be a phenomenologically cogent distinction between what is human and what is divine is for the experience of the authority of both society and individuals to be that of finite entities.[128] No individual or society itself can claim to be the exclusive conduit of divine authority in the world. God's authority is revealed, instead, in the limiting interaction of these two domains. It only shines between the cracks. Thus the rights of individuals, both individual human persons and individual Jews, intend a source other than the individual person himself or herself (autonomy) and other than society itself (heteronomy). The autonomy of the individual person and the heteronomy of society are relative to each other, hence limited per se. The authority of God as the maker of the covenant and giver of the law (theonomy) must

---

[127] See Maimonides, *Mishneh Torah*: Melakhim, 12.5.
[128] See Novak, *Law and Theology in Judaism* 2:15ff.

always be experienced as essentially different from what is human, be it individual or collective.[129]

Because of all this, the proposal of any society governed by Jewish law must convince the vast majority of the Jewish people that what is being proposed is authorized by the power that transcends all human power, whether collective or individual, and thus establishes both types of human power as legitimate finite domains. Thus the power of society is limited by individual rights just as the power of any individual is limited by the rights of society. All power and all rights are gifts from God. Neither party can ever claim to have a monopoly on their exercise or distribution. Indeed, the institution of human rights is not only something positive democratic experience has taught most Jews is in their best interest, it is also something that a true understanding of both creation and the covenant require the theory and practice of Jewish law to pursue as a theological desideratum here and now. The renewed government of Jewish law in civil society, of which the institution of individual human rights must be developed, can only come when there is a true renewal of the covenant by the vast majority of the Jewish people with their God.[130]

[129] See Novak, *Jewish Social Ethics*, 45ff.
[130] See Neh. 10:1ff.

Bibliography

Classical Judaic Texts

Abrabanel, Isaac. *Commentary on the Torah*. Warsaw: Lebensohn, 1862.

———. *Commentary on the Former Prophets*. Reprint. Jerusalem: Torah ve-Daat, 1956.

Abraham ben David of Posquières. *Commentary on the Mishnah*. In *Talmud Bavli*.

———. *Commentary on Sifra*. In *Sifra*. ed. Weiss.

———. *Commentary on Maimonides, Mishneh Torah*. (Hasagot ha-Ravad)

Abraham ben Yom Tov Ishbili. *Hiddushei ha-Ritva*. 3 vols. Reprint. New York: Otsar ha-Sefarim, 1970.

Albo, Joseph. *Iqqarim*. Edited and translated by I. Husik. 5 vols. Philadelphia: Jewish Publication Society of America, 1929–30.

Alfasi, Isaac (Rif). Digest. In *Talmud Bavli*.

Apocrypha and Pseudepigrapha of the Old Testament. Edited by R. H. Charles. 2 vols., Oxford: Clarendon Press, 1913.

Ashkenazi, Judah. *Beer Heitev*. In *Shulhan Arukh*.

Avot de-Rabbi Nathan. Edited by S. Schechter. Reprint. New York: P. Feldheim, 1967.

Bemidbar Rabbah. In *Midrash Rabbah*.

Beresheet Rabbah. Edited by J. Theodor and C. Albeck. 3 vols. Reprint. Jerusalem: Wahrmann, 1965.

Biblia Hebraica. 7th ed. Edited by R. Kittel. Stuttgart: Privileg. Württ. Bibelanstalt, 1951.

David ibn Abi Zimra. Notes. In Maimonides, *Mishneh Torah*.

———. *Teshuvot ha-Radbaz*. 2 vols. Warsaw: n.p., 1882.

Devarim Rabbah. In *Midrash Rabbah*.

Edels, Samuel (Maharsha). *Hiddushei Aggadot*. In *Talmud Bavli*, ed. Romm.

Emden, Jacob (Yavets). Notes. In *Talmud Bavli*, ed. Vilna.

Fraenkel, David, *Qorban Ha'Edah*. In *Talmud Yerushalmi*, ed. Pietrkov.

Gersonides, *Commentary on the Torah*. 2 vols. Venice: n.p., 1547.

———. *Milhamot ha-Shem*. Riva di Trento: n.p., 1560.

Hagahot Maimoniyot. In Maimonides, *Mishneh Torah*.

Halevi, Judah. *Kuzari*. Translated by Y. Even-Shmuel. Tel Aviv: Dvir, 1972.

———. *Selected Religious Poems of Jehudah Halevi*. Edited by H. Brody. Philadelphia: Jewish Publication Society of America, 1924.

Hayyim ibn Attar. *Or ha-Hayyim*. In *Miqraot Gedolot*: Pentateuch.

Heller, Yom Tov Lippmann. *Tosfot Yom Tov*. In *Mishnayot*.

Hizquni. *Commentary on the Torah*. Edited by C. B. Chavel. Jerusalem: Mosad ha-Rav Kook, 1982.

Horowitz, Isaiah ha-Levi. *Shnei Luhot ha-Berit*. 2 vols. Amsterdam: n.p., 1653.

Ibn Ezra, Abraham. *Commentary on the Torah*. Edited by A. Weiser. 3 vols. Jerusalem: Mosad ha-Rav Kook, 1977.

Igeret Rav Sherira Gaon. Edited by A. Hyman. Jerusalem: Boys Town Publishers, 1967.

Isaac bar Sheshet Parfat. *Teshuvot ha-Rivash.* Lemberg: n.p., 1805.

Isserlein, Israel. *Terumat ha-Deshen.* Reprint. B'nai Brak: n.p., 1971.

Isserles, Moses (Rema). Notes. In *Shulhan Arukh.*

―――. *Teshuvot ha-Rema.* Edited by A. Ziv. Jerusalem: n.p., 1970.

Jacob ben Asher. *Tur.* 7 vols. Reprint. Jerusalem:Feldheim, 1969.

Jacob ibn Habib. *Ein Yaaqov.* 3 vols. Reprint. New York: n.p., 1953.

Joseph Bekhor Shor. *Commentary on the Torah.* Edited by J. Nevo. Jerusalem: Mosad ha-Rav Kook, 1994.

Joseph Boaz. *Shiltei ha-Gibborim* on Alfasi (Rif). In *Talmud Bavli,* ed. Vilna.

Josephus. *Contra Apionem.* Translated by H. St. John Thackeray. Cambridge: Harvard University Press, 1926.

Karo, Joseph. *Bet Yosef* In *Tur.*

―――. *Kesef Mishneh.* In Maimonides, *Mishneh Torah.*

―――. *Shulhan Arukh.* 7 vols. Lemberg: n.p., 1873.

Kimhi, David. *Commentary on the Former Prophets.* In *Miqraot Gedolot*: Prophets and Writings.

Lampronti, Isaac. *Pahad Yitshaq.* 10 vols. Venice: n.p., 1750.

Loewe, Judah. *Gevurot ha-Shem.* Krakow: n.p., 1582.

Luria, Solomon. *Yam shel Shlomoh.* 2 vols., Krakow: n.p., 1646.

Maimonides, Moses. *Commentary on the Mishnah.* Translated by Y. Kafih. 3 vols. Jerusalem: Mosad ha-Rav Kook, 1964–67.

―――. *Dalalat al-ha'irin.* Edited by S. Munk. Jerusalem: n.p., 1931.

―――. *Guide of the Perplexed.* Translated by S. Pines. Chicago: University of Chicago Press, 1963.

―――. *Iggeret Teman.* Translated by B. Cohen. New York: Jewish Theological Seminary of America, 1952.

―――. *Maamar Tehiyyat ha-Metim.* In *Igrot ha-Rambam,* edited by I. Shailat. 2 vols. Jerusalem: Ma'aliyot, 1987.

―――. *Mishneh Torah.* 5 vols. Reprint. New York: E. Grossman, 1957.

―――. *Mishneh Torah*: Sefer Shoftim. Edited by M. D. Rabinowitz. Jerusalem: Mosad ha-Rav Kook, 1962.

―――. *Moreh Nevukhim.* Translated by Samuel ibn Tibbon. Reprint. New York: Om Publishing Co., 1946.

―――. *Sefer ha-Mitsvot.* Edited by C. Heller. Jerusalem: Mosad ha-Rav Kook, 1946.

―――. *Sefer ha-Mitsvot with Notes of Nahmanides.* Edited by C. B. Chavel. Jerusalem: Mosad ha-Rav Kook, 1981.

―――. *Teshuvot ha-Rambam.* Edited by Y. Y. Blau. 3 vols. Jersualem: Meqitsei Nirdamim, 1960.

Mekhilta de-Rabbi Ishmael. Edited by H. S. Horovitz and I. A. Rabin. Reprint. Jerusalem: Wahrmann, 1960.

Menahem ha-Meiri. *Bet ha-Behirah*: Baba Batra. Edited by B. Y. Menat. Jerusalem: n.p., 1971.

―――. *Bet ha-Behirah*: Ketubot. Edited by S. Sofer. Jerusalem: n.p., 1968.

―――. *Bet ha-Behirah*: Kiddushin. Edited by A. Sofer. Jerusalem: n.p., 1963.

Midrash ha-Gadol: Beresheet. Edited by M. Margulies. Jerusalem: Mosad ha-Rav Kook, 1947.

Midrash ha-Gadol: Leviticus. Edited by E. N. Rabinowitz. New York: Jewish Theological Seminary of America, 1932.

Midrash Rabbah. 2 vols. Reprint. New York: E. Grossman, 1957.

Midrash Tehillim. Edited by S. Buber. Vilna: Romm, 1891.

Miqraot Gedolot: Pentateteuch. 5 vols. Reprint. New York: Otsar ha-Sefarim, 1953.

Miqraot Gedolot: Prophets and Writings. 3 vols. Reprint. New York: Pardes, 1951.

Mishnah. 6 vols. Edited by C. Albeck. Tel Aviv: Mosad Bialik and Dvir, 1957.

Mishnat Rabbi Eliezer. Edited by H. G. Enelow. 2 vols. New York: Bloch, 1933.

Mishnayot. 12 vols. Reprint. New York: M. P. Press, 1969.

Moses of Coucy. *Sefer Mitsvot Gadol*. 2 vols. Reprint. Brooklyn: n.p., 1959.

Nahmanides, Moses. *Commentary on Canticles*. In *Kitvei Ramban*, vol. 2.

———. *Commentary on Job*. In *Kitvei Ramban*, vol. 2.

———. *Commentary on the Torah*. Edited by C. B. Chavel. 2 vols. Jerusalem: Mosad ha-Rav Kook, 1959–63.

———. *Hiddushei ha-Ramban*. 2 vols. B'nai Brak: n.p., 1959.

———. *Kitvei Ramban*. Edited by C. B. Chavel. 2 vols. Jerusalem: Mosad ha-Rav Kook, 1963.

———. *Torat ha'Adam*. In *Kitvei Ramban*, vol. 2.

Nissim Gerondi (Ran). Commentary. In *Talmud Bavli*: Nedarim, ed. Vilna.

———. Commentary on *Alfasi* (Rif). In *Talmud Bavli*, ed. Vilna.

Pesiqta Rabbati. Edited by M. Friedmann. Reprint. Jerusalem: n.p., 1963.

Pesiqta de-Rav Kahana. Edited by B. Mandelbaum. 2 vols. New York: Jewish Theological Seminary of America, 1962.

Phoebus, Samuel. *Bet Shmuel*. In *Shulhan Arukh*: Even Ha'Ezer.

Qohelet Rabbati. In *Midrash Rabbah*.

Rabbenu Hananael. *Commentary*. In *Talmud Bavli*, ed. Vilna.

Rashbam. *Commentary on the Torah*. Ed. A. Bromberg. Jerusalem: n.p., 1969.

Rashi. *Commentary*. In *Talmud Bavli*, ed. Vilna.

———. *Commentary on the Torah*. Edited by C. B. Chavel. Jerusalem: Mosad ha-Rav Kook, 1982.

———. *Commentary on the Writings*. In *Miqraot Gedolot*: Prophets and Writings.

———. *Teshuvot Rashi*. Edited by I. Elfenbein. New York: n.p., 1943.

Reischer, Jacob. *Teshuvot Shevut Yaaqov*. Reprint. Jerusalem: n.p., 1972.

Ruth Rabbah. In *Midrash Rabbah*.

Saadiah Gaon. *Book of Beliefs and Opinions*. Translated by S. Rosenblatt. New Haven: Yale University Press, 1948.

———. *Emunot ve-Deot*. Jerusalem: Mosad ha-Rav Kook, 1993.

Sefer ha-Hinukh. Vilna: n.p., 1912.

Septuagint. Edited by A. Rahlfs. 2 vols. Stuttgart: Privileg. Wurtt. Bibelanstalt, n.d.

Sforno, Obadiah. *Commentary on the Torah*. Edited by Z. Gottlieb. Jerusalem: Mosad ha-Rav Kook, 1984.

Shabbtai ha-Kohen (Shakh). Notes in *Shulhan Arukh*.

Sheiltot de-Rav Ahai Gaon. Edited by E. M. Kenig. Jerusalem: n.p., 1940.

Shemot Rabbah. In *Midrash Rabbah*.

Sifra. Edited by I. H. Weiss. Vienna: Schlessinger, 1862.

Sifre: Bemidbar. Edited by H. S. Horovitz. Leipzig: Gustav Fock, 1917.

Sifre: Devarim. Edited by Louis Finkelstein. New York: Jewish Theological Seminary of America, 1969.

Solomon ibn Adret. *Hiddushei ha-Rashba*. 3 vols. Warsaw: n.p., 1902.

———. *Teshuvot ha-Rashba*. 5 vols. Reprint. B'nai B'rak: n.p., 1958.

Talmud Bavli. 20 vols. Vilna: Romm, 1898.

Talmud Yerushalmi. Edition Pietrkov. 7 vols. Reprint. Jerusalem: n.p., 1959.

Talmud Yerushalmi. Edition Venice/Krotoschin. Reprint. New York: Yam ha-Talmud, 1948.

Tanhuma. Jerusalem: Lewin-Epstein, 1962.

Tanhuma. Edited by S. Buber. 2 vols. Reprint. Jerusalem: n.p., 1964.

Targum Jonathan ben Uzziel. In *Miqraot Gedolot*: Pentateuch, Prophets, and Writings.

Targum Onqelos. In *Miqraot Gedolot*: Pentateuch.

Teshuvot ha-Geonim. Edited by A. Harkavy. Berlin: Meqitsei Nirdamim, 1887.

Teshuvot Rav Sar Shalom Gaon. Edited by R. S. Weinberg. Jerusalem: Mosad ha-Rav Kook, 1975.

Tosafot. In *Talmud Bavli*, edition Vilna.

Tosefta. Edited by M. S. Zuckermandl. Reprint. Jerusalem: Wahrmann, 1937.

Tosefta: Berakhot-Baba Batra. Edited by Saul Lieberman. 5 vols. New York: Jewish Theological Seminary of America, 1955–88.

Vayiqra Rabbah. Edited by M. Margulies. 5 vols. Jerusalem: Ministry of Education and Culture, 1953.

Vidal of Tolosa. *Magid Mishneh*. In Maimonides, *Mishneh Torah*.

Yalqut Shimoni. 2 vols. Reprint. New York: Pardes, 1944.

Yom Tov ben Abraham Ishbili. *Hiddushei ha-Ritva*. 3 vols. Warsaw: n.p., 1902.

Zohar. Edited by R. Margaliot. 3 vols. Jerusalem: Mosad ha-Rav Kook, 1984.

Modern Judaic Texts

Ahad Ha'Am. "Al Shtei ha-Seipim." In *Kol Kitvei Ahad Ha'Am*, 2nd ed. Tel Aviv: Dvir, 1949.

Baron, S. W. *The Jewish Community*. 3 vols. Philadelphia: Jewish Publication Society of America, 1945.

Benor, E. *Worship of the Heart*. Albany: State University of New York Press, 1995.

Ben-Shlomoh. *Torat ha'Elohut shel Rabbi Mosheh Cordovero*. Jerusalem: Mosad Bialik, 1965.

Bleich, J. David, "Abortion in Halakhic Literature." In *Jewish Bioethics*, edited by J. D. Bleich and F. Rosner. New York: Hebrew Publishing Co., 1979.

Borowitz, Eugene B. *Renewing the Covenant*. Philadelphia: Jewish Publication Society, 1991.

Brown, Francis, Samuel R. Driver, and Charles A. Briggs, *A Hebrew and English Lexicon of the Old Testament*. Oxford: Clarendon Press, 1952.

Buber, Martin. *Between Man and Man*. Translated by R. G. Smith. Boston: Beacon, 1955.

———. "Guilt and Guilt Feelings." Translated by M. Friedman. In *The Knowledge of Man*, edited by M. Friedman. New York: Harper and Row, 1965.

———. *I and Thou*. Translated by W. Kaufmann. New York: Scribner's, 1970.

———. *Ich und Du*. Heidelberg: Verlag Lambert Schneider, 1962.

————. *Kingship of God*. Translated by R. Scheimann. New York: Harper and Row, 1967.

Buber, Martin, and Franz Rosenzweig. *On Jewish Learning*. Translated by W. Wolf, edited by N. N. Glatzer. New York: Schocken, 1955.

————. *Die Fünf Bucher der Weisung*. Cologne: Verlag Jakob Hegner, 1954.

Chajes, Zvi Hirsch. *Kol Kitvei Maharats Chajes*. 2 vols. Jerusalem: Divrei Hakhamim, 1958.

————. Notes. In *Talmud Bavli*, ed. Vilna.

Cohen, Boaz. *Jewish and Roman Law*. 2 vols. New York: Jewish Theological Seminary of America, 1966.

Cohen, Hermann. *Ethik des reinen Willens*. 4th ed. Berlin: B. Cassirer, 1923.

————. *Religion der Vernunft aus den Quellen des Judentums*. 2nd ed. Darmstadt: Joseph Melzer Verlag, 1966.

————. *Religion of Reason Out of the Sources of Judaism*. Translated by S. Kaplan. New York: Frederick Ungar, 1972.

Cohn, Haim H. *Human Rights in Jewish Law*. New York: KTAV, 1984.

Cover, Robert M. "Obligation: A Jewish Jurisprudence of the Social Order." *Journal of Law and Religion* 5 (1987).

Eisenstadt, Zvi Hirsch. *Pitehei Teshuvah*. In *Shulhan Arukh*.

Elazar, D. J. *Covenant and Polity in Biblical Israel*. New Brunswick, N.J.: Transaction Books, 1995.

————, ed. *Kingship and Consent*. Washington, D.C.: University Press of America, 1983.

Elon, Menachem. *Ha-Mishpat ha'Ivri*. Rev. ed. 2 vols. Jerusalem: Magnes Press, 1978.

————. *Jewish Law*. Translated by B. Auerbach and M. J. Sykes. 4 vols. Philadelphia: Jewish Publication Society, 1994.

Encyclopedia Talmudit. 21 vols. Jerusalem, 1955–93.

Epstein, Yehiel M. *Arokh ha-Shulhan*. 8 vols. Warsaw: n.p., 1900–1912.

Falk, Z. W. *Erkhei Mishpat ve-Yahadut*. Jerusalem: Meisharim, 1980.

————. *Law and Religion*. Jerusalem: Meisharim, 1981.

Faur, J. "Reflections on Job and Situation Morality." *Judaism* 19 (1970).

Federbush. *Mishpat ha-Melukhah be-Yisrael*. 2nd ed., rev. Jerusalem: Mosad ha-Rav Kook, 1973.

Feldman, D. M. *Birth Control in Jewish Law*. New York: New York University Press, 1968.

Finkelstein, Louis. *Jewish Self-Government in the Middle Ages*. 2nd ed., rev. New York: P. Feldheim, 1964.

Fox, Marvin. "Maimonides and Aquinas on Natural Law." *Dinē Israel* 3 (1972).

Ginzberg, Louis. *The Legends of the Jews*. 7 vols. Philadelphia: Jewish Publication Society of America, 1909–38.

Goodman, L. E. *On Justice*. New Haven: Yale University Press, 1991.

Halivni, David Weiss. *Peshat and Derash*. New York: Oxford University Press, 1991.

————. *Revelation Restored*. Boulder, Colo.: Westview Press, 1997.

Herzog, Isaac Halevy. *Tehuqah le-Yisrael al-pi ha-Torah*. Jerusalem: Mosad ha-Rav Kook, 1989.

Heschel, Abraham Joshua. *Torah min ha-Shamayim b'Ispaqlaryah shel ha-Dorot*. 2 vols. London: Soncino, 1962–65.

Heschel, Abraham Joshua. *Who Is Man?* Stanford, Calif.: Stanford University Press, 1965.

Hirsch, S. R. *The Pentateuch: Translated and Explained.* Translated by I. Levy. 2nd ed. rev., 5 vols. New York: Judaica Press, 1971.

Jacobs, Louis. *Religion and the Individual.* Cambridge: Cambridge University Press, 1992.

Kahane, Meir. *Never Again.* Los Angeles: Nash, 1971.

———. *Uncomfortable Questions for Comfortable Jews.* Seacaucus, N.J.: L. Stuart, 1987.

Katz, Jacob. *Out of the Ghetto.* Cambridge: Harvard University Press, 1978.

Kaufmann, Yehezkel. *The Religion of Israel.* Translated by M. Greenberg. Chicago: University of Chicago Press, 1960.

Klein, Isaac. "Teshuvah on Abortion." In *Conservative Judaism and Jewish Law,* edited by S. Siegel with E. B. Gertel. New York: Rabbinical Assembly, 1977.

Kohut, A. *Aruch Completum.* 9 vols. Reprint. Tel Aviv: Shilo, 1970.

Konvitz, Milton R., ed. *Judaism and Human Rights.* New York: W. W. Norton, 1972.

Leibowitz, Yeshayahu. *Yahadut, Am Yehudi u-Medinat Yisrael.* Jerusalem: Schocken, 1976.

Levenson, Jon D. *Creation and the Persistance of Evil.* San Francisco: Harper and Row, 1988.

Levine, B. A. *The JPS Torah Commentary: Leviticus.* Philadelphia: Jewish Publication Society, 1989.

Lieberman, Saul. *Hellenism in Jewish Palestine.* 2nd ed. New York: Jewish Theological Seminary of America, 1962.

———. *Tosefta Kifshuta.* 12 vols. New York: Jewish Theological Seminary of America, 1955–88.

Lifschitz, Israel. *Tiferet Yisrael.* In *Mishnayot.*

Malbim, Meir Leibush. *Commentary on the Torah.* 2 vols. Reprint. New York, 1956.

Margolis, Moses. *Pnei Mosheh.* In *Talmud Yersushalmi,* ed. Pietrkov.

Novak, David. "Buber and Tillich." *Journal of Ecumenical Studies* 29 (1992).

———. *The Election of Israel.* Cambridge: Cambridge University Press, 1995.

———. *Halakhah in a Theological Dimension.* Chico, Calif.: Scholars Press, 1985.

———. "I dritti religiosi dell'uomo nella tradizione ebraica." *Conscienzà e Libertà* 27 (1996).

———. *The Image of the Non-Jew in Judaism.* New York: Edwin Mellen Press, 1983.

———. *Jewish-Christian Dialogue.* New York: Oxford University Press, 1989.

———. *Jewish Social Ethics.* New York: Oxford University Press, 1992.

———. *Law and Theology in Judaism.* 2 vols. New York: KTAV, 1974–76.

———. "Maimonides and the Science of the Law." In *Jewish Law Association Studies,* vol. 4, edited by B. S. Jackson. Atlanta, Ga.: Scholars Press, 1990.

———. *Natural Law in Judaism.* Cambridge: Cambridge University Press, 1998.

———. "Parental Rights in the Marriage of a Minor." In *Jewish Law Association Studies,* vol. 9, edited by E. A. Goldman. Atlanta, Ga.: Scholars Press, 1997.

———. "Philosophy and the Possibility of Revelation." In *Leo Strauss and Judaism,* edited by D. Novak. Lanham, Md.: Rowman and Littlefield, 1996.

———. "Privacy." In *Natural Law and Public Policy,* edited by D. F. Forte. Washington, D.C.: Georgetown University Press, 1998, 13ff.

————, "Religiöse Menschenrechte in der jüdischen Tradition." *Gewissen und Freiheit* 46–47 (1996).

————. "Religious Human Rights in Judaic Texts." In *Religious Human Rights in Global Perspective*, edited by John Witte, Jr., and Johan D. van der Vyver. The Hague: M. Nijhoff, 1996.

————. *The Theology of Nahmanides Systematically Presented*. Atlanta, Ga.: Scholars Press, 1992.

Plaskow, Judith. *Standing Again at Sinai*. San Francisco: Harper and Row, 1990.

Rosenzweig, Franz. *On Jewish Learning*. Edited by N. N. Glatzer. New York: Schocken, 1955.

————. *Star of Redemption*. Translated by W. W. Hallo. New York: Holt, Rinehart and Winston, 1970.

Rubenstein, Richard L. *After Auschwitz*. 2nd ed. Baltimore: Johns Hopkins University Press, 1992.

Schechter, Solomon. *Some Aspects of Rabbinic Theology*. New York: Behrman, 1936.

Schepansky, Israel. *Ha-Taqqanot be-Yisrael*. 4 vols. Jerusalem: Mosad ha-Rav Kook, 1991–93.

Scholem, Gershom, *The Messianic Idea in Judaism*. New York: Schocken, 1971.

————. *On the Kabbalah and Its Symbolism*. Translated by R. Manheim. New York: Schocken, 1969.

Schreiber, Moses. *Teshuvot Hatam Sofer*. 5 vols. Vienna: n.p., 1855.

Shir ha-Shirim Rabbah. In *Midrash Rabbah*.

Simon, Ernst. "The Neighbor (*Re'a*) Whom We Shall Love." In *Modern Jewish Ethics*, edited by M. Fox. Columbus: Ohio University Press, 1975.

Spira, Hayyim Lazar. *Teshuvot Minhat Eleazar*. Bratislava: n.p., 1922.

Tushnet, L. *The Pavement of Hell*. New York: St. Martin's Press, 1972.

Urbach, E. E. *Halakhah*. Jerusalem: Yad le-Talmud, 1984.

————. *Hazal*. Jerusalem: Magnes Press, 1971.

Waldenberg, Eliezer. *Ramat Rahel*. In *Teshuvot Tsits Eliezer*, vols. 4 and 5. Jerusalem: n.p., 1985.

Weiss, A. *Women at Prayer*. Hoboken, N.J.: KTAV, 1990.

Werfel, S. *Sefer ha-Hasidut*. Tel Aviv: Z. Leinman, 1947.

Wolfson, H. A. *Crescas' Critique of Aristotle*. Cambridge: Harvard University Press, 1929.

General Texts

Ackerman, Bruce. *Social Justice in the Liberal State*. New Haven: Yale University Press, 1980.

Andelson, R. V. *Imputed Rights*. Athens: University of Georgia Press, 1971.

Anscombe, G. E. M. "Modern Moral Philosophy." In *The Is-Ought Question*, edited by W. D. Hudson. London: Macmillan, 1969.

Apel, Karl-Otto. "Normative Ethics and Strategical Rationality: The Philosophical Problem of Political Ethics." In *The Public Realm*, edited by R. Schürmann. Albany: State University of New York Press, 1989.

Aristotle. *De Anima*. Translated by W. S. Hett. Cambridge: Harvard University Press, 1936.

————. *Metaphysics*. Translated by H. Tredennick. 2 vols. Cambridge: Harvard University Press, 1933.

Aristotle. *Nicomachean Ethics*. Translated by H. Rackham. Cambridge: Harvard University Press, 1926.

———. *Politics*. Translated by H. Rackham. Cambridge: Harvard University Press, 1932.

———. *Prior Analytics*. Translated by H. Tredennick. Cambridge: Harvard University Press, 1938.

Augustine. *De Bono Coniugali*. In *Writings of Saint Augustine*, vol. 15, translated by C. T. Wilcox. New York: Fathers of the Church, 1955.

———. *De Civitate Dei*. In *Basic Writings*, vol. 2 edited by W. J. Oates. New York: Random House, 1948.

Berdyaev, Nikolai. *Slavery and Freedom*. Translated by R. M. French. New York: Scribner's, 1944.

Berger, Peter L. *The Sacred Canopy*. Garden City, N.Y.: Doubleday, 1969.

Berlin, Isaiah. "Two Concepts of Liberty." In *Four Essays on Liberty*. Oxford: Oxford University Press, 1969.

Brunner, Emil. *Justice and the Social Order*. Translated by M. Hottinger. New York: Harper and Row, 1945.

Cherbonnier, E. LaB. "The Logic of Biblical Anthropomorphism." *Harvard Theological Review* 54 (1962).

Cicero. *De Legibus*. Translated by C. W. Keyes. Cambridge: Harvard University Press, 1928.

Descartes, René. *Meditations*. In *The Philosophical Works of Descartes*, Translated by S. Haldane and G. R. T. Ross. 2 vols. Cambridge: Cambridge University Press, 1967.

Descombes, Vincent. "The Socialization of Human Action." In *The Public Realm*, edited by R. Schürmann. Albany: State University of New York Press, 1989.

Didache. In *The Apostolic Fathers*. Translated by K. Lake. 2 vols. Cambridge: Harvard University Press, 1912.

Donnelly, Jack. *The Concept of Human Rights*. New York: St. Martin's Press, 1985.

Dupré, Louis. *The Philosophical Foundations of Marxism*. New York: Harcourt, Brace and World, 1966.

Dworkin, Gerald. *The Theory and Practice of Autonomy*. Cambridge: Cambridge University Press, 1988.

Dworkin, Ronald. *Taking Rights Seriously*. Cambridge: Harvard University Press, 1978.

Feinberg, Joel. *Rights, Justice, and the Boundaries of Liberty*. Princeton: Princeton University Press, 1980.

Ferry, Luc. *Political Philosophy*. Vol. 1, translated by F. Philip. Chicago: University of Chicago Press, 1990.

Ferry, Luc, and Alain Renaut. *Political Philosophy*. Vol. 3, translated by F. Philip. Chicago: University of Chicago Press, 1992.

Feuerbach, Ludwig. *The Essence of Christianity*. Translated by George Eliot. New York: Harper and Row, 1957.

Finnis, John. "Law, Morality, and 'Sexual Orientation.' " *Notre Dame Journal of Law, Ethics, and Public Policy* 9 (1995).

———. *Natural Law and Natural Rights*. Oxford: Clarendon Press, 1980.

Freeden, Michael. *Rights*. Buckingham, U.K.: Open University Press, 1991.

Fried, Charles. *Contract as Promise*. Cambridge: Harvard University Press, 1981.

Freud, Sigmund. "The Most Prevalent Form of Degradation in Erotic Life." In *Collected Papers*, vol. 4, translated by J. Strachey. London: Hogarth Press, 1952.

Geertz, Clifford. *The Interpretation of Cultures*. New York, 1973.

Gewirth, Alan. *The Community of Rights*. Chicago: University of Chicago Press, 1996.

Gilkey, Langdon. *Maker of Heaven and Earth*. Garden City, N.Y.: Doubleday, 1959.

Glendon, Mary Ann. *Rights Talk*. New York: Free Press, 1991.

Golding, Martin P. "The Concept of Rights." In *Bioethics and Human Rights*, edited by E. L. Bundman and B. Bundman. Boston: Little, Brown, 1978.

———. "The Primacy of Welfare Rights." In *Human Rights*, edited by E. F. Paul, and J. Paul, F. D. Miller, Jr. Oxford: Blackwell, 1984.

———. "The Significance of Rights Language." *Philosophical Topics* 18 (1990).

Grisez, Germain. *The Way of the Lord Jesus*. Vol. 1. Chicago: Franciscan Press, 1983.

Habermas, Jürgen. *Between Facts and Norms*. Translated by W. Rehg. Cambridge: MIT Press, 1996.

———. *Communication and the Evolution of Society*. Translated by T. McCarthy. Boston: Beacon, 1979.

———. *Knowledge and Human Interests*. Translated by J. J. Shapiro. Boston: Beacon, 1971.

———. *Moral Consciousness and Communicative Action*. Translated by C. Lenhardt and S. W. Nicholsen. Cambridge: MIT Press, 1990.

———. *Theory and Practice*. Translated by J. Viertel. Boston: Beacon, 1974.

———. *The Theory of Communicative Action*. Vol. 1, Translated by T. McCarthy. Boston: Beacon, 1984.

Hart, H. L. A. "Are There Natural Rights?" *Philosophical Review* 64 (1955).

———. *The Concept of Law*. Oxford: Oxford University Press, 1961.

Hartmann, Nicolai. *Ethics*. Vol. 1. Translated by S. Coit. London: G. Allen and Unwin, 1932.

Hartshorne, C., and W. L. Reese. *Philosophers Speak of God*. Chicago: University of Chicago Press, 1953.

Hauerwas, Stanley. *Suffering Presence*. Notre Dame, Ind.: University of Notre Dame Press, 1986.

Hegel, Georg Wilhelm Friedrich. *Phänomenologie des Geistes*. Edited by J. Hofmeister. Hamburg: Felix Meiner Verlag, 1952.

———. *Phenomenology of Spirit*. Translated A. V. Miller. Oxford: Oxford University Press, 1977.

Heidegger, Martin. *Being and Time*. Translated by J. Stambaugh. Albany: State University of New York Press, 1996.

———. "On the Essence of Truth." Translated by J. Sallis. In *Martin Heidegger: Basic Writings*, edited by D. F. Krell. New York: Harper and Row, 1977.

———. *Sein und Zeit*. 15th ed. Tübingen: Max Niemeyer Verlag, 1979.

Hillers, D. R. *Covenant*. Baltimore: Johns Hopkins University Press, 1969.

Hittinger, Russell. *A Critique of the New Natural Law Theory*. Notre Dame, Ind.: University of Notre Dame Press, 1987.

Hobbes, Thomas. *De Cive*. Edited by S. P. Lamprecht. New York: Appleton-Century-Crofts, 1949.

———. *The Elements of Law*. Edited by J. C. A. Gaskin. Oxford: Oxford University Press, 1994.

Hobbes, Thomas. *Leviathan*. Edited by M. Oakshott. New York: Collier Books, 1962.

Hohfeld, Wesley N. *Fundamental Legal Conceptions*. Edited by W. W. Cook. Westport, Conn.: Greenwood Press, 1964.

Homer. *Odyssey*. Translated by A. T. Murray. 2 vols. New York: G. P. Putnam, 1919.

Hume, David. *An Inquiry Concerning the Principles of Morals*. Edited by C. W. Hendel. New York: Liberal Arts Press, 1957.

———. *A Treatise of Human Nature*. Edited by L. A. Selby-Bigge. Oxford: Clarendon Press, 1888.

Husserl, Edmund. *Cartesian Meditations*. Translated by D. Cairns. The Hague: M. Nijhoff, 1960.

———. *The Crisis of European Sciences and Transcendental Phenomenology*. Translated by D. Carr. Evanston, Ill.: Northwestern University Press, 1970.

Ingram, A. *A Political Theory of Rights*. Oxford: Clarendon Press, 1994.

Jackson, Timothy P. "Love in a Liberal Society." *Journal of Religious Ethics* 22 (1994).

Jonas, Hans. "Ontological Grounding of a Political Ethics: On the Metaphysics of Commitment to the Future of Man." In *The Public Realm*, edited by R. Schürmann. Albany: State University of New York Press, 1989.

Jones, Peter. *Rights*. New York: Macmillan, 1994.

Justinian. *Corpus Juris Civilis*. 3 vols. Berolini: Weidmann, 1915–28.

Kant, Immanuel. *Critique of Judgment*. Translated by W. S. Pluhar. Indianapolis, Ind.: Hackett, 1987.

———. *Critique of Practical Reason*. Translated by L. W. Beck. Indianapolis, Ind.: Bobbs-Merrill, 1956.

———. *Critique of Pure Reason*. Translated by N. Kemp Smith. New York: St. Martin's Press, 1929.

———. *Groundwork of the Metaphysic of Morals*. Translated by H. J. Paton. New York: Harper and Row, 1964.

———. *Grundlegung zur Metaphysik der Sitten*. In *Kants Werke*, vol. 4, Prussian Academy edition. Berlin: Walter de Gruyter, 1968.

———. *Kritik der praktischen Vernunft*. Edited by K. Vorlander. Hamburg: Felix Meiner Verlag, 1929.

———. *Kritik der reinen Vernunft*. Edited by K. Schmidt. Hamburg: Felix Meiner Verlag, 1956.

———. *The Metaphysic of Morals*. Translated by M. J. Gregor (Cambridge: Cambridge University Press, 1996).

———. *Religion innerhalb der Grenzen der blossen Vernunft*. In *Kants Werke*, vol. 6, Prussian Academy edition. Berlin: Walter de Gruyter, 1968.

———. *Religion within the Limits of Reason Alone*. Translated by T. M. Greene and H. H. Hudson. New York: Harper and Row, 1960.

Kelsen, Hans. *The Pure Theory of Law*. Translated by M. Knight. Berkeley: University of California Press, 1967.

Kierkegaard, Søren. *Fear and Trembling*. Translated by H. V. Hong and E. H. Hong. Princeton: Princeton University Press, 1983.

Koester, Helmut. "NOMOS PHUSEOS: The Concept of Natural Law in Greek Thought." In *Religions in Antiquity: Essays in Memory of Erwin Ramsdell Goodenough*, edited by J. Neusner. Leiden: E. J. Brill, 1968.

Kojève, Alexandre. *Introduction to the Reading of Hegel.* Translated by J. H. Nichols, Jr. Ithaca: Cornell University Press, 1969.

Koyré, Alexandre. *From the Closed World to the Infinite Universe.* Baltimore: Johns Hopkins University Press, 1957.

Levinas, Emmanuel. "The Rights of Man and the Rights of the Other." In *Outside the Subject*, translated by M. B. Smith. Stanford, Calif.: Stanford University Press, 1994.

―――. *Totality and Infinity.* Translated by A. Lingis. Pittsburgh: Duquesne University Press, 1969.

Locke, John. *Second Treatise of Government.* Edited by G. B. Macpherson. Indianapolis, Ind.: Hackett, 1980.

MacIntyre, Alasdair. *After Virtue.* Notre Dame, Ind.: University of Notre Dame Press, 1981.

Marcel, Gabriel. *Being and Having.* Translated by K. Farrer. New York: Harper and Row, 1965.

―――. *The Mystery of Being.* Translated G. S. Fraser. 2 vols. Chicago: Henry Regnery, 1960.

Maritain, Jacques. *Man and the State.* Chicago: University of Chicago Press, 1951.

―――. *The Person and the Common Good.* Translated by J. J. Fitzgerald. Notre Dame, Ind.: University of Notre Dame Press, 1966.

―――. *The Rights of Man and Natural Law.* Translated by D. Anson. San Francisco: Ignatius Press, 1986.

Marx, Karl. "On the Jewish Question." In *Marx-Engels Reader*, 2nd ed., edited by R. Tucker. New York: W. W. Norton, 1978.

―――. "Zur Judenfrage." In *Werke*, vol. 1. Berlin: Dietz, 1964.

Mayo, Bernard. "What are Human Rights?" In *Political Theory and the Rights of Man*, edited by D. D. Raphael. London: Macmillan, 1967.

Merleau-Ponty, Maurice. *Phenomenology of Perception.* Translated by C. Smith. London: Routledge and Kegan Paul, 1962.

Mill, John Stuart. *On Liberty.* In *Utilitarianism, Liberty, and Representative Government.* London: Everyman Library, 1993.

Narveson, J. "Human Rights: Which If Any Are There?" *Human Rights: Nomos* 23 (1981).

Nelson, B. *The Idea of Usury.* 2nd ed. Chicago: University of Chicago Press, 1969.

New Testament. Translated by E. J. Goodspeed. Chicago: University of Chicago Press, 1923.

Niebuhr, Reinhold. *Moral Man and Immoral Society.* New York: Scribner's, 1934.

Nietzsche, Friedrich. *The Will to Power.* Translated by W. Kaufmann and R. J. Hollingdale. New York: Vintage Books, 1968.

Novak, David. *Suicide and Morality.* New York: Scholars Studies Press, 1975.

Novum Testamentum Graece. 24th ed. Edited by E. Nestle Stuttgart: Privileg. Wurtt. Bibelanstalt, 1960.

Nozick, Robert. *Anarchy, State, and Utopia.* New York: Basic Books, 1974.

Orr, Susan. *Jerusalem and Athens.* Lanham, Md.: Rowman and Littelfield, 1995.

Otto, Rudolf. *The Idea of the Holy.* Translated by J. W. Harvey. New York: Oxford University Press, 1958.

Pennock, J. R. "Rights, Natural Rights, and Human Rights—A General View." In *Human Rights: Nomos* 23 (1981).

Plato. *Crito*. Translated by H. N. Fowler. Cambridge: Harvard University Press, 1914.

———. *Euthyphro*. Translated by H. N. Fowler. Cambridge: Harvard University Press, 1914.

———. *Gorgias*. Translated by W. R. M. Lamb. Cambridge: Harvard University Press, 1925.

———. *Laws*. Translated by R. G. Bury. 2 vols. Cambridge: Harvard University Press, 1926.

———. *Phaedo*. Translated by H. N. Fowler. Cambridge: Harvard University Press, 1914.

———. *Philebus*. Translated by H. N. Fowler. Cambridge: Harvard University Press, 1925.

———. *Republic*. Translated by P. Shorey. 2 vols. Cambridge: Harvard University Press, 1930.

———. *Symposium*. Translated by W. R. M. Lamb. Cambridge: Harvard University Press, 1925.

———. *Timaeus*. Translated by R. G. Bury. Cambridge: Harvard University Press, 1929.

Popper, Karl. "Falsification versus Conventionalism." In *Popper Selections*, edited by D. Miller. Princeton: Princeton University Press, 1985.

———. *The Open Society and Its Enemies*. 5th ed., 2 vols. Princeton: Princeton University Press, 1966.

Rawls, John. *A Theory of Justice*. Cambridge: Harvard University Press, 1971.

Raz, Joseph. *The Morality of Freedom*. Oxford: Oxford University Press, 1986.

Ricoeur, Paul. *Fallible Man*. Translated by C. Kelbley. Chicago: Henry Regnery, 1967.

———. *Oneself as Other*. Translated by K. Blamey. Chicago: University of Chicago Press, 1992.

Rotenstreich, Nathan. *Order and Might*. Albany: State University of New York Press, 1988.

Sandel, Michael J. "Justice and the Good." In *Liberalism and Its Critics*, edited by M. J. Sandel. Oxford: Blackwell, 1984.

Scheler, Max. *Formalism in Ethics and Non-Formal Ethics of Value*. Translated by M. S. Frings and R. L. Funk. Evanston, Ill.: Northwestern University Press, 1973.

Schleiermacher, Friedrich. *The Christian Faith*. Translated by H. R. Mackintosh and J. S. Stewart. Edinburgh: T. and T. Clark, 1960.

———. *On Religion*. Translated by R. Crouter. Cambridge: Cambridge University Press, 1988.

Schneewind, J. B. *The Invention of Autonomy*. Cambridge: Cambridge University Press, 1998.

Schutz, Alfred. *The Phenomonology of the Social World*. Translated by G. Walsh and F. Lenhart. Evanston, Ill.: Northwestern University Press, 1967.

Selbourne, David. *The Principle of Duty*. London: Sinclair-Stevenson, 1994.

Smith, Tara. *Moral Rights and Political Freedom*. Lanham, Md.: Rowman and Littlefield, 1995.

Spinoza, Baruch. *Ethics*. Translated by W. H. White and A. H. Stirling. New York: Hafner, 1955.

———. *Tractatus Theologico-Politicus*. Translated by S. Shirley. Leiden: E. J. Brill, 1989.

Stoljar, Samuel. *An Analysis of Rights*. London: Macmillan, 1984.

Stout, Jeffrey. *Morality after Authority*. Notre Dame, Ind.: University of Notre Dame Press, 1981.

Strauss, Leo. "Natural Law." In *International Encyclopedia of the Social Sciences*, vol. 11.

———. *Natural Right and History*. Chicago: University of Chicago Press, 1953.

———. *What Is Political Philosophy?* Glencoe, Ill.: Free Press, 1959.

Tacitus. *Histories*. Translated by W. H. Fyfe. Oxford: Clarendon Press, 1912.

Thomas Aquinas. *Summa Contra Gentiles*. Vol. 1, translated by A. C. Pegis. Garden City, N.Y.: Image Books, 1955.

———. *Summa Theologiae*. In *Basic Writings of Saint Thomas Aquinas*, translated and edited by A. Pegis, 2 vols. New York: Random House, 1945.

Tierney, Brian. *The Idea of Natural Rights*. Atlanta, Ga.: Scholars Press, 1997.

Tillich, Paul. *Systematic Theology*. Vol. 1. Chicago: University of Chicago Press, 1951.

Tuck, Richard. *Natural Rights Theories*. Cambridge: Cambridge University Press, 1979.

van Buren, Paul. *A Theology of the Jewish-Christian Reality*. Vol. 1. San Francisco: Harper and Row, 1987.

Walzer, Michael. *Spheres of Justice*. Oxford: Blackwell, 1983.

Warren, Samuel D. and Louis D., Brandeis. "The Right to Privacy," *Harvard Law Review* 4 (1890).

Weber, Max. "Bureaucracy and Political Leadership." In *Economy and Society*, vol. 3, Eng. trans. New York: Bedminster Press, 1968.

Weinreb, Lloyd L. *Natural Law and Justice*. Cambridge: Harvard University Press, 1987.

White, A. R. *Rights*. Oxford: Clarendon Press, 1984.

Witte, John, J. *From Sacrament to Contract*. Louisville, Ky.: Westminster Knox Press, 1997.

Wittgenstein, Ludwig. *Philosophical Investigations*. 2nd ed. Translated by G. E. M. Anscombe. New York: Macmillan, 1958.

———. *Tractatus Logico-Philosophicus*. Translated by D. F. Pears and B. F. McGuinness. London: Routledge and Kegan Paul, 1961.

Wolfson, H. A. *The Philosophy of Spinoza*. 2 vols. Cambridge: Harvard University Press, 1934.

Index

Note: When "Rabbi" appears in parentheses after a proper name, it denotes a Sage mentioned in the Talmud and related rabbinic literature, who is called there either "Rabbi" or "Rav." When a Hebrew phrase appears in parentheses after a proper name, it denotes the more readily known abbreviation of the name of a post-talmudic rabbinic authority (often preceded by "R." for "Rabbi" in the notes) or his major literary work by which he is more readily known. When a Hebrew phrase appears in parentheses after a common name, it denotes the original Hebrew term of which the English term is a somewhat arbitrary translation.

NEW FORUM BOOKS

New Forum Books makes available to general readers outstanding original interdisciplinary scholarship with a special focus on the juncture of culture, law, and politics. New Forum Books is guided by the conviction that law and politics not only reflect culture but help to shape it. Authors include leading political scientists, sociologists, legal scholars, philosophers, theologians, historians, and economists writing for nonspecialist readers and scholars across a range of fields. Looking at questions such as political equality, the concept of rights, the problem of virtue in liberal politics, crime and punishment, population, poverty, economic development, and the international legal and political order, New Forum Books seeks to explain—not explain away—the difficult issues we face today.